THE ETERNAL DANCE

About this Book

The Eternal Dance is "the Dance of Life" . . . "the Dance of the Soul" . . . "the Dance of All Creation." It's all these things . . . but most of all it is a book about the Universe and about YOU . . . a book that will change YOU and how YOU see the Universe, and your place in it.

A Journey to the Beginning

It is a book designed to help the reader enter an Altered State of Consciousness and EXPERIENCE, as well as comprehend, the multi-dimensional World of the Cosmos—taking the reader on a journey through Space & Time to the Beginning: to witness the Creation of the Universe, to witness its evolution through the interaction of the two Primal Forces (mistakenly labeled "good" and "evil"), and to know the origins of Consciousness and the real history of Humanity.

YOU—in the New Age

Through this book you will learn that YOU are an intrinsic part of the evolutionary process, and through this book—as you understand your true origins—you will learn how to RE-PROGRAM YOURSELF: tapping your subconscious mind to learn from it, to remember past lives, and to understand and resolve traumas (karma) from the past. You will learn to work with your mind, and to develop it constructively. You will learn the TRUE NATURE OF THIS "NEW AGE"—which is more than the transition into Aquarius, *for we are moving out of the involutionary arc into that of EVOLU-TIONARY RETURN!*

THE ETERNAL DANCE

Act I
Cosmology & Cycles of Life

Act II
Relationships & Karmic Recall

Other Works from the Authors

THE PAST LIFE MEMORY PROGRAM, 1977
How Past Lives Affect the Present
How to Use the Power of Hypnosis
Journey Into the Past With a Loved One
Finding Solutions to Present Life Problems
Discover Hidden Talents, Abilities & Knowledge

This five-hour series of cassette tapes is
available from Llewellyn Publications.

**For information about Correspondence Studies, Past-Life Readings
or Personal Appearances by the authors, please write:**
Collegians International Church
P.O. Box 929
Fairbanks, AK 99707
Please include $1.00 toward cost of materials, postage & handling.

THE ETERNAL DANCE

by LaVedi Lafferty and Bud Hollowell, Ph.D.

Foreword by Carl Llewellyn Weschcke
Introduction by Patricia-Rochelle Diegel

1985
Llewellyn Publications
St. Paul, Minnesota, 55164-0383, U.S.A.

International Standard Book Number: 0-87542-436-8
Library of Congress Catalog Number: 83-80135

First Edition, 1983
First Printing, 1983
Second Printing, 1985

\

Cover Art: Greg Guler
Inside Illustrations: Bill Smith, Bill Berry

Produced by Llewellyn Publications
Typography and Art property of Chester-Kent, Inc.

Published by
LLEWELLYN PUBLICATIONS
A Division of Chester-Kent, Inc.
P.O. Box 64383
St. Paul, MN 55164-0383, U.S.A.
Printed in the United States of America

Dedicated to
the memory of
MARCIA MOORE
and
perpetuation of her work
in astrology & reincarnation

ACKNOWLEDGEMENTS

We would like to give our heartfelt thanks to all of our many friends who helped make this book possible, including Gilbert Gibson, who suggested it; Patricia-Rochelle Diegel, for her introduction and encouragement through the years; Rachel MacPherson, who persevered in transcribing it; Bill Smith, who interpreted our humor in his illustrations; Dean Gottehrer, University of Alaska, for editing; Patrick M. Carter for indexing and proofing; Linda Aronow-Brown for proofing; Liz Berry for contributing the illustration by her late husband, Bill Berry; and we extend our gratitude to the many people who contributed material both directly and indirectly.

FOREWORD

The Eternal Dance is the "Dance of Life" . . . of the Soul . . . of All Creation . . . of the Universal Christ Consciousness beyond all religions. It is the *Dance of Shiva,* the Indian God who dances upon the body of his Consort, who is also Himself, who is also the Creation and Divine Power within Creation.

Here we have a symbol for all that is—God as active and passive, as male and female, and of creation as both involutionary and evolutionary. For us in transition to a New Age, it also symbolizes this new cycle of evolution in which we become the dancers, i.e. active players, and the dance is—as all dancing should be—one of joy, of worship, dance that both expresses and arouses Life itself.

As Shiva is also Shakti, God and Goddess, Creator and Created, so Man/Woman is also Divine, and in this new cycle assumes the more responsible role of active participation in the Evolutionary Drama. No longer passive, no longer the observer only, no longer a single spark in the Cosmic Fire, the New Age Person must know himself/herself as a *continuum* of the stream of consciousness reaching back to the beginning and forward to ultimate destiny.

This book is about the Universe as created, and about the New Age Person as the carrier for creation as we enter upon the evolutionary arc back to the Source.

How may Man/Woman fully awaken the Divine power and consciousness flowing through him/her? *By remembering!* As we remember events from our present lifetime, we learn the lessons intended; as we remember those of past lives, we learn the lessons left unlearned (karma) and carried forward to the being and circumstances of this life. As we remember, we release the hold the past has on us, and free our creative powers to more fully express the fullness of the Self within and fulfill the opportunities of being an Awakened Person.

The message of this book is that we should learn and understand the nature of the world we live in, and should perceive the conditions of our personal existence, that we may awaken, and take personal control and responsibility for our lives, both now and to come. With consciousness there is responsibility, with responsibility there is power, and with power there is destiny. Your destiny is to be more than you were, to become more than you are.

Remembering is the way. The *Past Life Memory Program* offered through this book is like a universal bus ticket that will take you anywhere, and from anywhere to everywhere! Remembering is the technique for *integrating* all that you have ever been and bringing it all together into shining Light. It is the awakening of the sleeping star within, for Man is the Microcosm, meaning that all that is in the cosmos *outside*, is also in the cosmos *inside*, and—as you take your place among the living stars—*that for which you were born takes place.*

Carl Llewellyn Weschcke, Publisher

ABOUT THE AUTHORS

Before the curtain goes up for the first performance, let me introduce the authors, LaVedi Lafferty and her colleague, Bud Hollowell. In setting the stage for their inevitable partnership, LaVedi (pronounced *lah-vay-dee*) was transplanted from Oregon to the Alaska wilderness. The rugged environment taught her independence and courage, while the tasks of surviving, raising a daughter and, later extending her education at the University of Alaska, majoring in English and journalism, supposedly kept her tremendous energy out of mischief. After these lessons, the surprising discovery that her physical body was not indestructible gained her attention and encouraged her to look inward and search for *Self*.

This search took her to England in 1969 and into esoteric studies, beginning her preparation for the future work with Bud. By 1977 she had become active enough in spiritual and corporate work to be included in *Who's Who in American Women*, having founded the non-profit Philosophical Heritage Institute (originally known as Vortex) in 1971, followed by Collegians International Church in 1977.

Meanwhile, Bud, as an All-American catcher, had been working through lessons on the baseball field of the University of Southern California. He was channeled into professional baseball as a player, coach and manager in the Los Angeles Dodgers organization, to allow him to release his past-life aggressions in a positive manner. More importantly, his athletic experience demonstrated to him the tremendous power of the mind to overcome self-imposed physical and mental limitations.

While Bud was playing out his athletic lessons, he was simultaneously run over the academic hurdles to earn a Ph.D. in physical education, with an emphasis in gerontology and the psychology of aging. This exposed him to the strengths and weaknesses of Western scientific thought, which, he was destined to find, failed to provide lasting

xi

substance in his life. This caused him to continue his quest for meaning elsewhere, and, surprisingly to him, it eventually led him to investigate hypnosis.

Professional baseball motivated him to seek out the possible uses of hypnosis in athletics, but once he learned the techniques, he realized how hypnosis could be beneficial for people in all walks of life. Slowly he had been brought to the realization that each "dancer" creates his own reality. Bud and LaVedi were now ready to meet in Alaska in 1974, finally to begin working together in 1976, when Bud began teaching hypnosis in Alaska. By then combining Bud's hypnotic techniques and LaVedi's training in clairvoyant skills, they began delving into past life work and creating easy to use methods of recall.

In *The Eternal Dance* they will share some of their findings with you and rapidly scan millions of years, while attempting to condense a variety of spiritual teachings into a comprehensive synthesis. It will be necessary to *stretch* your imagination to attempt to comprehend the large spans of time involved, bearing in mind that some civilizations overlap, while large time gaps exist between others.

Bud and LaVedi would like to emphasize that they do not want you to simply accept their perceptions, but rather to learn how to experience your own reality, truth and inner knowing. They can only share their research and intuitive findings, providing what they hope will be a springboard into your own voyage of discovery. Numerous resources are given to provide the intellect with information, but the real benefit to you should be the construction of a bridge from your *conscious mind,* through your *subconscious mind*, to your *soul consciousness* and eternal *Self.*

Now, on with the "dance." Allow yourself the privilege of experiencing consciousness as an unlimited, infinite spirit, beyond time and beyond space—an *immortal soul.*

The Director

Act I

COSMOLOGY & CYCLES OF LIFE

Meet the Director
Space Flowing Through Space
The Cosmic Egg
The Days of Creation
The *Yin* and *Yang* Forces
The Basis of the Twelve Astrological Signs
The Basis of the Seven Rays
In the Beginning Was the Word
Made in the Image of God
The Evolution of Consciousness
The Consciousness of the Atom
The Collective Unconscious
The Wheel of Rebirth

All Aboard for the Milky Way
The Formative Elements
Mother Earth Fails
The *Fallen* Angels
The First Man Adam
Hyperborian Atlantis

Act II

RELATIONSHIPS & KARMIC RECALL

INTRODUCTION
by
Patricia-Rochelle Diegel, Ph.D.

Patricia-Rochelle Diegel has given thousands of Immortality Consultations (past-life readings), taught many people to open the inner-doors to their past-life experiences in "Trinity" groups, and has lectured widely on reincarnation, spiritual unfoldment and New Age subjects for over twenty years.

The Eternal Dance has more information in it about *cosmology* as formative patterns of creation and *reincarnation* than any book I have ever read. It is easy to read and you will move through it very rapidly because the subject matter is so fascinating. Once you have read it, you will want everyone you know to read it, so you can discuss the many ideas it will spark in your mind. I feel it will become a source of deep discussion by serious students of Life and by all who are ready to move upward in consciousness.

The SOURCE of all consciousness, wishing to create in order to evolve and fulfill the *Law of Rhythmic Balanced*

Interchange, follows a design throughout all levels of life and in all dimensions. It *involves* into matter, toward its ultimate creation—humankind. All patterns repeat themselves in the scheme of things and perfected humanity will mirror a perfect universe. As the pattern of *involution* was set, so step by step the human creation reflects that pattern in evolution back to the Source. Whenever a human takes a sideroad or a detour from the perfect pattern, return is made through another body. Progress is the *Law of Life.* No person or thing ever stands still or is destroyed, but changes into another form of energy.

The Path of Evolution with the *Perfect Pattern* as a guide, must be studied and followed to lead the animal-man out of chaos, disharmony, fear and ignorance and into a condition of balanced living. Animal-man passes through many heavy traumas as he breaks or bends spiritual laws, so he continues to incarnate until he has worked out his "karmic debts" and severed "karmic ties." He repeats the same problems over and over until he releases guilt and gives forgiveness to self and to others. He must repeatedly go through birth and all of the re-learning: bottled, diapered, crawling, walking, dependent, independent, mastering language and relationships all over again . . . a waste of so many years and energy.

The animal-man stays on the straight and narrow for fear of going to hell or jail. After many lifetimes of trying and working on his personal evolution, he reaches a point on the evolutionary scale where *conscience* is developed. Instead of acting from fear of punishment, the human seeks to help others by doing "right" and starts to become a real human being. Realization develops that, by working in groups for the betterment of all, personal growth is made on the Evolutionary Path, while all of humanity benefits from the efforts. Welcome—from the animal kingdom and into the Human Race.

Evolution assumes a different purpose for the newly emerged human, helping him to become more sensitive and to increase his awareness of the world around him. The human turns to a variety of pursuits: gaining knowledge, examination of needs and desires, exploring new ideals and ideas, development of creative talents and clairvoyant faculties, plus using other levels of mind.

The Search for Inner Peace and Tranquility is a glimmering *light* at the end of a long tunnel, but . . . now . . . the human is aware that it is there. With the re-balancing of the personal self, the human becomes ready to move forward again towards a higher goal—working with more enlightened beings. Learning from those on a rung higher and helping those on rungs below, for all life now seems to be a vertical ascent up the Ladder of Life. At this point in evolution the human becomes aware that there is more than one embodiment, and that there is a soul which moves through many suits of clothes (bodies) over many thousands of years, or even hundreds of thousands of years. With the discovery of these other lifetimes, the human adds to potential in the present life. All of the talent, knowledge and abilities from other lifetimes can be regained and utilized in the current body.

Now the human with a conscience, who is knocking on the door of consciousness, can become the composite of all those past incarnations through the process of meditation and inner-dimensional awareness. As the human becomes totally conscious of immortality, then evolution is accelerated. Understanding is gained of the difference between reality and illusion, and the human knows he is not the Way, but merely a Wayshower. He knows that with the severing of all karmic ties and the release of karmic debts by helping others on the Path, he can move towards the *light*.

The final stages of evolution takes the form of Spiritual Initiations. When the human discovers the secrets behind these Initiations (which duplicate the patterns of *involution* or the coming into form), then, and only then, can the human make his way back to the Source within one lifetime. *The Eternal Dance* is so written that all of the clues to this *return* are in it. You will read and re-read the book many times, because hidden within its pages are the *Secret Patterns* you must follow, if you want this life to be the most important life you have ever lived.

This life is your chance to unlock the door and move forward on the Evolutionary Path towards the Ultimate Goal, completing all Initiations of the earth experience. Then you can have the choice to reincarnate or not, returning only if you want to experience life again or help humankind in some new way.

Patricia-Rochelle Diegel

ACT I

Cosmology
&
Life Cycles

All things in Cosmos are parts of Cosmos, and most of all is man the rational animal . . . after the image of the Cosmos and having mind beyond all earthly lives.

God maketh Aeon; Aeon, Cosmos; Cosmos, Time; and Time, Becoming.

(Corpus Hermeticum, VIII, Hermes).

1

OVERTURE

1

Overture

(Meanwhile backstage . . . .)
        O.K., let's take it from the top again.
Thunder! *rumble-rumble-rumble* . . . .
    Lightening! *FLASH-CRACKLE-FLASH!*
        Trumpets! *RatataTataTAAAAAA!* Cut! A little
           less volume and a little more

                        pizazz, O.K.?
Chorus, are you ready? Fine. Once again, now . . .
           This is live.

                  Quiet in the Cosmos!
Thunder! *rumble-rumble-rumble* . . . .
    Lightening! *FLASH-CRACKLE-FLASH!*
Trumpets!   *RatataTAtaTAAA!*
        As it was in the beginning,
        Is now and ever shall be,
        World without end. Amen. Amen.
    (shh . . . , quiet now.) Very good. Now, CURTAIN!
Scene One, with LaVedi center stage . . . .

3

MEET THE DIRECTOR

You are about to enter the exciting and powerful world of your own creative intelligence. You will have the opportunity to experience your transformation into a vibrant being of radiant *light* able to transcend time and space, and together we will explore the secrets hidden in unconscious levels of mind. We will learn how to reach Cosmic Consciousness and find out why it is so important an accomplishment. Together we will trace written and *unwritten* records that reveal the origin of life and humanity.

You will join me in this adventure into *inner-space* and other dimensions by extending your imagination to the Cosmic Stage, where performances never cease. I will ask you to leave behind earthly limitations, but at the same time I want you to keep your sense of humor beside you. On this stage tragedies turn into melodramas over time. The ability to laugh at yourself and with others is an essential part of releasing old unconscious emotions. As the past unfolds, you may be reminded of the good-natured embarrassment you feel from your baby pictures, or the fun and excitement of seeing yourself reflected by ancestors in an old family album. That is the light side. Families have serious sides, too, so we will be covering subjects as varied as human sacrifices by the "Sons of Darkness" to how to work with "elemental beings."

I am going to ask you to accompany me in a re-creation of a journey I first made into that endless sea of creative potential known as the *Great Unmanifest,* or *Void,* in 1971. This will set the stage for our experience of the creative process during the first great formative period referred to as the *First Day*.

We will practice experiencing the Cosmos from a state of altered-consciousness, because from our normal three-dimensional state of awareness we can only perceive intellectual concepts. To comprehend the multi-dimensional world of the Cosmos, it must be experienced. Later, at your leisure, you will be able to meditatively re-create portions of our exploration and experience them more deeply. This is part of a process that can put you in contact with your higher *soul-consciousness*. So you are invited to not only read, but become an active participant.

Now, if you are ready, I am going to ask you to relax, settle back where you will not be disturbed and prepare for an experience of altered-consciousness. Here we go . . . .

You are totally relaxed, all tension gone, but your senses are clear and alert. You are highly aware of your surroundings and thoughts. We will leave awareness of the physical body and earthly restrictions and enter a world of mind where *imagination* becomes reality, for imagination is a form of creative thought.

Imagine now that you have a shimmering body of all-inclusive *light*. You are becoming a being of brilliant translucent *light*. You pause for a moment, as if suspended and separated from your physical body, and then you shoot away like a speeding bullet. You can feel the pressure of atmosphere left behind and hear the rushing sound caused by your tremendous speed. Finally, after what seems an interminable length of time, you stop abruptly, but gently, at your destination. You discover you are floating in a great black silent sea. It feels velvety soft, but with no sensation of weight or gravity, so we tumble about each other, laughing and responding to the tremendous feeling of freedom and joy that bubbles up from our very core of being-ness.

We are immersed in the boundless spatial sea of the *Great Unmanifest*.* It reminds us of a great becalmed sleeping ocean with no pressure. Intuitively we know that it possesses an overwhelming and latent power, and we are startled to discover that this great sea is beginning to stir. We sense it is going to *awaken*. Within it we feel like cosmic ballet dancers, momentarily suspended in mid-air before descending once again into motion. Without resistance we begin to move along with the flow, our finite consciousness filled with uncomprehending awe.

SPACE FLOWING THROUGH SPACE

We feel only a smooth silken movement through absolute silence and realize that unmeasurable aeons will pass as this emanation, precipitated from the "dynamic field" of Space, flows on. The closest comparison we can make is that Space, reacting to its own unknown pressures, condenses itself into what becomes a continuing line of "spatial particle" exchange. This produces an *emanating current* that grows in potency from its movement.

"The prime duality is 'space' and 'movement.' "† Re-

---

* Known by many names including: Boundless One, Space, *Ain-soph, Nirvana, Tsi-tsai* (Self-Existent), No-Thing and referred to as sea or water(s). In physics *space* is now understood to be a *dynamic field*, where "virtual particles" are continually appearing and vanishing spontaneously. Space contains the potential to produce all of the sub-atomic particles that result in manifestation.
† *The Cosmic Doctrine*, Dion Fortune, Helios Book Service, Cheltenham, England, 1966.

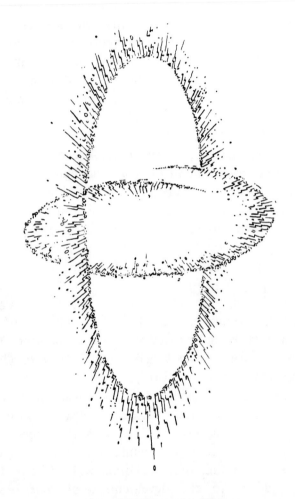

"Space Flowing Through Space"
The force generated by the motion of the spiral causes a reaction from the surrounding space and a second current begins to flow around the first one at a right angle.

maining in our *light bodies* and a timeless state, we move forward again, until we realize that the flowing emanation has begun to form an enormous curve.* The natural law of motion, involving the momentum and inertia inherent in *Space*, produces this reaction. The flow continues, but inertia causes it to curve back past itself, eventually forming a spiral that flows on and on.

Finally the force generated by the motion causes a reaction from the surrounding Space. A second current begins to flow around the first one at a right angle. In the beginning, because it is larger, it is slower, but after more aeons of endless rotation, the outer emanating flow reaches the speed of the original one. It begins to attract an aspect of the *force* flowing on the inner spiral. The positive and negative forces flowing in these two emanations makes them mutually attracting and repelling. Arcs form between them of positive and negative force, creating circuits and a "force field," known esoterically as the *Ring-Pass-Not.*†

An outer boundary forms, known as the *Ring Chaos*, along with an inner one, called the *Ring Cosmos*. The attraction between these two produces a *limitation* that allows the *Cosmos* to become self-contained. The "unmanifest" *chaotic* pre-matter particles of Space (continually appearing and vanishing) are held within the force field. Space will be able to begin "manifesting" or ordering itself into atomic combinations. This order will evolve in direct correspondence to the development of *consciousness*

---

* Einstein's general theory of relativity holds that space has degrees of curvature.
† A similar curved force field is known in astronomy that prevents light from escaping certain stars; it is called an "event horizon."

by the *Cosmos* ("cosmos" meaning to produce order from unordered space).

Intuitively we realize that the tendency of the inner Ring Cosmos is to *contract or condense* itself, a tendency that will eventually produce matter by combining sub-atomic particles and create "gravity." The tendency of the Ring Chaos is to *expand or diffuse* into Space and will cause the Cosmos to expand. In the multi-dimensional world of the Cosmos, expansion and contraction can occur simultaneously.

As we have seen by now, the two primal forces, or formative emanations, are two essential aspects necessary to form one unity: the *Cosmos*. They are God manifesting Self, yet humanity has labeled one as *GOOD* and one as *EVIL*. Good is held to be that which is positive, "Godly" or cosmic. *Evil* is seen as that which is negative, "material" or chaotic. Actually the problems arise from *imbalance* of these two forces, and since we are dealing with matter, imbalance leans toward the negative polarity. But consider that opposition must be present to create any balance or relatively stable condition. We would have difficulty evolving without some semblance of *stability*. Conversely *limitation* provides the "traction" or "pressure" necessary to overcome inertia and produce *motion*.

THE COSMIC EGG

A delimiting Cosmic "gyroscope" is now spinning through Space. Frequently we see it symbolized as a *Cosmic Egg*, illustrated by a serpent twining around an eggshell. This represents the macrocosm, with man, the microcosmic reflection, to emerge from the fertilized egg. The *snake* represents the limiting force created by the Ring Chaos. Within man the corresponding forces are present as electrical flows, known as *kundalini,* and are symbolized as a coiled snake at the base of the spine.

The use of symbols helps us to relate to our *Cosmic Source* unconsciously. Bombarded by the influences of our manifest world, our normal state of consciousness is limited or finite. We can overcome this by relaxing the conscious mind and reaching into the unconscious, where symbols provide a common language between the two aspects of mind. Our exploration of the Cosmos is a visualization that speaks to the unconscious and forms a *bridge* from the finite to the infinite.

Throughout the ages mankind has either consciously or unconsciously symbolized the three primal aspects of the Cosmos as a *HOLY TRINITY.* This remembrance has been reflected by worship of trinitarian sets of entities containing a pair of opposites that produce a third. A male figure appears representing the Ring Cosmos, a female figure represents the Ring Chaos, and the product of their union reconciles, unifies and transcends.

Trinities have existed worldwide with variations including: Father, Son and Holy Ghost; holy families such as the Hindu *Brahman, Shiva* and *Vishnu;* the Egyptian *Osiris, Isis* and *Horus;* the Christian *Jehovah, Mary* and *Jesus;* and planetary relationships such as the paternal *Sun,* maternal *Moon* and *Earth.* In Jewish *Kabbalism* a system of manifesting trinities, or *Sephiroth,* exists, beginning with *Kether, Binah* and *Chokmah* and descending to man.

THE DAYS OF CREATION

Symbols of serpents and dragons appear continually in religious allegories. They mean much more than evil forces that must be destroyed. They have qualities that have been used throughout history symbolically. The three main correlations we need to consider are the periodic shedding of skin (cyclic renewal or rebirth), the undulation of movement (emanating force) and the tendency to coil (encase in a spiral and constrain).

Worldwide heroes have attempted to conquer the reptilian force. In India the Hindu Krishna dances on the head of the king of serpents, until the serpent's power is broken. In Greek mythology the sun god, Apollo, kills the serpent monster, Python. In the *Bible* the bruising of the serpent's head is prophesied in Genesis, while Isaiah (27:1) says, "the Lord . . . shall slay the dragon that is in the sea."

The serpent symbol is not only to remind us that it limits consciousness, but also that the Cosmos experiences cycles. At times the snake contracts, and at times it relaxes and sheds its skin. This corresponds to the tendency of the Ring Chaos to expand and the Ring Cosmos to contract. At times one Ring is dominant and then the other. This creates a cyclic alternation between these two tremendous forces, resulting in the *Greater Days and Nights of Creation,* or, by correspondence, *death* and *rebirth.*

As the Hindu *Upanishads* teach:

All the worlds, and even the heavenly realm of Brahma, are subject to the laws of rebirth. . . . There is day, also, and night in the universe . . . (When a new world is born) Day dawns, and all those lives that lay asleep come forth and show themselves mortally manifest. Night falls, and all are dissolved into the sleeping germ of life. Thus they are seen, O Prince [Arjuna] and appear unceasingly, dissolving with the dark, and with day returning to the new birth, new death.

Science is giving serious consideration to the possibility that such great universal cycles exist, alternating between long periods of expansion and equally long periods of contraction. An article that appeared in the December 15, 1956 New York Herald Tribune describes it especially well:

New scientific findings indicate the universe may be pulsing like a gigantic heart, expanding and contracting in periods of many billions of years. . . . If the universe is, indeed oscillating, the inference will be that it has gone thru many births and deaths. Since its latest rebirth . . . the universe has been steadily evolving.

We are an integral part of this evolutionary process. Manifestation appears during the creative *Day*. We microscopically reflect this and build during our waking hours. During the *Day* the positive energy of the Ring Cosmos is dominant. Then, like our life forms, when its energy has been expended, it falls into a quiescent slumber to be recharged. Cosmic *Night* falls, with the Ring Chaos dominating. This "sleep" is primarily a static condition of balance between the two great potencies, which allows the restoration of force to the Ring Cosmos. Eventually the outward pull of the Ring Chaos upsets the balance and its persistent expansion brings a new *Day* into being, with the Ring Cosmos reacting and awakening ready to build again. We are experiencing one of these *Great Days* now, science estimating that our universe has been expanding for about 10,000 million years, assuming a constant expansion rate.

Our heroes, battling the various reptiles, are really conquering consciousness and freeing themselves from earthly cycles. They attain the *wisdom of God,* manifested by the serpent power encircling the Cosmos (bringing order from chaos). They conquer the illusion of *knowledge,* resulting from the limitation surrounding man, and merge with their Source, or as the Hindi *Upanishads* state:

> But, behind the manifest and the unmanifest, there is another Existence, which is eternal and changeless. This has been called the Unmanifest, the imperishable. To reach it is said to be the greatest of all achievements.

In Eastern philosophy, Cosmic Consciousness is spoken of as a heightened state of awareness that extends experience of the world. "These states seem to create an awareness of the interpenetration of space and time at a macrocosmic level . . . similar to the physicists' conception. It is a dynamic conception of things as ever-changing processes." (*The Tao of Physics*). Supporting this interactive concept the *I Ching* tells us the natural laws "are not forces external to things, but represent the harmony of *movement* immanent in them."

We have been exploring the first stage of the Unmanifest becoming manifest. To continue on we need to return once more as beings of omniscient *light* to the evolving Cosmos. As we relax and increase our awareness, we return to the Cosmos after many aeons have past. We find that change is beginning to occur. Emanations of *Light* are swirling toward the center of the apparently empty sphere. This *Light* is not light as we know it, but is pure force flowing.* We will visualize this *Light* as the light we are familiar with to help establish a mental image.

In the middle of the swirls a hub of *Central Stillness* forms, creating an *eye*. We have come to know this *eye* as the "all seeing eye of God." This eye is where we began, it is our *Source*. Eventually we "return" through our evolving consciousness, becoming One with the Cosmic Consciousness. It seems a very long distance from such a beginning to life on Earth. To unravel the mystery, we must continue our observation.

THE *YIN* AND *YANG* FORCES

We watch as the eye becomes a Central *Light*; it seems to synthesize the flowing *Light* into *rays*. The next reaction is especially important: the inner Ring Cosmos starts sending positive force along a ray to the Center in a centripetal action, similar to the concentration in the eye of a hurricane. From the Center, the centrifugal pull of the Ring Chaos will pull the force outward to the periphery, making it negative in the process. Since the force is flowing through

---

* In physics, light (and all matter at the atomic level) is considered to have a dual nature consisting of particles and waves. *Particles of light,* traveling through space, appear as vibrating electric and magnetic fields exhibiting wave characteristics. Sometimes the particle aspect dominates (stability), and sometimes the particles behave like waves (motion). The Theory of Electrodynamics shows that light is nothing but a rapidly alternating electromagnetic field traveling through space in the form of waves. *Visible light* is a very small part of these electric and magnetic fields oscillating at different frequencies.

"The Yin and Yang Forces"
Since the force is flowing through the revolving rays with swirl-like motions, the result is a giant "S" shape flowing across the Cosmos. As the S-shaped flow is drawn back across the Cosmos, it forms a double S-shape, or figure "8", upon completing its journey.

the revolving rays with swirl-like motions, the result is a giant "S" shape flowing within the Cosmos, bearing in mind that the Rings are continually turning over and over upon themselves during this process. This S forms the Taoist *Yin-Yang* symbol for the universe. The positive *Yang* is balanced by the negative *Yin* and circled by the Ring-Pass-Not, or cosmic boundary. In Chinese philosophy everything in the universe depends upon these two great opposite polarities. In Taoism, the *Tao* is the principle which unites and transcends these two opposites.

Returning to the evolving Cosmos, we see that when the force reaches the periphery, the S-shaped flow is drawn back again by the positive Ring, becoming positive force again. From the Center it again is drawn outward by the negative Ring, becoming negative force in the process. Only this time as it completes its journey, it forms a double S-shape within the sphere, or a figure 8. We know this as the *infinity symbol*, representing the never-ceasing flow. This form now contains two positive rays and two negative ones, charged by the flows.

THE BASIS OF THE TWELVE ASTROLOGICAL SIGNS

The cosmic evolution is responsible for many familiar symbols, including the zodiac. Closed circuits cannot occur in the Cosmos, due to its continual rotation. As a result, when the force completes its first figure 8, we see that the position of the Cosmos has changed and a new figure 8 is formed, until eventually we see three pairs of infinity symbols within the cosmic sphere. They form twelve rays that appear to radiate from the Central Stillness. Gazing down

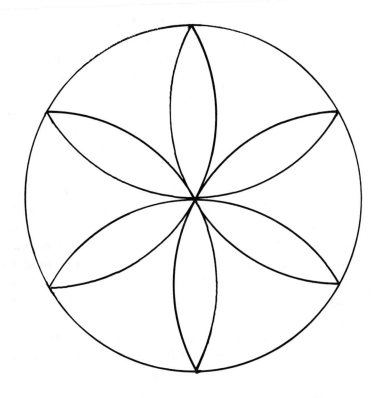

"The Basis of the Twelve Astrological Signs"
The flows across the Cosmos form three sets of figure 8's, or
infinity symbols, forming twelve *rays*. Gazing down upon these
they resemble the six-petaled lotus blossom, the symbol of an enlightened individual.

upon them, we see that they resemble the six-petaled lotus blossom, the symbol of enlightened man. The awakened consciousness is centered in the lotus, while the stem of the flower extends through the "waters" of space to the roots anchored in the "mud" of physical manifestation.

These twelve rays form the archetypal foundation for the twelve astrological signs of the zodiac. From them emanated the twelve *basic* expressions of all life, affecting all forms, both animate and those apparently inanimate, seen and unseen. The ancients referred to astrology as the "soul of nature, which gives form and order to life." The archetypal symbols of the zodiac reflect qualities of energy and ensuing manifestation into matter. When Buddha died he is reputed to have said, "*Spirit* is the sole elementary and primordial unity, and each of its rays is immortal, infinite and indestructible." Modern astrology is a weak and blurred reflection of these great forces flowing into manifestation.

People exhibit predictable behavior patterns or responsive reactions that are beyond conscious awareness. Carl Jung called these universal formative principles, or *archetypes*, patterns or models that all creation follows, including human thought. He said the archetypes, "might be compared to the axial system of a crystal, which as it were, preforms the crystalline structure in the mother liquid, although it has no material existence of its own."

This concept finds support in physics. Quantum theory shows that sub-atomic particles are *interconnected probability patterns*. Particles are considered to be "energy bundles" or "dynamic patterns." These are the "patterns" that form nuclear, atomic and molecular structures that build into material forms and appear "solid." Sub-atomic "pre-matter" is permanently "colored" by its ray origin, maintaining an affinity to like matter and a responsiveness to the ray influence.

Astrologers have empirically known this for centuries and have demonstrated that they see invisible patterns behind human thoughts and actions. Astrology provides a guide to the archetypal patterns. In *Astrology, Psychology and the Four Elements,* Stephen Arroyo touches upon this, stating these principles appear in mythology and astrology, with those of astrology "emphasizing the archetypal principles themselves reflected upon life. . . ." He mentions that Jung referred to these psychic substratum as the Collective Unconscious, while the archetypes are universal principles that underlie and motivate "all psychological life, individual and collective."

Applied astrology is both an art and a science, and has been subject to much abuse by the unscrupulous or naive. For those unfamiliar with astrology, remember that the scientific method is to test and investigate, not reject from prejudice.* An old rejoiner by Sir Isaac Newton to doubters is, "I have studied it, have you?"

Today a modern form of astrology has developed, known as *humanistic astrology*.† This updated form is

---

* Recommended as introductions to astrology: *The Compleat Astrologer,* Derek and Julia Parker, McGraw-Hill Book Co., 1971 (oversize paperback available) and *The Case for Astrology,* John Anthony West and Jan Gerhard Toonder, Coward-McCann, N.Y., 1970 (a compilation of assorted scientific support related to astrology).
† Reference works of Dane Rudhyar, such as *The Astrology of Personality,* Doubleday & Co., 1970 (original edition 1936).

rapidly gaining popularity in psychological counseling and psychiatric work, being proved a valuable and reputable tool. Jung would no doubt have approved the trend. Andre Barbault, in an interview for the French magazine Astrologie Moderne of May 26, 1954 said:

> One can expect with considerable assurance that a given well-defined psychological situation will be accompanied by an analagous astrological configuration. Astrology consists of configurations, symbols of the collective unconscious, which is the subject of the powers of the unconscious.

The mode of manifestation of these influences upon us is basically defined by natal charts cast for the time and place of birth. We are strongly influenced by the "stamp" of our "energy pattern" at birth, but past-life study reveals there is still more to this than appears on the surface. In a study of charts for past lives, as well as the present, a remarkable discovery appears. While our charts do change, basic influences will reappear life after life. We are reborn under energies that are harmonious to our basic composition. The lessons will vary, but the "desk" remains essentially the same.

We are interpenetrating parts of the evolutionary process of the Cosmos, connected and interrelated. "For just as in the visible world of the vegetable and animal kingdoms, so in the visionary world of God: there has been a history, an evolution, a series of mutations, governed by laws."

BASIS OF THE SEVEN RAYS
Once again I must ask you to relax yourself and ex-

pand your consciousness with me back to the evolving Cosmos. The rotation of the Cosmos has continued and we find that something else has begun to happen. Belts of dimensional motion, somewhat like the layers of an onion, are forming outward from the Center. Seven dimensions are forming, each revolving at a different speed.

The twelve rays continue their flow back and forth across the Cosmos, but now they begin to encounter the changes of speed and their flow experiences deflection. This creates huge dual vortices of motion that interlock and form *primal atoms.* * These appear as enormous gyroscopic units and are *sound-producing,* much like spinning tops. Some of these spinning units will eventually evolve into universes (bodies united by rotation) within the Cosmos.

Each of the primal atoms revolves within a geometric pattern resulting from the force of its impact with the motion of the belt of its origin. Those formed on the slower first belt gyrate in a three-sided triangular pattern. Those from the next belt move within a cubical four-sided pattern, and so on up to nine facets. These primal sound producing units of motion form the basis of the science of numbers, the Law of Harmonics and the "music of the spheres."

The number seven appears repeatedly throughout nature, in religion and philosophy. The study of the "Seven Rays,"† refers to the seven basic dimensional differentia-

---

*   Reference: the "M.R. Scripts," communications from the "Master R." through the Axminster Light Center, 3 Willhayes Park, North St., Axminster, Devon, EX13 5QL, England, (on man and cosmology).

†   Reference: *Esoteric Psychology - The Seven Rays,* Dr. Douglas Baker, 'Little Elephant' Essendon, Herts, England, 1975.
Esoteric Psychology, Volumes I & II, Alice Bailey, Lucis Publishing Co., 1962 and 1970.

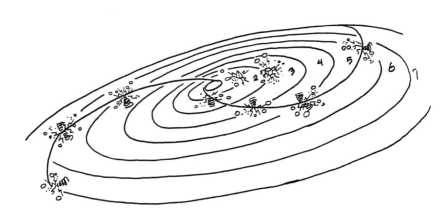

"Basis of the Seven Rays"
As the twelve rays flow across the Cosmos, they encounter
deflections of their flow, resulting in huge sound-producing vortices
of motion.

tions of the twelve rays. "They are the seven breaths of the one Life, the seven basic energies; they streamed forth from the centre formed by the impact of the will of God on divine substance, and divided into seven streams of force." (*Esoteric Psychology*, Vol. I).

Referring to the results from the creative rotation of the Cosmos, the *Yin-Yang Doctrine* flatly states:

> The cyclical movement itself produced the empirical and abstract forms of the cosmos. The oscillation between the Yin and Yang forms the correlation in all phenomena extending to the realms of time, space, number and ethics.
>
> (Encyclopaedia Britannica, 1973.)

IN THE BEGINNING WAS THE *WORD*

The primal sound-producing atoms each become a creative *Word* bringing forth manifestation of God, each in accordance with the dimensional motion of its belts. Individuals may become aware of the sounds of these notes ringing in their ears, called the *Om* or *Aum* in Eastern philosophy. All life, forms and human thought begin with the *Word*.

Christianity tells us that man arose from the *eye* and *Word* of God. St. Clement, one of the Fathers of the Christian Church, taught:

> We were in being long before the foundation of the world; we existed in the eye of God, for it is our destiny to live in Him. We are the reasonable creatures of the Divine Word, therefore, we have existed from the beginning, for in the beginning was the Word.

This is important, we have existed *from the beginning of the Word. What* existed? We have seen that only emanations, forces and evolving motions exist so far in the Cosmos. Where are we? To find out we will have to return to the Cosmos and watch the next stage, the evolution of the *Words*.

We see the primal atoms on each belt begin attracting other atoms, gradually forming clusters. As a *primal atom* gathers other atoms, it becomes a *composite atom,* held together by its own internal stresses. The composite atoms remain on their own belts until they become so massive that the laws of motion move them out along the rays. Now they become *traveling atoms* and they begin attracting more atoms from each belt they go through. They continue this process, gathering clouds of sub-atomic "pre-matter" around them until they have made the full circuit of all the rays and come to rest in the Central Eye.

When all of the traveling atoms have completed their circuit and gathered in the Central Stillness, the Cosmos reaches a state of equilibrium. The *First Day of Creation* draws to a close and *Night* (Pralaya) descends. This *Night of God* lasts until, renewed with force, the Ring Chaos upsets the balance. Movement begins again and the *Second Day* dawns. Each primal atom, or *Word,* now has all of the structural forces of a universal body within it.

With the new *Day* these great bodies are again pulled out along the rays. As they pass through the belts, they cause the creation of *secondary atoms,* or vortices, on each belt. Collisions of these atoms with each other creates still more atoms, and so on. A similar reaction occurs when "cosmic rays" collide with air molecules in Earth's atmosphere. The collision produces a variety of secondary particles that spray into streaks and spirals.

MADE IN THE IMAGE OF GOD

As the *Words* move through the Cosmos, their gyrating motion, or "cosmic dance," creates a permanent "track" in space, most easily visualized as a spiraling tunnel of permanent motion. We might crudely compare it to a wind tunnel, with a fan that keeps air continually moving along the tunnel. The motion will move objects through the tunnel, or turn a second fan at the opposite end.

Emanations of *Light* from the *Eye* begin to follow these "tracks" established by the Words. These emanations become the *Divine Sparks* of Cosmic Fire that constitute the *spirit* of man. It is most accurate to visualize these as "threads of *Light*" created by emanations of passive thought energy following the object manifested (the *Word*). Through our *Divine Sparks* we are permanently connected with the Cosmic Center.* Within man the Spark becomes a point of Cosmic Fire, the "flame of the soul," or the *Seed-atom*.

These Seed-atoms (atomic nuclei) will each eventually reflect the archetypal construction of the Cosmos, creating enveloping "bodies" of atomic particles from each dimension and following cosmic patterns. Through millions of years some will gradually emerge as man, "made in the image of God." In the Hindu *Katha Upanishad*, Yama, the god of death, tells us, "Smaller than small, greater than

---

* Reference: *Reincarnation & You*, Patricia Diegel, Ph.D., Prism Publications, 3453 East Poinsettia, Phoenix, AZ 85028.

great, this *Self* is hidden in the heart of man . . ." This *Self* is the Seed-atom united by the Divine Spark with the Central Stillness. Yama continues:

> Know that the *Self* is the lord of the chariot, the *body* verily is the chariot, know that the *soul* is the charioteer, and the *emotions* the reins. They say that the bodily powers are the horses and the external world is their field. (author's italics).

THE EVOLUTION OF CONSCIOUSNESS

The evolution of the Cosmos so far has involved continuous repetitious patterns of motion. These form the fundamental basis of consciousness. *Consciousness results from reaction plus memory, and memory results from repetitious motion.* In the beginning there is only motion, so the first awareness of the Cosmos is *unconscious,* a subjective awareness, first of the spiraling motion, then of the flowing forces and the dimensional belts.

This is the level of awareness when the *Second Day* draws to a close. The developing universal bodies and other bodies of motion stabilize and the Cosmos sleeps again. What happens next is especially important to us. We find that the slumbering Cosmos is unconsciously projecting "dream" images (thought energy) of the various repetitious activities that occurred through the *Day*. These unconscious thoughts travel out along the "tracks" and are received unconsciously by the universal bodies as impulses. They respond by ordering themselves after the archetypal (energy) patterns being projected. This process continues through the *Night* until once again the Ring Chaos upsets the balance.

With the *Third Day* the Cosmos begins to consciously perceive the *repetitious reactions* of the universal bodies. A reciprocal relationship begins developing between the Cosmos as the *knower* and the universal bodies as *objects known.* The Cosmos becomes *conscious of the reaction,* though not of the process. The first step toward purposeful thought to elicit a specific response has been taken.

As we watch, we see that the universal bodies seem to be responding to the Cosmic impulses and manifest the cosmic processes within themselves. Ultimately they also begin to gain awareness of *reactions* within themselves from *their reflection* of both the Cosmic input and their unconscious thoughts. While eventually becoming aware of reactions within their universal bodies, they remain unaware of the Cosmic influence. In this process a chain reaction is established whereby the evolutionary experience of each evolving body "climbs on the shoulders" of the previous one, accelerating the speed and complexity. This intensification eventually produces manifested matter as we know it. H.P. Blavatsky refers to this in *The Secret Doctrine:*

> Our "universe" is only one of an infinite number of Universes . . . each one standing in the relation of an effect as regards its predecessor . . . and this stupendous development has neither conceivable beginning nor imaginable end.

Within the sea of the Great Unmanifest there need be no limits upon the number of Cosmoses and universes, each mirroring the former and elaborating upon it. Our solar system is such a universal body, sending thought impulses into lesser bodies, including both planetary and human forms. Human consciousness having been built around cosmic patterns, we respond predictably, with one variant: "free-will." As man developed the ability to think and become his own creative agent, he also learned to direct his will himself. Problems arose when this will was not directed in accordance with the Divine Will and full consciousness was not gained, leaving man in a strange predicament.

The average human consciousness is prodded into *reaction* by unconscious motivation (*e-motions* causing movement). To become fully conscious and *Self-motivated,* you need to extend your consciousness beyond the powerful grip of your unconscious and illusions of reality. You have built up an unconscious body of thought and emotions through many lives, and are probably carrying a lot of hindering excess baggage you do not need. It is time to lighten the load and free yourself.

You can accomplish this and conquer the serpent by expanding your consciousness *through* your *unconscious,* your *soul-consciousness* and your *Divine Spark* to the *Central Stillness. Return to the Source* does not mean literally going back, or "annihilation" within the Void. It does mean *expanding* Cosmic Consciousness throughout the Cosmos. The beginning is the release of the egoic grip, centered around two-dimensional consciousness. From there uncomprehensible powers of mind can be reached. The rest is experience and development, which is what this book is about. You can learn to look back through the "chamber of mirrors" within your own mind and you can also look forward and learn to influence your present and future.

THE CONSCIOUSNESS OF THE ATOM

Cosmic order is reflected in all manifestations, from the atom and its components to great galactic bodies. The atoms we are familiar with consist of *three* particles with mass: protons, neutrons and electrons. Some of the sub-atomic particles known include the photons (massless units representing electromagnetic radiation), neutrinos (also massless) and antiparticles of opposite charges. Many more sub-atomic particles are known and stable interactions have been found to be very orderly, *oscillating* in rhythmic movements. The sub-atomic particles are not considered independent entities, but as *dynamic patterns* that are integral parts in a *network of interactions.* The patterns are said to fall into four categories of interaction: weak, strong, *electromagnetic* and *gravitational.*

It seems we can look at the unity of the Cosmos from two directions: from sub-atomic particles to formation of the Cosmic forces, or from the development of archetypal patterns that extend to the smallest atom. Either way represents interactive unity.

Looking at the atom still another way, we find that the electrons orbit around the center (nucleus), reminding us of a miniature solar system. The rest of the atom contains "empty space," dotted with negative electrical charges. Recalling the Cosmic belts, we find that the orbiting electrons also appear to be arranged in belts around the nucleus. Each of these belts, or shells, as they are known, is only able to hold a specific number of electrons, with a maximum of *seven* shells. The uranium atom, the most complex known, has seven shells reflecting the cos-

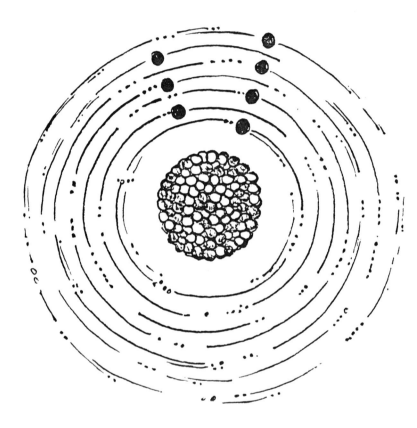

"The Consciousness of the Atom"
The atoms we are familiar with consist of three particles with
mass: protons, neutrons and electrons. The electrons orbit around
the central nucleus, resembling a miniature solar system, with belts,
known as shells, numbering up to a maximum of seven.

mic order.

The idea of the atom reflecting the universe is not new. In Chaldea the atom was called *Anu,* meaning the concealed deity or One. Vedantic philosophy describes *Parabrahm*, or *Anu* (smallest of the small), as "smaller than the smallest atom and greater than the greatest sphere or universe."

THE COLLECTIVE UNCONSCIOUS

So far we have found cosmic patterns and interactions appearing on several levels of manifestation. All forms may be thought of as *corresponding* to unconscious impulses related to the formation of the Cosmos. As human, we have received and responded to Cosmic impulses through our unconscious minds. We carry our personal history with us unconsciously and we have continual access to the Collective Unconscious of humanity. Beyond this we can extend our consciousness to Universal Consciousness to obtain objective and analytical history about ourselves, and through our divine aspect we can commune with the Cosmic Stillness.

You need to be aware that the Collective Unconscious, like your personal unconscious, contains an accumulation of information distorted by the experiences, opinions and emotions of humanity over millions of years. Unconscious mind is not an accurate source for objective information; this can only be obtained by drawing from Universal Consciousness. Our goal is to begin drawing more from the higher levels and less from collective levels.

As a sleeping/waking creator of your world, you have

mirrored cosmic processes, so in your unconscious memory are built-in reaction patterns you have added life after life, from death to rebirth. These in turn are permanently colored by your evolutionary stages of development in the universe and your ray origin influences. Your reaction patterns are built into *seven* interpenetrating layers, or "bodies," each of a different dimensional constitution. These fall into four main categories: spiritual, mental, emotional and physical. They were constructed during your travels as a Seed-atom, collecting sub-atomic matter to yourself on each dimension. Basically you incarnate by merging the higher vibrational bodies into a physical form, giving it the qualities of life, feelings and intelligence. Through life experiences you have continually added learned abilities, aptitudes, attitudes and motivations to your *soul-bodies.*

The door to your *soul-consciousness* is through your unconscious mind. Once you realize how powerfully it may be directing your life without your knowledge or desire, you can begin taking conscious action to reverse the situation. You can tap your unconscious, learn from it, work with it and develop it constructively. Bear in mind you cannot misuse the creative power of your mind without it turning on you (what you send out returns). Abuse can also create a misalignment or separation of the bodies, intentional or not. This is the cause of much sorrow, illness and other undesirable side-effects. In the cosmic perspective *disorders* can only be corrected by bringing them into line with *cosmic order* or under the stimuli of the higher levels of *Self.*

Once you realize you are your own creative agent and self-responsible, you can begin the rewarding project of reprogramming your own unconscious. You will learn that you cannot "blame" anyone else for your life experiences, past or present, and you will become increasingly aware that you are creating your future *now*.

As you begin to draw from the various levels of consciousness you will find symbols increasingly important. To tap these reservoirs of knowledge, the best keys are symbols that will be understood by both your conscious mind and the unconscious. A study of symbols becomes helpful for use in meditation, visualization and contemplation. Symbolical studies include dreams, myths, astrology, the *Tarot* and the *Kabbalistic Tree;* all are good starting points, dependent upon your particular interests.*

Many have gone before us to show that mastery of consciousness is possible. The greatest hurdle is overcoming the illusion that the conscious mind is self-directing, while in truth it is blind to its thought processes. We are "caught upon the wheel of rebirth" because of this blindness that tangles us in a evergrowing web of emotional (unconscious) desires. A Japanese Hymn from the 8th Century A.D. describes the plight:

> Blind, blind are sentient creatures all,
> Yet know they not their blindness,
> Again, again they are reborn
> To darkness and sadness,
> Again, again they pass and die
> Blinded by sense externally.

---

* Recommended: *Edgar Cayce on Dreams;* Harmon H. Bro, Ph.D., 1968; *Psychosynthesis*, Roberto Assagioli, M.D.; *Adam and the Kabbalistic Tree*, Z'ev ben Shimon Halevi; *B.O.T.A., Waite-Rider* or new *Golden Dawn Tarot* decks.

This is our predicament, blind to *Self,* until the ego is willing to accept the condition of its poverty and release responsibility to the eternal *Self.* In *The Yoga Aphorisms of Patanjali,* this great teacher says, "When the mind no longer conceives of itself to be the knower, or experiencer, and has become one with the soul—the real knower and experiencer . . . the soul is emancipated."

The plight of humanity, then, is the imprisonment of the soul by forcing it to submit to our *conscious* expression of free-will extended to our limited environment. The higher spiritual aspects may go so far as to withdraw in Self-defense, until such time as the individual intelligence actively seeks and petitions for its *Presence.* The human potential is to *direct the mind through will,* thereby drawing from all aspects of consciousness under the direction and guidance of Divine Will. The result is Oneness in awareness and purpose.

As you work on this, results become obvious when emotions improve, purposes grow, attitudes change and awareness increases. We learn objectively by finding that it works. Reflecting the cosmic process, we observe that our thoughts have brought responses within us and in our life, and we learn to use our creative power.

THE WHEEL OF REBIRTH

Ye suffer from yourselves. None else compels
None other holds you that ye live and die,
And whirl upon the wheel, and hug and kiss
Its spokes of agony. . . .
Before beginning and without end,
Is fixed a Power divine which moves to good,
Only its laws endure.
    —An excerpt from *The Light of Asia,* by Sir Edwin Arnold, 1897.

We are now coming close to understanding the principle behind rebirth. We have seen that the Cosmos appears to sleep and wake. Science agrees that there may be great cycles of universal death and rebirth, but this doesn't completely explain reincarnation cycles. Surprisingly science may have the answer to this also.

A major controversy has been waged among astronomers about whether our universe is *open* or *closed*. If it is *closed* and surrounded by a force field (as we have discussed), it would recycle everything in it. According to the 1978 edition of the *World Book Encyclopedia*:

> If the spread-out density of matter in space were as much as 100 atoms of hydrogen in 10 cubic yards . . . , the universe would be *closed*. A light beam sent into space in this kind of universe would return to its sender many billions of years later.

A light beam, a thought, a motion or action—each represents expenditure of energy that can be transformed but not destroyed. A *closed* universe means that expended energy would eventually return to its source. This also implies that we must eventually return as emanation (thought energy) to our Cosmic Source, and that we recycle our thought energy again and again within our own personal force fields. This is logical, since at physical death only the denser aspects "die," while higher dimensional aspects (including our intelligence) live on within their encompassing force fields.

To break the reincarnation cycle, we have to develop the habit of centering our thought in *soul-consciousness* and with the *Self.* Meditation, positive thought and study are all *processes.* So is past life memory, or karmic recall. When unconscious memories come into the light of consciousness, they tend to lose their unconscious power to motivate. Eventually when enough memories have been assimilated, a *soul-trend* may emerge, and you will have the unique opportunity to discover the *individuality* behind the *personality.*

The time to act is while you have conscious awareness. If you "put it off until tomorrow," it might be too late. Next time when you reincarnate you probably will not remember what you know now, and the unconscious will have to "prod" you to learn all over again, but you might not listen. You will find, as you start to work on developing consciousness, that there will be cycles up and down. Sometimes you may be keen, and at other times you may feel like you are getting nowhere. This is normal; it is part of the *process,* as long as you maintain your objective.

When you begin this process many experiences may come your way at different stages of advancement. These will largely depend upon your past life experience and training. Like any school, sometimes there may be lessons that are not easy but essential. It will be up to you how far and how fast you advance.

There are times when knowledge is released and human evolution leaps ahead. Now is such a time in human history. Tremendous opportunity is present for *individual and collective* advancement. This is being demonstrated today by the worldwide mushrooming of interest in spiritual growth, Eastern religions in the West, and an incredible number of *New Age* communities of all types. The desire, in fact the *impulse,* humanity is *responding* to is the call to "return," understood or not. Those who are ready are taking *action* now. They are consciously seeking the Divine Will of return. Regardless of your lifestyle, you can probably incorporate the principles of *Cosmic Consciousness* into it without radical changes.

> The SELF is the Lord of self, what higher Lord could there be? When a man subdues well his self, he will find a Lord very difficult to find . . . Him I call a Brahman who knows the mystery of death and rebirth of all beings, who is free from attachment, who is happy within himself and enlightened . . . . Him I call a Brahman who knows his former lives, who knows heaven and hell, who has reached the end of births, who is a sage of perfect knowledge and who has accomplished all that has to be.
>
> (From the *Dhammapada Commentary* of Buddhist Canonical Literature, translated by F. L. Woodward).

DRESS REHEARSAL

2

Dress Rehearsal

Places! Places everyone!

> Excuse me, but where do I go?
> Central Casting just sent me over to do the
> fallen angel series.

Right, just move over by
that small solar system, third planet
from the sun, you can't miss it.

> Wait a minute, don't you
> want to see my fallen angel routine?

Your what?

> Watch this. Ready?
> Ahhh . . . they got me. . . . . KLUNK!

What are you doing now?

> My fallen angel . . . .

I don't believe this . . . . Hey, where's Adam?
Has anyone seen Adam?

> Quiet in the Cosmos!

> Ahhhhh . . . . KLUNK!

(Good grief!)

ALL ABOARD FOR THE MILKY WAY

The Cosmos has evolved now to the point of having all of its basic motions and forces established, and universal systems have begun to settle on the various dimensional belts. We will return now to one of these, our future solar system in the Milky Way Galaxy. We will watch the evolution of our universal primal atom, as it follows the patterns established by the Cosmos and elaborates upon them, producing our planet and its mineral and life forms.

As we return we find that the universal body is arranged and divided just like the Cosmos, and rays of *light* are beginning to swirl toward the center. This is *light* that is more familiar to us, resembling intense explosive flashes and atomic in nature. In the middle of the continually rotating body a central stillness forms and *light* begins to grow within it. In Western traditions this is known as the *Solar Logos* (central light), or *Logos,* meaning *Word* (thought and will) in Greek and Hebrew, the first creation and creating agent of God.

The spinning primal atom develops its own unconscious body of thought in the stillness and continually receives impulses from the Cosmos. The *Logos* begins creating in response by reflecting these impulses to the accompanying Seed-atoms which take up the evolutionary work. "In the beginning was the Word, and the Word was with God, and the Word was God." (John 1.1)

The *Logos* is considered to be the "Greater Adam," known as *Adam-Adami* in Chaldean scriptures and *Adam Kadmon* in the Jewish *Zohar* (light of Kabbalism). The prefix, *"ad"* in Assyrian means "father," and in Aramaean

"One." The suffix "*am*," as well as "*om*," in most languages means divine or deity. To human consciousness the *Logos* is perceived clairvoyantly as an old man's face, surrounded by streamers of white "hair" flowing out from it. This has resulted in titles such as the "*White Head*," the "*Ancient of Days*" and the "*Ancient of Ancients.*"

In Buddhism the *Logos* is the universal *Buddhi*, or root of divine intelligence. The *Logos* becomes an evolving body of creative consciousness, surrounded by its own *ring-pass-not*, and unaware consciously of the Cosmic Source. The *Logos* only "sees" within *Self*, becoming an egoic body of the Cosmos. The Seed-atoms have essentially the same level of awareness as the *Logos* at this point, but as they leave the *Logoic Center* and venture out into the universe, they 'forget" their *Cosmic-Logoic Sources* and each *wave* develops its own egoic body of collective unconscious thought.

To follow the progress of the Seed-atoms, we had better continue watching from our *light* bodies. They begin to leave the *Logoic Center* in *waves* and flow along the universal rays, traveling again in a gyrating motion or "atomic dance," and producing another track in Space permanently connecting them with the *Logos*. They now have two tracks, one connected to the Cosmic Source and one connecting them with the *Logos*. Confusion results, somewhat like trying to listen to two radio stations at once, and is compounded by the *Logos* sending reversed cosmic images like the reflections in a mirror.

To solve the problem the Seed-atoms begin to "collect their thoughts" and store them in thought forms, where they will be sorted out.* They leave a glowing spherical body of thought-energy on each dimensional belt of the universal body. In the distant future these will evolve into planetary bodies.

THE FORMATIVE ELEMENTS

There will be seven *waves*, but the first three are "angelic" and the "human" waves have to wait until these complete their work. The first *wave* of Seed-atoms is only able to instill awareness of electricity and forces. As this thought energy is impressed upon the thought-form of collective consciousness, functional aspects develop and the electromagnetic forces and stresses of a planet are begun. When these reach a balance, the Seed-atoms have nothing more to impart, and the functions become automatic. The Seed-atoms have embued the "laws of physics" into the thought-form.

These Seed-atoms become known as the angelic *Lords of Fire,* and rulers of the *element of Fire.* The *Bible* tells us, "And he made His ministering Spirits a flame of Fire," and "flames of Fire were His ministering Spirits." The term angel, (*asdt* in Hebrew, meaning *emanation*) is translated as "messenger." Genesis 1:2 says, "And the earth was *without form* and void, and the darkness was upon the face of the deep. And the spirit of God moved upon the face of the waters." (Recall that "spirit" is the *emanating* contact through the Divine Sparks and "waters" an analogy

---

* Reference: *Thought Forms,* Annie Besant and C.W. Leadbeater, Theosophical Publishing House, 1967 (originally published 1925).

for Space.)

While using our past-life memory techniques a student, Rachel MacPherson, slipped back into one of these formative periods. (She had not known about them prior to her recall and a later reading of this manuscript.) This is how she described her experience in her own words:

> Formless—void—flame—fire—form just beginning to shape, a helper or assistant to a very high energy. Creating, transferring, transforming—seemed to be carrying particles (?) or elements. Fire seemed to be positive, yet destroying to transform.

> There seemed to be no thought or memory, only purpose. The purpose was to transform—to create. That is all there was—one-pointed purpose. Seemed to be in a group, not individualized at all.

> I couldn't get any one planet, there seemed to be a number of them each yielding a different substance, particle, or chemical (?) to be transferred.

The second *wave* Seed-atoms encounter the thought-forms left by the first wave and simply tune-in. However, since something new has been created in the universe, they begin reflecting awareness of *form* from the *Logos.* As they "think" about this, they cause small forms to develop. Again these are thought-forms, with motions that follow cosmic patterns. They are geometric patterns that will become chemicals as they attract and hold atomic matter by their electromagnetic and gravitational fields.

The Seed-atoms also develop vortices within themselves (*chakras*) that will attract and surround them with sub-atomic matter. The planetary forms already have vortices that were built-in by the first wave, so they are ready to attract sub-atomic matter and build chemicals from the forms created by the second *wave*. "And God said, 'Let the waters under the heaven be gathered together and unto one place, and let the dry land appear;' and it was so." (Genesis 1:9).

This *wave* of Seed-atoms responds now to another impulse, and begins the first cycle of "death and rebirth" by shedding the forms they have collected to themselves and leaving them on each planet as pre-matter. After each "death" they are attracted back to the *Logos*, then they return to their last planet, re-form bodies and go on to the next planetary body. This results in a mixture of dimensional pre-matter deposited on each planet by the Seed-atoms as they progress.*

The bodies the Seed-atoms build are similar to man's seven interpenetrating bodies. Those of higher vibrational material are not normally visible to human sight, but they are being photographed, by a method known as Kirlian photography, in all life forms.†

The planets are electromagnetically connected by atomic pre-matter, as well as the tracks left between them by the Seed-atoms. The interpenetrating nature of the Cosmos and the accumulative process of building inter-

---

* Reference: *The Cosmic Doctrine*, Dion Fortune.
† Reference: *The Kirlian Aura*, Photographing the Galaxies of Life, Stanley Krippner and Daniel Rubin, Anchor Books, 1974, (with an extensive list of reference works); *Psychic Discoveries Behind The Iron Curtain*, Sheila Ostrander and Lynn Schroeder, Bantam Books, 1970.

penetrating bodies from each dimension by the Seed-atoms are important factors in astrological influence. Earth is continually interacting with the sun and other planets. Angular degree relationships between the sun and planets as they move through the heavens are continually changing. These relationships can strongly support or interfere with Earth's reception of energy flow between the sun and planets.

A demonstration of this is the use of these planetary positions to predict the quality of radio reception in communications. John Nelson, an electrical engineer, found that most magnetic storms causing radio interference occur consistently under certain planetary relationships. He also found disturbance free fields existing in relation to the sun.

An article appearing in *The New York Times* noted that these effects seem "to indicate [that] the planets and the sun share in a cosmic electrical-balance mechanism that extends a billion miles from the center of the solar system. Such an electrical balance is not accounted for in current astrophysical theories."

These Seed-atoms become the *Lords of Form,* and also of *Death.* They begin the production of matter by confining sub-atomic matter within patterns of form, ultimately resulting in death through friction and disintegration. By the time they leave each planet all the functions to create forms have been permanently built into the planetary thought-form and the process continues automatically.

Two "elements" result from this process, *Earth* and

Water forming the basis of chemistry. Each element has its own collective consciousness built into the Collective Unconscious of the planet and keeps repeating its functions much like a record playing over and over. Try to visualize that we are really watching emanations, waves and particles of light carrying the *Cosmic-Logoic* impulses into various dimensions of motion and energy. The creative process is all interactive and interrelated, starting from the "virtual particles" of the Void and the forces of the manifesting Cosmos and focusing down to the elaboration of intelligent manifested energy forms, or our known *life* forms.

Now it is the third wave's turn. They arrive at the thought-form, tune-in and discover the emerging pre-matter forms. The *Logos* having perceived this latest development, provides the Seed-atoms with the impulse to conceive of combinations of these pre-matter forms to produce larger *composite units.* These units each develop individual force fields from their motions and the electromagnetic and gravitational ability to attract and hold combinations of chemical pre-matter. They are, however, still essentially patterns in preparation to the formation and collection of denser atomic matter (representing the science of biology).

The creation of these separate units with their own force fields is the step that will allow the *individuation* of life forms to develop and permit the evolution of consciousness in each form as a reflection of *Logic* consciousness. The third *wave* Seed-atoms become the angelic *Lords of Mind,* and of *Will,* laying the groundwork for the evolution of humanity, destined to individually reflect the "Greater Adam" and develop group functions (representing the science of sociology). The *third wave* Seed-atoms are responsible for the "element" of *Air*, corresponding to mind.

The evolution of units affects the elemental kingdoms and divisions occur here, also. They have to expand their functions to include each new form and division as it evolves, so many sizes and types of elementals result. While still functioning automatically from the collective consciousness, each kingdom is said to consist of elementals, meaning innumerable elemental units, each performing its own job. These elementals will evolve parallel to human evolution, but remain a lower form, separate and different. They will imitate man, drawing from the Collective Unconscious, and some will develop personalities, but they are not *individualized* through Divine Sparks.

Each planet is considered a Planetary Being, or Intelligence, formed around its interpenetrating bodies of thought. Its evolution is always behind that of its forms, since it depends upon them to continually feed thoughts into the Collective Unconscious. Our planet has been referred to in this sense as *Mother Earth*, and is capable to a degree of creating on her own.

MOTHER EARTH FAILS

The first three *waves*, finished with their work, leave *Mother Earth* on her own for a time. The various elemental functions continue under the developing planetary consciousness, containing the fundamental impressions of cosmic principles, archetypal patterns and individuation.

According to ancient traditions, the elemental kingdoms, responding to the primitive creative thought of *Mother Earth,* begin to chaotically create mismatched units of form.

*The Book of Dzyan** says the result was, "The water-men terrible and bad she (Earth) herself created from the remains of the others." "Water-men" would refer to their pre-matter composition and "the remains" probably refers to the matter deposited by the second *wave* Seed-atoms and disintegrating matter of other forms.

This development is also described in *The Chaldean Account of Genesis.*† It speaks of an "abyss of waters," where hideous beings resided, men with wings, four and two-faced men, human, with two heads and the legs and horns of goats, hippocentaurs, bulls with the heads of men, dogs with the tails of fishes, men with bird's heads and so on. These monstrous forms were not what the next four waves of future human Seed-atoms were meant to enter or work with, and tradition says the angels eventually destroyed them.

THE *FALLEN* ANGELS

Millions of years pass as the first three *waves* of angelic Seed-atoms return to the *Logos,* where they gain full consciousness of the *Logoic Will.* They become One in

---

* Sanskrit manuscripts reproduced in *The Secret Doctrine*, H.P. Blavatsky, Theosophical University Press, 1963, reprint from 1888.
† *The Chaldean Account of Genesis,* George Smith, as translated from cuniform inscriptions in the 1870's; reprinted by Wizards Book Shelf, Minneapolis, MN, 1977.

mind and purpose with the *Logos, Holy Powers* and *Arch-angels* ("arch" meaning primordial or chief). The angels, now conscious of the Divine Will, are "commanded" to reflect cosmic order under the *Logos.*

It is the *Logoic Will* as the "Greater Adam" to create alter egos that perfectly reflect the wisdom, power and purposes of the *Logos.* An archetypal Adam is meant to evolve on Earth. Agreement varies on exactly what happens next, but this is when the "war in heaven" occurs and Michael, the *Archangel of Fire,* and his celestial host drive one-third of the angels from heaven, condemning them to the lower realm. Why one-third?

It is said the *spirits of flame* could not help; the duty fell to the *Lords of Mind* to salvage the human evolution. They were the closest to future man. They had absorbed the knowledge of the first two *waves*, elaborated upon it and were responsible for the evolution of *individuation, mind* and *will.* The *Divine Will* was for them to finish what they had started and properly prepare the Earth to evolve man.

These angels are said to have taken the *Logoic* reflection from themselves, creating *light* bodies from their own substance for the arriving Seed-atoms. By so doing they attached themselves to these forms and condemned themselves to remain on Earth until all of their reflections "return" as conscious individual creators to their Source.

THE FIRST MAN ADAM

The early angelic creations of human form are referred to as "projections" or "shadow-men." *The Book of Dzyan* states, *"Seven times seven* shadows of future men were born, each of his own color and kind . . . " and "these *seven* gods, each of whom created a *man,* or a group of men," were "the gods *imprisoned* or incarnated."* The Japanese have a tradition that they came from "gods amounting to *seven* . . . said to have reigned an almost incalculable number of years . . . [they] were spiritual substances, incorporeal. They were succeeded by *five* terrestial spirits . . . . " After this the Japanese people are said to have emerged.

The races of men are consistently stated to have appeared worldwide simultaneously. Edgar Cayce says that their color "partook of their surroundings . . . in the manner of the chameleon." He mentions *five* racial aspects all "projected" and corresponding to the five elements or, "the attributes to which he (man) may become conscious from the elemental or spiritual to the physical consciousness."† The early shadow-bodies become the highest spiritual body of man and are eventually absorbed into the next bodies as they evolve.

Adam is not just one man, but all the races of men. The prefix *"ad"* may be followed by a variety of adjectives or modifiers. Like the *Logoic Adam Kadmon* of the Kabbala, and *Adam-adami* of the Chaldeans (One Father or creator), *Ad-am* is a collective name. As George Adams says in *The Chaldean Account of Genesis,* "The word

---

* Seven refers to the seven rays, and "times seven" is the forty-nine sub-rays of the *Logoic* universe.

† *Edgar Cayce on Atlantis,* Edgar Evans Cayce, Paperback Library, 1968.

Adam used in these legends for the first human being is evidently *not a proper name, but is only used as a term for mankind."* Variations on the name have included: *Admi, Adami* and *Adamu* (the latter a dark race in Babylonian legend).

Though humanity appears worldwide, some areas have become renown for their evolutionary developments. The first forms are said to have reached their highest evolution in "The Sacred Land." Tradition holds that this place still exists and that humanity will one day *return* to it. Examining early history may provide the meaning of this.

The early forms, though individualized, functioned collectively. Individual consciousness did not exist yet. They have been called the "Mind-born sons of *Brahma*" and the *"Yogic* Race," *yoga* meaning yoked together in mind. Hindu philosophy says the angels were the celestial *Yogis*, who seeing the mindless predicament of their projections, entered into the "curse of incarnation" and the lengthy cycle of rebirth to help the forms evolve. The Mexican *Popol Vuh* speaks of these early beings as men "whose sight was unlimited, and who knew all things at once," descriptive of their *yogic* collective consciousness. Evolved man, having achieved individualized consciousness, must return to a *yogic* condition with the *Logos*. A steady flow of guidance regarding this has come from the East, especially from Tibet and northern India. The *"Masters,"* those evolved entities who help oversee the development of mankind have largely worked from this "sacred area," having achieved their evolution there during the early *waves* of human Seed-atoms.*

Something very important happened when the "shadowmen" were projected. Like the emanating "tracks" between the *Cosmic-Logoic Sources,* a similar connection is formed between the angels and their projections. This connection has been known variously as the *Watcher, Oversoul, Superconscious, Higher-Self* or *Ego,* etc., a part of, yet separate from, the *individual.* In the highly evolved entity, it "appears" as a glowing sphere of light overhead (giving rise to "halos"). Having overseen many incarnations, it has absorbed only that worthy of divine thought through the ages.

On the next step up Jacob's Ladder, it ascends to the *Atman,* where man reaches the *Logos,* for the two are *One.* Such an individual will belong to one of the *Heirarchal ashrams* or schools, and a "group." As any individual advances, so does the group, and with the group all life moves up in consciousness. Remember *interpenetration.*

During the early period of angelic projections, *groups of forms* were created as needed. As Cayce says, "the ruling forces . . . create . . . or make the channel for . . . the projection of an entity or soul . . . such were not as households or as families . . . but rather as groups."† This was the beginning of the common phenomena encountered today of people repeatedly incarnating with "soul-mates" and in "soul-families."

---

* Recommended: *The Education of Oversoul No. 7,* Jane Roberts, Pocket Books, 1976, a *novel* designed to stimulate, inform and increase awareness.
† Edgar Cayce on *Atlantis,* Edgar Evans Cayce, 1968.

HYPERBOREAN "ATLANTIS"

Often confused with later Atlantis and Lemuria, the next area is actually the Hyperborean *Land of Meru*. Frozen by one of the turns of the globe, this formerly tropical land curved from the present Bering Straits to the British Isles. Now it is mostly in the arctic and sub-arctic North (*Meru* means "white island" in the old traditions, referring to the polar cap, ice and snow). The *Hyperboreans* of myth were "a people beyond the north wind in a region of perpetual sunshine."

Now the forms begin to exhibit "human characteristics." They can "stand, walk, run, recline and fly."* Still of noncorporeal substance, "the Breaths had life, but not understanding." Soul means to "contain the Breath of Life," reflecting the rhythmic oscillation of all forms from the Cosmos to atoms. This is the period the Bible speaks of when Adam has received the "Breath of Life"; he enters a "deep sleep" indicative of the lengthy time before he develops conscious thought or gains "knowledge."

An intermediary period develops when some of the arriving Seed-atoms fail to occupy the shadow-bodies, refusing the first forms. This leaves some of the projections as "soulless shadows," without Divine Sparks to provide them with individual *Cosmic-Logoic* contact.

Instead these Seed-atoms, attract matter to themselves and build their own bodies that are denser and more defined than the shadow-bodies. Reproduction among

---

* *The Secret Doctrine.*

them begins as a process called "budding," an amoebic-like division from their own "fluid" bodies. The "soulless," meanwhile, begin to co-mingle with the equally ethereal elemental and animal forms. The result is somewhat like the descriptions of the water-men. They produce mindless automatons of various combinations of human and animal forms, labeled by Cayce as the *things*. The *things* are able to reproduce themselves, so they proceed to evolve into deeper matter along with the "humans," and their intermingling probably gave rise to the Lilith legend. This tells that "Adam's" first wife is Lilith, a woman with wings and talons for feet who has "orgies with elemental spirits and sand demons, producing demon children by the score." She is said to be irresistible to mortal men and to bring death to human children.*

The Seed-atoms who reject the early projections become known as the "Sons of Darkness," "Sons of Belial," or "sons of men," having unwittingly rejected the spiritual body that would have given them *Logoic* contact through the angels. They will have to attract spiritual matter themselves to construct their spiritual envelopes. Those who do take on the "projections" become the "Sons of Light,"† "Sons of One," and the "Sons of Wisdom." They gain the tremendous advantage of the angelic "at-one-ment" with the *Logos.* While both groups have Divine Sparks, these only provide them with unconscious motivation. Eventually

---

* *The Book of Goddesses and Heroines*, Patricia Monaghan, E.P. Dutton, 1981.
† Referred to in *The Dead Sea Scrolls* as the "sons of light" and the "sons of darkness."

the shadow-men merge into denser forms, but the "Sons of Darkness" are considered not to be "of the pure strain."

As evolution continues, the Watchers begin descending onto Earth to reign over men, "who are themselves" (the Sons of Light). They become the *gods* of mythology, the *priest-kings, avatars, initiators, educators and protectors* of humanity. The Sons of Darkness, lacking the others' comprehension of divine purpose, grow envious and begin to use the *things* as slaves, increasing their responsibility toward them.

Evolution into denser matter progresses unevenly. The *things* continue to co-mingle with elementals and animals until limited to "kind" by complexity of form. Eventually they become unable to reproduce themselves at all, but not before these unfortunates become the cause of the the first open struggle between the Sons of Light and the Sons of Darkness. Emerging human consciousness begins to understand the wrong done to the *things*, reflecting Divine Will, but the Sons of Darkness, desiring to "be as gods," begin exercising their free-will to gain power and control.

This is the beginning of a period termed *epigenesis*, an evolutionary interval of *involution*. The "fall" gains momentum. The descent into matter is self-accelerating, desire producing unconscious thought and speeding the formation of denser and more complex forms. This process, triggered by the exercise of free-will for self-interests, continues until the nadir is reached and the "tide turns." This occurred with development of monotheism (Judaism).

The emergence of the "Sons of Darkness" was not a

normal evolutionary event and resulted in Earth becoming an unusually intense "universal school" among the *Brotherhood of Solar Logoi.* As evolution progresses, entities will arrive from many other star systems to conquer the Earth experience, seldom realizing what they are getting into and how difficult the process is.

As the descent into matter increases, reproduction goes through evolutionary changes. The first forms are sexless, or as Cayce says, "among . . . thought projections . . . the physical being had the union of sex in the one body." The early human and animal forms were hermaphroditic and of assorted shapes and sizes including giants. Plato's *Symposium* speaks of the giants as "androgynous" and "terrible in force and strength" with "prodigious ambition." The Persians taught that man grew in androygnous pairs, and both Judaism and Christianity speak of the early Adam as having, "*two* faces and *one* person, . . . from the beginning he was . . . male on one side and female on the other . . . "*

The earliest forms being non-physical, left no remains, so physical evidence of their existence is not available. Unfortunately most of the remains of the later forms with bones are buried beneath oceans or layers of earth from planetary cataclysms. Finds have been made, however. The Hindus speak of an earlier race of giants. Gigantic human bones, whose formation resembles the monkey more than man, have been found in caves of Tibet. The

---

* *The Secret Doctrine.*

creatures were related to a primitive humanity . . . "*
While much ancient Central American history is said to be
"taken up with the doing of an ancient race of giants called
Quniames."†

In India the ape is honored as the living descendent of
some of the early human forms that failed to evolve before
division of the sexes and materialization. Attracted once to
a huge sorrowful looking gorilla, sitting quietly in a corner
of his barren zoo cage, I couldn't help but sympathize
with his plight. I stopped to commune with him and sent
him some nature visualizations. As I stood before him, he
concentrated upon me and we locked gazes. After a time, I
was startled to receive a "spark" of white light, burning
ever so dimly in his consciousness. It was a startling and
deeply moving encounter.

Blavatsky says of the anthropoids, "They have a
spark of the purely human essence in them; man on the
other hand, has not one drop of pithecoid blood in his
veins. Thus said old Wisdom and universal tradition."

The New York Times, in its "Science in Review" section on August 10, 1958, carried an article on the discovery
of a humanoid skeleton found 600 feet down in an Italian
coal mine. This discovery was not accidental. In 1872
a French paleontologist had found humanoid fossil
fragments in Tuscany. Dr. Heurzeler became interested in
the fragments, and with the support of Dr. Helmut De Terra
(then of Columbia University) the two headed a research

---

* *The Great Initiates.*
† Atlantis: The Antediluvian World, Ignatius Donnelly, 1882, London (*origi-nal version*, unabridged).

team of scientists under a Wenner-Gren Foundation grant. They searched for 28 months before finding the skeleton. Its age was established at 10,000,000 years old, being found among the remains of other plants and animals known to be this old. According to Drs. Heurzeler and De Terra:

> If man did have a common ancestor it was neither an ape-man nor a man-ape. It was a creature with characteristics of neither a man nor an ape, that lived at a very early age of mammalian evolution, possibly as far back as 100,000,000 years ago. . . . no one has any idea of what this primordial "lump of clay" from which man and ape evolved looked like. What to look for is the next big problem. It will not be for a nonexistent "missing link" but for a primordial "lump of clay" from which incipient man and incipient ape emerged and went their separate ways on the road of their respective evolutions.

Other remains found have included a human skull found in a quarry west of Budapest, believed to be 500,000 years old; humanoid bones found in Tanganyika, Africa, dating 1,850,000 years ago; and an elbow bone found by a Harvard paleontologist estimated at between 2,300,000 and 3,300,000 years old.

Surprisingly even some of the *things* apparently evolved into fully dense bodies, but only those of the sea, mermaids and mermen, seem to have survived into recent centuries. According to *Man, Myth and Magic*, encyclopedia volume 13, "In 1830 a mermaid was on show at the Egyptian Hall in London, and in the 1870's Phineas Barnum's Greatest Show on Earth" included a mermaid. Until the Royal College of Surgeons was bombed in the Second World War, two stuffed mermaids were kept in a showcase there." And, "In 1403, it is said, a mermaid was found becalmed in the shallow water at Edam in Holland. She became accustomed to life on land but never learned to speak. She lived for some 15 years after her capture, and was given a Christian burial."

Most likely the majority of their counterparts were destroyed or buried with the early humans in the various earthly catastrophes. The sea would be the only place where survival might have been natural.

Awareness of our evolutionary past, the complex content of the Collective Unconscious and the dynamics of relationships are all important to self-understanding and personal growth. The ancient formative periods rarely appear in doing past-life work, because they are so collective and have a minimal direct effect on modern man. Our more recent personal histories have much stronger individual impact, though this doesn't eliminate our connections with the greater planetary cycles and various groups.

The *akashic* (spatial light) *records* are available to all who wish to search them clairvoyantly, but the many extant records and traditions available are easier to study and compare. They are rewarding in themselves, as much seldom heard history and ancient philosophy is available through them.

For example, throughout most of the old teachings the symbol of a *tree* appears. In the *Bible* it is the *Tree of the Knowledge of Good and Evil*, in Kabbalism the Sephirothal *Tree of Life*; in the *Popol Vuh* the Mexican race comes from a *Tzite tree*, the Norse *Ases* bring the forms of men from an *Ash tree*; and the Persians taught that man was the product of a *tree*, growing in androygnous pairs. Usually within the tree a *serpent* appears, representing the manifestation of knowledge (thought) made possible by the containment by the serpent power and order brought from the chaos of Space. *Microscopic man* must overcome the illusion of personal consciousness. He "falls" by eating the fruit of the tree (attaining individual consciousness) and as illumined man becomes the fruit of the tree. Its limbs are our "family tree" (or "Jacob's Ladder").

The Forgotten Books of Eden begin with the *Third Day* and tell us that:

> . . . God planted the garden in the east of the earth, on the border of the world eastward, beyond which, towards the sun-rising, one finds nothing but water . . .
>
> And to the north of the garden there is a sea of water clear and pure to the taste, like unto nothing else . . .
>
> And when a man washes himself in it, becomes clean of the cleanness thereof, and white in its whiteness—even if he were dark.*

The teachings of Patanjali state that concentration, meditation and contemplation are the means to "destruc-

---

* From *The Forgotten Books of Eden*, written during the Greek, Hasmonean and Roman Periods of about 200 B C. to A.D. 100 and derived from copies either in the original language (Hebrew, Aramaic or Greek) or translated from versions found in archaeological excavations. This translation from Egyptian. Crown Publishers, 1980, a reprint of a 1927 edition.

tion of impurity," opening the way for the "understanding-light."*

The "Eighth Book of Hermes Trismegistus" tells us that "the greatest evil in man is the not knowing God." This says, "Such is the hurtful Apparel, wherewith thou art clothed . . . that thou canst neither hear what thou shouldst hear, nor see what thou shouldst see."†

In the *esoteric* and traditional teachings of both Eastern and Western philosophy a strong current of consistancy is apparent. Illustrations and phraseology may change, but fundamentally they carry the same messages.

---

* *How to Know God*, the Yoga Aphorisms of Patanjali, translated by Swami Prabhavananda and Christopher Isherwood, New American Library, 1969.

† *The Divine Pymander of Hermes Mercurius Trismegistus*, translated by Dr. Everard from the Arabic (1650), Wizards Bookshelf, San Diego, CA, 1978.

FIRST NIGHT

3

First Night

How'd you like my fallen angel routine?
It was just fine, fine. Listen,
everyone take your places for opening night.
All the Seed-atoms over here working on
their soul bodies.
Do you want to see my fallen
angel routine again?
No, not right now, thanks. O.K., a little
more waters of the firmament over there.
Good, good. All you *elementals* and *gnomes*,
check your costumes.
Ahhh . . . . KLUNK!
I think someone in Central Casting
needs some time off.
Wanna see it again?
No, no thanks, just move over by . . . ,
KLUNK!
Sigh! This is going to be challenging.

Where was I? Oh, yes, *Scene Three.* Listen, LaVedi, you're
rolling. Do a few more scenes by yourself,
while we get ready for your partner.
Places everyone!

THE GARDEN OF EDEN

The *Garden of Eden* we think of as the birthplace of
man (in the Tigris-Euphrates Valley) was only one of such
"gardens" on the earth. Traditions teach that China had
the garden of the "Dragons of Wisdom," while the Himalayas held the "Garden of Wisdom." In Great Britain it
appears the "Isle of Avalon" may have been another birthplace of humanity. These special sites are only some of
those used as reception and anchor points for input of
Divine Will and knowledge into the Collective Unconscious
of the planet. Many of these energy points, also referred
to as *power points*, are still active today and are used as
channels for transmission from other dimensions.

When Adam is "driven from the garden" his form has
become too dense to continue sustaining itself from the
pranic or *light* energy of the atmosphere alone. He must
begin to eat physical "food."

When we left the races of Adam evolving around the
world, they were in a variety of evolving hermaphroditic
forms, though still of non-dense physical substance. Personal intellect must develop next, so it is time for "Eve"
to appear. Conscious mind does not emerge until after
Adam separates Eve from himself; then they "eat of the
Tree of Knowledge." Adam and Eve "see" each other and
become *self-conscious*. They begin to recognize individ-

uality, and correspondingly, with the development of personal consciousness, they lose contact with the collective consciousness and "at-one-ment" with God. They are no longer able to "talk with God."

"Eve," like Adam, is not a single woman. She is the manifesting *mother principle* of the Cosmos, and necessary to the next stage of human evolution. In Sanskrit Adam is "*Adima*" (first man) and Eve is also "Ivi," "Evi," "*Heva*" (that which completes life) or "Hovah" (female).

We should bear in mind that we are condensing time spans of millions of evolutionary years. Man was not instantly "created" overnight, but neither did he evolve Darwinian style, except as related to his own species. There were a number of basic influences, including the *seven rays*, the *sub-rays*, varying *planetary energies*, varying *stellar affects* and other factors affecting each of the interpenetrating human bodies as they developed over many incarnations in different locations. Each wave of Seed-atoms also contributed special attributes. Human make-up is complex, but breaks down into four basic components: spiritual, mental, emotional and physical (divisions within these result in the seven interpenetrating bodies of man). All of these are interactive and continually influence our actions, while our actions create *karma*.

KARMIC CYCLES

The "Law of Cause and Effect" (action and reaction), or *Karma*, results from the thoughts and desires of man as they feed into the Collective Unconscious and into other collective and individualized energy fields. *Karma* means that every action (or thought energy) will produce a corresponding reaction. Like the flashlight beam sent into the *closed* universe, all energy expended (thought, action, emotion, etc.) produces energy impulses that recycle in the force fields surrounding you.

As an individual, this means a recycling within your personal energy field and your unconscious mind. But many other types of collective bodies of thought can develop force fields, too, including civilizations, nations, races, neighborhoods and families. These usually result in forms of group karma.

Consider how it feels when you, as a stranger, enter a group of unfamiliar people. At first you may feel like an outsider and be uncomfortable. The group may even feel cold, until they consciously invite you into their energy field or collective thought form. If you are compatible and it is an established group, you may become a permanent member, or you may be an *old* member returning. On the other hand, we have all experienced "the silent treatment" at one time or another. A silent person holds his energy field closed and refuses to admit you, which is why this sort of situation is more uncomfortable than seems logical.

Karma does not mean some mysterious body of judges somewhere dispensing punishment to sinners. Under the guidance of *guardians,* (who may modify karmic impact) we each reap the harvest of the seeds we have sown life after life. Personal *karma* manifests itself in your psychological and emotional make-up, your health and personality, all pouring forth from the unconscious and the soul. The next strongest karma is family and relationships. We usually are members of "family groups" and reincarnate over and over with various members in a variety of exchanged roles. These two types of karmic cycles are the most powerful because of their closeness. We are unconscious of them, so we react subjectively and must work hard to gain objectivity.

The larger cycles, especially national and planetary, seem more abstract, since our relation to them appears small and impersonal. Their importance to *you* will depend upon how much influence you have wielded in the past, the effect it had and how you relate to larger collective groups. People with racial, religious or political prejudices, for example are advertising that they have a *collective* karmic problem. These are emotional, not rational, reactions, that stem from unconscious motivation. Similar reactions might have been perfectly sensible at one time, perhaps related to being enslaved or sacrificed by some tribe, but under different circumstances they become inappropriate and illogical. Unfortunately such memories can incite reactions that create a ping-pong effect life after life, as various participants take turns attacking each other. The old family feuds are a good manifested example of this perpetuation, with warring going on generation after generation, probably long after the original cause of the fighting has been forgotten.

The key to overcoming any *karma* is to rise above it, accept it if necessary, but do not attempt to fight it (emotional reaction). To end any karmic entanglement you must *genuinely forgive* all involved (even if it takes years), realizing that those involved have their own karma to work through (motivations they are not conscious of). Only you can decide when to end any *karmic* problem. Doing so may require a change of environment or association. This might be mental, emotional or physical in nature or a combination, but you will *act* when your *desire* to correct any given karmic difficulty is strong enough.

To understand your personal evolution, you need to know how you fit into various karmic groups and into the larger cycles. Examining your feelings about people and places will reveal a lot. Then recalling past lives helps explain details, group and personal relationships and karmic trends. National karma tends to be carried forward for lengthy periods. For example, many Americans carry Atlantean karma from their experiences there and abuses of knowledge and technology. America is Atlantis "reborn."

LEMURIA

Lemuria, or Mu (Moo), becomes the Motherland for millions of years, encompassing what is today Australia, Southern Asia, Europe and much of Africa. (Teachings and remnants from this cradle of man are partially preserved in Japan, China, Tibet, India, the Middle East, Egypt and Great Britain, as well as in many other scattered sites.) Lemuria leads the development of man, and while united under one consciousness, she acts as the seat of government for the entire world.

The people are still without speech, communication being telepathic. They are spoken of as the people of "one language and one lip," but this does not stop them from building great cities and nations under the tutelage of the Sons of One. The Sons of One "come into" the bodies of evolving mankind to guide and educate them and to perfect their physical forms. During this period visitors from other star systems begin to arrive, but most have little interest in the primitive Earth life at this stage. Some do stay, however, and add their advanced knowledge to that of the Sons of One.

The strongest rush into matter occurs in Lemuria and this is where the Sons of Darkness most devastatingly manifest their exercise of free-will. Many fascinating legends and traditions exist regarding this time. An interesting one appears unexpectedly from a clergyman in 1776 who met a group of Indians from west of the Mississippi who, "informed him that one of their most ancient traditions was that, a great while ago, they had a common father, who lived toward the rising of the sun, and governed the whole world; that all the white people's heads were under his feet; that he had twelve sons, by whom he administered the government; that the twelve sons behaved very bad, and tyrannized over the people, abusing their power. . . . . "*

THE SECOND FALL

Until the time of Adam and Eve, or division of sexes, the Sons of One and the Sons of Darkness reproduced without mixture, since male and female were in one body.

---

* *Atlantis: The Antediluvian World.*

But as division occurs, and procreation requires the union of separate individuals, the children of the "pure strain" begin to mingle with the "children of men." This produces the *second major fall*. The *Bible* tells us, "When men began to multiply on the face of the ground, and daughters were born to them, the sons of God saw that the daughters of men were fair; and they took to wife such of them as they chose."

The Sons of One, or "children of God," (the pure strain through the shadow-men and the first androgynous forms), begin to unite with the animalistic "children of men" (sirens, satyrs and giants of mythology) resulting in the "fallen ones" (the *Nephilium*). The *Bible* continues, "There were giants on the earth in those days, and also after that, when the sons of God came in unto the daughters of men, and they bare children to them. These same became mighty men which were of old, men of renown." (Genesis 6: 4, King James Version).

The Sons of One have taught the people for thousands of years, using allegories, symbolic mysticism and oral traditions suitable to their developing minds. Those who showed special capabilities were "inititated" into the mysteries of life and the universe. Others were taught the sciences, agriculture, architecture and the arts as they were ready. The *Logoic* knowledge shared by the Sons of One had to be preserved and protected from abuse by the Sons of Darkness. This effort is successful, until the children of God begin mixing with the children of darkness, after division of the sexes.

The offspring of these unions are natural *adepts*. They

learn the creative knowledge of the elemental forces and secrets of life and death from their parents. At this time all are still strongly telepathic. The *secret knowledge*, intellectual capacity and size of the *Nephilium* make them leaders in the land. They become powerful, but they lack understanding and awareness of the Divine Will and do not have the maturity to use knowledge wisely.

They seek personal power versus the collective good of previous times. Lacking communication *with* God, they choose to become *as* Gods. They believe they have the power and knowledge of God, so why not take his position? They incite the people by providing them with alcoholic beverage and by telling them they have a right to equal knowledge with the priestly Sons of One. To gain followers and worshipers, some begin to establish their own *ceremonies* to compete with the temple rites in the land. The first *black rites* are born.

The *black rites* are a mockery of the temple ceremonies, but the emerging *black priests* must convince the people of their godlike powers—equal to the Sons of One. They adopt the symbol of the serpent (symbol of wisdom or God manifesting knowledge) and use it in opposition to the sun symbol of the *One Logos*. They pervert the meaning of the serpent and use it as their authority to bring "knowledge" (the secrets of nature) to the people; or as a chant of the Delaware Indians says, "All were willingly pleased, all were easy-thinking, and all were well-happified. But after a while a snake-priest, Powako, brings on earth secretly the snake-worship (*Initako*) of the god of the snakes, *Wakon*. And there came wickedness, crime, and unhappiness. And bad weather was coming, distemper was coming, with death was coming. All this happened *very long ago, at the first land, Netamaki,* beyond the great *ocean Kitahikau.*"* The "fruit of the Tree of Knowledge" has been eaten.

The desire for individual power, corruption and satiety spreads throughout the land. The people flock to the ceremonies of the *dark priesthood,* but as power decreases among descendents of the *Nephilium*, their avarice increases and the former animal sacrifices become *human sacrifices.* In *black magic* some of the subtle bodies, as they leave the dying physical form, can be used for *magical* purposes. The *ectoplasm* from the blood of the victims is used in particular to create and activate *elemental demonic forms.* The priests then used these to do their dirty work against the living. This ancient practice is why countries, such as India, cremate their dead to prevent the "theft" of souls. Various death ceremonies (funerals) are connected with this protection. The more souls the *black priests* could enslave, the more *demons* they could send out to plague the children of God.

Such *demons* are no joke, they can provide an attack that will *rebound* onto the physical body, causing death, illness or insanity. I found myself forced to do battle one night with several of the likes of these. They had been sent by a "son of darkness" to "collect" the *astral* body of a young woman, while she slept. Though halfway around the world, I was "summoned" to destroy them. The man

---

* *Atlantis: the Antediluvian World.*

who had sent them was known for his practice of luring young attractive women to his classes in "spiritual development" to form sexual relationships with them. After using their "energy" he would be done with them. Some wound up institutionalized as insane. The fight was fierce, but *light* always wins when the *One Will* is with it. In the morning I had a huge repercussion bruise several inches across on one thigh to remind me it had really happened. There was further substantiating evidence, as shortly afterward the person left the area, following many years of residence. His demons destroyed, his power was gone. The young woman he had attempted to reach was my teenage daughter.

It pays to be very careful in choosing any kind of spiritual instruction. Remember, "by their fruits you will know them." Never be impressed by "spiritual talk," innuendos that you are somehow inferior or claims that theirs is the "only way." Always examine motives and feelings carefully. We have a great deal of protection, if we only allow it to help us. There are the "invisible helpers," "guides," sometimes concerned relatives acting as "guardian angels," and others on up to the Masters, the Watcher and our Oversoul.

I had this knowledge strongly impressed upon me one summer night in the wilderness of Alaska. I was spending the summer in my cabin near McKinley (Denali) National Park and had gone to bed as usual. Then in the middle of the night I felt this weight on my legs. Being very sound asleep, I tried to kick it off, but it wouldn't leave. Finally I came awake enough to see what it was and was shocked to see a dog laying on my bed. My immediate reaction was, "How did you get in here?" Whereupon I turned to the door and found it was standing wide open. I jumped out of bed and slammed it shut. It had a warp in it and must not have caught when I closed it for the night.

Then I turned to the dog. It was gone. My first impression had been that it was about a two-month-old grey pup, weighing about 15 pounds. But its appearance was unusual, it had the pointed nose and long pointed ears of the *Anubis*. Realizing what had happened, I saw it was a brilliant way to wake me, not frighten me and make me see the door was open. Why was the door so important? I had a neighborhood grizzly who regularly raided my garbage can. On this night, he arrived shortly after I closed the door. Sitting on my kitchen counter was a favorite grizzley treat, an opened can of bacon. If I hadn't closed the door I would have had a most unwelcome houseguest. Why the *Anubis?* Perhaps because he balances the scales of life and death. It wasn't time. Yram in *Practical Astral Projection* mentions that white or grey dogs are used as "watchers" and appear as "an image which inspires confidence."

The Hawaiian Islands are a remnant of ancient Lemuria and the practices of *black rituals* can be traced up to modern times. Some of the Hawaiian *Kahunas* ("wise-people") have taken the responsibility to "*cleanse*" the old sacrificial sites. I have worked with two different parties in Hawaii, clearing such sites that we "accidently" found. One of them has even been turned into a public park, its true identity deliberately covered up by a false story. My ex-husband, Lawrence, and I encountered this place on an outing and had its history thrust upon us. The dissected *auric* remains of dozens of human forms were "floating" in the air, guarded by elemental creations and an energy field. This was an interesting example of "psychic encounters," and of how teams can work together. I *see* on the *mind's screen,* while Lawrence *saw* on the actual *etheric-astral* level of substance. Working back and forth and comparing reception provides substantiation and training. In this case we found further evidence; a few days later an old Hawaiian cab driver confirmed that the park was a former sacrificial site, covered up by officials to promote tourism.

Such sites may be found worldwide. They usually involve the elements, represented by the sea, cliffs, water, rocks, etc. Great Britian has numerous examples, such as "Chalice Well" in Glastonbury (used to drown victims) and the sacrificial cave at Brean Down.* This latter one is still dangerous and is better not visited. I have even seen a site in the open desert of Arizona (now another park). A sacrificial rock slab is often the obvious give-away, carved or shaped to accomodate the flow of blood. Some of these are on display in the British Museum in London.

The serpent worship spread around the world from the Lemurian *black priesthood.* Biblical allegory rises again regarding sacrifices and serpent worship. Adam and Eve had three "children:" Cain, Abel and Shem. It is Cain's

---

* Reference: *The Sea Priestess,* Dion Fortune, Samuel Weiser, 1972. "The Sacrificial Tide" an article by LaVedi Lafferty, *Beyond Reality,* 1980.

sacrifice that God turns away from. Cain then *kills* Abel. "Cain" appears worldwide representing the serpent. According to LePlongeon,* "The family name of the king of Nazax was *Can* (serpent) as *Khan* is still the title of the Kings of Tartary and Burman, and the governor of provinces in Persia." In Japan the *Can* family is deified and so on. Abel, the good *son,* dies out with the advent of sexual division and "mixed-marriages." The caste system in India is a tradition that tried to prevent this, but rebirth mixed and separated above and beyond the efforts of men.

With the "twin children" of God no longer born together, Shem, the third *son* represents the resulting mixture, becoming the prototype for modern man. When twins, or hermaphrodites, were later born they were sacrificed. They still appear occasionally, but now their condition is usually corrected surgically. The Sons of One no longer exist as a pure strain, but a new humanity is evolving.

> Referring to this evolutionary process, Hermann Hesse, in *Magister Ludi*, relates a Hindu myth that speaks of the world in the beginning as "divine, radiant and happy . . . a golden age." Then the world grows sick and degenerates, becoming "more and more coarsened and wretched," until, after aeons pass, it is ready to be destroyed under the dancing feet of Shiva in preparation for the birth of a new world. After the old world dies, the next one will begin "anew from the smile of the dreaming Vishnu. . . . "†

---

* *Sacred Mysteries Among the Mayas and the Quiches,* Augustus LePlongeon, reprint of 1886 edition, Wizards Bookshelf, Minneapolis, 1973.
† Quoted from *Reincarnation: The Phoenix Fire Mystery,* by Joseph Head & S.L. Cranston, Julian Press/Crown Publishers, 1977.

THE FLOOD

There is a traditional tendency to personify events. For example, Noah *"floating on the waters,"* may also be Nuah of the Chaldeans, *"the Spirit moving on the waters."* In Guatamala he becomes the "Father of the Thlinkithians," and to the Hindus he is *Vaiswasvata.* The early people experienced devastating earthly cataclysms and the Sons of One repeatedly forecast these and preserved the rudiments of civilization (in "arks" upon the waters). "Arks" have represented sacred religious *vessels of God* to the Hindus, Jews and Mexicans.

Such legends abound. Among the Indians of the Great Lakes there is a tradition that, "In former times the father of the Indian tribes *dwelt toward the rising sun.* Having been warned in a dream that a deluge was coming upon the earth, he built a raft, on which he saved himself, with his family and all the animals. He floated thus for several months. . . . At last a new earth appeared. . . ."*

By the time of Adam and Eve the earth has already seen severe cataclysms. According to Hindu doctrines two *Pralayas* occurred: one was universal and the other partial. Blavatsky says these refer to geological cataclysms that occur at the end of each minor global cycle. . . . "New races of men and animals and . . . flora evolve from the . . . precedent ones."† The earth has not seen just *one* flood, but repeated cataclysms and upheavals.

The reign of Lemuria was very long, with numerous

---

* *Atlantis: the Antediluvian World.*
† *Isis Unveiled,* H.P. Blavatsky, Theosophical University Press, 1960.

migrations prior to catastrophic upheavals. A major cataclysm occurred around 800,000 years ago and another major one about 200,000 years ago. A final one, between 80,000 to 50,000 years ago broke up the continent and the governmental unity, bringing the end of Lemuria as a nation. Atlantis and other colonies and societies became separate and independent.

Prior to the final devastation of Lemuria by severe volcanic eruption, earthquakes and fumes, many fled to South America (then an island), Western North America (as far north as Alaska), to Atlantis, Africa and various oceanic islands. In South America they become the *People of the Sun,* and further north they are related to the Mayans, Aztecs and the *mound builders.*

A document exists that is believed to describe the final cataclysm that destroyed Lemuria. Known as the Troano Manuscript, it is preserved in the British Museum of London. It contains an account of a continental cataclysm as translated by Le Plongeon, and is thought to have been written over 3,500 years ago by the Mayans in the Yucatan. It reads:

> In the year 6 Kan, on the 11th Mulac, in the month of Zac, there occurred terrible earthquakes, which continued without interruption until the 13th Chuen. The country of the hills of Mud, the land of Mu, was sacrificed; being twice upheaved it suddenly disappeared during the night, the basin being continually shaken by volcanic forces. Being confined, these caused the land to sink and rise several times and in various places. At last the surface gave away and *ten countries* were torn asunder and scattered; unable to stand the force of the convulsions, they sank with their 64,000,000 inhabitants."

Notable island remnants of Lemuria, besides the Hawaiian Isles, include Easter Island, the Philippines and Madagascar. Histories of great cataclysmic floods are recorded in the *Popol Vuh* of Mexico, the *Chimalpopca Codex* of the Aztecs, and in legends of the Delaware Indians, Mistex and Mexicans, as well as in Chaldean, Hindu, Oriental and Christian.*

In the study of past lives Lemuria appears with moderate frequency, but the majority of *readings* relate to more recent periods from the latter days of Atlantis forward (after consciousness has developed and free-will is being expressed).

THE LEGENDARY ATLANTIS

For a million years or more the paths of Lemuria and Atlantis are parallel, with the exception that *black magic* rises to prominence faster and earlier in Lemuria. Atlantis suffers along with Lemuria during the earthly cataclysms. Prior to the upheavel, around 800,000 B.C., the continent is large—encompassing most of America, reaching far into the Atlantic and extending as far as present South America. This cataclysm splits the continent, with one coast line roughly following the present eastern United States' coast. Included is land in the present gulf of Mexico and the northern portion of South America.†

---

* For a detailed study of evidence: *Atlantis: The Antediluvian World,* Ignatius Donnelly.
† *Atlantis, Autobiography of a Search,* Robert Ferro and Michael Grumley, Bell Publishing, N.Y., 1970, (evidence found in the Atlantic of ancient civilization).

The next catastrophe, around 200,000 B.C., divides Atlantis into three large islands. One covers the present United States and New Foundland, another is in the Atlantic (the Azores are all that remain) and a smaller island appears between Africa and South America. The South American region separates into an independent island.

Finally, when Lemuria is broken-up, the continents emerge much like they are today. All that remains of the Atlantean civilization is primarily on one island left in the Atlantic, *Poseidonis.* *

Dates are difficult to establish *reading* clairvoyantly from these early periods, in the sense that time doesn't exist, or varies in concept. Dates or periods must usually be established by supplemental information. In the distant past this might be found through astronomical data, types of animals, plants, architectural design, clothing styles, etc. This is often the most reliable way to establish time, along with supplemental information from research. *Readings* should prove essentially consistent with known history and sciences. Getting accurate dates can be work, but it is rewarding to see confirmation unfold and fill in the gossamer memory images.

The Atlantean history is long and complex, civilizations rising and falling with the abuses of magic and global destruction. Many fractional groups, tribes and city-states develop and war with each other, Atlantis and Lemuria.

---

* Historical details: *Red Tree Insight into Lost Continents of Mu and Atlantis,* Christine Hayes, The Naylor Co., San Antonio, TX, 1972. *The Story of Atlantis and the Lost Lemuria,* W. Scott-Elliot, Theosophical Publishing House, 1968 from originals 1896 and 1904; *Atlantis: the Antediluvian World,* Ignatius Donnelly, 1910.

Through it all man is evolving, much of the time without speech.

The people are basically simple and collective. Parallel groups still exist in primitive peoples who retain contact with collective consciousness. They may mystify modern man by telepathic awareness or communication, such as the Australian aborigines exhibit by strange appearances and disappearances. Such people tend to shun the *limited* minds of other men.

Atlantis is said to have had a *Golden Age* lasting over 100,000 years, before free-will, evolving consciousness and the practices of the *black priests,* destroy it. Egypt (Eugypt) becomes an independent nation from Lemuria prior to the 200,000 B.C. catastrophe and the knowledge of Atlantis is preserved there. The priests, knowing Atlantis is doomed, reconstruct Atlantean pyramids and the Sphinx in Egypt.* The Sphinx is part of a temple, and along with the pyramids was used to develop the mind, the will and their application.†

Using the hypnotic *past-life recall technique* we have developed, Bud assisted me into an altered state of consciousness. We did the following past-life *reading* for a man in Fairbanks, Alaska, that revealed some of the ways consciousness was trained using the focused energy of pyramid structures.

---

* Reference: *The View Over Atlantis,* John Michell, Ballantine Books, 1969 on history of the pyramids and other surviving engineering works.
† *Atlantis to the Latter Days,* H.C. Randall-Stevens, The Order of the Knights Templars of Aquarius, Jersey, Great Britain, 1966.

Bud: Is there a karmic connection that ties in to the North American continent?

LaVedi: Well, I see another people, this is much older, not Indians in the sense of, as we know Indians. I see a bronze color skin, not red, bronze, almost golden.

Bud: Could this be toward South America, Mexico? Perhaps Inca?

LaVedi: I believe they were in this time period farther north, I believe the land was different then, we are back in Atlantean period . . . These people were apparently involved in some of the pyramid type structures in South America, they did the same thing on Atlantis. And what is found in South America and Mexico is carried over from their Atlantean experience.

Bud: Was this entity involved in the construction?

LaVedi: Yes, not only the construction, but the usage.

Bud: What was the usage of the particular pyramids?

LaVedi: As they used them, they were involved in the worship of the sun, in the focusing. These people had extensive knowledge of the heavens, and of solar energy, the lunar, and while some things might appear ritualistic, they knew formulas for extended travel . . .

Bud: Extended travel, on the earth plane?

LaVedi: Off of the earth plane and on the earth plane, control of magnetic forces.

Bud: Were these pyramids built for the use of this particular knowledge?

LaVedi: Yes. These that they worked with were not particularly large, they were designed to magnify the energies; focus, focus of the mind with some natural energies, and how to use it ... And it was not abused ....

Now the pyramids that they used there were not the Egyptian variety, these were square ziggurats. What I see is like huge blocks and the blocks are laid out in pyramidal shape, with a perfect square at the top, which is slightly different than any that I know of now. They incorporated some metals in this to increase the energies.

I see them doing some rather unusual things. I see them directing it in a form of mind power, in education. I see a school they had, where they magnified the power of learning. And those who came out of this, came out of it with an enormous amount of mental power, developed mind, concentrated will. They directed this. Their whole area was quite remarkable, in how they manifested the energies on the earth plane. This was quite a beautiful city.

Bud: Was the structure of the pyramids at that time, did the structure have anything that offered spiritual growth? Was it involved with energy that could be channeled by the will?

LaVedi: There were decided spiritual overtones in what they did. They viewed the Sun as the Central Source.

Worship of the Sun becomes the normal Atlantean practice, since the people are unable to understand the concept of the *Logos* represented by the Sun. A common symbol is converted to the god through lack of understanding or education. I learned an interesting thing about this type of misplaced devotion and ignorance, during one of the first life *readings* I did for myself with the guidance of an old "soul-mate." What was revealed was that if the *intent* is pure, *an image* may act much like a telephone, regardless of the conscious development of the person "placing the call."

The life in question occurred in Atlantis, where I found myself as a *Priest of the Sun.* The person assisting me was an excellent trained *reader* and she viewed the scenes along with me and added confirmation. In the mornings, at sunrise, it was my duty to "greet the Sun," and pass along the blessing to the people of the land. I acted as a *receiving vessel* and a *conduit* for *Logoic input* via my unconscious mind into the Collective Unconsciousness, receiving, anchoring and dispersing through application of will.

This lifetime was during one of the latter periods of Atlantis, and the government was no longer overtly run by the priesthood. Instead a ruler was "chosen" from a selected group of youths of the populace. Another of my duties was to "train" one of these boys, (the priests already knew who would be chosen). I had to teach the boy *out-of-body* as he slept, for the people had rebelled against the division resulting from the priestly educated. The future king had to be taught without even his conscious knowledge that it was happening.

During this life I was also an historian, and with a team of scribes, spent much of my life compiling a complete history of Atlantis up to that time. This was for use in the educational system of the period (similar to a university). I have been told that this history will "return" to me when it is "time."

Now, regarding worship of images, when I died as an old man, a large stone statue was erected resembling *Horus*, the falcon. It was perhaps twelve feet tall, of dark stone and was stylized, with folded wings. As we watched (from the present), we saw people coming to the statue with gifts of flowers and food and making requests. Then we *saw* that there was a group of entities, "invisible helpers" active around the statue. They were seeing to requests and carrying messages to higher powers as was needed. Such "invisible helpers" are usually people between incarnations. They may well have been helping their own friends and relatives, unbeknownst to them. Thus sincere supplication *through* an image may act like a telephone call, tapping not only the soul, but the help of entities assigned to the area.

This was my last life in Atlantis, as the nation's time was drawing near. I remember some other lives there, though, such as one as a simple oarsman spent in open galleys; I had heavy thickly calloused hands. In another I was a young peasant girl in the countryside near the sea. It was a magnificent land, with beautiful buildings, somewhat like Grecian styles, but much more grand.

"Its broad avenues shaded by great trees, its artificial hills, the largest surmounted by governmental palaces, and pierced and terraced by the avenues which radiated from the city-center like the spokes in a wheel. Fifty miles these ran in one direction, while at right angles from them, traversing the breadth of the peninsula, forty miles in length, were the shortest avenues."* This was the "City of the Golden Gates," described also by Plato in *Timaeus,* as related to him by Solon who was taught by a priest of Sais in Egypt.

For long periods of time the Atlantean government was theocratic, but as the *dark priests* gained the support of the people, the government that had provided adequately and equally for all subsided. Another past-life *reading* Bud and I did showed how greed spread over the land. Bear in mind that Atlantis was heavily involved in trade and commerce with the world during periods of development:

Bud: We are searching for the entity . . . . We wish to understand his source of power and why he is uncomfortable with it in the present.

LaVedi: He was . . . in Atlantis.

Bud: In male form?

LaVedi: Yes.

Bud: What was his position of power there?

LaVedi: I find him as a trader, a goods merchant, dealing with import and ships, financial trade.

Bud: A fairly well-to-do trader?

* *A Dweller on Two Planets,* Phylos the Thibetan, Neville Spearman, Great Britain, 1970 (as taken down in 1884 by F.S. Oliver, with many modern inventions, unheard of at the time of writing, described).

LaVedi: Yes. I think it is a period of war. Also the ships were used for transporting, bringing in soldiers, troops. I think it is a period tied in with revolt, or civil war. It seems to have been quite a destructive thing, because it divided and weakened the country . . . .

Bud: Did the entity have direct influence on this revolt through his occupation?

LaVedi: He had political power and money, quite wealthy. He wasn't actively in government as we know it. In the position he was in, he was the power behind the scenes; not particularly behind the scenes, he was pretty open.

Pretty chaotic, they seemed to take the city sort of by surprise, very well planned, bringing in these soldiers from somewhere and took the city unaware . . . It was a power move, and that they . . . , of course, this gave them access to many energy sources, this particular city's energy resources which were quite large. It seems that power sources of Atlantis were coordinated and had reached their peak (capacity) . . . as revolt and individuals, groups, political unrest, took over, it (coordinated control) became broken up . . . . this threw the balances all out of control; they were no longer harmonized with each other.

In other words, they would use them to their own ends and purposes, to any extent or level that they chose, not realizing, and refusing to accept, the danger of what they were doing. This was connected with the final destruction.

Atlantis had power sources that we today are only beginning to approach. They concentrated energy in what appear as large crystals, perhaps two feet by three. These crystals gave off such a brilliance that they are nearly blinding to look at. They were sequestered underground at various sites and maintained by the Children of Light. Cayce speaks of these crystals also " . . . there was the creating of the high influence of radial activity from rays of the sun that were turned on crystals in the pits that made connections with internal influences of the earth." It is very possible that, in non-technical language, this is a description of the use of nuclear energy.

The Sons of One held the knowledge of the universal energies and the elemental forces of the planet and maintained their balance. With the take over by the Children of Darkness the balance was lost and destruction by volcanic upheaval was the result.*

> The continent of Atlantis was an island, which lay before the great flood, in the area we now call the Atlantic Ocean. So great an area of land that from her western shores sailors turned to the South and North Americas with ease, ships with painted sails; to the east, Africa was her neighbor, across a short strait of sea miles. The great Egyptian age is but a remnant of the Atlantean culture; the antideluvian kings colonized the world. All the gods that play in the mythological dramas, in all of the legends, gods from all lands, were from fair Atlantis. Knowing her fate, Atlantis sent out ships to all the corners of the earth. Hail Atlantis!
>
> —As sung by Donovan.

---

* *The View Over Atlantis,* John Michell, Ballantine Books, NY, 1969, gives a comprehensive view of the old knowledge, and the evidence remaining today, regarding the energy flows of the earth as protected and utilized in former periods.

THE LATTER DAYS

By now you should be reminded of the many prophecies about the "latter days" and the time we are living in, including radical earth changes, floods, famine, volcanic eruptions, etc. Many are occurring as predicted, largely a repeat result of man's ignorant and determined abuse of the planet. All that is preventing these from being far worse is the rapidly growing awareness of evolving minds. The *Light Network* has become strong around the planet through the co-operative efforts of many during the decade of the 1970's.

Unfortunately we still have the Children of Cain with us. They may be highly intelligent and brimming with *knowledge,* but they lack *wisdom.* Often self-indulgent, power and wealth hungry, they may succeed again in bringing disaster to mankind. The Children of Shem, have been learning their lessons though. No longer duped, they are resisting harmful technology, nuclear power, pollution and abuses of nature. These intense efforts are having a strong affect on the Collective Unconscious of the planet.

A tidal change is underway in the Collective Unconscious of the planet, but serious imbalances have already been set in motion. Another series of upheavals are probably inevitable as humanity goes through another major evolutionary change. The Children of Light and many of the Children of Shem are moving up a vibrational notch to where they will be unaffected by physical events.

As to the future of earth, physically it may be desolate, but on another dimension many have seen cities that surpass our present imagination. Motion, once again, is by thought or travel in airborne capsules. Structures are circular, of pale colors and appear to be of smooth molded construction. Life is once again peaceful, consciousness is both universal and individual.

DOUBLE FEATURE

We mentioned before that the elemental kingdoms are evolving parallel to humanity. As primordial thought creations, they have been responsive to human thought. Like the stages of human evolution, the elemental kingdoms have followed along imitating human traits and personalities. As entities, most are not individualized, but they are good mimics. They can even "clothe" themselves with human imaginings about them, such as appear in fairy tales, while continuing to tend the elemental processes of the planet and forms.

A hierarchy of angelic beings exists who oversee the elementals under the oversight of the Archangels. Those with specific earthly duties are usually spoken of as *devas* (angels in Sanskrit). The elementals are usually known as *gnomes* (Earth), *salamanders* (Fire), *undines* (Water) and *sylphs* (Air). While the elementals are evolving steadily, they are still under control of their collective consciousness and under angelic direction.

Each element has its symbol, astrological ruling sign and ruling archangel as follows.

ELEMENT	GLYPH	SIGN	ARCHANGEL
Fire	Lion	Leo	Michael
Earth	Bull	Taurus	Auriel

Water	Eagle	Scorpio	Gabriel
Air	Man	Aquarius	Raphael

The four glyphs should be familiar from the Biblical vision of John (Revelations 4:5).

> And round the throne, on each side of the throne, are four living creatures, full of eyes in front and behind: the first living creature like a lion, the second living creature like an ox, the third living creature with the face of a man, and the fourth living creature like a flying eagle . . . . and day and night they never cease to sing,
>> "Holy, holy, holy is the
>> Lord God Almighty,
>> who was and is and is to
>> come!"

There are also *devas* in charge of the "group soul" for each species of plant and animal on the globe. Seen clairvoyantly these *devas* appear with the form of the species visible within their *light* body. Cayce mentions these as "thought bodies (that) gradually took form and the various combinations . . . of the forces that called or classified themselves as gods, or rulers over—whether herds, or fowls, or fishes, etc."*

Devic entities are located in many places on the globe, some acting as guardians over special locations, especially planetary vortices (reception points) and sacred sites. The Ojai Valley in California is one such example, where a *deva* towers over the valley from the high bluffs of Mt. Topa Topa. The valley itself is incredible, with between 20-30

---

* *Edgar Cayce on Atlantis,* reading (364-11)

spiritual organizations (not counting regular churches) with headquarters or branches located in it. "Ojai" means "the nest" in the language of the original Indians, and it certainly is one.*

A few of the better known organizations include: The Krotona Institute of Theosophy; Meditation Mount (world servers); the Krishnamurti Foundation; the Ojai Foundation and the Ananta Foundation (founded by Marcia Moore, without whose help this book might not have been written). This valley, like the valley of Sedona, Arizona, has been recognized as sacred before the arrival of the first white settlers. Such centers are *power points,* and attract, hold and distribute energy (thought and knowledge):

> Be deeply quiet and listen
> The mountains and the valley are sounding
> with a great and mounting joy.
> The sounding is of synthesis
> of a high and quiet power,
> an orchestration of intention.
> Why are we drawn to the valley—
> protecting walls, enfolding quiet,
> far reaching vistas?
> What is its secret? Why have we come?

> > *The valley is an ark,*
> > *preserving the fires*
> > *of continuity*
> > *for the Lords of Evolution,*

---

* *The Kingdom of the Gods,* by Geoffrey Hodson, 1952 and *Regents of the Seven Spheres,* by H.K. Challoner, 1966, both by the Theosophical Publishing House are good sources of illustrations of the devas and elemental entities.

> *fires of renewal,*
> *fires of ongoing,*
> *fires of sacred purpose.*
> *The valley is a listening post,*
> *a focus of reception,*
> *a channel of transmission.*

On Meditation Mount in the heart of the valley in the shadow of Topa Topa sacred to the valley, we meet in recognition, each lending his note, each adding his fire, each yielding his will to the Great Pattern and the Great Purpose, and with a sure knowing that *together* we build.
Broodings on Meditation Mount by G.C.

MODERN ELEMENTALS

Elementals may take many forms and are evolutionary partners man should learn to cooperate with, but not attempt to identify with. Direct contact can result in an evolving elemental entity trying to jump over into the higher life stream by usurping a human *individuality*. Humans must remember that elementals are a lower life stream. Man combines *all* of the elemental qualities, plus a fifth. Approach to the elemental kingdoms should be done through the angelic hierarchy so that they are under the control of their Lords. Contact by humans that is not in direct accord with the Divine Will can lead to trouble. Properly approached cooperation is both helpful and rewarding.

In 1972, while living in Hawaii, I was introduced to the highly evolved personality of a ruling *salamander*, or fire elemental. Morna Simeona, a Hawaiian *Kahuna*, has established a long standing and close relationship with Pelé,

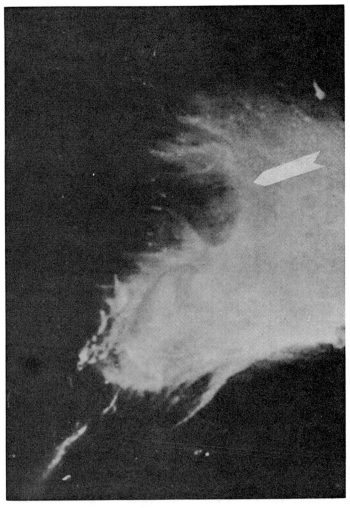

"Double Feature."
The face and shoulder of Pelé, the volcanic fire elemental on the Island of Hawaii, is clearly visible in this photograph taken during an eruption by *Kahuna* Morna Simeona.

the famous "goddess" of Kilauea Volcano on the island of Hawaii. Pelé correctly denies this title, understanding exactly who she is. The story goes, however, that she did preempt the volcano by ousting the former elemental guardian and taking over. The position is a key one, since this volcano is located in the center of what is called the *Pacific Ring of Fire*. This refers to the many volcanos surrounding the Pacific Ocean, extending from South America, to Alaska and the Far East. Pelé is in charge of balancing these powerful volcanic energies and her volcano often rumbles during distant eruptions.

I have a rare photograph of Pelé, taken by Morna. Pelé's face is clearly visible as a beautiful young woman within the blazing flame of an eruption. In the lodge on the volcano rim, an oil portrait of her perceptively shows the same beautiful young woman smiling through flames. My ex-husband has also seen her and confirmed the legend that says she is only young and beautiful when the volcano is active. During quiet periods she hovers over it, appearing as an old hunched crone in puffs of whispy smoke.

On the other side of the world, in northern Scotland, I encountered the air and water elementals that govern the fluids and gases of the planet. There is much more to the much maligned "rain dances" of native *shaman* ("doctors") than modern man suspects. They were a way of building up emotional energy and thought to communicate with the elementals. Such communications can be profound, as a group of us found while visiting the Findhorn Community.* This *New Age* community is famous for its successful cooperation with the nature kingdoms, producing remarkable gardens, even under adverse climatic conditions.

We were, however, visiting during the most severe drought in Great Britain in many years. Plants, trees and even giant elms were dying all over the land. Water rationing was strict.

On the evening of our communication experience, we had been seriously disturbed by an exchange between some humans and an elemental kingdom that we strongly disapproved of. We were *emotionally upset,* so we decided we should go out into the starry night and meditate beside the Findhorn "power point," where an earth vortex exists. The five of us stood hand-in-hand, contemplated our concern and then entered the silence. After about twenty minutes, we suddenly felt a fine spray of water shooting over us, coming from the direction of the "power point." Startled, we returned from our meditation, shared our impressions and went to bed. We felt that the problem that had disturbed us had been resolved.

That night the first rain fell in many months over the entire nation, ending the history making drought. "Coincidence?" Or had we stumbled upon a disturbance in the nature kingdoms that was appeased by our *expressed group concern* and contact? The elementals are our silent partners and we should never forget this fact. It is important to our global welfare.

---

* *The Magic of Findhorn,* Paul Hawken, Harper & Row, 1975.

THE LITTLE PEOPLE

Most cultures have stories about the "little people." Even the Eskimos of Alaska tell about meeting them on the open expanses of the northern tundra and warned against accepting gifts from them (believing this resulted in being "taken"). The work of the *gnomes* is to build mineral, metal and gem forms on the next dimension.

One day while meditating, I suddenly found myself being taken deep into the bowels of the earth. As I descended through layers of rock, I began to hear the little people hammering away. It grew hot as I continued deeper and deeper, arriving at what seemed an endless tunnel. Finally I reached the end, where a kingly figure was seated upon a golden throne at the barren end of the tunnel. He introduced himself as "King Alfred" and gave me an audience, explaining the work of his people. When he had finished, I thanked him and returned to my normal dimension.

This was an unusually evolved gnome. He appeared to have full consciousness and considerable personality. The more typical gnome personality is gruff and with no patience for the "stupidity" of man. A friend of ours in Alaska encountered one of these stern types when she became lost in the woods. Stumbling through brush and over logs and walking in circles, she finally resorted to asking the nature kingdoms for help. She has a good rapport with the elementals, but a glowering disapproving gnome partially appeared before her and grimly pointed to the way *out*. She followed his instruction and soon crossed an old road that led to a highway.

"The Little People."
A glowering disapproving *gnome* appeared to our friend, when she was lost in the Alaskan woods, and grimly pointed the way *out*.

A friendlier gnome was discovered at our former site in the countryside near Fairbanks, Alaska, while Peter Caddy from Findhorn and some clairvoyant friends from Anchorage, Alaska were visiting us in 1977. The gnome's name was Lor and he was unusually tall, nearly five feet, with a typically long gray beard. He was in charge of a vortex of energy focused through a remarkable spruce tree. The great trunk of this tree divided about twelve feet above the ground into four tall symmetrical, fully limbed tree trunks. Lor was quite proud of "his tree" and the area surrounding it had a very special atmosphere, so much like a sanctuary that we used it for outdoor ceremonies, such as Bud's marriage. It was a lovely grove, with Lor apparently acting as the overseer of the elemental caretakers in the area.

The proper approach to the nature kingdoms is always one of cooperation with the Divine Will for the planet. This produces their cooperation in return, for this is their duty. Today this cooperation is vital to overcome extensive abuses of nature. Part of human evolution is to reach the point of becoming an example of cooperation. Their awareness depends upon what has been impressed upon them by the angelic hierarchy and mankind. We have not been a very good example, so its little wonder if our weather acts strange, volcanos erupt and other "natural" disasters plague humanity. If our example is to destroy, they might just take us up on it.

Cooperation with the kingdoms is fun. Visual contact is not necessary, or even desirable, but it is still possible to communicate through the *intelligence* within everything. For example, talk to your plants, even weeds. If you need to remove some, explain to them why they must go. Talk to your car, appliances and other equipment. Give them names and personify them and they will respond by working and avoid breaking down. When you need to use an unfamiliar tool, what do you do? Did you know you can communicate with it? You can tune into the thought form connected with it and the tool will teach you how to use it. Try it! You may be surprised by the results. Cooperation with the elementals is enjoyable, but do not become infatuated with it.

The elementals exist on the astral (emotional) realm. We contact them through the emotions, (e-motion meaning *to move* something). To elicit a direct reaction from an elemental kingdom requires human *emotion,* so care must be taken that your will is in accord with the One Will. Asking the elementals to do something, is very different from simply cooperating with them and sharing their collective consciousness.

To measure your elemental balance consider the four essential qualities: *Earth,* willingness to accept *responsibility; Water,* willing *flexibility* to "do Thy Will, not mine;" *Air,* a steady *vision* of Oneness in being and purpose; *Fire,* freedom from personal desire manifesting in *zeal* to do the One Work. Unless these are sincerely present and a part of your consciousness, you should not attempt to solicit personal responses from elemental personalities. Do cooperate with their work and draw information from the *devic* level of collective consciousness. This is not saying direct contacts are wrong in any way. They just should not be attempted by the untrained.

"MUSIC OF THE SPHERES"

4

Music of the Spheres

Aaa . . .   . . . round   wor . . . ld   eight
                    the   in   . . . y days . . .

What are you doing now?!

        I'm warming everyone up for the
        next scene.

By singing?

        Certainly.

How can you enjoy . . . oh, never mind.

        Please don't let me interrupt you.

        Thanks. Just move back and
        give me room. That's it. Now, feast
        your celestial ears on this!

Wait a minute . . . . ,
    what are you doing with that
    electric guitar?!

        Just be patient . . . ,
        remove yourself to a safe distance
        and enjoy.

"You ain't nuthin' but uhh HOUND $^{DAAWWG . . . "}$

103

. . . KLUNK!

                                          What was that . . . ?

        I think another angel
        just fell.

                        Oh, yeah? Say . . . , that reminds me of when
                                I joined this show . . .
Yes, well, now it's time to get on with it.
        Where's the lady . . . ? LaVedi! You're on!

CELESTIAL CHORDS

So far we have primarily looked at the evolution of
our own solar system within the Cosmos and considered
the Seed-atoms that originated with it. Now we need to
consider how Earth has been affected by the evolution of
other star systems as well. Man is not alone in the Cosmos,
and we are becoming increasingly aware of this. Extraterrestrials as they are commonly called, have always been
involved with Earth's evolution. The populated worlds
are interactive; when a world or a universe dies, the occu-
pants migrate to other systems and planets. Other worlds
also send "students" to earth to individually learn from
the earth experience and to collectively absorb the experience of these emissaries.

Earth has then a universal population that includes a
mixture of her own protégé, and a conglomeration from
other star systems. The extraterrestrials have varied from
the highest evolution of multi-dimensional teachers to
exiles sent to Earth as a last resort (like a penal colony).
Others simply failed to complete their evolution on their
own spheres and immigrated here to continue the process,

just as those who do not complete their evolution on Earth will eventually go on to new worlds. The process is simply one of transferring consciousness and our higher dimensional incorporeal bodies. Interdimensional travel can be done by the physically living or the "dead," and it can be done on different levels (body involvement).

We have already seen how all matter is interpenetrating and how forms have geometric (mathematical) and sound (musical) correspondences. As Hellenbach says in *Magie der Zahlen,* about chemical variety, "so far as we can grasp its inner nature, depends upon numerical relations, and we have further found in this variety a ruling law for which we can assign no cause; we find a law of periodicity governed by the number *seven.*" We are surrounded by natural laws involved with the orderly structure and action of atoms, and these relate to interdimensional travel. For example, an electron will jump from one shell, or belt, if enough energy is applied. In this sense, matter, when exposed to the frequencies of specific sound waves can be stimulated to change vibration and dimension.

In the Cosmos we saw how essential motion was in the original creation process, and we saw how when the flowing rays met the dimensional motions of the belts they formed vortices of motion (the Words). This meeting is said to produce a *squaring* of dimensional motions and this squaring follows rules of music and mathematics. All form is said to be "frozen music."*

---

* Reference: *Music of the Spheres,* Guy Murchie, Dover Publications, 1967 (matter, atoms, waves, radiation and relativity).

An English physicist, Henry Gwyn-Jeffries Moseley, demonstrated the harmony between matter and vibration by a process of X-raying the diffraction of most of the chemical elements. He found corresponding order in the square roots of their vibrational frequencies and these frequencies conform precisely to the periodicity of the series of atomic numbers (beginning with "1" for hydrogen).

The frequency of a musical string's vibration also varies directly with the square root of its tension, (though inversely with its length and the square root of its weight). This was discovered in 1636 by the French mathematician, Marin Mersenne, while Pythagoras the Greek mathematician, discovered the laws of harmonic numbers. Flammarion, in *Astronomical Myths,* gives an account of Pythagoras' discovery:

> It is stated that one day Pythagoras, passing near a forge, noticed that the hammers gave out very accurate musical concords. He had them weighed, and found that of those which sounded the octave one weighed twice as much as the other; that of those which made, (an interval or), a perfect fifth, one weighed one-third more than another, and in the case of fourth, one-quarter more. After having tried the hammers, he took a musical string stretched with weights, and found that when he had applied a given weight . . . to make any particular note, he had to double the weight to obtain the octave . . .

Pythagoras concluded from this that the planets, which both weigh and move, must also produce individual sounds or celestial music. Euripides then wrote, speaking to Earth:

> Thee I invoke, thou self-created Being, who gave birth to Nature, and whom light and darkness and the whole train of globes encircle with eternal music.

Sound ratios govern the wave-like motions of atomic particles. The effect of sound on matter is easily demonstrable. Most everyone is familiar with the phenomena of a wine glass being shattered by someone singing "high C." The vibrations of musical notes have been scientifically measured, showing for example, that "middle C" consists of about 262 pressure waves per second and that *any* regular vibrations at this speed will produce this note. Interdimensional travel (and levitation) are connected with these laws.

In *Isis Unveiled,* Blavatsky mentions that as she and her companions traveled for the first time in the East they met sages of the orient with "mysterious powers" and "profound knowledge." She says they showed them the existence of God and man's spiritual immortality could be demonstrated through a combination of religion and science.

The time has arrived to take the "mystery" out of religion and the ancient secrets. We have the scientific knowledge to do so, all that really stands in the way is prejudiced superstition on the part of the scientific community that forces investigators to either take an unpopular stand or work unknown behind the scenes. When man entered space beyond Earth, he announced that humanity was ready. We will never be the same again.

Dane Rudhyar, in *The Sun is Also a Star,* mentions this new direction, resulting from man's changing view of the universe. He writes that it "demands the acceptance of a *new dimension of reality.*" Rudhyar was referring to the "fourth dimension," which he writes can best be defined by "INTERPENETRATION . . . all there is interpenetrates everything . . . "*

We are composed of continually moving, changing, interpenetrating energy patterns. Why should we think it impossible, or even difficult, to separate or alter the rates of vibration involved?

According to Joseph Goodavage, even the formal *Journal of Medical Electronics* has pointed out "that *everything* is composed of electromagnetic fields . . . . " He also quotes Dr. Lloyd Graham of Grants Pass, Oregon as stating the human body consists of an "orderly arrangement of electromagnetic light wave vibrational patterns in gravitational and radiational motion." Goodavage goes on to state that everything, animate or inanimate, is "frozen" electromagnetic light wave patterns or energy "pressed" into forms.†

COLONIZING EARTH

There seem to have been several influxes of extra-terrestrials to Earth that especially influenced the development of ancient civilizations, technology and human evolution. Tradition holds that the first colonization on Earth was in the area now known as the Gobi desert.

---

* *The Sun Is Also a Star*, Dane Rudhyar, E.P. Dutton, N.Y., 1975.
† *Astrology: The Space Age Science*, Joseph F. Goodavage, Parker Publishing Co., 1966.

Highly evolved entities created a multidimensional city there, known as the "crystal city," or Shamballa. This allowed them to live in their own dimension, yet appear to humans in what seemed to be "physical forms" at will. *"Material-izations"* are really just "thought-forms" of varying strength.

The *records* indicate that this paradise may have lasted until nearly 300,000 years ago, when the physical structures were destroyed by what was possibly a form of atomic warfare. The higher dimensional aspect was removed to the vicinity of Tibet, from where Divine Will is still distributed to humanity through what is termed the Hierarchy. We see here a mixture of evolved entities, from Earth and other systems united in One Purpose, identity being irrelevant. For more on this the writings of Alice Bailey are recommended.

During Atlantean times a migration arrived from "Mizar." Patricia-Rochelle Diegel, my longtime friend and time-traveler (over many lives) came from there. She tells how she arrived with a large group of intergalactic immigrants when their planet become uninhabitable. Mizar had a highly evolved society and the Mizarians became a strong influence on Atlantean society. Having had horses and races at home on Mizar, they developed them in Atlantis. They also brought sciences to earth as a *reading* for a former Mizarian revealed:

> Bud: Let us move on and explore the relationship of the entity . . . with the Titan.
>
> LaVedi: He appears among them [referring to the Atlantean

Titans or giants], had some difficulty adjusting to different bodies.

Bud: What was the purpose of his incarnation as a Titan?

LaVedi: This was a vibration that he would acquire. There was resistance to taking on the earth form, which . . . made it difficult, created a problem for himself. As a Titan form he was given the opportunity to accomplish the egoic need and to express a certain energy brought from his source, that would have been compacted, compressed too much in the other earth forms. It is like he needed the size of the . . . larger form before he could funnel down into a normal size body on this planet.

Bud: What is the original source of the entity?

LaVedi: I see a ship and the entities in front of it. And they are like collecting specimens . . . intergalactic specimens, plants, life forms.

Bud: May we have more on the Titans?

LaVedi: Moving back to the Titans on the earth plane . . . extraordinary large size.

Bud: Moving back to that scene. How large are they?

LaVedi: About eight feet . . . it seems that they gave rise to many myths because of their size and their power.

Bud: Physical power? . . . Would it be called psychic power?

LaVedi: There is something more . . . work because of their size; there are things on earth today that man cannot explain, they were done by the Titans.

Bud: Could this relate to the statues on Easter Island?

LaVedi: An early outpost; there is more advanced work later. Their civilization existed for a span of time.

Bud: Was it extensively populated?

LaVedi: No, like colonies. And where they went they established many new sites—we know as power points—because of their ability . . . they went to locations that had direct earth works and created like a conduit around the world, through the earth.

Bud: Middle of the earth?

LaVedi: I see like tunnels reaching down into the earth, possibly volcanic tunnels, possibly other tunnels; I am not sure, but it is like a circulatory system, possibly a physical one in the earth, and to which the power points are connected.* One of these colonies was in Alaska, or in a portion of same that existed at that time.

Bud: Was this particular location in the Seward peninsula?

LaVedi: In that area.

Bud: Is this the particular reason for "the Titan " (a "Master") to be working in Alaska? Is it a strong power point?

---

* Note: I have since found reference to mysterious tunnels said to exist in Mexico and thought to possibly connect with endless tunnels in Brazil, Peru and the Andes. Others have been found in Egypt and tradition holds they may link up with others in Tibet.

LaVedi: His interest isn't all in the one—because it is unrecognized.

Bud: Has "the Titan," as we call him, directly related in any fashion to the entity ———?

LaVedi: In the sense that like student to a teacher, yes.

Bud: On the inner planes?

LaVedi: Both.

Bud: He has been in incarnation during the Titan period? Are there certain yet to be discovered soul talents of the entity, ———— , from this life experience that he should learn to use?

LaVedi: Begin developing sensitivity of the hands, vibration attunement that can be developed in relation to healing radiations from the earth or sources of vitality . . . . this can be utilized in much more practical ways in smaller spaces, also in larger areas, for picking out again major power places, in other words, there are major power points, and many minor ones. It is like large chakras, and many, many minor chakras, and he can develop the hands to feel both, and also feel emotions, or read the quality of the energy they offer.

Bud: How may he practice and develop this talent?

LaVedi: First learning the feel of many objects. Hold the hand or hands above many forms of matter until you can *feel the vibration* . . . . Learn the different sensations. You will be looking for degrees of feelings.

The references to Alaska appeared again in a *trinity*

*reading** I did with two other people in Fairbanks in May 1978. We found ourselves aboard a submarine-like ship, traveling the Pacific Ocean. The ship was powered some-how by sound and had delicate instruments on board to interpret earth energies and locate power points. One such point appeared in Alaska, again on the midwestern coast, where a colony was formed much like an old fort, or a radar station today. The region was tropical and the colony was protected by a surrounding "sound-barrier" and high sloping wall.

The northern portion of the globe has an importance that is seldom recognized. The beneficial input coming in-to Earth, Cosmic and interdimensional is drawn through the northern vortex at the pole and flows southward around the planet on the "Van Allen Belt." The ancient Hyperborian continent, Meru, mostly buried under the polar ice cap, was where early man began to develop into androgynous forms.

The Titan, also known as *Prometheus* and the Venusian Master, is considered to have been the *generator* of humanity, because he "kneeded" the clay to provide the first formed bodies. As Prometheus, he suffers con-tinual torture on Mt. Caucasus, until mankind learns to use the gift of "sacred fire" he gave to them. He is one of the *Seven Regents*; in myth there were seven Titans, re-ferring to the seven sub-ray divisions of Prometheus (one ray).

---

* Effective technique developed by Patricia-Rochelle Diegel, utilizing fo-cused group energy in collective recall of past lives and events.

He still reigns over the Land of Meru, waiting on humanity, and governing the Cosmic Forces of Chaos on the higher and lower realms. *Pro-me-theus* means "he who sees before him," or the future. The gift he gave to man was his future enlightenment and desire for *return* (Union). The *individualizing* force flows through Prometheus that develops concrete consciousness in preparation for reunion within the One Consciousness, as an individual creating agent. A future is set aside for the North that relates to evolved humanity.

Alaska has a powerfully concentrated individualizing force. It's the place to come when personal identity and individuation is being developed. Collective activities are most successful in connection with growth of the rational intelligence aspects of mind and the arts (again connected with individuation). Persons who need this are attracted like a magnet.

Another large group of immigrating star travelers came from Sirius and vicinity. Quoting from another *reading* Bud and I did for a fellow Alaskan, we found:

> LaVedi: He has training in what would be the equivalent of an astronaut today, in that he came here from another world as a space traveler and understands from this level of consciousness planetary communication and energies that we haven't thought of yet.
>
> Bud: Where was the entity's original source? Before this planet? ... A star system?
>
> LaVedi: A galaxy to the northeast of Sirius.

Bud: Why did the entity select this planet?

LaVedi: 'I am looking for a new planet to inhabit. Our own is dying.'

Bud: Was this particular entity in what would be considered humanoid form?

LaVedi: Yes.

Bud: Were there any distinguishing features other than normally found?

LaVedi: They appear actually to be interdimensional beings, smallish. They also entered this world to enter into manifested dimension, which was . . . , had not been possible on their planet. For some reason they seemed to function out of both dimensions.

Bud: Did the spacecraft actually land on the planet? This was before Atlantis?

LaVedi: Yes.

Bud: Much before, or Lemurian times?

LaVedi: Very early, very early, at the time before this manifestation. Their ship was not too large. There were only a few. Another ship followed. This was interdimensional travel.

Bud: Interdimensional travel that presupposed the speed of light?

LaVedi: Yes. Leaving that experience, that life. There is one area that is very interesting; this ship is not in a sense what we think of as a ship—a container.

Bud: Could we more accurately call it a time machine?

LaVedi: Yes. It seems it could be used either way.

Bud: Do you see any explanation for how this functioned? Vibration?

LaVedi: Yes . . . , sound. That could be the answer, vibration.

There is a good sized Sirian population on Earth today. Rachael MacPherson, in doing a *reading* following our techniques to delve into her origins, reported how she came from Sirius "B" to Earth as follows:

> Beginning journey to earth, by way of Venus. No sex . . . no speech between other beings. Telepathy, direct knowledge, one mind, one thought. Purpose of leaving—sent out to gain all possible experience, eventually to return having gained it. An assignment. To describe Sirius B impossible with words, only direct knowledge.

Rachel next notes that the "Master Serapis" is from Sirius, and that he is asking those from that realm to tune into him through hypnosis and meditation:

> . . . to make assimilation of experience immediate, rather than taking thousands of centuries. There will be a turnover, a turning around from earth thinking and knowledge, because the time is at hand, and we beings of light have to shed all the earth shells and become what we essentially are. Those who cling will be removed to other spheres. Only beings of light can

inhabit Sirius B, because of the heaviness (density) of that planet.

To leave, to re-colonize, meant materializing bodies suitable to Venus, then to earth, in stages. Bodies: physical, mental, astral, (are) only *instruments of adaptability*. We descended into matter to bring light, to lighten, to resurrect, to 'principle.'

Rachel noted, after the above, that Sirians arrived during the time of the Lemurian epoch. In the *Zohar* these early space travelers are spoken of as the *Ischins,* the "lower angels" and as the *Malachim,* the "good Messengers," or commonly as the *B'ne Aleim.* The *Zohar* goes on to say, "the Ischins, the beautiful B'ne Aleim . . . *mixed themselves with mortal men because they were sent on earth to do so."* These "men-spirits" brought civilization and world evolution to mankind, but it is not correct to consider them as "angels," for these are two different streams of evolution.

HOME SWEET HOME

Most extraterrestrials living on Earth in human forms are becoming aware, as the possibility is brought to their attention, that they are nonearthlings. For the most part they appear like everyone else, though they normally have high intelligence and creative talents. They also have a persistent sense of somehow "not belonging here," and are often haunted by the inexplicable feeling that they are somehow sojourners in a foreign land. These feelings are becoming very strong now, as they are being "recalled" home. Conscious awareness is beginning to merge with the unconscious memories and contact, as their term on Earth draws to a close.

One of these individuals, a lady from Sacramento, California, who I assisted in a *reading* about her home planet, described an atmosphere of love and great knowledge. The forms of the entities, as she saw them, were human-like, but taller, very beautiful and of incorporeal substance. Communication was by thought transference, and their clothing appeared as robes and gowns in exquisitely vibrant colors. The woman felt that she left her world as a young girl, but was sent by her teacher to both help and learn. Her longing for "home" brought tears of loneliness to her eyes, while she mentally "visited" her old friends.

Another *reading* that compliments this one was done by Marcia Moore with one of the founders of the Ananta Foundation, Dr. Richard D. Willard, M.D. Their findings appeared in the formerly published "Hypersentience Bulletin "*

> I found myself a young man by earth standards, standing beside some buildings. The dwellings were simple, yet all were of a complex geometric design . . . . This planet is called Lemuric, which means Sea of Divine Love. Governments, laws and regulations are unnecessary in this place. The entire planet is surrounded by an aura of light which radiates from the *heart-energy* generated by the inhabitants.

> Monetary systems of barter and exchange as earthlings know them are non-existent. Attraction exists between masculine and feminine entities. The attraction is satisfied by

---

* *Hypersentience*, Marcia Moore, Bantam Books, 1976, (describes the "hypersentience" recall techniques and case histories).

periodic interpenetration of form—a simultaneous fusion of body, mind and spirit. While there are no rulers or administrators, instructors are present to serve as advisors.

I was unable to find a point of nonexistence on Lemuric. At first I was concerned and somewhat apprehensive. Then like a flash it dawned on me. *I have not yet died on Lemuric.* I co-exist in both places simultaneously. As this enlightenment swept over me, the entity on Lemuric disclosed a smile of sapient approval.

I was immediately aware that I had chosen to follow the path of the student—a path which would eventually lead to my becoming an instructor. I had progressed in my studies to the point where the next step was to learn about human beings. That is where I began my incarnations on the planet Earth.

I get the distinct feeling that rather soon, as we here count time, my basic entity on Lemuric will be drawing this aspect of itself—that is me—back inside itself. Because I will have performed the task of gathering knowledge and awareness, and he will have this knowledge to draw upon.

The similarity of these experiences is remarkable, considering that these quoted all occurred independently and among diverse people. Contact with "home" can also occur spontaneously, as happened to one of my former students at World University in Ojai, Rahn Jensen. Rahn reported that one evening he couldn't get to sleep and:

. . . my awareness seemed to expand and I found myself *gazing* at a distant horizon of mountains. I saw a *blue light* coming over the horizon—it was kind of like a blue sun, but almost transparent. (This is a highly typical clairvoyant transition to an altered state of Cosmic Consciousness as taught by our *Past Life Memory Program*.)

The next thing I knew I was walking down a street in a small rural town . . . . with some "skeptics" and I looked up and saw a huge ship floating in the sky directly above the street.

I said, "See, now you can't deny they exist, your own eyes are proof." By now the ship has turned on its end and settled on a long narrow part that balanced the rest of the massive ship above it. Quite a number of people had gathered and there did not seem to be hysteria or confusion.

A door opened in the bottom of the column it had landed on, and several people got out. They looked just like earthlings, but the faces in some cases were a little different. It was almost like they could change their features—and did so in order to see what kind of reaction it would cause. I could feel the love and warmth radiating from them as they reached their arms out toward the crowd. I was drawn forward and found myself embracing one, and then several of them.

As the group from the ship came out, it seemed that all of them were male, or at least they were so similar in appearance that no difference was noticeable . . . They wore very bright clothes. One, who seemed to be a leader of sorts, began walking into the crowd. He pointed to one lady in the crowd, nodded and said, "She's one." He passed on by her and also several others, and then pointed to me and said, "He's one."

The crowd dispersed and I had the feeling that even though they had witnessed the landing, they had refused to believe it had happened. All this time I kept saying to myself how wonderful it was to be experiencing this, and *knowing* that it was *not* a dream.

Next we were in a large room seated around a table. I was standing behind the first person I had reached out to when they first came out of the ship. This person had now taken on a masculine appearance. He very closely resembled a light skinned negro, was bearded and very nice looking; but like the others it seemed that he also changed his appearance . . . . their skin tone was brighter and shinier, the facial structure was fuller, almost voluptous, but changing. I seemed to see, within the tremendous amount of love and warmth they projected, a subtle unchanging appearance that was very beautiful.

The person who had apparently taken me in charge was writing very rapidly in a strange scriptic manner that seemed to go up-down-sideways, all over the paper at the same time. He had me hold the tip of the pen while he moved the end. When we had written awhile the paper was full and the result was quite beautiful. It was almost as if it was a picture, but I knew it was writing.

It seemed I was in a classroom and he was trying to show me, or tell me where they were from and to instruct me in their writing. We did not talk, we exchanged thoughts and when I inquired as to where they were from the answer that kept coming into my mind was "Futura." My feeling was that this was not far away . . . I am not sure of what I thought of as being, "very far." At this time he was showing me a drawing that resembled a galactic map of sorts.

I asked him if he would write my name in his language. He said, "Yes," if I would write mine down for him. I picked up the pen and started to write, but could not. I tried many, many times . . . it became very frustrating . . . My frustration seemed apparent to my instructor. I stood up and thought,

"I am not worthy." As soon as this thought came into my mind
the feeling came back that it didn't matter. He reached out his
arms and I felt myself dissolving within his being. It was a
wonderful feeling and very energizing.

Whether Rahn merged with an aspect of himself, or
with friends and an instructor from his "home" is not clear,
but he does *know* that he is not an earthling.

One final point regarding communication between
persons from other planetary systems, is that they have a
communication situation very similar to that described for
the Seed-atoms. They are also receiving from their *Logoic
Source* via their *light* threads. We did a *reading* for an
entity sent to Earth specifically to establish contact
between our collective consciousness and his Logos:

> LaVedi: An entity . . . in another sphere of experience . . .
> and regarded as a teacher, (perceived as the 'Ancient of Days,'
> with streamers flying from the head . . . , like waves of energy),
> he is working . . . it is very hard because there is a veil of
> words . . . , but, in a sense, exchange of energies . . . , through
> mind.

> Bud: What is the basic purpose of this entity on the earth
> plane at this time?

> LaVedi: . . . the entity receives instruction in the form of ex-
> change from his Source, and in receiving this awareness of
> exchange, not knowledge in the sense that we think of knowl-
> edge; awareness of existence beyond what we know, and by
> receiving this exchange, the entity brings this awareness to this
> planet. When he becomes able to bring this to his conscious-
> ness, he will have accomplished his purpose.

In the *reading*, I went on to explain that, as he becomes aware that he is receiving input from his Source, and begins to know what he has received consciously, he will then be able to share this with others. Bud then asked if there was a meditation technique that would help him to accomplish this:

> LaVedi: I see a world within a world, within a world, and in the center, consciousness like a telescope.

I suggested that he visualize this image in contemplation for information, to greatly accelerate his awareness; by entering the *Void,* layer by layer, world within world.

As for myself, I am not an "earthling" either and have also experienced multi-dimensional existence in other worlds. I entered during the Venus cycle under Prometheus (the Titan), during the manifestation of the androgynous forms. These are related to Venus, representing manifestation of the generative (procreative) *principle*. These early forms were referred to as the Titans, and this was known as the "Titanic Age." The Titans awoke the "fires of passion," or the Cosmic Fire made manifest in man, Venus symbolizing "love."

Venus-Isis-Eve are one, representing the Divine Will recreating cosmic principles in man. *Isis* says, "I am the Queen . . . I am she who rises in the constellation of the Dog [Sirius, the "Dog-star] . . . *Isis-Osiris* are older than the ancient Zodiac painted on the ceiling of the temple of Dendera in Egypt. For humanity *Osiris* represents the regathering of the parts and union with the Sun *principle* (the Greater Adam, the Logos). This results in *One*, symbolized by *Horus.*

Human union is a reflection of the creative force (Fire) of the Cosmos. When a child is conceived, the emotions between the parents produce a "vortex" of attraction that draws an incarnating soul to its "quality." In a similar way, when an *individual* begins to unite with *Logos*, the process forms a "vortex" of energy. The seeker then progresses through periods of "gestation," "birth-pangs," assimilation, symbolic "death" and Union ("rebirth").

In one of my Egyptian lives, I was a temple seeress and "kept the *records.*" This was during a period of political upheaval and our temple was overthrown. Before they burst in upon us, we secreted away many papyrus scrolls under the fitted stone flooring to preserve and safeguard the sacred knowledge. A few years ago an oracle, apparently from this long ago time, was "returned" to me. This is exactly as I "received" it:

Sek-ar-rhet

Sek-ar-rhet, child of pharaoh,
   Born to be lonely,
Star-walker of the night,   [sleep]
   And mower of the meadow of the moon. [unconscious]

The cornflower nods to thee,
   As you journey through the seas of time,
Seeking your lost one,
   Mate of Eternal Day.

When the sands run dry,

The Sun will return.
And shine upon the night of Sek-ar-rhet.
Seeker of the Lotus Flower of the Heart.

The "cornflower" puzzled me, until recently. Corn is ruled by Venus and sacred to the priesthood, but the cornflower is a blue star-like bloom. I understand this correlation to the "blue" we use for a focus in the mind's eye in doing time travel, but there is more. The cornflower grows among the corn and its stems are so tough it dulls the reaper's sickle (symbol of Saturn and death):

Thou blunt'st the very reaper's sickle and so
In life and death becom'st the farmer's foe.

As well as being ruled by Venus , the Titanic Age was under the constellation of Capricorn, therefore I repeatedly incarnate in connection with this sign. Surprisingly, Capricorn is associated with Venus. Human descent is related to Lemuria born under the influence of Saturn, (ruled by Capricorn). It is Saturn that brings *conscious* awareness to "Adam," through creation of "form," and limitation (ruled by Saturn). At the same time Saturn rules death and time (Father Time). This is the "blessing" of death that permits us to resume our immortality.

The sign of Capricorn is generally not understood. In the Hindu zodiac this sign is *Jala-rupa* (water-form) or "sea-dragon, half-dolphin and half-antelope. (Appropriately my first early form was a type of "water nymph.") In Egypt, Capricornus was symbolized by the crocodile, due to the animal's habitual rising from the waters of the Nile with

the first morning's sunbeams. This personified a devotee
of the *Solar Logos,* the highest aspect of the soul to the
Egyptians.

Osiris was called the "double crocodile," with several
meanings. It refers to death and rebirth, first in human
form and then as the Unified One, and it relates to Capricorn being the tenth sign of the zodiac, or double five.
In Sanskrit, the name of the sign is *Makara* (dolphin
and antelope), derived from *ma,* related to the number
five and to *kara* meaning "hand." This corresponds to
the *five elements* doubled, or the macrocosm made manifest in the microcosm (man), with two "creative hands."
The dual aspects of the amphibious animal, also refers
to this double aspect, living both on "earth" and in the
"water." The symbol of *Makara* in Hinduism appears
representing Venus, because *Makara* is connected with
birth through love (the mind-born sons of God and the
children of men), and with death and *rebirth* into the
Universal Estate. Birth (Venus) and death (Saturn) are
irrevocably connected.

These two basic influences add to clarify and deperson-
alize the emanations related to the principles of form and
enlightenment (Venus springing from the ocean with the
lotus in her hand). Or as the Egyptian *Book of the Dead*
says of transformation, "I am the pure lotus, emerging from
the Luminous one. I carry the messages of Horus. I am the
pure lotus which comes from the Solar Fields." Osiris and
Isis, children of Cronus (time without end), become the
parents of man as Horus, and of the God Horus, regen-
erated. The instruction through Isis-Osiris-Horus dates

from this early Venusian period.

In the past I have been particularly connected with Horus, with preservation of Wisdom Teachings, oral and written histories and the arts. Similar to Blavatsky, Bailey and Fortune, I seek to work in cooperation with those forces seeking unity of East and West through Wisdom and understanding, and the collective change in consciousness at this time.

> There has never been a period in our planetary history in which opportunity has loomed so large or when so much spiritual light and force could be contained and utilized by humanity.
>
> (*Discipleship in the New Age,* Vol. II, by the Tibetan through Alice Bailey).

THE *KABBALISTIC MAP* OF RETURN

The *Kabbala* of Judaism is said to represent the hidden wisdom of the *Old Testament,* compiled by rabbis during the Middle Ages of older secret doctrines. The Hebrew word, *Kabbal* means "to receive," while the derivative, *Kabbala* (spelled variously as *Kabalah* or *Qabbala*), indicates "a thing received." In the *Talmud,* it is stated that " . . . the words of the *Kabbalah* are just the same as the words of the law," referring to the written law received by Moses upon Mt. Sinai, (fol. 19, col. 1).

Going back further, tradition holds that the Kabbalistic Mysteries were *principles* taught by God to the angels before the fall of man. These secrets were then revealed to "Adam" so that "through the knowledge gained from an understanding of its principles fallen humanity might regain its lost estate."*

To students of the *Kabbalah,* the *Tree of Life* represents (as does the cross) a map or pattern to merge all aspects of Self: spirit, soul, mind and body. It is not necessary to go into complex or detailed studies to utilize the *Tree.* It does require dedication and purpose, but if you have decided you want to raise your consciousness the *Tree* is a proven way to do it in a balanced way. There are many "systems" used and assorted symbols, but as is often the case more direct methods are easier and at least as effective as others. Once you understand the *principles,* the rest is up to you. Because everyone is different and individual, there is no *one* way. The pattern of the *Tree* is adjustable to fit you and represents a way of life.

We have already seen the basic elements symbolized by the *Tree.* It contains ten Sephiroth (circles) connected by "paths," with the circles on seven levels. Beginning from Earth and man, the levels ascend through angels, archangels, the rays (as the color spectrum), Limitless Light (Logos), Absolute Light (Cosmos) and the Absolute of the Void (Space).

The *Tree* is meant to be an experiential map to dimensions and all levels of consciousness, from the mind of man, through the unconscious (including intellect and emotional desire), to the Collective Unconscious and Universal Consciousness. From this it should be apparent that the *Tree* is a capsulated pattern of the Cosmos. Like

---

* *The Secret Teachings of All Ages*, Manley Palmer Hall, The Philosophical Research Society, 1962.

the acorn, if you choose to plant it in your unconscious and water it regularly it will grow into a mighty Tree you can climb to "heaven."

The feeding and watering, as with any diet, involves certain nutritional elements. This *Tree* requires: meditation, contemplation, prayer and practice. Through meditation we commune with the Stillness; in contemplation we train the mind in symbols and visualization; through prayer we express methodology and willing devotion; while practice is our thoughts and actions daily. All of this interpenetrates. The more we practice, combining all levels, the sooner we become *One.* The combination speaks to each level of *mind* and primes the pump, so to speak. The unconscious, being much like a computer, finds itself being programmed from all directions at once.

The *Tree,* of course, in itself is only a map, *not a consciousness or object of worship.* This belongs only to God, not the angels, archangels or any other beings or things. The *Tree* is a tool, a tried and true means to attain the goal of *At-One-Ment.** It is a process of experiential education under the guidance of your personal hierarchy, from the *Logos* through your soul and layers of mind. To receive it, however, *you* must, through your directed will and thoughts, reach out for it.

---

* Recommended for study: *The Ladder of Lights,* William G. Gray, 1968, Helios Book Service, 8 The Square, Toddington, Nr. Cheltenham, Glos., England and *The Mystical Qabalah,* Dion Fortune, 1957, Ernest Benn Ltd., 25 New Street Square, Fleet St., London EC4A3JA, England (orig. 1935). *Twelve Steps to Spiritual Enlightenment,* Israel Regardie, 1969, Sangreal Foundation, P.O. Box 2580, Dallas, TX 75221.
The Rainbow Bridge, Two Disciples, 1975, New Age Press, P.O. Box 1216, Black Mountain, NC 28711.

The ten Sephiroth, or *Lights* of the *Tree of Knowledge*, are considered to represent the prototypal body of Adam Kadmon, or the Celestial Adam, corresponding to aspects of human development and parts of the universe. Numbered from one to ten, they are as follows with some of their archetypal and Kabbalistic correspondences:

Sephiroth	*Correspondences*
1. Kether - the Crown	The Ancient One/the Monad/the Star/Atman/I am
2. Chokmah - Wisdom	Buddhi/Inner Intellect/Jehovah/Father/Adam/Uranus
3. Binah - Understanding	Outer Intellect/Mother/Eve/Jehovah Elohim/Saturn
4. Chesed - Mercy	Inner Emotion/King/El/Jupiter
5. Geburah - Judgment	Outer Emotion/Warrior/Hero/Mars
6. Tiphereth - Beauty	Self/HolyGuardian Angel/Son/Groom/Sun
7. Netsach - Endurance	Woman/Victory Venus
8. Hod- Glory	Hermaphrodite/Mercury
9. Yesod - Foundation	Ego/Unconscious/Moon
10. Malkuth - the Kingdom	Body/Bride/Virgin/Earth

THE CORPS DE BALLET

5

The Corps de Ballet

I'm getting the feel of this now.
Who do I play this time?

I've got just the part for you!
You play a Catholic Puerto Rican raised
in Ireland by Jewish parents,
who immigrate to Japan
to open an Italian pizza and
eggroll shop!

Ahhh, come on . . . . . .

It gets better!

I sure hope so.

Since you can't speak Japanese,
you go to night school and meet
this German . . .

you gotta be kidding . . . !

Nope. It's your chance to
see the world.

A pizza and eggroll shop.
(How did I get into this?)

133

MOTHER EARTH'S SECRETS

We have seen how the angels built natural laws into the planet and how important collective bodies of thought are. These have influenced the development of races, distinctive nationalities and communities, but this is not the whole story. Even considering collective bodies of thought, there seems no logical reason why they should vary so widely across arbitrary boundary lines, making radical differences in language, temperament, culture and politics.

The answer is in the energy patterns of Earth and her interactions with the sun and planets. The knowledge of how the electrical and magnetic flows of energy circulate around and through the earth, affecting all life upon the planet, is a lost science. In ancient times specialists were trained and these flows were understood. They were channeled and utilized to influence life on Earth. You might say these specialists were like "planetary physicians," who kept the planet healthy by keeping its circulation stimulated and directed. This kept Mother Earth calm and channeled distinctive influences to various areas.

The early study of the earth flows has been called "geomancy," and was related to geometry (form, measuring land and computing ratios and proportions). The early geomancer, aware of the various incoming cosmic energies and types of flows, then *channeled* them proportionately around the earth by constructing physical conduits, lines and relay stations. Where possible, natural earth constructs were used, but when necessary they were created.

Like so many of the ancient sciences, geomancy is now thought of only as fortunetelling (*geo-*, earth and *-mancy*, divination). This study relates to reading dots and lines drawn in the earth and has its place, but is only a remnant of the ancient reading of the lines of the entire planet. Agrippa's De Artium, 1569, said, "There is also another kind of Geomancie, that which doth diuine [divine] by certaine conjecture taken by the similitudes of the crakings of the Earthe." This appears to be more closely related to the original science, though still evidently used for "event divination." We should not confuse this with the art and science of the old *geomants*.

"A great scientific instrument lies sprawled over the entire surface of the globe . . . almost every corner of the world was visited by a group . . . who came with a particular task to accomplish. With the help of some remarkable power . . . they could cut and raise enormous blocks of stone . . . pillars . . . pyramids . . . underground tunnels, cyclopean stone platforms, all linked together by a network of tracks and alignments, whose course . . . was marked by stones, mounds and earthworks." (*View Over Atlantis,* John Michell). We are affected by this ancient work today far more than we realize. Much of it may be buried and forgotten, but it is still alive, as we shall see.

Bud and I did a *reading* for a modern day aspiring geomant. She was seeking information about this little known knowledge:

Bud: We wish to make contact with the entity _____ .

LaVedi: The entity was among those ancient ones, mound

builders, on the North American continent, and at that time had the knowledge of the earth flows that has long been lost . . . .

The mounds were created in animal forms, reptile forms, [she was] particularly connected with one shaped like an alligator. Some investigation into the works of the mound builders will supply this old information, there are mounds in the midwest, and in the west-northwestern states.

Investigate that which is known about them and visit them for that which you will learn when you are upon the site, for then you will both remember and be taught. Investigate the energies related to orgonomy and visit those who know about it, who are seriously working with it, for the principles similar to those used in the construction of the mounds to relay and direct earth energy . . . .

Appear to have been Indian origin, the red-skinned people.

Bud: Is this after Atlantis?

LaVedi: Seems to be Atlantean . . . .*

Bud: These were the mound builders?

LaVedi: Yes. And their groups reached across the Atlantic and to some degree around the world, and the energies are still felt . . . they had legends then, even as now we have legends of those who had the knowledge of the planet. . . . They established their earth works to communicate.

---

* This refers to an Atlantean period considerably later than the time of the Titans and their mammoth works. The mound-builders were of a different stage of human evolution.

Bud: To communicate with whom?

LaVedi: It was not fully understood who they were communicating with, they thought they were communicating with the planet, and in a sense this was correct, indirectly. In a sense they used a reflection system, like a mirror system, you might say. They were receiving through the earth reception center the influences of the overlord of the planet, directing its development and growth, and in receiving the energies. They [the energies] were distributed around the globe much like a grid network, north and south, east and west, and feeding the planet.

Bud: So the mound builders had a definite working knowledge of geodesic?

LaVedi: Yes. This was done purposely in connection with directions, and mineral deposits, and knowledge of water, and the ability to read the land, mountains, rock strata. It was a complex knowledge, a considerable amount of geological knowledge, as well as psychic . . . there were those who were considerably groomed . . . to act as receptors or readers . . .

Bud: Was the construction of the mounds specifically related to geomancy?

LaVedi: Yes.

Bud: Were they in location of absorption points—the function of the mounds themselves?

LaVedi: Reception centers.

Bud: Were they built of any special material?

LaVedi: Yes, stone and earth, constructed in layers.

Bud: What type of energy may be said to have been transferred?

LaVedi: Magnetic and electrical.

Bud: Is this referred to as "power points" today? The locations?

LaVedi: They were in a sense power points, you might say magnified the natural earth energies, key points chosen. Sometimes it was necessary to pick places like relay points, but it was not a natural power point, just a chain, a feed around the earth directly. They were very sensitive. The well-being of the planet depends on balance, and today we still need the balance.

Bud's next question was an important one, "Did this determine the creation of certain villages or cities?" I confirmed that energy points could, indeed, stimulate population centers around them. Most large cities of the world are located around major *power points*, with each one having its own special combination of energies. For example, the focus of energy in London is St. Paul's Cathedral; during World War II bombs fell all around it, demolishing the area, but the cathedral remained "miraculously" untouched. If you visit St. Paul's, stand in the center of the nave, where the structure forms an architectural cross. If you are at all sensitive, you will probably feel a physical reaction from the powerful energies focused there, then, possibly feeling a little "strange," you may need to move out of the flow. Direct contact with strong power points can have a transforming effect upon a person physically, emotionally, mentally and spiritually.

In another major city in Great Britain, Edinburgh, Scotland, energies are focused through a tiny chapel known as St. Margaret's. This lovely little chapel overlooks the city and is appropriately reached by a wide, spiraling cobblestone approach through the royal castle on the top of The Mount. One of my favorite hobbies is to seek out *power points*; I do this by "picking up the thread" and following it. This may involve great or short distances. In the case of St. Margaret's we were following the energy from Glastonbury and London. When we got off the train in Edinburgh, I was immediately drawn up the hill to the chapel. This particular pilgrimage led next to the Isle of Iona, a very special *point*, and then on to Findhorn. In the Findhorn library, I discovered confirmation of my finds in unpublished special studies, entitled, "The Plan of Light," "The Iona Report" and "A Lecture on Power Points by Roc [Robert Ogilvie Crombie]."*

Returning to the geomantic reading, Bud and I next found the entity in China.

Bud: Shall we continue?

LaVedi: Yes. I find her in the mountains, connected with a group of people. This is apparently in northern China, quite a mountainous area .... They are doing stone work again. They seem to go down into the ground, and also above ground, like towers. I think it is functioning on the principle of the pyra-

---

* Also reference: *The Magic of Findhorn*, Paul Hawken, Harper & Row, 1975.

mid, but a different shape, and they seem to [have] . . . tunnels
or roots reaching down, the tower open . . . .

Bud: Like an hourglass, perhaps?

LaVedi: More straight . . . , if they still exist they must be
hidden or are not recognized for what they are.

Bud: Was the entity involved in building these?

LaVedi: Yes, it was almost like expeditions into mountainous
regions to build these. They are not known simply because
they are in the mountains of Asia . . . , the Chinese were very
aware of the ancient laws, the contoured landscape, the whole
country to direct these flows. These towers, these root towers,
were like wells. Again, reception points . . . surplus energy
would be held in a reservoir and then mentally directed, as
well as magnetically attracted to other mounds, mound type
structures or forms.

Bud: Does this connect in any way to the tower in the Himalayas?

LaVedi: Yes . . . investigate archeological finds to locate one
of these towers . . . probably inaccessible now. There was one
that would have remained—a monastery in Tibet. There are
others, many of them underground.

The Chinese were highly knowledgeable in geomantic
science. J.H. Gray's *China* notes, "The houses are built
according to the principles of geomancy." And John Michell
in *View Over Atlantis* wrote, "Not only was every sacred
building magically sited, but the Chinese geomantic principles are known, for the practice . . . was carried on well

into this century." It was called the science of *fung-shui*, "wind and water." The magnetic currents were known as the *yin and yang* "dragon currents." The positive *yang* was channeled over the rougher high lands and the negative *yin* over gentle low hills. The ideal proportion was considered to be 3/5 yang and 2/5 yin. The Chinese intent was to landscape the entire country to these specifications, and no construction was allowed, unless it supported geomantic balance.

The grid-work of energy flows follows lines around the planet much like our conception of latitudinal and longitudinal lines. They vary in strength, quality and influence, but occur approximately every twelve feet. The natural flows appear as wavy lines of glowing energy, whereas those influenced by man appear straight. These latter especially have come to be known as *ley lines,* or *straight-tracks.* They appear over the whole of Great Britain, stretching between the old villages, churches, along roads and hedgerows. The names of many towns end with the suffix "-ley" (or a variation), meaning they are on *ley lines.* I took great pleasure in living and studying on one of them in a village near Cambridge. It was a vibrant site, with a feeling of verdant fertility.

Overall we have become completely unaware of these flowing currents and of our response to them, but respond we do. Why shouldn't we? We are just smaller bodies, with energy flows traveling through us, too. We are beginning to realize this now, thanks to Chinese acupuncture. The meridian lines of acupuncture could be equated to the planetary energy flow lines, while the acupuncture points might be equated with the *power points*. Just as man can block up and disrupt his own energy flows and cause illness, he can also disturb the planetary flows, causing planetary upheaval.

ELEMENTAL HUMANITY

While the races are understood to have appeared simultaneously worldwide, there is much more to this than simple manifestation. The races evolved on their various sites in response to their local environmental conditions, including earth flows, and cosmic and planetary (astrological) influences that vary from place to place.

We are continually affected by energies exchanged between Earth, the other planets and the sun. As an example, illustrating the close connection between human reaction and the sun, the following excerpt appeared in the April 25, 1968, *New Scientist:*

> At a recent session of the Popov Radio Engineering and Electrical Communication Society, Dr. A.K. Podshibyakin reported that research carried out over a number of years at the Tomsk Medical College had found a relation between road accidents and solar activity . . . the day after the eruption of a solar flare, road accidents increased, sometimes by as much as four times above the average . . . similar findings had also been obtained by workers in Hamburg and Munich. He also claimed that human response is generally slower during a solar flare than at other times.

The article goes on to mention that solar flares produce large amounts of ultraviolet radiation, this then increases the ionization in Earth's atmosphere, and short-wave communication is often disrupted. Solar flares have been just one of the obvious influences upon us. Now consider the nearby moon, traditionally the opposite polarity of the sun:

> In the last few years some strange and inexplicable links appear to be emerging between lunar phase, rainfall, meteoric impact, magnetic storms and mental disturbances. It seems as though we are moving through a series of scientific fantasies to a proof of the ancient belief in the connection between the moon and lunacy.
> (London *Sunday Times,* Sir Bernard Lovell, March 15, 1963).

Not unlike geomancy, astrology is a science and an art that has been little understood in modern times. Originally it was the study of major cycles and effects as these related to the planet as a whole and nations in particular. It was not a primitive study, but one of the schools of knowledge taught by the Sons of Wisdom and the "star people." It is primitive now by comparison, but fortunately computers may soon change this.

The races are divided by the five elements, but are, for our purposes under the four fundamental elements: Water, Fire, Air and Earth. The fifth relates to evolved humanity. These correspond to the major spectrum of the races: black, red-brown, yellow and white, and also reflect the four primary divisions of our interpenetrating bodies.

Similar to the division of bodies to accelerate physical evolution, the entire human race seems to have divided into sub-races to emphasize the development and expression of necessary qualities. Most of us have incarnated many times in all of the races to assimilate the predominant characteristics and overcome "weaknesses" peculiar to each race. Eventually we must merge them all into the One again, or the fifth element.

When humanity settled around the globe, it became subjected to planetary energies that varied by location, due to geological factors. These were compounded by Earth's interaction with the sun and planets. For example, a place with heavy gold deposits would attract concentrations of energy from the sun, while heavy tin deposits would attract energy from Jupiter. It is much more complex than this, but this is the general idea. Combined local conditions concentrate and result in energies that affect all who live there. Over time obvious features, qualities and characteristics develop and become national or racial traits.

Wide-spread, deep-rooted concepts exist about the qualities of the races. At one time these related to collective characteristics; now they have much less meaning due to much mixing and individualization. As a group, the black races have represented *Water,* the emotional aspects of man, and have been known for outer passivity, passions and strong self-expression through vibrant colors, music and rhythm. They frequently have hidden inner power (including magic), all *Water* characteristics.

The red-brown races, including Atlanteans, Egyptians, North American and East Indians have represented *Fire,* the spiritual aspect of man. These races have held the ancient knowledge and developed the spiritual faculties of man. They have frequently been nomadic travelers, "preserving the sacred."

The yellow Oriental races have been most noted for their philosophical approach to life, their abstract thought typifying the element of *Air*. They developed the art of mind over matter, reaching a peak for the individual in the martial arts. Lastly we have the white races, most strongly recognized for their development of materialism, personal property accumulation and individualism. They signify the element of *Earth*, and have a regard for concrete consciousness that approaches worship, with a tendency to disregard the spiritual, emotional and intuitive. Obviously these are broad generalizations, but they have basis in the quality of vibrations found in the physical composition of racial bodies. The hardest to master is the Caucasian body, being the densest and most material, but each race provides essential qualities and lessons.

The energy flows of the earth contribute to the force field of the planet, forming an *aura* containing the cosmic pattern of the archetypal rays. This *planetary aura* is stimulated by its relationship and energy exchange with the other planets. Before planetary energies affect us individually, they affect the earth's energy field. We are then influenced in turn through our smaller energy fields, including our personal ones. The planetary field is affected by numerous planetary and stellar cycles. The largest is the *Precession of the Equinoxes*, which determines the *Age* we are in by the direction the North Pole is pointing. Since an entire cycle takes nearly 26,000 years, each *Age* is approximately 2,000 years long. The smallest cycles used are called "planetary hours," relating to cyclical planetary influences throughout each day. There are other cycles we know very little about, such as those connected with comets.

NATIONAL STARS

Nations, similar to the races, respond to the energies peculiar to their region, but there is a difference. A nation is an entity, conceived (as a thought-form) and born at the time of its founding. As with a person, it may be "reborn" at the time of a revolution or other radical changes, but it will always carry forward all that it has ever been in its history, even if unconsciously.

At each birth there will be certain planetary influences that will affect it from that time on. In the past the study of the stars was primarily used to predict the future of kings, nations and the planet. Many wars have been waged under the guidance of astrologers, including World War II. Hitler relied on astrologers, and England counteracted Hitler's moves by employing astrologers to predict what the German astrologers were advising.

A few examples may make the astrological influences on countries more meaningful. The birth of the United States on July 4, 1776, makes us a Cancer nation with the Sun, Jupiter, Venus and Mercury all in this highly home-oriented sign. The combination of these planets is reflected by American pride in family, home ownership and luxury items.

Our ascendant is frequently given as Gemini, however, using the completion time for the signing of the Declaration of Independence, which was shortly after noon, the correct ascending sign is Libra. Considering that we are a nation dedicated to "Liberty and Justice for All," this seems quite appropriate, since Libra rules law and justice. The U.S. Saturn is in Libra, in a difficult square aspect to the Sun, thus we have repeatedly gone to war overseas for causes of justice. The Gemini influence so often noted is more likely a carry-over from Atlantean times and the Age of Gemini. Esoterically we are taught that this ancient influence is important, especially as the New Age dawns and the inhabitants of North America repeat Atlantean karmic patterns.

With Libra ascending, the U.S. has its Moon placed in Aquarius in the fifth house, ruling children and education. This is highly appropriate for a country that has also offered "Education for All" as a right, for the purpose of safeguarding its freedom (very Aquarian). The U.S. does have Mars in Gemini in the ninth house, indicative again of war on distant shores and of corporate industry, especially the manufacture of steel and autos.

Another national example is France, which presents a remarkable sequence of astrological carry-through from government to government (a national equivalent of reincarnation). Beginning with Bastille Day in 1789, we find the karmic North Node position at *25° Scorpio*. Thereafter the Scorpio influence appears dramatically through two empires and five republics. The First Republic (1792) was formed with *Mars* at *25° Scorpio* and *Jupiter* at *2° Scorpio*. This was followed by the First Empire of Napolean the First (1804) with *Neptune* at *25° Scorpio*. At the formation of the Second Republic (1848), *Mars* appears again in *Scorpio*, along with the *Sun*, and *Mercury* is at *23° Scorpio*. It is apparent that the sign of Scorpio and this degree position are highly influential in the history of France.

Continuing with the formation of the Second Empire (1852), we find Venus in Scorpio, with Saturn, Uranus and Pluto in the opposite reciprocal sign of Taurus. The charting date for the Third Republic is cloudy, but it appears Mars may again have been in the latter degrees of Scorpio. The Fourth Republic is definitive, with Jupiter, Mercury and Mars all in Scorpio and the Moon in Taurus. Finally, the Fifth Republic was formed with Jupiter and Neptune in Scorpio.

The history of France has been riddled with revolutions, wars and grandiose attempts to conquer other nations, all typical of a power-seeking Scorpio influence, goaded by the war-like energy of Mars, excessive Jovian expansiveness and spiced with Neptunian illusions. This pattern was strengthened even more by many of the above planets appearing in neighboring Libra or Sagittarius, when they were not in Scorpio for the times in question. The repeated formations of governments by France affords an unusual opportunity to observe this transfer of national energies from period to period.

Any legal transaction that results in forming a structure, ranging from the creation of a nation to the building of a house, produces a signature date from which an astrological chart can be cast. Individually we are attracted to those places which have energies anchored that are harmonious to our own. We will tend to be most successful in such locations, so it *pays* to listen to your intuition.

ATLANTIS REBORN

> Reincarnation being the great law of life and progress . . . .
> Individuals and nations in definite streams return in regu-
> larly recurring periods . . . . And as the units in nation and race
> are connected together . . . large bodies of such units . . .
> reunite at different times and emerge again and again . . . as the
> cycles roll their appointed rounds.
> (*The Ocean of Theosophy,* William Q. Judge, 1851-1896).

People not only tend to reincarnate in family groups,
they may also come en masse into communities or nations.
For all practical purposes, America is Atlantis reborn. Our
civilization is built over that of Atlantis, so we are not only
American, but Atlantean. It is unavoidable. With the rise
of affluence, technology, educational rights and religious
freedom it is extremely reminiscent of old Atlantis and the
quest for the Atlanteans. And, to ice the cake, America
is facing similar dilemmas related to technology and energy abuse. We are told the astrological aspects approaching are very similar to those that brought the final destruction some 10,000 years ago and relate to the sign of
Gemini.

Edgar Cayce made a number of predictions about the
United States, and its present and impending crises, that
included massive continental earth changes within this
century. In 1934 he said the western part of America
would be broken up, Japan lost to the sea, Europe suddenly
changed and that land would rise off the eastern coast
of the United States.

He said, "There will be upheavals in the Arctic and in the Antarctic "resulting in the eruption of volcanoes in the Torrid areas." He went on to predict that the poles would shift again, making the arctic areas (including, therefore, the Land of Meru) tropical. " . . . these will *begin* in the periods '58 to '98" and were predicted to be "periods when His Light will be seen again in the clouds" (reading 3976-15).*

Edgar Cayce is only one among many through the centuries who have made predictions about the time we are living in. The famous and incredibly accurate prophet Nostradamus, wrote his first book of predictions in France in 1555. As translated by Steward Robb, Nostradamus predicted our time period would see a "great human exhaustion" with "Plague blood," famine, pestilence and problems involving milk and iron. He wrote fire would be seen in the sky, with a "long running spark."

We are probably in this period, where human exhaustion is growing great. Plague blood may well be the military usage of serum to create deadly diseases. Milk could refer to the "infant formula" scandal, as well as other problems with milk, such as atomic fallout. Famine is certainly serious, especially in all of the third world countries. Iron could refer to the radical changes occurring in this industry, strongly affecting world economy, while we have plenty of pestilence, such as epidimic levels of pollution and chemically caused cancer. The sky fire may be Halley's Comet of

* *Edgar Cayce on Atlantis.*

1986. Interestingly this comet in ancient times was viewed as the diety of salvation.

In another remarkable quatrain, he wrote that from where famine was expected supplies would come, and from the sea an "eye" would watch like a "greedy dog," while one would give "the other oil, wheat." This certainly applies to the present, with the controversy worldwide over oil and wheat supplies and the watching radar and nuclear ships.

Then a quatrain appears that is often contemplated about the end of this century. This one states that a "great king of terror" will come "from the skies." The date Nostradamus gives for this is "1999, seventh month." It seems to indicate that England will be struck and states that "Mars will reign for the good cause." I suspect the king of terror may be another comet or heavenly body hitting the earth. After all of our fears, our anticipated "disaster" may be a natural one.

Esoterically we are taught that we are approaching transit with another universal body that is not visible to us. Such transits are accompanied by comets (the origin of comets). This great periodic passage is the cause of cyclical cataclysmic earth changes and the impetus of human evolutionary change. At this time it is greatly increasing our vibrational rate, raising awareness and placing additional stress on the planet.

There is nothing to protect us from collision with heavenly bodies, except statistical odds, and these have run out. We may be in a race now between blowing ourselves up, or having nature do it. Nostradamus, however, says, "Mars will reign for the good cause," ruling out war, signified by Mars. Mars does rule the military though, and anyone who has ever been in a natural disaster, knows the immense rescue efforts exerted by military personnel and equipment. The prophecy sounds like a natural disaster and ensuing military rescue operations.

As to the effect of this on Great Britain, Nostradamas predicted a government head would come from America, even though "America" did not exist at the time of his prophecy. He also refers to the "Island of Scotland," and said it would be paved with ice. This concurs with Cayce's prediction of change in Great Britain, and it sounds as though America steps in to salvage the remains. Nostradamas went on to say Great Britain would have a "Reb for King," and that this would be a "false Antichrist." He called him the "third Antichrist." and refers to a "bloody war" that lasts 27 years.*

The *Bible* speaks of the "Battle of the Great Day of God Almighty," when the "Kingdom" shall be established. And it tells us of the various plagues we have continued to adjust to for the sake of wealth and industry at the cost of countless lives: diseases, poisoned waters and droughts. Then "the sixth angel poured his bowl on the great river Euphrates . . . to prepare the way for the kings from the east . . . to assemble them for battle. . . . "

---

* *Prophecies on World Events by Nostradamus,* Stewart Robb, Liveright Publishing Corp., 1961.
Recommended Reading: *The Great Pyramid Decoded,* E. Raymond Capt, (Archaeological Institute of America), Artisan Sales, P.O. Box 1497, Thousand Oaks, CA 91360.

We have chosen to miss the point that the Antichrist represents our intense and deadly materialism, throwing the world into economic chaos and growing steadily more fatal. The Battle of Armageddon is not a war fought with weapons, it is a battle of consciousness—Christ (Cosmic) Consciousness against the Antichrist (Earth/material) illusions. These two polarities will produce the third, the "Kingdom."

The finale, according to Revelation 16:17, is " . . . a great earthquake such as had never been since men were on the earth, so great was that earthquake. The great city was split into three parts, and the cities of the nations fell. . . . And every island fled away . . . and great hailstones, heavy as a hundredweight, dropped. . . . "

A comet or other heavenly body striking the earth could cause a sizable planetary "convulsion," earthquakes, tidal waves and "hailstones." The face of the globe may be changed again, to prepare for a "new world." So we are warned to prepare for judgment day. However, we should change our thinking on this. Fear has been used to attempt to "convert" men and has unfortunate consequences. This is a time of opportunity for those who will take it. For others, if Earth is unsuitable for them, they will go on to other worlds. The *yogic Kingdom* will be coming to pass for this planet.

THE BERMUDA TRIANGLE
One of Cayce's predictions that has generally been believed to be unfulfilled was that portions of Atlantis would "rise" again, "—expect it in '68 and '69—not so far

away." This was given in 1941. As is so often the case with prophecy, people put their expectations upon the meaning, when in reality there are usually multiple levels of fulfillment. There has been a measured rise in land in this area, but this is of less import than the find of a group of treasure hunters in 1968, working in the Bermuda Triangle.

They were searching near the great tongue of the Bering Islands off of Ambrose. They thought that excessive magnetic influences in the area might be accounted for by old sunken ships. Using an aerial magnetometer, they mapped the section (fifteen by five miles) of the ocean into a grid and then began systematically sinking test holes up to 20 feet deep over the entire area. Failing to find any treasure ships, and running out of funds, they had to stop their investigation temporarily.

Two years later, one of the original treasure hunters, Dr. Ray Brown, Ph.D. (a doctor of homeopathic medicine), returned with a new crew to try again. At the site they were caught overnight in a powerful storm. The next morning they only had enough compressed air left for an hour's diving, so they went down to have a quick look at the area in question. They were amazed to find that the storm had done their excavating work for them. It had uncovered an entire submerged city, extending over the whole fifteen by five mile rectangle.

Since Dr. Brown's find, some twelve other groups are said to have come in contact with parts of this ancient city, including Peter Tompkins, who is said to have discovered pillars in this area. Robert Ferro and Michael Grumley also found portions of what were believed to be pillars and a possible rock roadbed in 1968 near Bimini.

Dr. Brown, a very unpresuming man and a quiet speaker, tells how, when he began exploring the city, he discovered a large pyramid. He estimated it to be about 400 feet tall, with only about eighty feet exposed above the sandy ocean bottom. The exterior had a highly polished white surface, with a capstone that appeared to be blue and gold lapis lazuli. As he swam around the pyramid he found an entrance; and, though it was risky, he swam in. Inside he saw a table surrounded by seven chairs, and upon the table rested a round crystal held by a pair of metallic hands. Above the crystal, suspended from the peak of the pyramid by an extremely hard golden metal rod, was a cut-garnet or ruby. The only thing Dr. Brown was able to remove was the crystal, which he is the custodian of today.

The energy field of the crystal is very strong, being readily perceptible some twenty to thirty feet away. Inside of the crystal three grayish pyramids are visible, and, if you switch up to an alpha state, a fourth one emerges. When photographed, winged balls may appear in the pictures, reminiscent of Egyptian symbology.

To my knowledge there is nothing written about the use of the crystal and ruby in the manner described by Dr. Brown. However, several years earlier I had clairvoyantly seen the combination used together in the manner he spoke of. This crystal was used primarily to magnify thought and disperse it over the land, a use confirmed by numerous clairvoyants, and related to the attempt to maintain unification. In variation, crystals were also related to

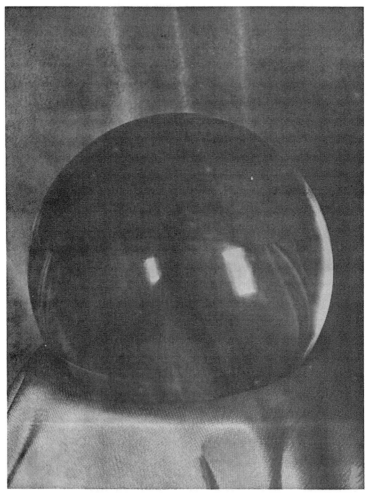

"The Bermuda Triangle"
The interpenetrating pyramids are sometimes clearly visible inside this crystal recovered from an underwater city in the Bermuda Triangle.

energy supplies and interdimensional travel.

The use of pyramids is based upon the four elements and mathematical principles in relation to the flow of the earth's energies. They act as collectors, with energy emerging from their peaks. You can test this yourself in a simple experiment. Place your open palm a few inches above a small pyramid that has been correctly oriented with one side to magnetic north. Within a few minutes or less, you should begin to feel a slight pressure, tingling or flow against your hand.

During World War II, planes were ordered not to fly over the Great Pyramid of Giza, because it would disrupt their navigational instruments. *Why* then, should a similar result over at least one other pyramid in the Bermuda Triangle be a surprise? Considering that the carefully designed pyramids, with their powerful energies, were sometimes used for interdimensional travel, the numerous disappearances in the Bermuda Triangle may be logically explainable.

THE ETERNAL SPHINX

A number of years ago I was clairvoyantly shown a great crystal or flame "burning" in the head of the Sphinx. Now, I would like to share a *reading* with you that Bud and I did in relation to the Sphinx and the Great Pyramid:

Bud: Moving back now, to the conception of the Sphinx in Egypt, moving back, over the oceans of time, to the land of Egypt, just before the construction of the Sphinx, on the count of ten down to one . . . What do you see or feel?

LaVedi: First there are large crowds of people cheering, yes, they are cheering the reception of someone . . . .

Bud: Are they in the desert? Is the Sphinx under construction at this time?

LaVedi: No. This is related to its completion. Seems . . . , I am not sure of the words to exactly describe . . . , apparently they have used it as a doorway . . . to bring entities through from another level, to a physical form . . . there was a specific source and channel of energy, and it still is, but it was built for this purpose, and that they would remember the possibility. There is a key to what they knew and were capable of doing between the planes, origins . . . .

The cheering was the revel of an entity anticipated, expected, which was their purpose in building the Sphinx, at least an understood purpose by those who labored in construction.

Bud: Could this person have taken earthly form? Did he take over a body that was presently on the earth plane?

LaVedi: No.

Bud: He created one himself?

LaVedi: The energies that were created in the Sphinx enabled this or made it much easier to do so, than it would have been otherwise. There is more between the symbolism: the lion, (the sun), the woman, (the moon) the sun and moon, positive and negative, and the balance between these two that allows communications and movement.

Bud: Is it still possible to use the Sphinx?

LaVedi: Yes.

Bud: Is this dependent upon groups of people performing proper mental attunement?

LaVedi: There is more and it is connected with the *Guardians of the Light.*

Bud: Is this *Light* for the benefit of mankind on the earth plane?

LaVedi: Yes. There is more to the "flame" than previously understood; it relates atomically to matter, healing, beyond physical, beyond that known physically . . . .

Bud: Is the Sphinx to be used as a rallying point or as a tool?

LaVedi: It is a channel to guide, like a radio, (one with tubes in it), by directly attuning perception is greatly increased. And therefore all work is made easier. The contact here, with those not on the physical level, is very helpful consciously. There is a chain, a reception on earth. This is a major receiver, receiving and sending point. Receiving not of the earth, but sending over the earth. This is not necessarily done through entities, but through the aura that has been built for this purpose.

Bud: The aura around the Sphinx?

LaVedi: Yes, this is a special energy field for this purpose.

The Sphinx acts as a major *power point* on Earth in combination with the Great Pyramid. They still function today. My ex-husband, Lawrence (Steven) Pipella, was especially interested in Egyptology and the secrets of the pyramid. He spent a night locked in the Great Pyramid and said it was a turning point in his life, for the old initiations still go on as they always have. As he said, "Everything Paul Brunton wrote in *Search in Secret Egypt* is true," only Lawrence didn't turn back, as Brunton did part way through the process. As Lawrence told the story:

> I arrived in Egypt with the purpose of doing what I had contemplated for many years. My objective lay in Giza, one of the oldest parts of Cairo. It was good to be back in Cairo, as my first visit had proven fruitless. Unlike Paul Brunton, the times had changed, and I was unable to make headway in acquiring the necessary permit to spend a night in the Great Pyramid.
>
> After a week in Cairo and frequent visits to Memphis, one afternoon I found myself wandering around the Great Pyramid and met a rather curious fellow, part Bedouin, I think. He inquired if I desired to enter the Pyramid, but having done this already I declined. He was insistent, though, so I went again into the Pyramid. While we were going through the chambers, I fell into conversation with him about his work. To my surprise, he informed me that he was the head man in charge of all the Pyramids in Giza.
>
> After finishing the tour of the regular chambers, I inquired if it would be possible to go into the well. He agreed, and after the Great Pyramid was closed to tourists, we proceeded to descend into the shaft, which is cut through 230 meters of rock. After going through the level part of the shaft, we finally ended up in the well room. Along the shaft, the guide showed me a vertical shaft that came down from the gallery. It was supposedly used by the workmen to escape from the Pyramid, but how they got out still remains a mystery.
>
> When we reached the top of the shaft again, I asked my

guide if it would be possible to spend a night in the Pyramid. At first he was surprised, but he saw that I was sincere. The arrangements were made for me to enter the Great Pyramid to spend a night alone!

It was chilly that night as I stood before the Great Pyramid, remembering that it was constructed of three million blocks of stone, each weighing an average of 2½ tons, with the largest weighing 54 tons.

Out of the corner of my eye, I saw my guide arriving; we then proceeded to the lower entrance. At this time, a thousand questions entered my mind, each challenging my sanity.

We arrived at the gate and the guide unlocked it, as the Pyramid is locked at night. I entered and advanced to the stairs. At that time I heard the gate close—it was too late to turn back; I was committed to spend a night in the King's Chamber!

I began to ascend the shaft to the lower part of the gallery. It took a few minutes, for the shaft is difficult to move through. As I moved, I thought about what awaited me in the King's Chamber. I arrived at the lower gallery, pausing to catch my breath, noting that the Queen's Chamber lay straight ahead. My appointment with fate, however, lay in the Chamber above. As I continued to climb, I couldn't help but notice that sweat was running down my spine. As the sounds resounded throughout the gallery, each step was amplified to instill additional terror. When I reached the top of the gallery, I turned around and the light from my flashlight was lost in the darkness. As I turned again, the King's Chamber lay before me. I was moments from my goal; it had taken 26 years of this life to return here. I couldn't help but recall Victor Hugo's words that one could not return to the ordinary path after beginning to tread "the path."

I bent over and started moving through the last aperture. Finally here I was—in the King's Chamber, on my right the great sarcophagus, the same that the Great Ones had been initiated in—leaders, great philosophers, and many others. I placed my light so it fell on the sarcophagus, and prepared my blanket on the stone bed. While getting ready, I could not help but notice that the air was very dry; it was filled with a strange polarity, with spirits and other unexplainable vibrations. I went to my light and turned it off. I immediately started praying, first out of fear, at the same time explaining my reason for coming there and intruding upon their domain. Out came all my hopes, desires, reasons for being, and upmost the desire to be of service to mankind. Finishing this, the pervading silence returned, all that I could hear was the beating of my heart.

As if guided, I entered the sarcophagus and lay down, awaiting what might come . . . .

At first my breathing and heartbeat increased, and it echoed down the chambers, but then calm overcame my mind. Many hideous forms and things came to challenge my faith, but I knew these to be hollow and of no consequence, so I banished them from my mind as illusions, and they were gone. Another form approached me, but this form I knew to be aware of my purpose and yet inquiring of my being there. It seemed to grasp more than this life, and began to materialize. The form was at first vaporous; then I noticed the eyes. They were like fire—I recognized who it was—the Guide of the Underworld, the Anubis. Along with the Anubis came priests, but at the same time I saw thousands of forms—Kings, Queens, priests, priestesses and many others. Then I left my body . . . .

But I cannot tell the rest, for each of you must seek the answer for yourself—it awaits you in the Great Pyramid!*

---

* "The Vortex Voice," P.O. Box 929, Fairbanks, AK 99707, Spring 1973.

Lawrence was sworn not to reveal what happened next, but he did say he was challenged many times, each time being led deeper into the ancient teachings of the Egyptian priesthood. When morning came he reluctantly returned to his body. In his words, "If they had found me dead in the morning, it wouldn't have mattered to me at all."*

The Great Pyramid is not alone; there have been many lesser pyramids, some known and others buried under jungle growth or the oceans. Other *transmitters* include great mountains, such as Mt. McKinley (Denali, meaning the "Great One") in Alaska, the highest mountain in North America; Mt. Shasta is another, shrouded by mysterious stories; the Himalayas, stronghold of monasteries and ancient repository of wisdom teachings; and the Andes, lost land of the "People of the Sun."

Then there is the incredible "Isle of Avalon" (Glastonbury) in Somerset, England, Home of the Holy Grail legend and King Arthur and apparently one of the Edens dating back to Meru. The energy field of Glastonbury is so powerful it "hit" me ten miles away. The origin of its name is lost in time, but the ancient Celts called it the "Crystal Island," while Glastonbury refers to a "fortress of Glass." Avalon is believed to be indicative of an "orchard island."†
In times past the area was surrounded by water.

An ancient civilization left its ruins in Britain to be found by the Romans, much as we now view the Roman remains. Traditions tell of a "Golden Age" when gods

---

* Suggested reading on the Egyptian priesthood and initiations: *Winged Pharaoh*, Joan Grant, Berkley Medallion Book, 1977. A "novel" of far memory written in the 1930's.
† *This Holyest Erthe,* Oliver L. Reiser, Perennial Books, London, 1974.

walked with men, " . . . but even these gods . . . had prede-
cessors—giants whom they overcame and whose kingdom
they took by storm."* Surrounding Glastonbury, the
ancients built the Somerset Zodiac, where the symbols of the
zodiac appear as man-made earthen hills. Some are as
much as two miles across, while the entire zodiac is some
ten miles in diameter. The symbolic astrological shapes are
visible from the air. A visit to this very old pilgrimage site
is an inspiring experience. The old geomants left us much
to marvel at and puzzle over.

Through the ages, between man's abuse and planetary
upheavals, the knowledge of Earth's many energy flows
has been forgotten or withdrawn. Today we have the
scientific, psychic and spiritual potential to regain this information and use it to accelerate our evolutionary progress. The possibilities far exceed present concepts.

Special centers, such as have been mentioned, receive
cosmic energies and transform them to planetary needs.
Multidimensional energies converge at these sites, making
the *veil* thin. This greatly accelerates contact between
dimensional intelligences at such points, and correctly
approached, they can be of enormous benefit to those
seeking service and return. Pilgrimages are of infinite value,
if done with understanding, devotion and respect.

---

* *Avalon of the Heart,* Dion Fortune, Samuel Weiser, NY, 1971, (1934).

STAR ATTRACTIONS

6

Star Attractions

Give me some thunder!

                     rumble-rumble-rumble

    Lightening! Let me have it!

                          FLASH-CRACKLE-FLASH!

       Now, trumpets!

                        RatataTAtaTAAAAAATA . . . .

Cut!   *tataTAA . . . .*

               Cut!   *Taa . . . .* Cut!

Excuse me, *you*, playing the first chair trumpet,

    can I see your union card? Thank you.

            What's your name? Gabriel?

            O.K. Gabe, where'd you learn to play?

    Cloud nine . . . ? Hmmm . . .

      See me after rehearsal!

  Meanwhile, when I cue the trumpets, just

                blend in nice and easy, kid. Right?

    Fine. Let's take it from the top again . . . .

      QUIET IN THE COSMOS!

    Give me some thunder!

                  rumble-rumble-rumble

"TOP BILLING"

Reincarnation . . . is interwoven with the cycles of karma
. . . . And along this road are the points when . . . cycles of
Avatars bring out the great characters who mould the race
from time to time . . . .

(The Ocean of Theosophy).

The cycles have brought, along with the energies of
each period, special teachers to guide evolving mankind.
For the 2,000 year Piscean Age the predominate figure has
been Jesus of Nazareth (known in the East as Lord Maitreya). Unfortunately much of the rich legacy he left us has
been shrouded by attempts to make it fit man-made dogmas and doctrines created by the Christian churches to
solidify an exclusive claim on Jesus as *their* savior. Even
so, his example of love and oneness has shone through,
and his esoteric teachings are available, if one searches for
them.

Jesus set an example that is important to us today,
but to better understand it we need to fill in the *Bible's*
missing years of his life and learn about his instruction and
preparation to become the Messiah. Evidence indicates
this was carefully planned and undertaken.

Today many students and authorities believe Jesus
was raised and educated by the Essenes, being initiated by
them into their *mysteries* both in Syria and in Egypt. They
were a mystery sect of Judaism, said to have had one
school in Egypt and another on the shores of the Dead Sea.
Their origin is not clear; some authorities tracing them to
schools of Samuel the Prophet, and others to the Orient or

Egypt. The term Essene is said to literally mean "possessed by a god," or in Syrian "physician." A highly pious people, they practiced the building trades and were frequently employed as tutors for Roman children in Syria. In their teachings they used so many symbols of builder's tools, that they are considered to be the forerunners of modern Freemasonry.

Meditation, contemplation, prayer and work comprised their lifestyle. "At dawn they communed with the Angels of the Earthly Mother, while at dusk they attuned to the cosmic energies of the Angels of the heavenly Father. At noon they paused in their activities for the contemplation of the Sevenfold Peace. They recognized that the Earth was a living sentient creature and the universe was a vast continuum of Mind. They knew that the oceans of Thought, Life, Love and Will permeated all etherial space and penetrated the world of matter." (*One Earth,* Vol. 2., Issue 3., "The New Essenes," Sir George Trevelyan).*

Josephus, the famous Jewish historian, said of the Essenes, "They teach the immortality of the soul, and esteem that the rewards of righteousness are to be earnestly striven for." Membership into the sect required a year's probation, then three initiation degrees were offered. Few candidates completed all three (the third probably related to the Egyptian initiation process). Both Mary and Joseph

---

* Reference: *The Gospel of the Essenes, The Teachings of the Essenes: From Enoch to the Dead Sea Scrolls* and *The Essene Gospel of Peace* (translated from IIIrd Century Aramaic Manuscript), Edmond Bordeaux Szekely.

are believed to have been members of the Order of the Essenes, and the incarnation of the Messiah was anticipated through their order.

And, quite contrary to common belief, the *Bible* does not indicate that Mary and Joseph were poor. Actually in the Jewish tradition, "Joseph was of noble and wealthy background, for he was a descendant of Nathan, a son of David, who trained his sons to be architects of synagogues, and as such were called the 'Carpenter Tribe'."* The knowledgeable practice of carpentry was more than a trade to the Essenes.

Among little-known early Christian writings are a number known as apocryphal, a term originally meaning "hidden" or "secret," not spurious as is commonly thought today. The apocryphal writings fell into disrepute because many of them belonged to Christian Gnostic sects, (gnostic meaning *to know* by revelation, as opposed to believing by faith alone). These Gnostics were early mystical Christians. They believed in reincarnation and their scriptures contain a wealth of information about the early Christians that has largely been ignored.

According to the apocryphal work, *The Protoevangelium* in the "Gospel of Pseudo-Matthew," Joseph is said to have been an aged widower with grown sons, while Mary was a child younger than his own grandchildren, dedicated in her infancy to the Lord. This writing states that when Mary turned 12, the priests met to determine what to do about

---

* Reference: *Blessed Among Women*, Arnold Michael, D.D., Ph.D, DeVorss & Co., 1973 (an "inspired" work from a remarkable clergyman).

her. The High Priest entered into the Holy of Holies for guidance, where an angel appeared to the priest and said, "Zacharias, go forth and summon the widowers of the people and let them take a rod apiece and she shall be the wife of him to whom the Lord shall show a sign."

Joseph is said to have collected the rods of the other widowers, but left his rod, which was only half as long as the others, behind in the Holy of Holies. The rest of the rods were returned to the widowers from within the Holy of Holies, but no sign was received. Joseph had not requested his back because of his age. An angel, however, is said to have appeared and instructed that the short rod be returned. When it was handed to Joseph a white dove flew from its end, lighting upon Joseph's head.

The symbology of this is important. A rod is the symbol of creative power, of the fire of life or *kundalini* force within the spine of man. Its elaborated symbol is the Caduceus, topped by the winged sphere. Joseph is said to be an old man, the shortness of his rod may have been referring to his shrunked stature and presumed lack of procreative power. The story, as recorded, may be a parable describing a visionary experience, when the "dove descended."

As to the controversial immaculate conception, Jesus and Mary are considered to have been twin souls, or the male and female aspects reunified in Mary. Normally an enlightened entity reunites with the twin aspect, not as two people, but as *one* in one body, which may appear as either sex. When Cayce was asked to explain the birth, he said it was brought about by spiritual self and mental being

"pushing itself into matter." The "immaculate conception" is the result of the physical and mental being "so
attuned to spirit as to be quickened by same."* Perhaps
this can be clarified by remembering that the earlier
androgynous forms did essentially the same thing, separating one body into two. Why should it not follow that a
reunified and enlightened manifestation could separate
again, using the current manner of reproduction?

Following the birth, Joseph and Mary logically fled
to Egypt, considering the Essene relationship and fulfillment of prophecy. After this the gap begins to appear in
the life of Jesus, unless legends and various records are
pieced together. Much of this information was probably
cut from the *Bible* in the 6th Century by the Church,
along with reincarnation, as being an "embarrassment" and
threat to the exclusiveness of the Church doctrines and
their power over the people.

According to Cayce, Jesus was first taught in Egypt
and then was brought back to Carmel through his early
teens to study the law and prophecies. Then he was sent
abroad, first again to Egypt, and from there to India to
receive the teachings of "those cleansings of the body as
related to preparation for strength in the physical as well
as the mental man." From there he traveled to Persia,
learning "the union of forces as related to those teachings
of Zu and Ra." Then he returned again to Egypt to pass
the initiatory tests based upon ways of all the teachers,
"For . . . the unifying of the teachings of many lands

---

* Edgar Cayce on the *Dead Sea Scrolls*, Glenn D. Kitter, Paperback Library,
1970.

was brought together in Egypt," as the center of the world. Cayce spoke of the initiation of Jesus in the Great Pyramid, and supports tradition, saying it was built "to be the Hall of the Initiates of that sometimes referred to as the White Brotherhood." In the initiation process the soul must pass through the same stages of development as have been experienced by the earth itself, or by humanity. The passages of the inside of the Pyramid are representative of this, ending at the empty tomb, signifying the release "of the soul from its bondage to the material world and death." From there he took his baptism in the Jordan and began his ministry as a Rabbi and Master.*

It is believed that Joseph of Arimathea, a trader and merchant, was the uncle of Jesus. He traveled by sea to both the Orient and the British Isles as a tin trader. Jesus is said to have gone with him as ship's carpenter and to have learned the mystical teachings of the Far East during his travels. A coin struck in his honor is supposed to have been found in India and early Christian records are said to exist in Tibet. And a Buddhist monastery in Ceylon is said to have a record indicating that Jesus stayed with them and learned their philosophy. He is also said to have studied in Greece, and in Great Britain visited the ancient monuments of early man (adopted by Druidic descendents). There he learned their tradition that a coming savior named *Yesu* was expected.†

---

* *Edgar Cayce on Jesus and His Church*, Anne Read, Paperback Library, 1970. Recommended: *The Aquarian Gospel of Jesus The Christ*, Levi, as written from the "Akashic Records," DeVorss & Co., 1964 (original 1907).
† *The Secret Teachings of All Ages*, Manley Palmer Hall and *Glastonbury Tales*, John A. Greed, St. Trillo Publications, St. Trillo House, 92 Hillside Road, Portishead, Bristol, BS20 9JL, England, 1975.

BRITISH LEGENDS

Much to my surprise, upon visiting and living in Great Britain, I found that it was rich in little known legends about the time Jesus spent there. They even teach that his grandmother, Anne, may have been born in Cornwall and taken at an early age to the Essenes in Syria. Her lineage was of the House of David through Soloman of the "Shepherd Tribe." The majority of British legends are found around Cornwall, Joseph shipping from the tin mines there, and Somerset (Glastonbury vicinity) where the world's supply of lead was mined. Sayings persist, such as in the small village of Priddy, near the lead mines, "As sure as our Lord was at Priddy." At another site, the location of the ancient sacrificial caves on Brean Down, we found the local people proudly telling us that "Christ walked upon the Down."

Glastonbury Abbey is said to have been first founded in A.D. 37, by Joseph of Arimathea. The *Bible* notes Joseph as the one who was permitted to remove the body of Jesus. The legend of the Holy Grail stemmed from Joseph catching the blood of Jesus in the cup that was used at the Last Supper. Since Pilate was willing to give the body of Christ to Joseph, it supports the claim he was a relative. He would not have given the body of a criminal to just anyone. They were normally disposed of outside the city in a special location.

Another part of the legend says that Jesus actually spent a winter in Glastonbury, marooned by inclement weather and living in a wattle hut. After the death of Jesus, Joseph was "instructed" to return by boat to England and found a church in Glastonbury. The original abbey is described as consisting of wattle huts, surrounding a central wattle chapel.

One of the first past lives that Bud and I discovered together, found us together during the time of the Holy Grail, when I saw it resting in what seemed to be the center of the wattle chapel. It gave off an incredible glow that filled the hut. This crude chapel was the first Christian Church in the British Isles—in fact, the first in the world. Sir Henry Spelman in his *Concilia,* wrote, "We have abundant evidence that this Britain of ours received the Faith, and that from the disciples of Christ Himself, soon after the Crucifixion of Christ."

The legend says that Joseph landed at Glastonbury (then surrounded by water) and drove his staff into the ground, where it became a thorn tree that bloomed at Christmas. To this date, the descendents of that original thorn tree still bloom at Christmas time, but only in Glastonbury. Stories are also found in other parts of Britain, such as in Forres, Scotland, where the transfigured Christ is said to have come and left energies anchored to be released in the latter days. Also tradition holds that Mary and Joseph were both brought to Glastonbury after the crucifixion. Joseph was buried beside what is now St. Mary's Chapel, with Mary later buried inside.

Now, we have to wonder why there appears to be such a strong connection between the Holy Family and Great Britain. The metal trade may have been the basis for it. Joseph of Arimathea was not the only Jew in Britain. Apparently many Jewish immigrants were attracted by the trade and may have been escaping persecution. In the *History of Cornwall,* Polwhele says the oldest smelting places were known as "Jews' houses," with references to "Jews' tin," etc. A most surprising source arises to substantiate the many legends—the English records of heraldry. Several Jews, evidently of Jewish royal birth, settled in Britain and married with British royalty. The records, while not conclusive, due to their age and minor variation, provide a clear trend.

Anne, the mother of Mary, married two or more times. A combination of traditions indicates that Anne was descended from both Cornish royal blood and the House of David, and supports that she came from Cornwall. One record states her first husband was Joachim (or Heli) who was the father of Mary. Jewish tradition also calls him Nakeeb Shab, and he is said to have been of the family that ruled Palestine when the Persians had control, and a hierophant in the school of the Magi. Anne's sister married Zacharias and was the grandmother of St. John the Baptist, agreeing with the *Bible* that John and Jesus were second cousins. Another record shows that Mary remarried after the death of Joseph to one Cleophas (but this is confused by a record that indicates that Anne also married a man named Cleophas).

In the British Museum a record shows the descent of Mary and Joseph from David and indicates that their fathers were brothers, making Mary and Joseph first cousins. This substantiates the view that Joseph of Arimathea was an uncle to both of them. His daughter Anna, would then have been a cousin of Mary. This Anna is recorded as having married King Beli (grandfather of King Lear), linking the

Holy Family with the British Royal Family, while Penardin, daughter of Anna and King Beli Mawr the Great, is said to have married King Lear himself. The line continues through King Arthur and the Knights of the Round Table; all claiming descent from Joseph of Arimathea (through Anna and a grandson, King Avallach).* Cornwall enters the picture again, as the area where Arthur was raised (or instructed) by the Druidic Merlin (Myrrdin).†

Arthur has lived in history and legend as the defending champion of the early Christian Church and civilization, having carried into battle an image of the Virgin Mary as a badge and the symbol of the cross. The legends of Arthur even make sense, when examined. For example, a explanation of the sword drawn from the "stone," may be a simple variation in translation. The words stone and Saxon are very similar, so it is probable he took the crown by winning a battle against the invading Saxons.

Even the mystery of his sword, Excalibur, may reveal itself through linquistics. *Ex* in Latin means "out of" or "from," while *cale* is an old British word for river or stream and *bre* is a variant for hill. There was a tendency to mix words and their meanings, so it is believed Excalibur may have meant the sword came from land surrounded by water, possibly the Isle of Avalon. This would have been looked upon as important, since water was used in temper-

---

* *St. Joseph of Arimathea at Glasonbury,* Lionel Smithett Lewis, James Clark & Co., Ltd., Cambridge, England, 1976 (orig. 1922), containing pedigree data from the English College of Arms, the Herald's Office, Roll 33, Box 26; the British Museum, Harleian MS. 38-59, f. 193b; and Jesus College, MS. 20.
† *Magical and Mystical Sites,* Elizabeth Pepper and John Wilcox, Harper and Row, 1977.

ing the iron and was believed to have an influence on the merit of a weapon.

Arthur was considered a general and also the Duke of Britain, with the Round Table being his grand council, an assembly of his commanders and subordinates. Malory writes that the "Table Round" and 100 knights were sent to Arthur as a wedding gift by King Leodangrance, when Arthur married his daughter, Guener. This was during the period of many battles to defend Britain from the Saxons, and while Rome apparently was still attempting to retain its control. Camelot also exists, thought to have been an ancient hill castle located near Glastonbury. The ruins can be visited and show the defensive structure of the old fortress.

Arthur remained the defender of Christianity until his death, recorded in 542, but he has lived in the hearts of many, symbolizing man's search for *Self*. The date of his death places his command immediately prior to the founding of the Iona Monastery in 563 and that of Lindisfarne (the Holy Island) in 634. These were, along with Glastonbury, among the first centers of Christianity. They are all valuable pilgrimage sites. Lindisfarne is only accessible across the sands at low tide, where majestic ruins and relics are preserved. Iona is more vitally alive and a dedicated spiritual community is fulfilling the prophecy by its founder, St. Columba:

> Iona of my heart,
> Iona of my love,
> Instead of monks' voices
> Shall be the lowing of cattle;
> But ere the world come to an end,
> Iona shall be as it was.

At Glastonbury, the abbey is slowly being rebuilt from the ruins. In 1190, while rebuilding following a fire, the grave of King Arthur and Guinevere was found. The bodies were buried 16 feet deep, placed in the hollowed-out trunk of an oak tree. The man's skeleton was exceptionally large, with 10 wounds in the skull. They were found between two stone pyramids carved with figures and inscriptions nobody could decipher, while nearby was a leaden plate. When translated it read, "Here lies interred, in the Isle of Avalon, the renowned King Arthur." In 1278 the remains were removed and entombed at the abbey in the presence of King Edward I and Queen Eleanor.

Glastonbury is a *jewel* and *repository* that has somehow gone unnoticed by the Christian community in general. Perhaps, this is because it is too revealing of the early Christian history in Great Britain and the common origin that Christianity has with all of the ancient religions, philosophies and wisdom teachings. I cannot emphasize how important I feel attunement to these very ancient sites is to those seeking human "roots."

AFTER THE ORDER OF MELCHIZEDEK

It is worthy of note that, in the New Testament, Jesus is referred to as, "called of God an high priest after the order of Melchizedek." The "Melchizedeks" are considered to have been the divine rulers of our planet before men were placed in dominion over it. Esoterically this reverts back to the original Seven Regents, the Melchizedek lineage being traced to the pre-Atlantean Titans of Meru. In the Kabbalistic writing, *The Source of Measures,* Melchizedek is referred to as the lord of the Ecliptic, or *balance,* or *line of adjustment.* . . . "*

"After the order of Melchizedek," Jesus was restoring balance considering the tradition that Jesus was also "Adam" and Mary his twin aspect, "Eve." This makes him the prototype of heterosexual man, and the member of the Seven Regents responsible for division of the sexes, necessary for man to evolve deeper into matter. As a Regent, there will be those who belong specifically to his ray and school; the rest of humanity is indirectly connected through the act of assuming male and female forms from that evolutionary phase.

Since Jesus had responsibility for guiding mankind into matter through division of the sexes (to complete a cycle that would culminate in each individual becoming *One from two*), he has the responsibility to guide them back. One with the *Logos,* he said, "I am the way. . . . " Then following the example of Melchizedek, at the Last Supper he performed the same sacraments—the drinking of the wine and breaking of the bread. Unfortunately much of the meaning of these acts has been overlooked, the concentration being upon death and resurrection. There is a much deeper meaning when we acknowledge that we received our bodies and life giving blood from the much earlier sacrifices of those who have overseen evolving humanity. Our realization should be that *our bodies are not ours; we are only caretakers* of these earthly temples grant-

---

* *The Secret Doctrine.*

ed to us to experience manifested life.

There is an additional ancient correspondence between the symbology of Noah and the Christian sign of the fish. Jesus, Vishnu and Bacchus (as a sun symbol) have each been called the "fish." The Hindu Vishnu guided an ark as a fish, following the same symbology mentioned earlier of saving a "sacred vessel" (Sons of God) from the waters, "deluges" being analogous to chaos or disorder. The order of Melchizedek represents those overseers who guide mankind through disorder back to balance, and balance brings us back to karma, sacrifice and the doctrine of atonement.

As with others of the Regents, the incarnation of Jesus was not his first. Cayce traces him from first Amelius, through "Adam," to Enoch (the father of Methuselah), Hermes, Melchizedek, Joseph, Joshua, Zen (the father of Zoroaster) and to a scribe named Jeshua, before the incarnation as Jesus. He came to teach, until it was time for the final incarnation. Then he opened a pathway for evolving humanity; those who follow him, his example and teachings come under his protection, atonement and guidance. As a christened "Son of God" (*Christos* in Greek meaning annointed or equivalent to *Messiah* in Hebrew), he was in union with the *Atman* (Logos). Anointing was a part of the mystical rites in the Mediterranean. His example was meant to be a demonstration of each person's potential, thus he said, "these things shall ye do and even greater."

The sacrifice of the Master Jesus was to provide a means of balancing the descent into matter and provided a turning point (connected with the *involutionary nadir*).

The scales were tipped upward by his input into the collective consciousness. It was not an easy process; we tend to forget that Jesus did not die alone. His birth and teachings have brought the deaths of thousands, all contributing to the transition. First the babes were killed by Herod, then the Christian martyrs through the centuries, culminating in the blood-bath of the Inquisition. "Who, for example, is aware that the Inquisition first came into being in the thirteenth century to destroy the Cathari?"* (Christian reincarnationists threatening the existence of the Catholic Church).

SAVIORS, CROSSES AND CRUCIFIXIONS

Through the ages many "saviors" have suffered at the hands of their fellow men either literally or allegorically. Besides Jesus, they include Prometheus, Krishna, Apollonius, Buddha, Chaitanya, Pythagoras, Mithras, Hercules, Osiris and Quetzalcoatal. A consistent theme emerges behind this that needs to be understood for its symbolic meaning.

Mythologically Prometheus was exposed to vultures and crucified on Mt. Caucasus for disobeying Zeus (father of the gods), and giving fire and immortality to mankind. Mithras, of Persia, was also put to death by crucifixion and was supposed to have arisen on March 25th. He was called the "rock born God," flashed from a Persian mountain as a

---

* Reference. *Reincarnation,* Joseph Head and S.L. Cranston, Causeway Books, 1967 and *The Cathars and Reincarnation,* Arthur Cuirham, The Theosophical Publishing House, 1970. Quote from *History of the Inquisition of the Middle Ages,* Henry Lea, 1888, reprint 1955.

radiant ray of light, representing primordial light personified and the male fire principle.

Krishna, the East Indian counterpart of Christ, and one of the major gods of Hinduism, is said to be the eighth incarnation of Vishnu. According to the Bhagavata-Purana, written in the 10th century AD, Vishnu descended to the goddess Earth to free her from her oppressing demons. Krishna was believed to be a divine incarnation because of his many miraculous deeds. Finally, when the time for his death arrived, Louis Jacolliot, in *The Bible in India*, describes how Krishna, was murdered as he prayed by the Ganges and was hung from a tree for vultures to eat. Upon word of his death, Arjuna, accompanied by a crowd, went to retrieve the body, but reminiscent of Christ's ascension, the body was gone and the tree where it had been hung had burst into bloom and diffused a sweet perfume.

Apollonius of Tyana is said to have been hung upon a "cross" until unconscious, as a part of his initiation into the Arcana of Egypt within the Great Pyramid. He was then removed and laid in the Pyramid, as if dead, for three days. The cross, or the arms outstretched, are meant to symbolize the four elements that must be conquered to attain the fifth, thus one had to symbolically die. In Egypt the aspiring Initiate usually left the body for three days, only the connection with the *silver cord* barely maintaining life.

Resurrection is also universal symbology for cyclic renewal, the reappearance by Jesus after three days in the "underworld," (he had not yet "appeared to the Father"), was still another demonstration of such renewal. *Resurrection* typically occurs at the full moon period of the sun in

Aries, or the sidereal new year, and is a ceremonial rite. Along with this rite comes the annual Hierarchal *outpouring* into the global consciousness for the year ahead.*

As to the literal hanging or crucifixion on crosses, however, it is possible, even probable, that the "crosses" were not actual crosses, but plain simple trees. The perfection of the symbology was probably an elaboration by the Church, along with many other dogmas that have clouded the history of Christianity. There is no *Biblical* or other early substantiation of the *cross* of Jesus, only of the death. To follow the consistent threads that weave the fundamental patterns of life, it is necessary to continually cut through the allegories and outright fictions created through the milleniums. The sacrificial tree is symbolic of the *Tree of Knowledge* and the battle of conscience between the pull of matter and the call of spirit.

The cross, like the Kabbalistic *Tree of Life,* is a symbol of ascent and a "map" of the Cosmos. The equal-armed cross specifically represents only the four elements: *Fire, Air, Earth* and *Water.* The unequal-armed cross, or *Cross of Sacrifice,* is a symbol of cosmic return. Properly proportioned it measures five units by eight units, and is also known as the "Golden Mean" or the "whirling square." If you take a rectangle of this measurement and draw a line through it, so the lower portion is a perfect square, you will have a smaller rectangle left. Draw another line through this one to form a second square, and you will have another

---

* To participate: Contact Lucis Trust, 866 United Nations Plaza, Suite 566-7, New York, NY 10017, or Meditation Mount, P.O. Box 566, Ojai, CA 93023.

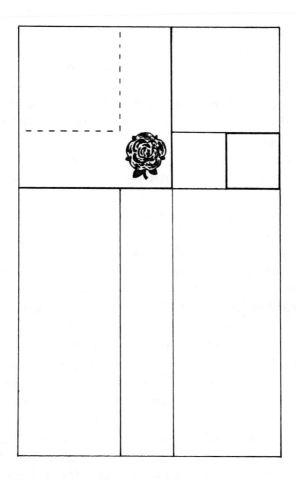

"Saviors, Crosses and Crucifixions"
The *Cross of Sacrifice,* properly proportioned, illustrates the "Golden Mean" or "whirling square," symbolizing world within world and the way of cosmic return.

rectangle. This demonstrates world within world, or the Path of Return to perfect balance.

While the Christian Church tries to behave as if it has some special claim to the cross, it simply is not so. For that matter, an examination of the older crosses will show the early Christians understood very well the elemental aspects of the cross. Many old crosses were constructed with engravings or illustrations of the cherubs representing the elements (man, bull, eagle and lion), each correctly positioned on the arms in accordance with the cardinal directions.

Until recent times all churches and temples were aligned with the cardinal directions, in accord with the elemental flows. The altar was carefully positioned facing East, toward the rising sun, while older churches were shaped like a cross in their inner construction. As I mentioned regarding St. Paul's Cathedral, the middle of the cross is a tremendous vortex of energy, where the four forces meet. In older crosses this mid-point is sometimes shown by a circle. In the true meaning a sacred building was to be a meeting, reception, anchoring and distribution point where man could approach the Holy of Holies and be enabled to commune with God. It was built on cosmic principles not unlike a powerful battery. Small wonder many churches today have a problem reaching their flocks, not unlike trying to start a car with a dead battery. There is no comparison between experiencing God and intellectually listening to someone attempt to tell you about Him, regardless of how sincere the speaker may be.

The use of the symbol of the cross is universal. It appears in Mexico, where Quetzalcoatl is said to have come to the Central American Indians from the "sea," described as wearing garments with clouds and crosses on them and carrying a cross. This pre-dates any Christian influences, the cross being a sacred symbol of the Mayas. When Cortez arrived in Mexico in the 17th Century, the natives thought he was Quetzalcoatl returned because he carried a cross.

Manley Palmer Hall, quoting from Godfrey Higgens (*Anacalypsis,* 1836) tells of Quetzalcoatl being depicted as nailed to a cross in the painting of the Codex Borgianus. Higgens also claimed the Incas possessed a one piece marble or jasper cross "three fingers in width and thickness," that was treated as sacred. And he remarked that Mexican temples were built in the shape of a cross, aligned with the four directions.

This universal symbolism of the cross, as mentioned earlier, appears in the Far East, too. An exceptional Oriental drawing portrays a crucified man (seemingly hanging in mid-air) with nail holes in his hands and feet and wearing a loin cloth. John P. Lundy, writing in 1876, commented on the strong resemblance to a Christian crucifix, with the exceptions that there is a crown on the head, no inscription, no visible cross and there are rays pouring down from overhead. He asks if this might not be the Priest or Victim-Man of Hindu mythology, who sacrificed himself "before the worlds were?"*

This latter speculation reverts back to the concept of the order of Melchizedek and the sacrifice by those intelligences who gave of themselves that humanity could evolve into corporeal form and individual consciousness.

---

* *The Secret Teachings of All Ages,* Manley Palmer Hall, 1962, Los Angeles, Calif.

We are surrounded by the ancient wisdom, if we but scratch the surface of our heritage and look with understanding. The modern veneer is really very thin.

The sacrificial crucifixions are meant to be examples to humanity that death is an illusion, but more, they represent the supreme service atonement to help mankind overcome the collective karma of the various periods of evolution. The same is true of the initiatory process, which is a forced evolution, not the slower and safer paths that the majority follow. During the three day period of "death," all aspects of the unconscious, personal and collective, must be overcome, including fears, phobias, memories, illusions, temptations, desires, errors of judgment, etc. The lower man must die to attain the *Higher Man.* Failure has brought physical death, or occasionally insanity or imbecility. It has never been a process to take lightly, but "once an Initiate, always an Initiate."

Since there is no turning back, the old initiations still go on, but most ceremonies now take place out-of-body in the dream state. The tests are taken in the field of "real life." This does not make them any less difficult, for the "dark night of the soul" must still be passed. This is again symbolic death, a "cutting-off" from all support, while the Initiate must conquer life alone. If inner certainty is not present, the result can be just as serious as in the ancient methods. This comes full circle to understanding and acceptance of all life experience as just and beneficial. The lessons must be seen and learned, without complaint, no matter how difficult or what appearances may seem. You cannot know causation and never have the knowledge to judge either self or others. What *seems to be* is only a min-ute fraction of any story at a given time.

WORSHIP ONLY GOD

Man has clearly been told to worship only God, not other men, angels, divinities or idols. Teachers always say, "Do not worship me, I do nothing of myself." They have continually tried to convey that all power is from God flowing through form and universally available to all. But humanity, persistent in its blindness, relates only to the manifest.

That other great leader, Mohammed, repeatedly told his followers not to worship him, yet today Islam con-siders his image so sacred it cannot even be portrayed. Gautama Buddha also continually referred the people to their inner teacher, warning them not to worship saints or gurus. Regardless of such emphatic instruction, the God within is continually confused with the outer form. Respect, veneration, love and honor are all due to those entities who have overseen humanity through the ages, but not worship.

When a seeker accepts any acknowledged entity as a teacher, guru or guide, he becomes a disciple under a Hierarchal chain of command flowing through the Regent, Masters, gurus and guides to a variety of "workers in the field." On the lower levels this can be confusing, as people don't know to what "school" they belong. It may require experimentation and experience to find out. Since in the end, all are *One,* they will benefit regardless. Through per-severance their particular "Path" will open for them. Most serious seekers have already made initiatory contacts through the ages, and these ties are never cut, regardless of outer appearances. Careful self-analysis and exploration are the best ways to find your Path. There is no "one way," anymore than there is a magic pill to enlightenment. Many expect to find the magical guru who will touch them, and all will be revealed. But the teacher comes when the student is ready. The student has no right to expect to waste a teacher's time, if the wealth of written instruction that is readily available has not been studied. "Know thyself" first is still paramount.

Knowledge in itself, is not an end. It must be balanced by the other aspects of soul through meditation, contemplation and daily actions to achieve wisdom. We have seen many examples of the result of "worshiping" knowledge and intellect in this century. The God-is-dead concept gained many followers within the academic community. God became science, ironically through the ancient knowledge of the four elements of physics, chemistry, biology and all of the physical sciences. Now, fulfilling the Antichrist prophecies, science is beginning to claim potential powers of life creation and human immortality—shades of Atlantis all over again.

To be fair, one can hardly blame members of the scientific community for rejecting the obvious fallacies of church dogmas. Many of them are an insult to intelligence. On the other hand, science has arrived at the turning point where it is beginning to confirm the original esoteric teachings, and a "new breed" of scientist is emerging. Another cycle is approaching completion. As in all things, there is a balance, a purpose and a fulfillment. *Negative force* is necessary to the *manifestation* of the divine.

The Oriental philosopher and former president of India, Sarvelpelli Radhakrishnan, summed up the predicament of achieving enlightenment and maintaining balance between the forces of the material and spiritual worlds. Considering Eastern and Western Paths, he wrote:

> Hindu and Buddhist thought, the Orphic mysteries, Plato and some forms of early Christianity maintain that it takes a long time for realizing the holy longing after the lost heaven . . . Man grows by countless lives into his divine self-existence. Every life, every act, is a step which we may take either backward or forward. By one's thought, will and action one determines what one is yet to be.
>
> The world process reaches its consummation when every man knows himself to be the immortal spirit . . . Till this goal is reached each saved individual is the centre of the universal consciousness . . . Salvation is not escape from life. . . . . It is to live in the world with one's inward being profoundly modified.
>
> (*An Idealist View of Life*).

STAR ATTRACTIONS TODAY

Humanity is never left without its greater and lesser teachers incarnate. We have had a number of remarkable ones over the past century. Taken chronologically, the New Age impulse began its manifestation with Helena Petrovna Blavatsky and the founding of The Theosophical Society. The work of "H.P.B." and other founders of the society has done more to unite the philosophy and ancient wisdom of the East and West than any other single group.

Today they are the largest publisher of New Age books and literature.

Immediately following Blavatsky in the first half of the 20th Century, came Alice A. Bailey (a first ray individual), who also devoted her life to the unification of Eastern and Western teachings. The writings of the "Tibetan," channeled through her intuitively, have formed the major foundation for *New Age* activities, including the worldwide Light Network. The organization she founded is Lucis Trust, which publishes her books and offers correspondence study to all seekers through the Arcane School. An offshoot of this is World Servers, working for unification and peace between all peoples, regardless of walk-of-life.

During approximately the same time period, Edgar Cayce was doing his remarkably accurate diagnostic medical *readings*, while at the same time touching upon many ancient historical periods and forgotten civilizations. By combining Christianity, mysticism and practical application, he may have reached more "average Americans" than any other western mystic. It is very common to find that someone returned to the Path through Cayce. I did, and I know Bud did; time and time again I hear, "I started with Cayce." The numerous books written around his *readings* are excellent basic instruction, covering material from reincarnation to meditation, spiritual principles and dreams. Most aspects of daily life are covered. Universal in concept, it is hard to find a better and more concise starting point. The Association for Research and Enlightenment he founded is still producing material researched from his *readings* in Virginia Beach. In Phoenix, Arizona, the A.R.E.

Clinic, founded by Drs. Gladys and Bill McGarey, has pioneered alternative medicine, using research information from the Cayce medical *readings.*

And we cannot forget the remarkable Mohandas Gandhi, who set such an example for the world. From his *Letters to a Disciple* we read:

> The more I observe and study things, the more convinced I become that sorrow over separation and death is perhaps the greatest delusion. To realize that it is a delusion is to become free. There is no death, no separation of the substance. . . .

> The form ever changes, ever perishes, the informing spirit neither changes or perishes. True love consists in transferring itself from the body to the dweller within and then necessarily realizing the oneness of all life inhabiting numberless bodies.

> Having flung aside the sword, there is nothing except the cup of love which I can offer those who oppose me. It is by offering that cup that I expect to draw them close to me.
>
> (*Young India,* April 2, 1931).

The early 1900s were such a fruitful period of knowledge release, we cannot possibly include everyone. But there are more we should mention, for example, Manley Palmer Hall, founder of The Philosophical Research Society, located in Los Angeles, California. This non-profit corporation provides a wealth of research material in its publications and its library is one of the largest and most complete in the West of esoteric literature.

Then there was Paul Foster Case, founder of Builders of the Adytum, also in Los Angeles. This organization still provides one of the best correspondence courses available for the study of symbology, the Tarot, meditation and contemplation. Also during this period, Max Heindel was responsible for the founding of The Rosicrucian Fellowship (not the same as the "Rosicrucians" or AMORC). Much of the work of this fellowship has centered around the teaching of astrology (correspondence course available), healing and the work of the invisible helpers.

Coming from India, Paramahansa Yogananda devoted his life to the union of Eastern and Western religion, founding the Self-Realization Fellowship in California. An excellent course of instruction is available by mail from the Fellowship, concentrating upon spiritual instruction and meditation technique. When Yogananda died in 1952, a published letter from Forest Lawn Memorial Park in Glendale, California, stated: "The absence of any visual signs of decay in the dead body . . . offers the most extraordinary case in our experience. No physical disintegration was visible in his body even twenty days after death . . . . " Science would probably say this is impossible, *but it happened*; it is not impossible for the transfigured body.

Other international figures from the East have been the Maharishi Mahesh Yogi and Yogi Bhajan. Though at times controversial, they have each had a wide reaching influence. The Marharishi brought meditation instruction and practice to the capitalistic West on a large scale— appealing to society's needs, not just spiritual seekers. This was no small accomplishment and has had an immeasurable effect on the planet, at a time when it was most needed. His courses of instruction continue to be available, as well as advanced studies.

The followers of Kundalini Yoga, founded by Yogi Bhajan, are mostly highly dedicated young people working in nationwide ashrams in the United States. We are used to seeing them wearing white Indian garments and turbans. They have been a major stimulus toward natural healing techniques and nutrition in the U.S., as well as being regular practitioners of *karma yoga*, by actively working in society.

Finally, there is an individual today who will have a profound effect upon the West. Driven out of Tibet by China, after centuries of seclusion, the Dalai Lama of the Temple of Lhasa has established the Tibetan government in exile in Dharmsala, India. Finally, in the late 1970's the United States gave him permission to visit this country, after repeated denials for political reasons. Tibetan monasteries are being established in many locations and academic interests are beginning to seriously work on collecting and translating the ancient wisdom. The Sons of Wisdom are beginning to walk the earth again. The tradition of this northern Buddhism is to continue service among mankind after achieving enlightenment, incarnation after incarnation, until all of humanity has achieved union.

The Dalai Lama is considered to be the 14th incarnation of himself, an embodied emanation of "Supreme Compassion." Known as an *Avolokiteshvara Bodhisattva,** he is an earthly representative of the "Celestial Buddha,"

---

* *The Discovery of the XIVth Dalai Lama*, Sonam Wangdu, Klett Thai Publications, Interpart Thailand Ltd., Bankok, 1975.

and an individualization of his spiritual first ray. His designation means "the Buddha Who Illuminates or Enlightens," and is synonomous with the *Christos,* or an annointed One.*

In this tradition there is always a *Buddha* incarnate, with Gautama Buddha being one of the lineage. Each such Buddha descends "like a flame spreading the eternal Fire," becoming "Universal Life on the Mundane Plane."† *Fire* refers to the "electricity" or *light* of *enlightened* entities, who should be recognized and honored as the "early achievers" who helped mold the rest of humanity.

Gradually the wisdom of Tibet is beginning to seep through the West. There have been major language and cultural gaps, but these are steadily being overcome, especially as India is an English speaking nation. This is a highly significant occurrence when considered in cyclic perspective.

STAR LIGHT

The *Seven Regents, (Dhyan Chohans* or *Rishis*), are also known as the *Seven Sons of Light* or *Stars.* They represent seven levels of manifestation with complex subdivisions, from undifferentiated essence to the corporeal, and are related to Ray Individuations who take charge of planetary spheres ("stars") following angelic (elemental) creation. They then appear through *human doubles,* or an-

---

* *Tibetan Yoga and Secret Doctrines,* W.Y. Evans-Wentz, Oxford University Press, 1975 (1959).
† *The Secret Doctrine,* H.P. Blavatsky.

nointed Ones, such as Prometheus, Buddha, Krishna, Jesus, etc.

Each of us entered manifestation under one of these *Stars* and permanently contain "essence" from the "Angel" of our *Star*. This *Star* is always with us; to the Initiate it becomes the "Twin-Soul," and the "Bright Image."* This is the blinding intelligent *light* described by so many who have clinically "died" and returned to tell about it. As one said, a "brilliant white light appeared to me. The light was so bright that I could not see through it, but going into its presence was so calming and wonderful. There is just no experience on earth like it."†

You may be aware of the *Star's* influence in your life in different ways. Since I can remember, I've always said, "I'm following my *Star*." I had no idea what it meant, but I knew it was *absolute* and not to be doubted. It has taken me through life's gyrations and around the world. Bud has an interesting manifestation of his; in his hypnosis work he often uses a "green door" (green ray), with a big yellow *Star* painted on it. You should, indeed, "follow your *star*."

CHANGE THE SET!

In a few short chapters we have covered billions of years, summarized the esoteric traditions regarding the origins of humanity and examined the importance of some major cycles. My experience shows that interest in esoteric knowledge and ability to apply it moves forward in stages,

---

* *The Secret Doctrine.*
† *Life After Life,* Raymond A. Moody, Jr., M.D., Bantam Books, 1976.

so interest in various portions of this book is likely to vary. The first half has been largely intended to expand consciousness and awareness.

The next half of our book changes pace and enters into the practical application of using *hypnosis* and *past life recall* to change your life and influence your evolution. You can enter this process from any background, as it does not require esoteric or technical knowledge. However, as you continue, you will probably find your hunger for knowledge growing. We have provided information and directions that can keep you learning and growing, just as fast as you desire.

The major karma we all have to deal with involves our relationships with others: friends, family and foes. So we will examine a number of typical situations and experiences to demonstrate how karma works in our lives. Once this is understood, you will be ready to seriously set to work on your spiritual goals and development of Cosmic Consciousness.

ACT II
Relationships
&
Karmic Recall

When the iron bird flies,
And horses run on wheels . . .
The Dharma will come to the Land of the Red Man.

(Padmasambhava, Eighth Century Tibetan Saint).

THROUGH THE LOOKING GLASS

7

Through the Looking Glass

Hey, c'mon, c'mon. Hurry,
     we're going to be . . .
          late!
               Okay, Okay . . . ,
                    I'm coming, I'm coming.
    Hurry, the second act is about to
      start. Forget your coat. You
    don't need that.
                    Oh, yeah . . . , I forgot.
Hurry up. . . .
      Did you check those things?
               What things?
    Shhh . . . C'mon, you know . . . , your limitations.
    You can't bring any old limitations
                    in here.
          Oh, yeah, right . . . ,
    SH   SH   SH
        SH

Okay, Okay . . . ,

Here he comes, that's Bud. He plays the
balding hypnotist in this drama.

SH   SH   SH   SH
       SH

Okay, Okay . . . ,
Shhh . . . , he's starting to
speak . . . .

WHAT HYPNOSIS IS . . . AND ISN'T

Okay, LaVedi, that's enough of the "cosmic stuff"!
I am now going to drastically bring things "down to
earth" for awhile to explain the fundamentals of our hypnosis technique. Actually, this chapter signals a change in
tempo of our presentation to you for the remainder of the
book. So sit back and get comfortable, relax and prepare
to enjoy the rest of the *dance.*

As you know, LaVedi and I use hypnosis and self-
hypnosis as effective methods for moving closer to *Cosmic
Consciousness* and to increase the potential for spiritual
growth. To show you how hypnosis can move you into
altered states of consciousness, I will take you backstage to
help you understand its simple, yet powerful, principles.
Then I will describe the technique we have developed to
gaze through the looking glass of time to explore your own
past lives—the history of your soul.

First, hypnosis is a method to *bypass the critical mind
in order to establish selective thinking.* It has no direct
connection with the theory of reincarnation other than as
a research method to investigate this theory more closely.

Instructors of yoga, meditation, prayer, guided imagery and medical relaxation use very similar principles of suggestion which are studied in depth in the art-science of hypnosis.

Hypnosis is not magic, it's not mysterious, or even unusual, once you understand how it works. And yet it is a proven scientific method which can allow you to more effectively use the power of your own mind to accomplish your goals. Hypnosis is used as a valuable tool in the areas of obstetrics, gynecology, criminology, dentistry, dermatology, epilepsy, alcoholism, psychiatry, radiology and even professional athletics.

Like all approaches that use suggestion techniques, the real work is always done by the individual having the experience. Thus *ALL* hypnosis is in fact self-hypnosis. Therefore, the professional hypnotist will seldom, if ever, accept the blame or the credit for an individual's failure or success. All the hypnotist can do is use his knowledge of how suggestions and imagery work most effectively to guide the individual toward success. The person CAN ALWAYS ACCEPT OR REJECT these suggestions and determine the amount of emotional power to be used to follow them. Keep in mind that all hypnosis is basically self-hypnosis.

A great many misconceptions concerning hypnosis have resulted from the tricks of stage performers and the fantasies of Hollywood movies. While these do make people aware that hypnosis is a real phenomenon, they also, unfortunately, create unrealistic expectations and unwarranted fears. For example, it is quite common for people

to expect me to *make* them stop smoking, *make* them overcome pain or *make* them lose weight. I have to explain
that hypnosis can not *MAKE* anybody do anything. You
have to voluntarily CHOOSE to follow the suggestions,
and then work to change yourself. You seldom accomplish
anything of value without working for it.

Many people feel hesitant to experience hypnosis for
fear of having someone "take over" their minds while they
are "asleep." But *HYPNOSIS IS NOT SLEEP;* it is a high
state of *AWARENESS* achieved through *cooperation* with
the given suggestions. With hypnosis you focus your attention to become more aware, more attentive and more in
touch with reality. Because you are more in touch with
reality, you only accept suggestions that are beneficial and
personally appropriate. Thus you would never violate your
ethics, morals or sense of well-being.

As to the unwarranted cries that hypnosis is dangerous,
as of this writing I know of no instance where anyone has
been directly harmed by using hypnosis. Keep in mind that
hypnosis is a *method* of treatment and certainly not a cure
in and of itself. Like any method or tool, it can be used in-
appropriately. Hypnosis is like the surgeon's scalpel that
can be used either to perform delicate surgery or to scrape
pots and pans. It is not the tool or method that is the issue,
but how it is used.

Let me repeat that hypnosis may be explained as beginning with the bypass of the critical mind, followed by
selective thinking. This simple definition is used by medical
hypnotist Dave Elman in his excellent book *Hypnotherapy*.
This does not disregard the genius of Milton Erickson or

the intellectual cleverness of Richard Bandler and John Grinder, but Dave Elman's simple and clear approach is more appropriate for our work. Simply described, the critical mind may be thought of as the conscious doubting mind, the mind that is logical and rational, the mind that is influenced by pre-programmed beliefs. This critical mind needs to be bypassed, or set aside for awhile, to open a more clear channel to the subconscious computer (we will use the term "subconscious" to differentiate this from your personal unconscious energy field). As this channel is relaxed open, you may more easily overcome your self-imposed subconscious limitations and fully realize that, as John Lilly wrote in *The Center of the Cyclone,* "Within the province of the mind there are no limits."

THE SUBCONSCIOUS AS A COMPUTER

Before discussing *how* to bypass the critical mind, we will first consider the computer programming aspect of the subconscious mind. The subconscious can be simply viewed as a computer, as Dr. Maxwell Maltz writes in *Psycho-Cybernetics.* In this excellent book he describes the subconscious as a goal-striving mechanism that operates like an impersonal computer. Now, that is not to say that you and I are computers, but only that we have these wonderful computers to use, and many of us are just poor (random and untrained) programmers.

A "program," in this sense, is an imaginary "thought habit" or "tape loop" that operates automatically, without our conscious initiation; hence it is *sub*-conscious. An example program might silently repeat, "I am shy, I am

shy . . . ." Or, another program might angrily repeat,
"The world is against me, the world is against me . . . . "
Still another might lovingly repeat, "Life is beautiful,
life is beautiful . . . . " Which one would you like to play?
As you practice your self-hypnosis, you may have the
growing suspicion that the difference between sadness
and happiness is really a DECISION.

To understand how the subconscious computer
can be reprogrammed, we need to briefly discuss the
engineering "principle of cybernetics." At the end of
World War II, Dr. Norbert Wiener, working on self-correct-
ing rocketry, clarified the principle of cybernetics. Cybernetics refers to a feedback goal-striving system, which may
be illustrated by a thermostat and a furnace.

If, for example, you set your thermostat in your
home for 70 degrees, it records this program and instructs
the furnace to turn on when the temperature drops to,
perhaps, 65 degrees; and conversely, to shut off when
the temperature reaches 75 degrees. The thermostat
in this example represents the computer storage apparatus
of the subconscious. The setting at 70 degrees represents
the thought habit, or tape loop. The furnace represents
the outward behavior that stays within the prescribed
limits, while the person setting the thermostat represents
the conscious programming mind. This basic pattern of
establishing the program, and of staying within certain
prescribed limits, generally explains how our beliefs about
the world, and our beliefs about ourself, are cybernetically
created and maintained.

YOU CAN CHANGE!

Obviously, we have many different views of ourselves depending upon our various roles: father, student, customer, lover, woman, baseball player or pizza eater. We tend to stay within the behavioral limits of each of these roles, as dictated cybernetically by our subconscious self-image programs. A bad result of *negative self-image programming* is the hyperactive child who, because of excessive energy, constantly distracts his teacher and classmates. He may soon be labeled a "troublemaker" and eventually begin to play this negative program in his subconscious computer. Unless he learns that he can remove this negative self-image (this lie about himself), it can lead to a great deal of unnecessary suffering for the rest of his life.

The first and most important program I encourage my students to consider using in their hypnosis practice is "I CAN CHANGE." If this is not part of your thinking and you believe, for example, that you will always have a bad temper, then you WILL always have a bad temper. Realize that all of these imaginary programs, both the good ones and the bad ones, are all "make believe." They are all flexible, changeable and far from being cast in concrete. So, in essence, YOU ARE RESPONSIBLE FOR CHANGING YOURSELF—for literally creating your own reality.

Once you take the conscious responsibility for creating your own reality (you have been doing it unconsciously all the time anyway) and then actively try to change, you may be surprised that you continue to have so many dark thoughts running through your head. Relax, and just keep in mind that most of these thoughts are simply due to old inappropriate programs in your subconscious. First, just acknowledge these negative thoughts when they occur as your opportunity to overcome your old self. You need to be ruthlessly honest with yourself to do this, but it will pay off. As soon as you identify the source of these thoughts or emotions, honor their existence and let them float by your mind. Simply allow them to dissolve back into the nothingness from which they came. Let them die from lack of use. Next, replace them with strong positive thoughts, such as forgiveness, kindness, compassion or love. The conscious goal is to THINK PERFECT THOUGHTS. Easy? No. Tough? Yes. Possible? Given enough lifetimes, we will all inevitably make it. How fast we progress depends upon the clarity of our thoughts held on the goal and the power of our desire to achieve it.

An example, of several I will share with you concerning good positive subconscious programming, was demonstrated by a friend who scored quite low on an I.Q. (Intelligence Quotient) test in high school. For awhile he actually accepted this potentially negative "make-believe" self-image program, and he wondered whether he might be destined to subcultural imprisonment with the rest of his black friends. But one day he rejected this constrictive subconscious program and replaced it with one that opened him to his unlimited potential. I later took two graduate classes in General Semantics from this man, who holds a doctorate and is now a professor at a major university in California.

Fortunately, at some point in his young life, the future professor had the courage and wisdom to take charge of his own life and make his own future or, in other words, to become a conscious subconscious programmer. You, too, can overcome your self-imposed limitations by carefully designing and correcting your own programs. You then build them into your subconscious computer with vivid imagination by using hypnosis. *Your thoughts provide the DIRECTION and your emotions provide the POWER to accomplish this.*

Another good example of strong positive programming has been demonstrated every fourth or fifth day on the pitcher's mound by former Cy Young Award winner, Tom Seaver, formerly with the Cincinnati Reds and, as of this writing, with the New York Mets. Let me share with you the unusual story of our first meeting while playing baseball in, of all places, Fairbanks, Alaska. Red Boucher, then coach of the Fairbanks Goldpanner ballclub and later Lieutenant Governor of the State of Alaska, had Tom picked up at the airport and hustled to the ballpark. Tom had to change into his baseball uniform on the way. He then hurriedly tossed a few balls in the bullpen and charged out to the pitcher's mound in the middle of the third inning. The three of us, Red, Tom and me (I was the catcher), introduced ourselves on the mound, got our signs straight for the pitches and went to work on the next hitter.

From then on it became obvious to me that this man had a great positive attitude, and that everyone played a little harder when he was pitching. He had great confidence in his ability and tremendous determination to challenge and overcome any hitter. As the pressure grew tough, he became twice as tough. He was a "winner." To have a man on your ballclub with this contagious positive attitude is worth a great deal more than what is shown by his individual pitching statistics. Whatever money he is paid today, his total contribution to the team makes him well worth it.

Most of us on our semi-professional ballclub assumed Tom Seaver would achieve whatever goal he set for himself because of his positive, aggressive and enthusiastic subconscious attitude towards life. As it turned out, he continued to channel his energies into baseball, but he probably could have raised cactus in Alaska and found some way to be successful.

Another example of positive programming, again from the sports world, is Tommy Lasorda, manager for the Los Angeles Dodgers. I first played for Tommy in 1965, my first year in professional baseball, and was impressed by his unbounding energy, his sense of humor and his never ending war cry (repetitious programming), "Ya gotta believe!" This spread through his players like the chicken pox at a nursery school.

All strong emotions are naturally contagious, and the symptoms of "Lasorda's Disease" are easily diagnosed when a Dodger pitcher walks to the mound with a glassy-eyed stare on his face mumbling something about, "This is my mound and my ball—get a hitter up there!" Another symptom of Lasorda's Disease is when one of the Dodger outfielders crashes into a wall chasing a flyball and, when the trainer wakes him up, the outfielder grasps the round blood pressure squeezer out of the trainer's bag and jumps up shouting, "I caught it, I caught it."

These sports stories illustrate how clear positive

thoughts focused on a goal, and multiplied by powerful desire, can change the subconscious computer to make success inevitable. Now, let's take a closer look at the phenomenon of imagination—the language of the subconscious computer.

IMAGINATION IS THE LANGUAGE

Einstein said, "Imagination is more important than knowledge." I believe the reason he said this is because once you understand how to program your subconscious computer by using powerful imagination, you can consciously work toward accomplishing ANY GOAL that is in your heart. Once you master this process, you realize that you have ALWAYS been creating yourself with your imagination every minute of your life, but never noticed it before. *YOU ARE RESPONSIBLE* for all that you are now and all that you will become, so you cannot possibly blame your parents, your friends or even your environment any longer. Life is a continuous story of self-creation written with the powerful language of the imagination.

Since the imagination is the language of the subconscious computer, everything you believe about yourself, associations and surroundings has been built into your mind through your thoughts and emotions, using imagination. Repeating some examples: if you *imagine* yourself to be shy, you will be; if you *imagine* the world is against you, it will appear to be; if you *imagine* that life is beautiful, it will appear so. Because the subconscious is highly responsive to creative thought (imagination), you can design new programs very deliberately to be successful. Since you are creating your own reality anyway, you might as well do it consciously and skillfully.

However, before you change or program anything, you need to decide clearly what you WANT. Most of us have a very clear imaginative picture of what we do NOT WANT, such as not to gain more weight, not to smoke or not to lose our job. *Forget what you do not want,* and instead get a clear picture of what you DO WANT. Word it in a short repeatable phrase or get it clarified by a vivid mental picture. Then use hypnosis to place it deeply through imagination in your subconscious computer. A sample program phrase is, "Everything is easy. Everything is easy . . . ." A sample picture is visualizing *white light* surrounding and blessing someone who is having difficulties.

To program the subconscious effectively I encourage my students to get a clear vivid "pay off picture" of the desired end result. Eliminate worry, which is negative imagination, and continuously keep the positive pay off picture and its corresponding emotions clearly in your thoughts and feelings. Since "mind is the builder," as Edgar Cayce so often said, build strong positive thoughts and emotions around your pay off picture and success is inevitable.

The work I really do in hypnosis classes is to teach people how to DE-HYPNOTIZE themselves from their old negative programs. When Mark Twain said, "It's not that people are ignorant, but that they believe so much that ain't so . . . ," he seemed to be expressing a basic truth about people. As it turns out, most of what we believe or imagine about ourselves "ain't so." If it momentarily "is so," it certainly does not have to "stay so."

BYPASS OF THE CRITICAL MIND

As I mentioned, hypnosis begins with the bypass of the critical mind. One way to accomplish this is to establish "eye closure." It was thought for many years that a person had to watch lamps or lights to establish eye closure before hypnosis would work. Dave Elman, a leader in the field of medical hypnosis, discovered that all watching lights did was to make the eyes so tired they would want to close. Today there are still a few hypnotists that may say dramatically to their subjects, "You are getting sleeeepy . . . . " This is fine, but "please close your eyes" will work just as well with most people. The following wording is a very effective way to get simple eye closure and achieve bypass of the critical mind. You may accomplish this quickly yourself by following these simple suggestions:

> Take a deep breath, hold it, and close your eyes. (You may find it rather difficult from this point on trying to read with your eyes closed!) Let your breath out slowly and completely, and relax your eye muscles. Relax your eye muscles so much that they will not work. Test them to make sure. Now, stop testing them, and take another deep breath. Let it out slowly. Now let that same relaxation go all the way down to your toes.

Another way to do this is to just "pretend" that your eyes are so relaxed that they just won't open. Either way you are demonstrating your cooperation and willingness to use your imagination, the language of your subconscious computer, by proving to yourself that your eyes will not open. You are bypassing your critical mind that is probably saying, "Of course I can open my eyes . . . . " But, if you do open your eyes, it is evident that your critical mind is still in control. This eye closure sequence allows you to know whether your limited critical mind or your unlimited creative mind is in control.

There is nothing magical about getting eye closure. In fact the eyes could remain open during hypnosis, as long as some method is used to bypass the limited critical mind. This is true because only three things will prevent hypnosis: an unwilling attitude, mental incompetence or fear. Whenever fear is present hypnosis gives way naturally to normal waking consciousness. So, whether the eyes are open or closed is of no particular consequence. However, it is preferred that they be closed to reduce visual distractions and improve concentration on the suggestions.

Once eye closure is established, good physical relaxation is accomplished by relaxing all parts of the body, from the toes to the top of the head. An Elman technique is then used to get mental relaxation. This is accomplished by counting backwards from 100 to 98, while doubling the physical relaxation with each number. This encourages you to become mentally involved in evaluating and deepening your own relaxation. At the same time you raise your level of cooperation, as you are "paced and lead" (terms used by Bandler and Grinder) deeper into hypnosis. From this point on the physical body should no longer be a distraction. Then the desired program, such as to lose weight, to improve memory or to raise the level of consciousness to view past lives, becomes possible. LaVedi and

I begin our work at this comfortable level of medium depth hypnosis.

PAST LIFE MEMORY TECHNIQUE

It took LaVedi and me over two years of continuous work to refine our technique to help you explore your own past lives with *SAFETY and CONTROL.* It should be pointed out that this is not a classical "age regression" technique that takes you back through your infancy, decreasing your conscious awareness of your present personality. To the contrary, our technique is designed to INCREASE your conscious awareness, rather than decrease it. While experiencing impressions of past lives, you remain aware simultaneously of your surroundings and your present personality. You are therefore always perfectly safe and in control.

Consequently you enter into each past life memory at a more objective and heightened overview, instead of plunging into emotional scenes that distort the memories. By operating at this higher mental level, which we call *soul consciousness,* you can maintain detachment from the powerful emotional level. This gives you more freedom and maneuverability. You can witness scenes, but do not need to emotionally participate, unless you CHOOSE to do so.

Personally, I have chosen to relive entire emotional experiences only in a few instances, to make sure of the information I was seeking. While the emotions can be very powerful and convincing, I do not encourage using the emotional level until you become skilled. I do want to make it clear that you have this OPTION, but it is not a requirement of our technique.

The *Past Life Memory Program* we have developed and made available on cassette tapes is based upon three sources of information: my knowledge of hypnosis, LaVedi's experience with meditation and clairvoyant recall techniques and information from a third *Source*, known to us as "The Timeless One." The Timeless One (*Logoic consciousness*) worked through LaVedi to help us combine the first two sets of knowledge. The result is a technique that allows us to bridge into *soul consciousness* by bypassing the critical mind and programming the subconscious mind.

We begin with the same basic three hypnotic procedures already explained: achievement of eye closure, good physical relaxation and mental relaxation. Following these three steps a cocoon of *white light*, symbolic of Christ Consciousness, God's Perfect Presence or your ideal concept of God and all that is good, is visualized surrounding your body. This strong positive influence literally raises your vibrational rate, preparing you to view scenes from past lives safely and easily, with compassion and forgiveness.

Next you concentrate on the particular situation or person that you wish to investigate in relation to a relevant past life. When using the memory tapes (after using Tapes No. 1 and 2), we recommend beginning with the guided past-life induction designed to help recall past lives with loved ones (Tape No. 3), because memories connected with people are usually the easiest to recall. The other tapes investigate present-life problems that may be based upon past-life causes (Tape No. 4), and expanded use of past-life recall to recover hidden knowledge, talents or abilities (Tape No. 5). These past-life experiences cover the basic needs and desires expressed by most of the people in our seminars and private sessions.

After a period of intense concentration upon the particular subject to be investigated, a *blue light* or *tunnel* is visualized, imagined or actually *seen*. This is viewed from the middle of the forehead (the "third-eye" or *chakra* that gives clairvoyant vision). Once this is *seen* or sensed, you allow yourself to move *into and through* this *blue light* or *tunnel* toward the other side of it, feeling yourself flow into the warm and comforting *space* that is *soul consciousness*. Guided suggestions are then given on the tapes to aid in the gathering of sensory and intuitive perceptions and impressions.

Because you enter your experiences at the higher level of *objective soul consciousness,* you will be free of attachment, guilt, fear, pride or other egoic emotions. Lower emotions are not felt by the *Self*. Contact with *soul consciousness* makes you aware that you are much more than the narrowness of the limited personality. Everyone is a piece of the divineness we call God. Pride, vanity, guilt and anger are just not felt at this level of consciousness. However, if you should feel yourself slipping down into some lower emotions for any reason, you only need to relax, center yourself and more lovingly visualize or imagine the *white light* surrounding you. The more you work with *soul consciousness*, the less power the lower emotions will have in your life. You will begin to see your spiritual goals more clearly and be able to move consciously and deliberately toward them, with as much speed and energy as your life pattern permits.

Working from this level of *soul consciousness* provides the positive benefits of safety and control, since while using these simple hypnosis procedures, you can return to normal waking consciousness at any time by just opening your eyes. Control is designed in, so you may move into or out of experiences, choose your level of emotional involvement, change time periods, ask your own questions and still be completely aware of your immediate surroundings.

BENEFITS OF KARMIC RECALL

The initial information that you may bring back from the past can produce ever increasing positive benefits in human relationships and present life situations. In most cases, this information helps to gain insight, forgiveness of others and forgiveness of self. *FORGIVENESS* is the bottom line message in almost all of our past-life work. As you learn how to experience your past lives, you will find forgiving others is easier than forgiving yourself, as we tend to judge ourselves more severely than we do others. Commonly self-condemnation lies at the root of many past-life problems that spill over into the present life. The subconscious can still be silently passing judgment, even though the "debt" may have been paid centuries before. Past-life recall abilities can give you an improved knowledge base to genuinely understand the importance of forgiveness. Forgiveness of self and others is *essential* to release the subconscious influences. Otherwise you will keep re-experiencing related problems, until you learn the universal lesson to not judge, but forgive.

The most powerful benefit of experiencing past lives, beyond gaining information, is the deep awareness that you never die. *YOU NEVER DIE.* Your physical bodies die from time to time, and you discard them like wornout garments, but the REAL YOU is much more than those bodies. The churches have been right all along about the immortality of the soul, but the corresponding message of the immortal cycles and rebirth has been largely lost in the West.

Another powerful benefit of experiencing even just one past life is the realization that the universe is exquisitely divine, moral and perfectly fair. You will see for yourself that all of us are in the process of uncovering our own divinity. Morality becomes more than a social issue, when it is recognized in truth as a reflection of God's logical and rational divine Law of Cause and Effect (Law of Karma). You will discover that not just wrong actions, but even wrong thoughts eventually come back to us—what we sow we do, indeed, reap. Therefore, learning how to think perfect thoughts is both sensible and imperative, and your efforts to achieve this goal can make your present life, and future lives, much more enjoyable.

Past-life experiences will also help you realize that a negative situation or crisis in your present life is actually an *opportunity* to learn compassion, forgiveness, courage or other positive qualities you need to overcome particular past-life tendencies. All such experiences can be *growth experiences* that expand the consciousness steadily toward *Cosmic Consciousness.* Only by learning and demonstrating positive or divine qualities can we hope to purify the consciousness and enhance the speed of the soul's evolution and *return.* LIFE HAS A PURPOSE—the growth and evolution of the soul and the ability to experience God consciously. The soul eventually graduates from its earthly limitations, to become an active, infinite and fully conscious participant in "the eternal dance."

ON TOUR TOGETHER

8

On Tour Together

Do I need to pack my fallen angel costume?
No, no, no . . . , just your normal
human equipment this time.

I got a lot of mileage out of this costume.
Ah, those were the aeons!
Will you put down that angel costume and
start packing! We've got a show to do.

How about just my bent halo?
Your . . . bent . . . halo?

Yeah, that was my own idea, very symbolic
don't you think?
(A . . . *bent* . . . halo! Hmm, from now on
I'd better check the list of members before

each tour.)

TOGETHERNESS

We rarely incarnate alone; our earthly stage is usually set with old friends, bitter "enemies," former relatives and loved ones. These are the people we have returned with through the ages and who eventually form our "soul-family." Even an orphaned baby will find its way on the tides of life to entities it has known before.

Attractive bodies were designed for us, but we get lonely in them, isolated from whom we really are. We can't quite remember why, but we feel like there is something missing. So we turn to other people for comfort, support and companionship, while we search life after life for the elusive *Self*.

Within our soul-families, we continually exchange roles. For example, your father today may have previously been your husband, mother, wife, sister, grandparent, friend, lover or enemy. Each soul-family contains a full cast of characters, all of whom are working out karma with each other that has been built through many lifetimes. The cast even includes animals, who will get into the act by returning to former loving owners or sometimes to enemies.

We found an example of a soul-family role exchange when we did a past-life *reading* for a couple seeking an answer to their present childlessness. As Bud used our hypnotic technique to heighten my consciousness, I began to view their last life together during the Roaring '20s.

> LaVedi: I find her coming from . . . wealthy family . . . I find her as a female; I see her blond, long hair. I think it is on the East Coast . . . her favorite sport at the time was tennis . . .

Bud: Is the entity known as _____, her husband, in that same life on the eastern seaboard?

LaVedi: I get that he is a younger brother, maybe ten, eight years (younger). The relationship between the two seemed to be good.

Bud: Does she marry in that incarnation?

LaVedi: She has a boyfriend . . . . What I see is a rather fast set of people . . . , like during the flapper days, and a really fast type of crowd.

She does seem to marry the boyfriend . . . , the impression I get is that she is not interested in a family, just in having fun; and he is not interested in having family. However, she does get pregnant; the child isn't wanted.

Bud: Is the child . . . born?

LaVedi: Well, there is a great deal of turmoil over this situation. He leaves her; she is left pregnant.

A great deal of arguing. A lot of tears. A lot of turmoil. The fancy fast life suddenly dissolves, and this interferes with the life style, which was a very shallow life style.

He leaves her for someone else; she is left pregnant. She commits suicide. She runs her car off a . . . . . .

Bud: Let's leave that scene for a minute.

LaVedi: She runs her car off of a cliff.

Bud: How does her brother at that time (her present husband) respond to this?

LaVedi: He seems to be of a different turn of mind, more serious. Of course, he was younger, wasn't in her crowd, but even
so, I see him at the funeral, cap in hand, head bowed, not overwhelmed by it, but very sad. He seems to be of a more philosophical turn of mind; more depth of life, even at that age. And
he was just very sorry about the situation and *wished that he
could have helped her.* . . . it was this very desire that caused
them to come together now.

In the present life the woman has very much *wanted*
to have a child, but after having killed herself, and her
unborn child previously, and having instructed her body then
that she did not want children, she has so far been unable
to conceive. Her former brother, from his desire to aid her,
became her husband this time to help her overcome the
impact of that former experience.

The subconscious carry-over from this life has been so
strong that, discussing the *reading* with Bud, the woman
told him she could not tolerate any portrayals of the '20s,
such as movies or television shows. They would cause her
to burst into tears. She also completed the description of
the car going off the cliff, before hearing it. . . .

In another *reading,* done by Rachel MacPherson, using
a memory tape, Rachel found herself looking down upon
tiled roof-tops from a grilled-in area. The scene was in a
crowded Spanish town during the Inquisition. She was
looking for a lifetime with her former husband, and she
found him in this period as her son.

In her notes, Rachel recorded, "He tortured during the
Inquisition: I feel torn between deep devotion to church
and son, a lot of guilt. I was in a heavy black costume

(almost like a nun's or mourning)." She went on to consider that the torture might explain her husband's excessive sensitivity to pain, especially to his fingers and back; why he was so extremely bitter toward organized religion; and why she felt the need to "mother" him. These two have lived many lifetimes and roles together.

We should be aware of the horrific impact the Church and the Inquisition has had upon people and relationships, creating powerful emotional carry-over. In this life, as LaVedi, I had to spend much of it struggling with anger. Finally I was shown a life during the Inquisition when I died hanging from a stone wall from manacles around my wrists. It was dark, dank and filthy, with a few light beams filtering in from a high narrow slit of a window. I was filled with consuming rage and hate, and died with a snarl to gain revenge against the injustice of the Church. Once I realized the source of this emotional dynamite, I was able to begin releasing it. An important aspect of such energies is that like will attract like, as a part of the purging process. So examine closely any energies around you that you dislike; they will be reflecting something within yourself that you may be totally unconscious of. Many couples are working out emotional tangles from the distortion of the Dark Ages.

Through the exchange of roles, we even out these emotional hills and valleys, releasing the pent-up carry-overs and helping each other. The more intense emotions can take years, or even a lifetime to work out, so perseverance is a must. Religion played a variation role in another *reading* Bud and I did for a married couple:

LaVedi: Well, I see these two as lovers . . . . At that time . . . both chose the Church instead of marriage to each other . . . .

Bud: Is there something in that experience with the Church that has influenced ＿＿＿＿ (his) attitude toward the Church in this incarnation?

LaVedi: There was in the latter part of that life a disillusionment with the Church, and this occurred for a reason—to set the entity questioning and seeking more—for it could not last upon the level he had reached; in the natural course of growth (it was) essential to create . . . dissatisfaction.

Today, following that life of sacrificial separation, they have married and have a daughter, another member of their soul-family. The life *reading* continued:

Bud: At this time we are searching for a karmic connection between the three entities . . . .

LaVedi: ＿＿＿＿ (the daughter) will teach you. You are to offer her balance, and, again, it is difficult to put into words, but you will offer her connection with the earth plane. Not one that holds her to the earth, but one that assists her in relating to earth with love. She, also, offers you a link with your Source, and will teach you many things.

There is a bit of karma to work out on the earth plane. In experiences ＿＿＿＿ (she) has acquired some ego karma, stemming from her magnetism; and ＿＿＿＿ (her present father) was drawn into this at one time; and she will attempt to manipulate or influence in this way, and this will be between these two. It is essential that he redirect her energies to her Higher-Self, and not this earth, (her lower inclinations when they manifest). The self-will aspect, which she will generate, particularly through a phase of childhood, can assist her, in helping her overcome this, so she will be free of it.

Though still an infant, this daughter is already using feminine wiles on her father to try to get her own way, just as she did in their former man-woman relationship. She is extremely personable and precocious. His task may not be easy, as she has a powerful personality, but they now have the opportunity to achieve new balance, love and understanding together. The parents remain strongly oriented in spiritual objectives and will be able to rely upon these to guide their daughter. Interestingly the mother still has strong past-life carry-over from the nun's vows, and wears no make-up or jewelry (with no desire to change this).

Sometimes soul-families are so "tight" that they even appear to keep coming into the same earthly family lineage, or at least this is what some Alaskan Natives believe. Dr. Ian Stevenson, of the University of Virginia, has reported several well-documented examples of such instances in his book, *Twenty Cases Suggestive of Reincarnation.*

One case involved a Tlingit (pronounced "Klink-it") Indian boy, Corliss Chotkin, Jr., who remembered his previous life, as Victor Vincent, his present mother's deceased uncle. The mother of Corliss had been a favorite niece of her Uncle Victor. On Victor's frequent visits to the Chotkin home, he is quoted as having said, "I'm coming back as your son and I hope I don't stutter as much then as I do now. Your son will have these scars," referring to a scar on his back, in which the small holes of the stitches remained visible, and another scar on the right side of his nose.

Eighteen months after Victor Vincent died, in 1947,

Corliss, Jr. was born, bearing the exact scars that Victor had said he would. These were later confirmed by Dr. Stevenson. Victor had also had an Indian name, Kahkody. At 13 months of age, when his mother was trying to teach the little boy his name, the child asked her, "Don't you know me? I'm Kahkody!"

In still another past-life *reading* for an Alaskan couple, Bud and I found they had been together repeatedly, including a time as thieves in the Old West. Then, as cohorts, they dangled from the ends of ropes beside each other. Today they still have rebellion in their hearts, but now they are channeling it into constructive pioneering in the Alaskan wilderness. We had an interesting confirmation of their past experience, when the wife commented that she could not tolerate wearing *anything* around her neck. This is a frequent reaction of people who have previously died by hanging or strangulation.

YES, EVEN PETS

Animals are evolving, too, and are subject to reincarnation and karma. They belong to overseeing "soul-groups" under their *devas*, according to their species, until they begin to individualize. Lacking personal power of individuation, they can only do it through their human companions. This is exactly what they do, by establishing a strong mental or emotional connection (thread). How often have you heard someone comment that a pet even looks and acts like its owner? It is no accident.

. . . You may sometimes catch the glance of a dog which lays a kind of claim to sympathy and brotherhood. What! Somewhat of me down there? Does he know it? Can he too, as I, go out of himself; perceive relations?

Ralph Waldo Emerson

We have such a pet in Alaska, a cat named Hera, who rules everyone, including dogs, like the mythological goddess she is named after. Born in London in 1970, she has been with us since. She puzzled us at first, because her actions were so atypical for an ordinary housecat. She would swagger through rooms with a funny rolling gait that was strongly reminiscent of a powerful lioness. She seemed to think of herself as large; laying in the middle floors spread-eagled on her back, totally oblivious to the danger of being stepped on. As a young cat, flying from Madrid, she endeared herself to the airline hostesses by sitting, unleashed, in her own window seat, curiously observing each take-off and landing. She behaved herself like a perfect lady during the lengthy flights, as if she had done it all of her life.

Finally, one afternoon in Alaska, several of us spontaneously decided to do a past-life *reading* for Hera. We found that she had, indeed, been a large cat. The life we discovered was in Egypt, where she had been trained and used by myself (a priest at the time) in temple work. At her death she had been mumified and the mumification had prevented her from reincarnating, until the mummy was destroyed during World War II. In 1977, when we visited the British Museum in London, we found confirmation that the Egyptians had mumified cats. There were several medium sized cat-mummies that had been added to their Egyptian mummy display.

Hera had first returned to us in 1968, as a large gray Siamese cat, but was accidently killed when she ran under a car. Following that brief incarnation, she came to us in London as a large black and white "alley" cat, after her mother "insisted" upon adopting us on the streets of London. She seems to retain influence from the Egyptian experience, for she loves to routinely join people in meditation, becoming highly indignant and noisy if any attempt is made to exclude her. As long as she is allowed to participate, she is very well-mannered. It appears she is resuming her evolution, and will not tolerate any interference.

In another past-life *reading* Bud and I did using our hypnotic method, we found a similar case that involved reincarnation between an individual and dogs. The person, now a man, had been a woman in China, where we found:

> LaVedi: . . . apparently they used dogs, as a kind of guard dog . . . , they were used to guard the grounds . . . .
>
> Bud: Was he strongly attracted to these dogs?
>
> LaVedi: Protected by them, not really guarded by them, appreciated . . . , and I get the scene; I am not sure what it is exactly, a temple or a residence . . . . It seems that life was saved by the dogs at some point. Created a strong link, a beginning in that era. It has been pursued since.
>
> Bud: Their particular dog, Sin-gin, is it possible that the same dog was in that particular incarnation?

LaVedi: I think so, I see it licking her face. Sort of like saying, "You recognize me."

This person was an old friend of Bud's, so he knew that the man and his wife owned several rare oriental Akida dogs, of whom they are inordinately fond, but I was totally unaware of this, until it came out in the reading.

Better take a second look at your pets, you never know . . . , and remember, you enable them to individualize by your example and attention. Abuse their development and you will share negative karma with them. Help your "little brothers" and you will be able to share pleasant future experiences together.

SOUL-MATES

Soul-mates may be able to trace their history back to an original soul-group, various periods of evolution, affiliations or other planets. We continually reincarnate with many of our soul-mates, while others are more casual friends who we simply have reunions with occasionally. There have been many cycles, and we tend to be permanently stamped with whatever the vibrational influences were at the time of our own particular earthly beginnings. These vibrations guide us down our own evolutionary path, with the assistance of the related overseers, so we naturally tend to group together. We have "family habits," interests and personality traits that reflect our group.

These habits are very similar to those of everyday family situations. They affect intellectual interests, religious preferences, hobbies, talents, eating habits, entertainment and so forth. Century after century the lives of our soul-families intertwine, karmically adding and losing family members on the complex journey through time. Families also have terrible fights and feuds. Just because we reincarnate with old companions does not necessarily mean all is sweetness and light. To the contrary, families are likely to have the worst fights due to the continual closeness of their interactions.

So, watch intense feelings, favorable or unfavorable, you may well be reacting to an old soul-mate, a member of your own soul-family. *Try to respond, instead of react,* and work at clearing up any negative emotions and *karma.* Help comes to us in many disguises, so we may not realize that someone who seems to be giving us trouble, may actually be doing so to help us learn about ourself. We need to take a close look and give careful consideration to anyone who causes us great unhappiness for any reason.

The most powerful situations tend to appear in parent-child relationships. There are several reasons for this. First, it is more or less inescapable. Second, childhood is more flexible, and difficult karma may be more easily worked out. And third, it is a lengthy period of interaction. Difficulty with a parent can be extremely charged with emotion and require persistent effort to work out. It may be impossible within the relationship, in which case the message is clear: cut the *karmic tie,* forgive and forget. A prayerful attitude is very helpful in this, as it can really be more than the emotions and consciousness can achieve alone. It works equally well for the deceased, a factor especially important when there is a need to deal with a situation involving deceased parents or others where difficult karma has been involved, but it is too late to do anything about it in person.

I had the power of such prayer dramatically demonstrated following a nasty and violent divorce. Some eight years afterward, I decided I should clean up this particular karmic connection. Since I had never seen him again and had no idea where he was, I used prayer to both send and ask for forgiveness (always do both). After working on this a few months, I suddenly received a very strange call from the East Coast. A man said his "conscience" had been bothering him, and he wanted to let me know my former husband had died two years before in Maine. He correctly thought that my daughter (my former husband's adopted daughter) was eligible for social security. The timing was excellent, we had just returned from Europe and were broke. If he had waited even a couple more months, he would never have reached us, as I never again had a telephone in that name.

During times of difficulty, we need to remember that ALL experiences are lessons, and ALL problems are opportunities to learn and grow. Soul-mates sometimes make great sacrifices to help each other, so do not be taken in by appearances. They can be extremely deceiving. We need to think much less about *karmic punishment*, and instead realize that situations are only difficult because of unwilling attitudes, unaccepting ideas, emotional desires, or negative approaches to life. Unhappiness is a warning flag. It says we have a faulty program in our subconscious computer and had better create a new program through positive thought.

Always give others as much understanding and "growing space" as you can muster, for neither you, nor the other involved, may know the real motivations behind actions or reactions. This is true of intimate family, friends, associates or bitter opponents. Try not to judge. Try to be lenient, just and honest, loving and helpful, regardless of how difficult the circumstances may appear to be. In fact, the harder it seems, the more important it probably is for you to be generous. Help your fellow "dancer" remember his steps, and you will be helping yourself, too. In fact, you will be helping to improve the entire human performance.

SOLO PERFORMANCE

9

Solo Performance

I've been thinking about this solo and
I don't feel ready, yet.
But you've been working up to this for
centuries; you'll be great.
You keep saying that, but maybe I peaked
with my fallen angel routine.
But this is your big break!
Big break?
Right!
Just picture yourself on stage, and for
the first time you suddenly realize that
you are totally alone . . . .
Totally?
Totally.
To discover consciously who you
REALLY are.
Oh, yeah, right. . . .

And then, everything that could go wrong
    does go wrong, to drive you to search
  for the meaning of life, to find your eternal unwavering
    Spiritual Self!
                     Got it! Spiritual Self . . . , unwavering.
                       Great idea! And then I'm
                       finished? Right?
No, not at all.
            Oh.
Now, you go through utter despair to motivate
  you to the ultimate action, to rip away the veil, to knock
down the barriers of illusion and grasp your Eternal Identity!
               Fantastic! I'll do it!
         Where's my script? Tell Scheduling I'm on my way!
             Rip that veil!
                Knock that barrier!
Here, hold my halo, I'll be right baack . . . . . (in a millenium
       or two).

WHY LONELINESS?

In karmic recall we frequently find that loneliness results from the abuse of others in some way. Love may seem to stay just out of reach, until the unhappy individual overcomes the sorrow from past transgressions against self and others. It is a process of purification, inner assimilation and attunement. Bud and I did a *reading* for a friend, a poet and spiritual seeker, that clearly demonstrated typical causes of loneliness, as well as the purpose and value of the experience. In this lifetime the individual has fought against drug and alcohol addiction, chronic and painful illness and continual failure in love relationships. Finally he turned to spiritual illumination to find his solution.

As Bud moved me into deep hypnosis, I began to report on this man's past:

LaVedi: I see an old man, he is tall, he stands straight, very gray, almost rags. He carries a staff.

Bud: Is this in the East?

LaVedi: Pilgrim. This man—he wandered, searching. There was a hardiness about him, a determination, a longing for satisfaction. He was perhaps in his 60s. At that time (he) satisfied his quest; and now, he is to find out why he was sent into isolation. This is the time the spiritual will exalt for this entity.

He was sent out alone, to search and not to find, a bitter experience. Aloneness. Lost. He built up a great longing.

Bud: These were from previous lives, or one and the same life?

LaVedi: Previous.

Bud: Does there seem to be a variety of causes?

LaVedi: . . . yes . . . , at one point strongly involved in sacrificial rites, another time I am picking up in Egypt . . . .

Self-gratification, indulgence. They were very ugly times, the priesthood was really bad, very complex situation between soul knowledge, death and soul knowledge, the physical being was of the lower vibrations. Ugly times, hard to recover from them.

Again, part of the struggle . . . taking on Western body, with its lower vibration in this cycle.

I see the pattern, a return to the East, to the source of enlightenment prior to the Western body. Now, blending with the vibrations, attunement . . . now possible.

Bud: Is the older man with the staff . . . ?

LaVedi: The result of previous abuse of money and abuse of others. There were many abused during those dark days. It is not necessary to dwell upon what was done. There was violence, death, abuse.

Loneliness has been the process of payment up to this time.

Bud: Should the entity consciously forgive himself for this?

LaVedi: Very important to understand; dwell upon his growth and present activity; in future work.

Bud: Is there a connection to this time period of the entity's present kaleidoscope?

LaVedi: A break in the auric sheath . . . there have been a lot of knives involved, both when he used them and he died by one . . . .

Bud: Is this particular pain a carryover from a previous . . . , a stab wound? Did he die from it?

LaVedi: Yes . . . connection with a previous killing by a knife . . . karmic carryover . . . lack of acceptance of the death, bitterness that his life was cut off at its peak . . . .

Bud: Was this a slow death that carried strong emotion with it?

LaVedi: Not so much a slow death, but the result of the emotional personality, a painful death; small bowel's involved.

He is (now) letting go of the desire. This is being done and forgiving the entity who killed him, and, of course, forgiving himself for having previously done the same to others (killed them), which is what he thought about at the time of that death.

A culmination of forgiving himself . . . he must forgive himself for that situation at his death, the desires, the other lives involved. All this in the West.

Loneliness plays a vital part in the tempering of the soul. The path is not easy. We do not come into incarnation to enjoy it, but to benefit from it and evolve. If all is easy or positive, less gain is made. Pressure must be present to motivate change, development and advancement. As Virgil, the Roman poet laureate, wrote in *The Aeneid*:

> And some are hung to bleach upon the wind
> Some plunged in waters, other purged in fires,
> Til all the dregs are drained, and all the rust expires.

FROM EAST TO WEST

Many individuals have found the transition from Eastern incarnation to Western difficult, as the Eastern bodies are of a more subtle vibration and finer attunement. Western bodies are denser in vibration and less sensitive generally. With the fall of Egypt, scores of entities who had risen to enlightenment in the East, fell to the tempting cycle of the re-emerging dark priesthood (the Sons of Darkness reborn). The situation was like the one that caused much of the Atlantean population to succumb.

Our friend was no exception; continuing the *reading*, we found:

LaVedi: I see a series of lives and deaths . . . .

Bud: These lives, that are part of his evolution in consciousness, made the fall in the Roman and Egyptian era that much more serious; is that correct?

LaVedi: Yes. It is like octaves. And then taking on the channel of another octave (Western incarnation), and not being able to make it on the first go-round; deciding to do a slower one . . . (he) must accept that which occurs on the evolutionary arc . . . , a part of the process.

I feel there is something we need to get from the East . . . through the Buddhic life . . . I see an old man, who was One with the Light, until the end. He attained a high state of Being, environment of a temple. In the vicinity a very large statue of Buddha . . . .

Bud: Does this account for the entity's strong desire to seek enlightenment once again? The memory?

LaVedi: Of course. He has to answer the soul on its long journey back. It is a route of relearning that he will take. Of course, he must refine the liberation of his body. Desires (emotions) are much stronger than in most bodies, and are, therefore, more highly charged.

Once conquered, of course, again by still higher seeking of
enlightenment, he must find a greater control of self, of mind
in matter. There is now an attachment to the Buddha . . . .

In his present lifetime this individual turned a few
years ago to Eastern teachings, where he found *Self.* His
problems may not be ended, but now he radiates love and
understanding and has become alive with *light.* The long,
"dark night of the soul" has been conquered and he is
steadily progressing back "up the mountain," reassimilat-
ing all that he has been and known before. He is sharing
himself now "like a flame spreading the eternal Fire."
He is no longer lonely, for once the reasons for his seeming exile from human relationships were understood and
accepted, love entered his life.

GUIDED BY DESPAIR

In life, if we are satisfied and comfortable, we have
very little motivation or incentive to seek change. Unfortunately, we still are prompted to self-improvement primarily by pain. To escape it we seek answers. In another
life *reading* Bud and I did for a talented male singer, we
came across a situation where loneliness and despair had
also been used in the past to prod the entity into seeking
enlightenment.

Bud: Let's seek out a life relevant to his spiritual growth at
this time. A life that will help his spiritual position.

LaVedi: . . . in India. I find him first a child. Extremely poor,
in the area that is swept by monsoons. He has a teacher, an
older man, who is keeping tabs on him. As a child he was left

at home, and the older man would visit occasionally to see
how he was progressing.

Bud: Was the old man a father or a spiritual leader?

LaVedi: A teacher. And, finally, as he grew a little older, he
began going with the old man, and he would beg for him.
They would sit for long hours, sometimes talking, also sitting
in silence. He (the old man) stayed with him until he was 27.

And then, the old man left. Just left. One day he was gone.
And then the search really began, for now there was no one
to answer the questions which occupied him. (He) suddenly
found himself without a master, and he felt lost.

Many feelings at that time. A mixture of confusion, questioning. He didn't know where to turn; finally (he) understood and
went within.

There is, again, a valid need to repeat the same experience. But,
it was a profound experience—the interior life—very little of it
was outward, a life devoted to the inner search.

And the attunement that was gained from that experience is
available; and this is what is sensed; and there is a desire to
regain the states of consciousness learned at that time. They
are within touch, and the attunement of consciousness that
was learned is certainly present in this lifetime.

The problem now is applying that to the present times . . . (to)
reconcile modern consciousness with the higher states of consciousness available.

In great contrast, we found this same entity later
leading an opulent life in France, a life that revealed a

strong sense of emptiness that has carried into the present. This dissatisfaction has caused him to question his pursuit of a musical career, and to try to reconcile music with spiritual purpose and growth. Returning to the *reading:*

> LaVedi: . . . a life in France, Marquis duBonnet. There is a connection with this experience in his present hesitation about the career in singing . . . , this was a life of wealth, of frivolousness, for show, for display. A life, however, not without value, because there was a certain appreciation gained of quality and development of self, of pride; an egoic development that was not native.
>
> I don't see that abuse was made of the life. It was enjoyed. But in many eyes it would not have been a particularly valuable experience, but yet it was . . . , he gained, but there was a carryover, a fear of repeating it, a residue . . .
>
> Bud: Did the entity have musical talents as the Marquis?
>
> LaVedi: He is a patron of the arts, . . . he wore long curled hair, carried a walking stick, somewhat heavy, in his early years he traveled quite a bit on the continent . . . .
>
> Bud: Was there a particular time period? Is that visible?
>
> LaVedi: The time of Antoinette.
>
> Bud: Tell us about the concern of this life in the present . . . .
>
> LaVedi: . . . the fear of emptiness that he has responded to . . . I don't find a wife. I think he had not been married and had no family. . . . He left his property to maintain and sustain a

school connected with the students, or entities, he was patronizing. He will "remember" himself on the banks of the Rhine.

The reconciliation of these widely different, yet lonely lives, will not be easy. The one in India was austere, in great contrast to the artistic dilettante in France, but both are equally valuable. The first connected him with his Higher-Self, the second grounded him in creative earthly expression, while both have acted as prods to create desires that are manifesting now, through his combined musical and spiritual interests. There is hardly a better way to express spiritual joy than through beautiful inspiring music.

Most great artistic works have resulted from either great emotional joy or deep pain. To know joy we must experience pain. To fly to the heights of ecstasy, we must grovel in the depths of Hades. To truly appreciate love we must bleed for it; then we will never take it for granted again. To find ultimate release from the pain of loneliness all recourses may be closed, to force us to go within; to seek our *Logoic Center.* Then we find eternal love, God and Oneness, in communion with our *Source* of creativity. The main shortcut to God for humanity is usually through pain.

Some try to escape by taking the selfish route, by trying to bury their sensibilities in material wealth, thrills, sensations or excesses. In this manner they may dull the emotions, but the effort will ultimately fail. This type of escapism only aggravates festering emotional wounds. It is far better to treat a wound before it turns to gangrene. The tragic life of billionaire Howard Hughes may be a classic case of the life energies destroying self through fear, greed and selfishness. The answer to personal satisfaction does not lie in materialism or emotionalism.

UNION IS WITHIN

The most frequent question asked any clairvoyant counselor is, "Am I going to marry?" Then follows, "Who, when and where?" Marriage is often a stacked deck for those most concerned about it, if they marry at all. They may be so disturbed about it, that they fail to give life a chance to flow. If you have love within yourself, then love will manifest in your life, too. The condition of your love life, and your attitude about it, reflects your own inner condition. "Seek ye first the kingdom . . . ."

Bud and I did a past-life *reading* for a woman who was very concerned about remarrying. Though she had several children and a busy life, all she seemed able to think of was remarriage. The *reading* went as follows:

Bud: At this time we are seeking to understand previous lives of _____ , relevant to the present situation.

LaVedi: At the moment I am seeing a life in medieval times. Pressures of life as a woman; and women have no rights. They are no more than chattels. This wasn't a poor life, and she was attractive; made her aware—acutely aware—of herself, as a woman.

In this life, she is working out, breaking away from, patterns of dependency, as well as, the feeling generated from those times, (and) through other lives, typically feminine ones, some that you would call "catty," (with) intrigue strong, but misdirected frequently.

The relationship to life seems to get confused in the feminine role. This goes back; definitely difficulty in relating to the feminine role, not in playing the role, but in relating to it positively.

. . . she found herself in the suppression situation, where it was necessary to use guile, or feminine charms, the mind, the emotions, to accomplish her ends, which was a naturally understandable thing at the time . . . , but this had an effect on the emotional body, that she has been working out in this lifetime, where we are gaining freedom in the feminine role.

So, it is the release of that karmic pressure (that) is (making it) possible to relate to the feminine role in a healthy way, to find it as a positive expression, to find it as a receptive vessel for insight into the spiritual Self.

She is growing in this manner in a very healthy way, approaching awareness as a potential with herself.

This woman was, in addition to the problem of loneliness, working out physical karma through illness and pain. The situation was summed up briefly in the *reading*:

Bud: In reference to the injury, the fall, related to the back problem, is there a karmic explanation for the fall?

LaVedi: To learn not to depend on the physical body . . . to understand that Self is not the body; to reawaken this awareness; Self is not the body, or its personality; (to) find out who she really is.

This was not a harsh indictment of the individual, for

we found she was a highly evolved entity and under pressure for good reason:

> LaVedi: This entity entered the earth plane in the ages of mountains we know as the Himalayas. At that time was a teacher. Apparently came from another dimension. Seems to be a direct translation from the subtle body to the physical body. And from this point entered into incarnation cycle. At that time, at that period of entry, it would not have been necessary, however, the choice was made to undertake this experience.

> Bud: What was the purpose of the entity entering into incarnation?

> LaVedi: At first the transmittal of knowledge, ensuing came the decision to stay and partake of this experience.

> Bud: From the subtle body. Is that the astral plane?

> LaVedi: Came through the astral plane. No, it is not the astral plane.

> Bud: Was the origin from a different galaxy, or system?

> LaVedi: . . . she evolved through a cycle of Venus. Part of her present problem involves the awakening of the Venus awareness.

> Bud: Was that particular cycle in Venus a similar karmic cycle to physical incarnation, as refers to the present?

> LaVedi: Physical pattern.

Bud: Is this what is referred to as the subtle body?

LaVedi: That is correct.

Bud: Can that be described in physical terms? Or, more in etheric . . . , the subtle body?

LaVedi: It is a different vibrational rate, therefore less dense.

Bud: In the 20th Century, are there subtle body incarnations on the planet Venus at this time?

LaVedi: Yes.

Bud: In what manner, then, may the entity relearn this awareness of her Venus source?

LaVedi: Through meditation . . . . When the decision is made of dedication, when the will is released and the desire is released, then this will be possible. The energies being received by the entity here, are more, at the time, than the body can tolerate, due to blockages. This will take time to clear, meditation will help . . . it is necessary to go through this period of the clearing of the bodies to restore the ability to receive the pure energies of Self. With this purification can come in with Self, it is this Union that is sought.

In this *reading* we see the combined factors of an entity who began life as a non-human, evolving through the *Venus cycle* in a subtle body less dense than ours. As an evolved entity she came to earth to help and then decided to stay for the physical experience. Caught now, in the emotions of earth life, she needs to recontact her higher nature by quieting the earthly consciousness through meditation. She is being forced to seek Self by her loneliness, forced back upon her own inner resources to reach an inner attunement.

The urge for love is the urge for *Oneness,* for re-mergence with friends left behind upon other dimensions, for *Union* with *Self* and God. We are all lonely for the reality we left to enter the state of separatism caused by physical incarnation.

Loneliness can be a spur to developing healthy independent thought and *individuation.* We must learn to stand independently upon our own two feet to accomplish our evolutionary purpose. Only then can we free ourselves for re-mergence with the *Whole.* As long as we insist upon leaning on others, we are not accomplishing full growth. There is a very real difference between depending upon others and sharing with others. Seek cooperative sharing and conscious awareness of your motives. Search your heart for your motivations and examine them continuously with ruthless honesty. Do this and you may discover a beautiful rose growing from a thorny crown of earthly lives, filling your life with loving warmth and the "bliss that surpasses understanding."

MUSICAL CHAIRS

10

Musical Chairs

Cut! Stop the music!
Very nice everyone. Now, switch partners.
Wait a minute, wait a minute.
I'm still working on my solo!
Your solo was fine, just fine.
A little more emphasis on planetary harmonics
in this next scene please.
Excuse me, again. But, maybe I could use
a little more despair?
Listen, your solo was very good, but in
this next scene we are pirouetting with
partners.
Twelve cosmic rays get ready!
But . . . ,
More light in that far galaxy please.
But . . . ,
QUIET IN THE COSMOS!
But . . . ,
Action!
(Rats!)

CHANGE IS GROWTH

"Change is the only certainty there is," but we spend enormous effort trying to arrange our lives just the way we think we want them. If we succeed in arranging our material life, we frequently find we are bored or dissatisfied. Or else disaster strikes: fire, flood, illness, divorce, death or some other transforming change. With life so unpredictable and unstable, we need to seek indestructible goals of permanent value, that will last life after life. We need to know how to turn apparent misfortunes or difficulties to our advantage.

Think of life as a continuing educational process and Earth as a school where we share many lessons with friends, family and classmates. Finish one assignment and you will receive another, possibly with a short recess in between. If you have earned it, you may even get a vacation, a pleasant life of "reward." The turmoils of living are your real lessons that vary with each student. But, as in our educational system, tests, grades and levels of advancement exist.

Our lives fall into a number of cycles, with greater ones affecting groups and the planet, while smaller ones, such as personal astrological cycles, affect us more directly. Through awareness of these we can anticipate when we will reach periodic crises that may motivate change. At such times, we may find ourselves forced out of old habit patterns and into making radical changes in relationships, career, home or philosophy. An excellent book on human cycles is *Passages* by Gail Sheehy. The crisis periods this writer describes so accurately for different age groups are the same ones the humanistic astrologer expects, as planetary relationships cyclically trigger critical periods in each individual life.

LIVING WITH THE PLANETS

We saw earlier how the planets had magnetic and electrical fields, galvanic stresses, and other manifestations of cosmic forces built into them, along with a collective consciousness for each planet. As we evolved through our Seed-atom exposure to these planets at different stages and to their fields of consciousness, we incorporated these influences into our interpenetrating *light bodies,* or *aura.*

Each of us has built-in electro-magnetic energies that resonate to the planets and other influences as they continually change positions and relationships. It is easiest to compare ourselves with radios, continually receiving broadcasts from the planets, while they in turn are influenced by the constellation energies. Remember that *space* is not "empty," but filled with an interpenetrating network of *Light* and creative potential in the constantly appearing and vanishing "virtual particles" that fill it.

We are continually receiving "music" from the planets, our *Star,* and Earth herself. The type of music and its qualities will depend upon interactive factors affecting each planet as it moves throughout the heavens and how this in turn relates to your natal astrological influences, as well as your soul's composition.

When you were born in this life, you were *physically* "tuned" for life—your first breath charged your body with all of the broadcasts of that instant: electrical, magnetic,

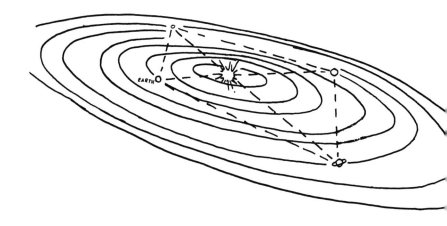

"Living With the Planets"

Periodically various planets form *square* or ninty-degree angles
to each other. When Saturn forms this aspect with the position
Saturn held at the time of your birth, or when it is opposite
that position or conjunct it, major changes normally occur,
corresponding to major life cycles.

vibratory, etc. This has made you receptive to some "stations," and more or less indifferent to others, all dependent upon your particular "programming."

We should realize that our response to specific planets is not just personal. A planetary interaction, or reception, is first established between Earth and its surrounding energy field with the sun and other planets. As Earth receives these influences, they then affect our particular local energies and finally we feel them personally. Astrology is far from the simple study it is often thought to be. Many factors are rarely or never calculated and seldom synthesized. One procedure that considers the global relationship of a person's birth is Astro*Carto*Graphy, providing an analysis that is worthwhile to understand the interaction between locale and the individual.* Based upon the rapidly changing relationships of location with the sun and planets due to the earth's rotation "relative to the local horizon," it is accurate and revealing.

The planets periodically form angular relationships that stimulate important changes in our lives. For example, major cycles are signified by Saturn. This planet returns from its journey around the sun to the position it occupied at your birth approximately every 28 to 30 years, and tends to form difficult (testing) angles every seven years. You will note that every seven years we tend to go through significant changes. These are especially obvious as children. Around age seven we start our schooling, at about fourteen we enter puberty and at twenty-one we "come of

---

* Astro*Carto*Graphy ®, P.O. Box 22293, San Francisco, CA 94122.

age." Then, between twenty-eight and our early thirties, we hit a make-or-break period, when we seriously decide what we want from life and change accordingly.

And so it goes, with each quarterly division of the Saturn cycle holding its own significance, and often inducing radical upheaval in our lives. It is not wise to resist a Saturn cycle by trying to hold on to things the way they were. Saturn induced changes are inevitable and are related to your karmic lessons, so try to accept them when they come, not fight them. If you seem to successfully resist initial changes in your life from a Saturn cycle, you may only be building yourself up for a real disaster when the next cycle rolls around.

The Saturn cycle is a major one, but there are many others that affect us regularly. A more technical example of planetary aspects in relation to birth charts appears using statistical techniques. "Wave analysis" is especially interesting in that it breaks data down into component *harmonics.* This technique is used to study natural cycles and phenomena related to both planetary and celestial cycles. Using wave analysis, a researcher, John Addey, studied "applying" and "separating" aspects. Applying means an angular relationship that is forming between two planets, for example Saturn and your Sun. Separating means they are still within a few degrees of each other, but pulling apart. An applying aspect, in either a natal chart, or as planets transit the heavens, traditionally causes increasing tension, whereas separating planets bring release and relaxation. The effects of any transit are strongest as the planets come within two degrees or less of each other.

The importance of Addey's study using angular relationships was to demonstrate that astrological principles are sound, including the aspects, houses, degree significance and planetary relationships. He did an initial study showing a significant number of separating aspects among 970 persons between 90 and 100 years old (indicative of relaxed attitudes). Then he followed this with a study of applying aspects among polio victims, who are recognized as having a personality type that is bright, nervous and active. The polio victims, as suspected, showed a preponderance of applying aspects. The significance of this was not astrological signs, but the pattern of recurrence and a *wave form* that corresponded to a *harmonic*. He found polio victims "tended to be born according to the twelfth harmonic, and, most strongly of all, according to the 120th harmonic." In other words, "a child born every third degree (irrespective of the zodiacal division) is 37 percent more liable to contract polio than a child born in the two intermediary degrees."

A similar result was found studying the results of a survey done by Donald Bradley, an astrologer and statistician. He collected the birth data of 2,593 clergymen looking for astrological correlations. He found peaks and troughs occurring in accordance with Sidereal Zodiac, but more importantly another harmonic appeared, indicating clergymen are more likely to be born on days corresponding to the 7th harmonic. Addey's work had shown that the principles of astrology can be demonstrated statistically. If this approach were taken extensively, surprisingly useful data would no doubt emerge. For the moment, it is one more way to demonstrate the validity of the "music of the spheres."

Another researcher, who set out to disprove astrological influences is Michel Gauquelin, a graduate of the Sorbonne in statistics. Compiling a test group of 576 professors of medicine, he attempted to disprove an earlier study indicating planetary aspects (angles) to the ascending and descending signs relating to career. Instead he found the charts of the professors to have strong Mars and Saturn aspects. Compiling another group of 508 eminent doctors, he found a similar result. "The odds worked out to 10,000,000:1 against this being the outcome of chance."* To deny such influences is unreasonable, while to utilize them wisely is very helpful.

Saturn is generally considered a key indicator of karma in any chart because it rules discipline and forces change. Actually karma when examined totally appears throughout the chart. However, if you are interested in a quick glimpse at a summary of your karma, look at the positions of the North and South Nodes of the Moon at the time of your birth. The South Node acts in a manner similar to Saturn, while the North Node resembles Jupiter. Martin Schulman's book *Karmic Astrology*† covers the major influences of these positions. In his words, "At one level these Nodes reveal the track that your soul is running in the current life, while the rest of the horoscope adds additional informa-

---

* *The Case for Astrology*, John Anthony West and Jan Gerhard Toonder, Coward-McCann, 1970.
† *Karmic Astrology*, Martin Schulman, Samuel Weiser, 1977, (1975).

tion as to how you are to make the journey."

Most important to look for, or seek through a professional analysis, is when you will be affected by major cycles, with consideration of how these have manifested earlier in your life. You can expect some repetition, with variation related to maturity. Competent astrological studies are an important first step to self-understanding and the understanding of others. Never make the mistake of thinking you are "beyond astrology." That is ridiculous. The question is *how* it is affecting you, not *if* it is. I should emphasize, however, that I do not mean fortune-tellers and soothsayers. Excellent psychologically oriented *humanistic* astrologers are available in most cities. If you do not know a local professional astrologer to consult, you can obtain competent assistance by mail, such as through Llewellyn's services.* Sometimes friendly amateurs can be excellent, if sincere, simply because they can spend more time with you, but they will lack the practiced "eye." Astrology is still a more or less unregulated service. Membership in the American Federation of Astrologers assures a degree of technical competency and requires an oath of ethics, but has no influence upon how the person applies his knowledge.

The best way to find a reliable astrologer in your area is to contact local or regional astrological associations and ask for the names and addresses of professional *humanistic* astrologers. Better yet, find one who is also a practicing

---

* Llewellyn Personal Services, P.O. Box 43383-ED, St. Paul, MN 55164-0383.

psychological counselor or specializes in karmic astrology. The general public does not yet realize that astrology, as most other fields today, has specialties. An astrologer who is also a psychological counselor should exercise a high degree of professionalism. Finding a karmic astrologer may be trickier, as he must have a good respect for the positive, as well as the negative aspects of karma. You want a total picture.

Knowing how cycles affect you, puts you one up on the game, again like school, when you know a test is coming, you get ready. Preparation pays off. But if you have been playing hooky, resisting life's pushes and nudges trying to guide you, or have flatly refused to cooperate and do your homework, you may find your walls tumbling down around you. If you refuse to respond to a tap on the shoulder, you may be hit by a cannon blast, so you have no choice but to take notice. By then you may be in the midst of a full-blown crisis. You cannot run away from your lessons. Eventually you will be caught when the energies you have created catch up with you.

You cannot escape your work, your karma, or your life's lessons. If you accept them willingly, life will flow harmoniously. If you shirk them, complain and try to force changes to suit self, then expect trouble. What happens when you skip lessons or tests? Progress doesn't stop and wait for you. No, school continues and the tests become harder. Can't pass them? Then you flunk, don't you? You are held back a grade, while all of your friends are moving on to graduation.

If you have a problem, take advantage of the many

human services around today. Numerous alternatives exist and there are people who really care about others always available. Counseling services have greatly expanded. Along with astrology, many professional counselors and doctors are using reincarnation and past life recall today.* We generally recommend that traditional means be sought first for serious problems to avoid using the past as an excuse. You are here to work out past lives *through the present.* Solutions should first be sought in the present to clear this life of recent complications. A beneficial series of steps exists that is important to personal development and self-responsibility.

A sincere *wholistic* approach will take advantage of all appropriate services to expedite personal growth and development. Set as your primary goal: *self-understanding.* The instruction to first "Know Thyself" was given to us by Hermes Trismegistus and reiterated by Socrates, and should be heeded. Then seek to understand *any* situation in which you find yourself. Don't fight against it. Look at it. What is it trying to tell you? You wouldn't be in it, unless you have something to learn from it, so quit struggling and look for the lesson. Don't try to rationalize yourself out of it, consider it an exception, or try to blame anyone else. Once you settle down and figure out how you relate to any given problem, you will be able to free yourself from it permanently. If you don't do this, it will return in a variety of ways.

---

* To locate a professional therapist we suggest inquiry at local bookstores, local related associations or writing to the Association for Past-Life Research and Therapy, P.O. Box 20151, Riverside, CA 92151.

TAKE COURAGE

In family or marital situations, alcoholism and drug addiction are two of the most difficult problems to deal with for all concerned. Basically addiction is an attempt to escape karmic pressure, an inability to forgive self and others, and a refusal to accept self-responsibility. While the addict must make a first step to self-help, if the loved ones understand the karmic involvement, they may be in a position to be more patient, supportive and influential. *Readings* can help to gain conscious understanding of subconscious motivations.

Bud and I did a *reading* for a lady who was divorced and remarried, but was still torn over her feelings about her first husband. She had divorced him because of his alcoholism, but was still concerned about him and thought she might be able to help, if she understood the karmic situation. We found they had been soul-mates for many lifetimes, but he was carrying a burden of guilt from the past and was unwilling to accept self-responsibility. The *reading* explained:

> LaVedi: I find again, also a complex of guilts built-up on ———— (his) part from old memories of a time when he was highly intolerant of other people and races. There is also a descent for him from Lemuria . . . . I find a life, it appears in South America, where he was involved in old sacrificial rites of . . . a black people, who were apparently descendents from Lemuria . . . . They were not typical rites; they were so old they were performed with a spear, not a knife . . . .
>
> Some of these concepts carried through to him into another time . . . the feeling that was generated there has carried forth

into one of guilt; and into a reversal of this, as idealism. realizing that injustice is a natural issuance of karmic cause and effect. And also, using that as an excuse. This is a very fundamental relationship to the alcohol problem. There is a need to gain perspective in relationship to this.

(He) has telepathic capacities he has not utilized. He has closed these with negativity; he has responded to them in a negative way. The idealism is correct as far as it goes, but his relating to it and manifesting it is in error. He has not understood the communications he receives . . . which, then, must of course, be translated into conscious thought.

If he will be aware that he has this assistance . . . always with him and available; he is not alone, as he so often feels, then the purpose of his life will begin to unfold. He will no longer need the crutch of escapism.

His understanding will grow; his comprehension will grow; he will open his mind to the positive manifestation of these ideals that he feels. However, because he has not been able to manifest them, because he feels the world cannot manifest them, he then has buried himself in guilt, a sense of incompetency, of both of these sides of his nature. This is partly what has confused _____ . She has seen the brighter side, and she has seen the negative manifestation, drawn by one and driven away by the other.

Bud: Should he make conscious effort to regain the telepathic power?

LaVedi: He should be aware of a quiet space within himself. He should learn to enter into this quiet space, within himself, without judgment, without expectation. If he will do this, without trying to assess, evaluate; then he will begin to establish a rapport with those who are with him always.

. . . It is a beautiful relationship that he has (telepathically). It comes from a distant world, which he has known. He remembers the ideals that were all possible. He has not related, as well as he could, to earth life. He needs to understand that earth life is different, unusual, and an opportunity in itself. That his negative thought only manifests negativity around him. That he is very decidedly creating his world and building the world of all humankind at the same time.

He should not be feeding negative thoughts into the earth sphere, about himself or anyone else. He should seek to understand the karmic balance. He should seek to understand the evolution of the earth and his place upon it. And learn the responsibility we all carry in the earth's evolution.

Bud: Is there any other advice at this time?

LaVedi: Only again: he should seek the spot within, and view it like a well, which will gather in knowledge and understanding slowly. As often as he will enter into it, just like turning on a faucet, gradually the water will build of understanding and awareness, until it overflows in his life. He should not rush this, but he should know that it is possible, and this is destined.

Here we have another non-earthling and a highly evolved soul suffering through his "dark night." He is not really alone, even though he feels so. There is no escaping the lessons, the music we have created or the tests. Only after we take our courage in hand and meet life's challenges head on, can we manifest our dreams and ideals. We have to earn them in many ways.

OLD SCORES

When we marry, we normally choose soul-mates, especially those we have established karma with over long periods of time. As a result marriage is rarely a "bed of roses." The idealistic view of marriages *made in Heaven,* where two really become one, refers to twin-souls returning to each other. In reality this seldom happens, unless they are particularly fortunate karmically or have special work to do together. Marriage then, is a ceremonial rite celebrating this potential and should be understood as preparation for the "real thing."

Why do we "fall" in love? The terminology is interesting, since the emotional rush or attraction has a lot to do with a flood of hormonal reaction to stimulation. But emotional-biological love is of relatively short duration, while the deeper long-lasting love doesn't wear out. Today we often confuse the former with the latter, hence a high divorce rate. If we had a better understanding of karmic relationships, we might not be in such a hurry to take vows.

Upon meeting an old soul-mate, we feel initial pleasure, resulting from the store of shared unconscious memories. But after this reaction cools off, the not so pleasant interactive patterns may begin to surface. Astrological composition and past-life memories mix to create "programming." We tend to respond to individuals who have astrological charts that harmonize with ours. In marriage relationships Saturn's influence usually manifests strongly, indicating degrees of permanence and possible difficulties to be resolved. Marriage should be taken much less romantically and much more seriously. A common situation is to think we are "in love" with a former foe or an individual we have wronged in a past life. The line between the powerful emotions of love and hate can be very confusing.

On the other hand, most encounters are not by chance. We are attracted to our soul-mates and those we need to work out karma with much like a magnet attracts iron filings. Distance is no factor; people find each other regardless of country, city or circumstance. Most of this occurs unconsciously, even when we think we are going somewhere or doing something that is in reality only a cover. We are often guided this way, "set-up," if you will, by our own karma.

> As when with downcast eyes we muse and brood
> And ebb into a former life,
> We say all this has been before,
> All this hath been, I know not when or where.
> Alfred Lord Tennyson, a poet-laureate of Great Britain.

An encounter I had with an ex-husband from a previous life illustrates the power of attraction over distance and despite former unhappiness. When I first went to London, in 1969, I met an American actor there. We saw each other every day and felt a strong mutual attraction. Hovering on the edge of a serious romance, we even debated about returning to his home city of San Francisco and the stage.

This man had been my husband, George Costairs, in London, during the late 1800s. We had both been on the stage together then, though we didn't consciously realize this at the time we met again in London. In that earlier life in Victorian London, as Julianne, I took advantage of his love for our children to influence him, unable to bring to my consciousness the deeper potential of spiritual love. It was a short and sorrowful life.

During our "reunion" in England, the former children were also present, again as English brother and sister. My ex-husband was now romantically involved with one of our former children, and despite basic incompatibility and age difference, he felt the urge to protect her. I felt close to the brother, as there seemed to be an intangible understanding between us of the situation. Meanwhile, between "George" and me was what felt like an insurmountable wall of energy that both attracted and repelled. So we parted, no doubt fortunately for all concerned. Otherwise, ignorant of our karmic relationship, we would probably have repeated a performance of the former tragedy we so strongly intuited.

William Ernest Henley (1849-1903), a British poet, editor and playwright, poignantly describes such *karma* in his poem dedicated simply "To W.A."

> Or ever the knightly years were gone
> With the old world to the grave,
> I was a King in Babylon
> And you were a Christian Slave.
> I saw, I took, I cast you by,
> I bent and broke your pride . . . .
> And myriad suns have set and shone
> Since then upon the grave

Decreed by the King in Babylon
To her that had been his Slave.
The pride I trampled is now my scathe,
For it tramples me again,
The old resentment lasts like death,
For you love, yet you refrain.
I break my heart on your hard unfaith,
And I break my heart in vain.

MIRROR, MIRROR ON THE WALL

A couple who are attracted by negative karma may well wind up in a divorce court, but first they should try to solve their inner problems involved. We are not attracted to each other by accident, we need to understand our karmic relationships and resolve them. This holds true for any life encounter.

All of life is a reflection of ourselves. What we see wrong in others, is a reflection of a problem within us. All too often, instead of facing such a problem, we try to run away, get a divorce, quit our job, or move. What we should do is seek help, get counseling, if necessary, and try to work out the karmic tangle. It isn't unusual for individuals to subconsciously seek self-punishment for old wrongs done to others centuries before. The result may be a guilt complex and reactions that unnecessarily bring suffering to all involved.

If you sincerely try, and a close relationship continues to fail, there is still time to end it, but hopefully with greater mutual and individual understanding. Part friends, if you possibly can, attempting to absolve your old debts to each other. There is no reason, karmically, to stay together in unhappiness; this is only likely to generate more negative feelings and future karma. Divorce or separation in this kind of situation is not failure. The important part is to try first by all possible means and with sincere effort, to genuinely understand and forgive each other.

But what if it's a one-way street? Perhaps, a marriage partner refuses to cooperate. Then seek help yourself and seek your own understanding. Never try to force someone else to do anything. *Assume self-responsibility.* Do try to communicate your feelings and thoughts. If you do—and if you do it lovingly—you can absolve yourself of any karma involved. If you aren't sincere—if you are angry, unforgiving or carry any other emotional baggage with you—you will continue the karmic connection. If you make a clean break, and know in your own heart that you did the best you could, then—*be free.* Your ex-mate will continue attracting whatever karmic situations are necessary for growth. It is no longer your karma or responsibility, if you can leave with a clear conscience. If you still feel residue from an experience, then use prayer, positive thought and objective evaluation to clear it up. Take as much time as is necessary to wipe the slate clean of karmic inscriptions. No limits exist to prevent you from prayerfully clearing old situations. Karmically we must *never* judge another's actions. It is impossible to pass judgment, because superficial appearances do not represent true facts.

Bud and I did a life *reading* for another woman in Alaska who was about to get a divorce. At the same time she was attracted to a second man. She wanted to know the karmic relationship between herself and both men in her life. This is a delicate type of situation, and typical of one that cannot be pre-judged. We found:

> Bud: Is there a karmic connection between _____ (wife) and _____ (husband)?

> LaVedi: He is one of many along the way; she rejected him at a previous time, not kindly done. You (wife) were in a position of authority at that time, and used his affection toward you, manipulating him to your own ends. There is ability yet to manipulate people. Beware that it is not done under the guise of good intentions.

> Bud: Is that the karmic lesson between _____ (them)?

> LaVedi: These tendencies still exist, yes, and it is something she should not do. It would be well to settle this account and cut the tie, preferably under terms of good will, if possible. If not possible, she needs to, at least mentally . . . send goodwill to him, and expect positive response from him, to release both of them, at least herself from this link.

> In this there is still the memory of the power she held in that life, as a woman; there is still the desire for it, like two threads running parallel—the memory of position, and the memory of obligation, created by not meeting obligation.

> There is a need to . . . not try to exercise power over people, to not feel superior to any other living entity, to become aware that she is part of the one whole and only a fraction of that whole. This is where true strength lies, not within one entity becoming a . . . possessing power (over another).

> Bud: We are searching for the karmic connection between _____ (wife) and _____ (the friend).

LaVedi: One who has been with her repeatedly, who has come in parallel to you (wife) to assist you. He has tried before and was unable to reach you. There is a dedication here. He is indebted to you from long ago, in more positive times, before you lost your direction.

You taught him in the ways you then understood of the truths, and set him upon what is called the Spiritual Path. And in turn he has chosen this way to repay you and assist you. If you seek it, you will remember the knowledge you held . . . .

She was in a dilemma requiring careful handling; you cannot hurt another for self-gain, without falling back into *karma*. The only solution to such a situation is sincere honesty and a real attempt to establish understanding with a potentially "injured party." If this is rejected, at least you tried. You must be vigilant and continually be aware of your actions and innermost motivations.

DECLARATION OF INDEPENDENCE

Change frequently comes to us through divorce and remarriage, especially today, with the divorce rate increasing nearly as fast as the marriage rate. Due to the expensive legal complications and rapid change of partners, many people no longer bother with marriage formalities. What is our karmic responsibility in intimate relationships, legal and otherwise?

First, we need to understand the principle behind union of male and female. It goes back to the basic cosmic polarity of the creative force flows. The male energy is symbolically, and for the most part literally, positive and active. The female energy is considered negative and passive.

Neither is greater or lesser. The two energies are equally
essential aspects of *One*. Positive and negative energies
are not, however, conveniently confined to just male or
female bodies. An independent, aggressive woman is
expressing positive energy, while a meek, unassuming man
is expressing negative energy, with a multitude of variations
in between.

In the past men and women have generally been expected to live according to their alloted sexual role, natural
or not. Today, no such sharp line divides masculine and
feminine, as the two energies begin to achieve degrees of
balance in both men and women. This is very important in
our evolution, for it means that *individuals* are growing in
wholeness, with less dependence upon a sexual partner to
supply the opposite polarity. Instead, balanced polarity is
becoming incorporated into each of us, individually.

This is evolutionary growth manifesting, wiping out
the illusions of difference and separation caused by physical incarnation. As these polarities gain in balance, women
become more spontaneous and independent, while men
grow gentler, more considerate and less concerned about
the egoic image of masculinity.

We tend to forget, in these modern times, that for
lengthy periods of our earth's history marriage has been
synonymous with men possessing women. Women were
little more than slaves. This situation has continued to
modern times, with women still fighting for equal and legal
rights. Equality is very important, not just for obvious reasons, but for the balance it will establish on our planet.
Suppression breeds suppression—that means karma. Men

who take advantage of women today will pay tomorrow (probably in female bodies), and so on, back and forth. The time has come to straighten out our polarity relationships. This correction is essential to full development of humanity's creative consciousness.

The stereotyped roles of housewife and breadwinner are being upstaged by flowing energies seeking balance and expression. Our evolutionary growth is reflected by the desire to manage our own lives as we individually *feel* is right, not as others have *told* us is right. This is the Aquarian energy manifesting, creating healthy new attitudes and independent thought, with equality for all.

Returning for a moment to our school analogy, as long as you are in the lower grades, you have to obey the teacher. But, as you advance you grow independent and able to work alone, without constant supervision to keep you out of trouble. At first you do what you are told, but as you gain responsibility for your own actions, you are given freedom. The laws and restrictions imposed by religion and society have served the same function for adults as the classroom does for a child. Without discipline, *involving* humanity would have wrought chaos. We have had to be drilled again and again to memorize what human behavior is all about.

However, when you graduate from school, you want to take charge of your own life. If you become your own boss, then you feel you have earned the right to dictate your own working hours and leisure time, as long as you get the job done. This also means you are entitled to make your own mistakes and to take full responsibility for them.

This is really the *key*: if you are ready to take charge of your own life, and ready to live as *you* feel is right, then you may be ready to take responsibility for your own karma. You are *individualizing*—breaking out of the over-shadowing group karma by accepting personal responsibility for your actions.

HEARING A DIFFERENT DRUMMER

In the past, an attempt was made to teach mankind love through spiritual laws. But without understanding, the *letter of the law* is empty. The motions of spiritual love and worship are meaningless without feeling, or comprehension of their inner meaning. In a past-life *reading* we did for a conscientious young woman in Alaska, and member of our group here, we found the time when she learned the difference between empty ritual and fulfilled reality:

Bud: We wish to understand the previous life that is relevant to the present situation.

LaVedi: I see a male, tall; this is a nomadic life, desert life. See power and energy around him. He walks with long strides, a shepherd of some sort. It is a dry country, rocks, also valley. There is water in the valley.

Bud: Does this seem to be in the Middle East?

LaVedi: I keep getting around the Mediterranean area, farther north than that, northeast . . . .

Bud: Is there a tribe? Perhaps, a leader of a tribe?

LaVedi: Yes. He seems to be the head of this group. Now, let us try to pick up his family connections. The purpose of this life. Seems to be Hebrew. This is back in the days of the Law. I see him making a sacrifice, so he also acted as a spiritual shepherd, in a sense.

Bud: Was he spiritually attuned at that time? Or going through rituals?

LaVedi: He seems to be sincere in following the Law he was given . . . and in other spiritual lines, harsh to an extent in this respect. . . now, at the time I am seeing him, he is middle-aged, gray. Up through this point he has followed the tenets of his faith, but there seems to be something that shatters his faith.

Bud: Is it an incident that has occurred?

LaVedi: . . . He hears of something in the land, of things that are more than just following the Law: a teacher, a leader. And, he has contact with this person, he meets this person. (He) seems to perform what seem to be miracles. And this individual has . . . followed the Law somewhat blindly, suddenly he comes face to face with the reality that he hadn't really seriously considered. It completely changes his feelings, his reactions. And thinking this, he leaves. He leaves everything behind.

Bud: To follow this man?

LaVedi: Yes . . . , he goes with the Israelites. He joins them in their journey and links his karma with the history of them in the founding of the Promised Land. Yes, at that time it was an awakening, an opening, an acceptance of a new role, no longer walking under the Law, under direction. But under love and purpose, an accepting and building of the new faith. Preparation, yes. I see a great deal of golden energy around him. There was an aura built up at this time, and this man lived to be quite old. His hair turned white, long, and he was a patriarch of the people . . . .

This was a turning point, the time when love was learned. An expression of it not before understood or experienced by this individual.

A NEW AGE VIEW

The New Age is an age of change, of freedom, of friendship, of human caring and love. We see it being expressed in the release of stale traditions and in the search for meaning in life. People are no longer content simply to sweat for their bread. They want food for the soul, and they want work that has meaning. They are no longer willing to endure empty relationships. They want to find fulfillment and meaning in their associations. As a whole, humanity no longer passively accepts its lot. We are beginning to ask more from life and we are finding it.

Equality emerges in many forms. Eventually I hope we will also see improvements in marriage and divorce laws. They need to be less penalizing and more in keeping with reality. At present they are inadequate, but we do need means to protect all involved. Just living together has complications, unless contracts are carefully drawn for business and financial arrangements.

People tend to forget that marriage is a contract. One solution raised in some state legislatures is renewable partnership (marriage) contracts that may be drawn up by couples for a stated number of years, instead of "for life."

For marriages not *made in heaven* this may be a realistic approach that protects legal rights. It would certainly be better than encouraging people to just live together, as the present system does.

If you do decide to marry, consider writing your own marriage vows, since all vows should be taken seriously. *A vow before God* should be one you mean, or the whole ceremony is hypocritical. It may be wiser to prepare a ceremony with words you believe, rather than mimic words that have lost their power. Many New Age Churches are willing to help with this and perform the ceremony. The Quakers have made it possible for many years.

Please remember, whatever life brings you, whatever changes fate decrees, try to be willing and accepting of it all. Seek the growth offered, step out and find your challenges. You may be amazed to discover "disasters" turning into gold mines of experience and blessings in disguise. What if you hadn't looked?

> Contemplate unceasingly the generation of all
> things through change, and accustom yourself to
> the thought that the Nature of the Universe
> delights above all in changing the forms that
> exist and making new ones of the same pattern.
>
> *Meditations.* IV, 36
> Marcus Aurelius Antoninus (A.D. 121-180)

IT TAKES TWO TO TANGO

11

It Takes Two To Tango

A little closer . . . ,
Hmmmm . . . ,
Closer yet . . . ,
Hmmmmmmmm . . . ,
Closer.
Hmmmmmmmmmm . . . ,
Ouch!
What's the matter?
You stepped on my toes!
That's because your toes are longer than your memory!
Oh, yeah?
Wait a minute,
Let's relax and try it again.
Right. First let me put my halo down . . . .
Here we go now,
a-one, and a-two, and . . .

283

MAY I HAVE THIS DANCE?

The subject of multiple births, twins, or entities working in tandem can be complex. Physical twins may be either twin-souls or soul-mates. They are usually working out a special karma, perhaps expanding the experience of the soul by entering into two or more bodies, or if only soul-mates they may be overcoming excessive dependence upon each other. A relationship can be worn-out through extreme closeness. Or, they may need each other's added support to gain inner strength and confidence, perhaps to overcome a problem. In the old tradition, identical twins would be considered as two aspects of an androgynous soul dividing or incarnating together. Wide variation exists, since two or more souls working this closely may be either drawing closer (to merge) or separating (to individualize).

At other times, instead of being born together, souls share one body, with strange results. For example, in Idaho in the '40s, a young child was playing in some construction diggings, when suddenly the earthen walls caved in and buried him in a ditch under rubble. As the boy smothered under the fill, another entity waited to be "born." The boy "died," and as the body was dug out, the second entity entered it. The child was rescued, appearing to be miraculously alive. Following the accident, the parents noticed that the young boy seemed to be quieter than usual and forgetful. They attributed this to shock, little did they know . . . . The second entity, however, remembered his strange "birth" and entry into the body. He told me about it some 20 years later.

This type of teamwork, or exchange, is not as unusual as we might think. The first entity apparently having completed his share of *karma* with the family, was ready to leave, and it became the second entity's turn to play the role of their son. The biggest problem encountered by entering late this way is lack of memory of the body's life to date. The newcomer does not share the former occupant's memories, so the past must be filled in by others, observation, questions and experience. Also the body is not astrologically "right" for the second inhabitant, so there is usually difficulty adjusting to it for the rest of the life.

Bud and I found a variation of this when we did a past life *reading* for a teenage girl in Fairbanks, Alaska, described in the following *reading:*

Bud: _____ has no recall from the age of eight, nine or ten. We need to find out during that period of her young life if there was another soul who entered her body at that time.

LaVedi: Is her father living?

Bud: No.

LaVedi: Ask her if someone died about that time. The entity that was born in the body chose to join someone who died. I think this was a relative.

It would be well for her to communicate with the original owner of the body, in the sense of asking forgiveness for entering the body. She wasn't supposed to; she took advantage of the opportunity. The original entity . . . is disturbed by it. There is a disharmony between these two.

Bud: Is the original entity staying close to the body?

LaVedi: In contact, yes. It isn't too pleased. If she will not try to establish a line of communication, but simply ask for forgiveness for having entered the body without (permission) . . . . She realizes she is responsible . . . ask the other entity to accept this with understanding, release her claim on the body.

The first one wanted to leave, and when someone else took it (the body) over, she didn't want to give it up. This should in time release the nervousness. There may still remain some tension; this isn't the natural body. She is slightly haunted by the original owner and she needs to realize the responsibility for the body she is in.

. . . I think primarily this discord is the specific difficulty with the body. The lack of memory perhaps bothers, but that is neither here nor there, those weren't her memories. She might possibly ask for them and receive some of them from the other entity.

In another instance, an acquaintance of mine was one of identical twin boys. One noticeable difference, however, separated the twins—one brother was an easy-going slow learner, while the other was quicker and brighter. During the bombing of Pearl Harbor in 1941, the smarter boy was killed. The surviving twin became aware of a decided increase in his own intelligence after his brother's death. His own feeling is that his twin merged with him in the remaining body, a supposition that is probably correct. In this case, as divided aspects of one soul, the karmic pay-off process may have been speeded up through the violent death of one body, while remaining in incarnation within the second one.

Siamese twins may represent the extreme of emotional attachment, so extreme that they actually create a union of their physical bodies. The pressure and experience of such a joint incarnation should create an intense desire for separation, thereby ending any excessive interdependency. At the same time, if they cannot be parted surgically, they may have to live with an intimate situation that requires continual consideration of another person. This could be called a crash course in cooperation and enforced "at-one-ment." Such a tragic union of bodies, from a wordly view-point, could actually offer enormous potential for evolutionary growth. Or, like normal twins, they may be aspects of one soul beginning to separate, but are not quite able to complete the process. They may be going through either a separating or a merging procedure.

Multiple births of all types offer a special challenge to parents, for there is a need to find a balance between encouraging independent action and over-stressing it. Twins should not be allowed to be excessively dependent upon each other, but they should not be pried apart, either. Unless the karma they are personally working on together is known, parents should play it by ear. A middle-of-the-road approach is safest. The twins themselves will have the best insight into their direction: mergence or separation.

TWO HEADS ARE BETTER THAN ONE

The division of the soul does not necessarily stop at dividing into just two personalities. What the soul can do once, it can repeat. In other words, there are not only twin-souls, but triplets, quadruplets and so forth, depending upon the need and purposes of the soul. We unexpectedly found an example of such a case in a *reading* Bud and I did for a young husband and wife in Fairbanks. From my altered state of consciousness, I first discovered we were dealing with twin-souls:

> LaVedi: . . . they have received considerable guidance, even manipulation on the physical plane . . . to come together. These two should be in love and develop, seeking from each other . . . .

> Bud: Could they be called twin-souls, or soul-mates?

> LaVedi: Yes . . . twin . . . twins don't come together very often on the physical plane; when they do, it is a special relationship. It is a tremendous working, growing together, evolving and . . . , if they choose, they can complete the earth cycle. This is a way down the road, not time yet, though it offers some potential.

> Bud: We wish to understand the karmic connection with _____ (the husband's young son); to understand the relationship between the twin-souls, _____ and _____.

> LaVedi: It seems he should also be with them, seems to be merging, also . . . I believe as he grows older he will be with them, and the three of them should be together . . . . It is rather unusual.

> Bud: Have they been together in the past a few times?

> LaVedi: They were one!

Bud: The twin-souls were three souls (triplets)?

LaVedi: That is what I get.

Bud: Perhaps we should try and investigate the origin, of the possibility of a triple-soul?

LaVedi: Aspects of one soul that is put off. _____ (the child) seems to be the original. It is very complex.

Bud: Does it seem that the situation is such that with three energies at work, more can be accomplished in the escaping the earth life at this time?

LaVedi: Well, it is like the original entity divided itself (as twins) and chose to come into incarnation, and the other (the original soul) came into incarnation later so the three are present . . . they had lives together, but it is more important in the sense of re-assimilation . . . .

Bud: Can this unusual triad be indicative of the unusual times of the Aquarian cusp?

LaVedi: Yes, that is the reason for the opportunity now.

Bud: Merging to a higher level?

LaVedi: It could culminate at this time, or at least lay the pathway for the coming together now, in recognizing each other. It doesn't require unusual stress (emphasis). The importance of this learning is to go to the quiet place within, so the wholeness becomes alive and that wholeness is living. And it seems they can do this very naturally.

The soul does not seem to find any great difficulty in

dividing itself into multiple personalities, within any number of incarnations, providing a variety of life experiences and opportunities. The more personalities it has, the faster it may be able to evolve, as long as it doesn't overextend itself. It is simply that two heads, or personalities, are more efficient than one. Also, when a soul has reached the end of its need for earthly incarnations, it may choose to divide and stay to be of more help to the rest of humanity, leaving a personality here to work. It may, at the same time, continue its advancing evolution in other realms or on another planet.

Another common reason souls subdivide, besides the opportunity to learn and experience more, is to isolate problems. We might say it is possible for a soul to develop an abcess, a serious personality defect or habit, that could hold up the overall evolution. So, instead of enduring the problem indefinitely, the soul isolates or splits-off a personality, concentrating the difficulty.

Other personality aspects of the soul can then continue developing without this particular hindrance, while the personality with the problem will be forced to "take a cure." This is just one more reason why we should never judge another. You simply do not know why a person *appears* as he does. Appearances, to the unaware, can be false. We are not usually conscious of our twin-soul personalities, sometimes even failing to recognize them when we meet. There is, however, a certain amount of "feedthrough" unconsciously. This may cause inexplicable moods, interests or impulsive reactions. In response to actions, thoughts or feelings from these unseen parts of ourselves. These parts may be personalities going through life parallel to us. Normally this is no problem, since the flow of awareness between *soul aspects* tends to stay stable enough to remain unconscious.

It does present an important reason to know yourself, and to watch your thoughts, feelings and moods: they may not always be your own. You may be picking them up from another part of your soul telepathically. After awhile, you can tell when thoughts are your own, or originating elsewhere. We really are receiving telepathically all of the time anyhow, on a subliminal level, from many sources around us.

If, at any time, you feel bothered by thoughts or moods you feel are not your own (for which you have no conscious explanation), then you can head them off mentally. An occupied mind is very difficult to influence, so get busy, do some work, go shopping, visit friends or read a captivating book. Don't give unhappy or unpleasant thoughts room to grow. Starve them out, just like weeds, with strong healthy thoughts and feelings.

PERSONALITY SHELLS

So far we have considered individual souls manifesting through multiple bodies, but there are also individual bodies that seem to have multiple personalities. Occasionally these "extras" cause trouble, making a person think he is mentally unbalanced, irrational or even possessed by another entity or a demon. Actually, the cause is often found to be self-haunting by a past-life personality "ghost," or more accurately, an old personality *shell*. We all carry over shells from previous lives, but we are usually not aware of them. They are like extra garments, hanging in our subconscious closet, until the time when we need to put one on, or the time when one or more becomes excessively energized for some reason.

In *Many Lifetimes* far memory researcher, Joan Grant, explains that while the physical body's only reality is the present, previous personalities are not affected by this law. As parts of the "supra-physical component," they are able to maintain independent identities as long as the personality supplies them with enough energy to accomplish this. It is unusual to find someone who does not have several co-existing "supra-physical" shells.

These old personality shells can be very useful. They can help us to identify with otherwise unfamiliar peoples, age groups or situations. They can also help us develop skills, remember talents or use our physical vehicle better. Contact with them may be stimulated by past memory and, once a life is remembered, it is easier to call upon the knowledge held by the former personality.

Exceptional stage performers seem to call upon this ability repeatedly and easily, seeming to magically reach inside of themselves to slip on character personalities as needed. Most of us have lived the major life roles available to us during one time or another. Child prodigies may be another example, appearing to be born knowing how to paint, play a musical instrument or express some unusual knowledge.

We should be aware, however, of the subtle difference between such shells of ourselves and actual overshadowing soul aspects. These may also manifest and influence us when they are not in incarnation. Shells are packages of energy following us around for better or worse. Some of them we will have to face and destroy when we go through the initiation process. They are the "dwellers upon the threshold," parts of ourselves that may be very difficult to accept. Our soul identities are different, vital and intelligent parts of ourselves. Those out of incarnation may merge with us as evolutionary strides are made, becoming *One* in incarnation and afterward.

EXTRA PERFORMERS

It is quite possible that, if knowledge of past-life shells were more widespread, we would be more effectively able to help with problems of mental illness, even schizophrenia. Highly intelligent, imaginative, sensitive people are the ones most likely to make a powerful contact with a past shell. If an individual is having emotional problems, he may slip back into a former personality to escape an unpleasant present experience. In the extreme, a shell may even supercede the current personality.

An example of this may be the case of Sybil, described in the book about her by that name. This woman, as a child, suffered unbearable atrocities and apparently slipped off continually into a surprising variety of shells "for necessary tests." As an adult, it took long patient medical assistance to get the extra personalities back in the closet and to convince the proper one to fully resume her life role.

How to proceed in the de-energizing of nuisance shells depends upon the situation. The first step is to try to find out why an old shell has appeared, since it may have either a past or present life cause. Normally, as soon as the reason for the dependency on an outdated shell is brought to the consciousness, the shell loses its subconscious control and retreats. The shell was probably called forth as a protective measure by a threatened ego. The threat needs to be identified if possible, since it is probably existing on a subconscious level and is reactivated when the present personality meets a place, person or event that stimulates the threatening memory. As soon as the current real or imagined threat registers subconsciously, the old shell may emerge, whether it is appropriate or not.

A common example is seen among people who "change personality" when they get drunk, becoming argumentative, abusive, defensive, etc. When these people lose conscious control an old shell may take over, usually resonating to a present life lack of self-confidence. It isn't unusual for the present personality to have no memory of actions while "under the influence." In these cases the initial problem may be a lack of present-life confidence, stemming from a subconscious guilt or other past-life carry-over. Restore self-confidence and the shell will probably vanish, being of no further service.

Most disorders and illnesses have more than the obvious present-life causes. This is why so many illnesses appear to be self-induced or psychosomatic. This may be correct as far as it goes, but what is missed is the cause of this—karmic recall hidden in the depths of the subconscious. Physical disorders will carry over life after life, either as "ghostly memory" or a reproduced disease or ailment. Root out the memory and emotional charge, and healing may appear to be miraculous.

CRASHING THE PARTY

Possession by outside entities is an entirely different story. These may be earth-bound ghosts, elementals or a variety of astral creations. They exist on a lower level of psychism that is most easily contacted by the use of Ouija boards, automatic writing and other mediumistic or occult dabblings in an *unsanctified* atmosphere. These should never be attempted by the untrained and unprepared.

In 1971 I received a letter from an old friend in London, who had gotten herself unpleasantly involved with an "other world" influence. Beside herself as to what to do, she wrote:

> I was a little sick and had spent the day in bed, since I was so disposed. R., C. and D. came to my flat instead of we going out and J. was already there. For some reason . . . there was nothing, no smoke, no drink . . . , and it was a full-moon. Of course, R., being so easily given over to crazy ideas for which he later abandons all accusations of responsibility, suggested that we have a séance.

> While everyone was joking at him, he cut out the letters of the alphabet with "yes" and "no," and ordered my round kitchen table to be taken to the tea room, and very soon the five of us were sitting round the table with our fingers placed very lightly on an upside-down glass. It took us awhile to concentrate, but after a short time we sat quietly thinking of nothing. Before long the glass began to shiver and then move.

I tell you I was scared. I didn't know what to believe, if one of the guys was moving it, or if it *was* another force. But I could see we were all a bit surprised, and we started to ask questions . . . .

. . . as far as we could gather each of us are watched all (of the) time by an individual spirit, that spirit can be either good or bad, but that does not make the person good or bad, respectively. It seemed the equivalent of the "guardian angels" idea. Well, naturally we started asking who had a bad spirit and who had a good spirit. I, D., C., R., had good spirits, J. had an evil spirit. Poor J., if you knew him I'm sure you would perceive a greater understanding, for basically I think he caters to the natural comforts of life . . . , he is the weakest, most dishonest, most perplexed tormented person out of my London circle of friends. It also said that he would die . . . .

Finally it had seemed to acknowledge everyone in the room except me. D. asked if it would like to say something to me and it quickly answered, "No," well, they all laughed and I was a bit offended and I said, "Do you want me to go," as a joke and it very promptly answered, "Yes," . . . so feeling somewhat dejected, I left the room. I thought perhaps it was because I was the only girl . . . but after the guys had asked some more questions . . . C. (asked if) the cross I wore on my ear had anything to do with why I was dismissed. It did not make "Yes" or "No," but started to circle around in a violent manner in the middle of the table. It did this several times in answer to other questions, so it was difficult to interpret the proper meaning. (The cross was something she had been advised to begin wearing the year before.)

For a long time afterwards I did not wear my cross ear-ring and I found I went through a very bad . . . period . . . (then) I wore the ear-ring again and my life . . . improved.

I mean no harm when I wear the cross, it has no religious meaning for me. The only reason I wear (it) is because I believe that life is a series of interchanging harmonious balances, i.e., when there is black, there is white; when there is white, there is black; if there is not black, there is no white. One balances off the other and without one there is not the other. And even if it offends spirits, surely it is good for offending bad spirits?

. . . (Then) one evening a girl sat down beside me and immediately started talking about herself and her strange experience . . . . She told me of a boyfriend who claims he was a child of the devil and that night she was visited by the spirit of a cat who attacked her . . . . I said perhaps she should wear a cross and she said that someone else most knowledgeable on the occult had given her the same advice . . . .

Now my head is alive with thoughts. I cannot differentiate between logical possibilities or wild fantasies. Sometimes I think I sense a presence of another force, usually at night in my room. I have laid with my eyes shut tight for fear of opening them and seeing what I feel so strongly. During the day if I drop a bottle of milk or continually goof I feel as if something is having a good joke. Last night I even slept with the light on. It appears I am becoming a spiritual neurotic . . . .

My friend had opened herself up to serious trouble. Even though I was in Alaska, between us we cleansed her flat of the intruding agency, she freed herself of fear and returned to her normal buoyant personality. Hopefully she learned her lesson.

Her experience is an excellent example of the power of wearing a cross, even though she herself placed no particular faith in it. While it did not totally prevent her encounter with the negative unseen, it certainly appeared to create a barrier that decidedly disturbed the communicating entity and through which it did not want to pass. If she had continued wearing it, the problem might have resolved itself. She was lucky. Others are not always so fortunate.

It is possible for a human body to be taken over or possessed by an elemental or demonic entity. When this occurs, the person is usually quite mediumistic and prone to negative thoughts and feelings. In former lifetimes the individual has usually had strong contact with black magic and misused developed psychic ability. In extreme cases the possessing entity cannot function properly due to its own *astral* (emotional) and mental distortions, and causes the human personality to appear insane. This is when exorcism may be called for, producing immediate relief.

Bud and I encountered a case of partial possession by an elemental demon during the fall of 1977. A couple had renovated a portion of an old dairy barn into living quarters, but they had one room they could not use because of a "presence" in it. Even a large German Shorthair dog they had owned had refused to enter the room, quaking and balking in the doorway. The wife was particularly susceptible to this presence, suffering from extreme depression and psychotic ailments. She had been under extensive psychiatric care for years. The couple asked Bud and me to exorcise the room and quarters to see if this would help her.

Before actually doing the exorcism, we did a *reading* for the woman to find out the initial cause of her problem, and then we inquired about self-healing and the alien presence:

> Bud: Would there be a particular meditation from the past, or one that could be prescribed, that would be suited to her mental and emotional growth?
>
> LaVedi: To visualize a cross in front of herself, glowing with light, shielding her from the darkness, shedding light all around her, protection and comfort. Impenetrable, giving love, forgiveness, mercy.
>
> Bud: Moving to a different line of thinking, the present experience in the home of the two entities; _____and_____ wish to find out if there are any entities still present out-of-the-body.
>
> LaVedi: There seems to be one who wandered in there. Didn't actually die there, but was attracted there by the energies of the animals, animals who were slaughtered, particularly. It has hung on, apparently drawing energy from . . . , place should be cleansed.
>
> Bud: Does it mean them harm, or is it seeking release?
>
> LaVedi: It isn't exactly that he means harm, just that he is hanging on, retaining. Hanging on by attaching himself. This is, of course, harmful.

We drove out to the place and looked around. The room had a definite feeling of oppression in it. I proceeded with a banishing technique, while Bud offered observant support from a corner of the room. (I never asked him why he chose the corner by the door.) Finally, as I was sending the entity away in a vision of flame, we began to hear it breathing in the corner of the room opposite from Bud. At first the breaths were loud but slow, then as I increased the psychic pressure they grew louder and increasingly rapid, until finally the entity was sucked away and the breathing ceased.

This was not a human ghost, but a distorted elemental type of entity that had been attracted originally to the barn by the energy from the cattle, then it had remained, attached to the negativity of the mental and emotional illness. The woman's condition has improved since, but she is still working on the original problems that attracted the foreign entity.

Healthy people cannot be possessed. When we speak of health we mean emotional, mental and physical. We need to be aware of our thoughts, feelings and actions. All forms of excessive or morbid negativity may open one to random contact with equally negative forces or entities. LIKE ATTRACTS LIKE. Learn to be a positive person, and you have no reason to fear possession.

Please avoid dabbling in psychism for curiosity. It's dangerous. However, if for any reason you feel you need to know more about protection from the unseen, I highly recommend Dion Fortune's *Psychic Self-Defense*. This is an aging classic, but is in print and as valid as ever. It is based upon elemental principles and their application. Your best defense, however, against all negative influences, past or present, is your own attitude. Lead a happy, healthy active life and approach all spiritual activities sincerely, *positively* and *prayerfully*. For most normal pursuits this is quite adequate. Remember, no dabbling. If you want to do psychic experimenting, be sure you have the assistance of a *competent* professional. You should then receive protection by association.

n excellent modern book on positive self-defense is *Psychic Self-Defense &
ell-Being,* by Melita Denning and Osborne Phillips, Llewellyn Publications,
N, 1982.

THE CHILDREN'S AUDITION

12

The Children's Audition

All right, that's it! No more heavy scenes
for awhile. Okay? I've been black, white,
Chinese, old, sick,
spindled, stapled and mutilated.
How about just a short part this time?
Even John Barrymore
can't play Macbeth every night.
Okay, okay, a short part . . . .
Let's see . . . , ah, yes, here's a good one.
You only have to make a brief appearance to
help a young couple face
the meaning of life and death.
That sounds pretty good.
May I see the lines?
You don't have any.
I don't have ANY?
Nope.
Not ONE? Not even a murmur?
Not even a murmur.

303

Isn't that a little too brief
an appearance? I mean are you
sure this is really in
the show?

Have I ever led you astray?

Well . . . , no . . . , but . . . .

THE SOUL TAKES A BODY

Having gone back to several of my own births, while in an altered state of consciousness, I recall being present before birth and observing the scenes. In one instance I was acutely aware of feeling like a very tiny condensed spot of brilliant light, but fully conscious. At that time, I waited in the room of my mother-to-be throughout the day and most of a night, watching the labor and listening to the talk. Finally, when the infant's body was born I momentarily lost awareness, and next, as the baby, I heard them saying, "It's an ill-omen to be born upon St. Jude's Day." The ill-starred life of Julianne Costairs, the London actress, had begun.

Past-life birth information is easy to retrieve by using recall techniques to return to the first day of your life in any given incarnation. The data obtained may be confirmed by preparing an astrological chart for the life in question and comparing that chart with the present personality's birth chart. We find that life after life the major influences the soul is utilizing will be represented and repeated with remarkable similarity. In other words, though the role may change, the characteristics of the actor carry through the centuries. We have found this type of comparison provides a documented history of the soul's expression.

Returning to the actual birth experience, especially in respect to abortion, a major controversy rages on about when the soul actually enters the body. Most adherents of an opinion about this acknowledge that the body is not the soul, yet they are concerned about depriving a soul of life. This is somewhat contradictory, in that the soul is accepted as immortal and, therefore, is not subject to death or murder. Only the body (one personality), can actually be deprived of physical life, and this only temporarily. However, we do not wish to nitpick. The legal system is honestly trying to solve the dilemma and determine when the fetus becomes an ensouled human with a right to life.

In most incarnations, our findings indicate the soul does not *fully* enter the body until after birth, and even then not necessarily at once. This intelligence has no reason to undergo the traumas of birth that the newborn body endures. So instead, the soul is usually present and *overshadowing* the situation. The physical vehicle, until fully occupied by its soul, possesses a measure of life and even memory by itself, and can, under some circumstances, maintain its life support systems indefinitely. It will appear to be mentally defective. But normally a soul merges more fully into its body within a few days, usually losing conscious memory then of its past. Consciousness becomes limited to its new life experiences.

The findings of past life researcher, Marcia Moore, agree with ours. In her excellent book, *Reincarnation*, she wrote about the implications of these delays by the soul in entering the body. She felt the evidence supported that a mother who has an abortion is not "murdering" a *soul*, "since until birth, or even shortly after, the soul is only loosely affiliated with the body." Marcia thought this might account for many infant deaths that have no explanation. The soul "may take a look around" and decide it does not want to experience this life, withdrawing instead of incarnating.

Bud and I found such a case of withdrawal with a set of twin fetuses, who decided to abort their future forms at the age of five months. One twin was a female and the other a male. However, after the female entity had motivated her future body to abort, she decided that she wanted to incarnate after all, so she connected herself to the remaining male body. This infant was born normally at full term.

In another case a couple was deeply concerned over a medically necessary abortion. Their *reading* revealed:

> LaVedi: . . . this experience is . . . something that draws them closer, and the entity that was the fetus wished to make contact for a time . . . it changed her physical body in some way . . . it seems to be acting in the capacity of a guardian angel, still within contact.

In this case the pregnancy was apparently never intended to come to full term. Its purpose seems to have been to influence a change in the glandular system of the mother by the entity who temporarily worked through the fetus. This entity seems closely concerned with the growth and evolution of these two. Remarkably as we transform our consciousness, a corresponding glandular and structural transformation occurs.

In still another *reading*, Bud and I found a very different situation, involving an infant daughter who died at the age of two months. The death had left the mother abnormally depressed for over 18 years preceeding the time she came to us for a past-life *reading*. We found that the present mother had, in an earlier life, been a man with the morbid responsibility of disposing of executed criminals by throwing them off of a cliff into a rocky valley below, where they were devoured by vultures and beasts of prey. Sometimes the criminals were not really dead, but in these cases he tossed them over anyway, without remorse or pity.

The entity at that time, had a daughter who was married to one of the less fortunate criminals who had been so cruelly and dispassionately disposed of. The same daughter, somewhat vengefully, appeared as the infant to stimulate the horror of those old memories and awaken feelings of loss and conscience. She accomplished this by her brief two months appearance. Subconsciously, for many years, this woman has fought with her "dweller on the threshold," wrestling with the ancient guilts that she must eventually resolve through seeking and giving forgiveness. She is fortunate to have a gentle loving husband (an old soul-mate), who has stood by her and patiently helped her. Assimilation of such memories can be slow and painful.

THE DECISION

In 1935, the May 26th *Sunday Express* reported the experience of Mr. W. Martin of Liverpool, England, who, in 1911 at the age of 16, was knocked unconscious by a blow to the head. While his physical body appeared to be unconscious, he actually remained fully conscious in an out-of-the-body state. During this time he visited his parents at home and on their way to him by train, and almost reincarnated into another body. The report continued with his experience:

> . . . I was again transported—this time it seemed to be against my wish—to a bedroom, where a woman whom I recognized was in bed, and two other women were quietly bustling around, and a doctor was leaning over the bed. Then the doctor had a baby in his hands. At once I became aware of an almost irresistible impulse to press my face through the back of the baby's head so that my face would come out at the same place as the child's.
>
> The doctor said, 'It looks as though we have lost them both,' and again I felt the urge to take the baby's place to show him he was wrong, but the thought of my mother crying turned my thoughts in her direction, when straight-away I was in a railway carriage with her and my father.
>
> I was still with them when they arrived at my lodgings and were shown to the room where I had been put to bed. Mother sat beside the bed and I longed to comfort her, and the realization came to me that I ought to do the same thing I had felt impelled to do in the case of the baby and climb into the body on the bed.
>
> At last I succeeded, and the effort caused the real me to sit up in bed fully conscious . . . .

Both she and Dad were amazed at my knowledge. Their astonishment was further increased when I repeated almost word for word some of the conversation they had had at home and on the train. I said I had been close to birth as well as death, and told them that Mrs. Wilson, who lived close to us at home, had had a baby that day, but it was dead because I would not get into its body. We subsequently learned that Mrs. Wilson died on the same day at 2:05 p.m. after delivering a stillborn girl.

We won't conjecture on all of the implications of this unusual situation, but it seems the entity may have rejected his death and an immediate rebirth and was then allowed to re-enter his body to continue his male incarnation. The most important aspect of the incident regarding birth is that his rejection of the infant girl's body caused it to be stillborn. Apparently no other entity was intended to ensoul the form or was available to do so.

LIFE IS INDESTRUCTIBLE
Karmically there may be many reasons for infant deaths, abortions (either natural or induced), and stillbirths. We should never carry around a guilt load over an infant's death. The potential ensouling entity involved has also had a degree of choice. This does not necessarily mean that abortion should be condoned, but rather that the potential parents should carefully consider their true motivations and then act according to their inner convictions without regrets. The soul of an infant knows what is in its mother's heart, and it is desirable for a baby to be

wanted, not born out of a sense of fear, duty or guilt.

In abortion the question may not be so much that of life, as of possibly preventing a member of a soul-family from joining its family group. However, abortion cannot prevent incarnation, at most it can only delay the soul's, and possibly the group's, evolution. Abortion may be a temporary side-stepping of karma, if the motivation is selfish, but all abortion situations are bound to be complex and require sincere self-responsibility. Rejection of a challenge may actually be a tremendous opportunity lost, veiled by apparent or imagined circumstances. Abortion is another one of those personal decisions coming about with the New Age. It is so personal that this decision should not have to be made by others, but for individuals to assume proper responsibility they need to fully understand what may be involved karmically.

Evaluation of such karma is very difficult and should be approached sincerely and prayerfully. If the potential parents vehemently do not want the child or simply would be unable to care for it, then abortion may be warranted. However, if the child is strongly wanted, regardless of apparent circumstances, then it probably should be born, even if it is not kept. Another factor that has been approached obliquely and inadequately is the *manner* of conception. An entity attracted to parents by love will be a positive personality. One attracted under negative circumstances or powerful emotions, such as terror, may be a very undesirable entity—one with negative emotional make-up.

Overpopulation is a real problem at this time on

Earth. Too many forms are being created to be cared for under our present social systems. Serious consideration should be given to why one is having a child. Unfortunately, people who will give the subject thought are probably the most eligible parents. Excess bodies do give numerous entities an opportunity to move upward into human evolution from other kingdoms, but with this comes more social problems. Many of these "young" unprepared entities become juvenile delinquents, due to their inability to cope with crowding, restrictions and regulations. These reactions are magnified by psychological and social pressures in our "concrete jungles." Entities unprepared for the shock of such living conditions may well behave like "savages." Other entities may reincarnate too rapidly, without assimilating previous life lessons. Or they may enter forms conceived under negative or undesirable circumstances and find them very difficult to handle.

Another question often asked is, "Why should *innocent* children die?" Sometimes they seem like "angels" taken away from an unseemly world and parents suffer deep grief from their loss. These children usually come into incarnation to complete some karma of their own, and possibly some karma also connected with the parents. They don't need a full lifetime to fulfill their purpose.

Bud and I found such an "innocent" involved in a karmic triangle between a man, his present wife and her ex-husband. His wife had been his beloved daughter in a former life. The *reading* revealed:

Bud: This time we will be able to move, or see, a life, a previous life of the entity ⎯⎯⎯ that relates to her present situation . . . .

LaVedi: . . . I have the entity . . . , now I see a young girl, perhaps five, six, she has curly hair, she is dressed in the style of probably early in the century. She is closely linked to her father. Their relationship is very close, she follows him, tags after him; she is his pride and joy. There is a karmic lesson here. ⎯⎯⎯ (the present husband was) the father, ⎯⎯⎯ (present wife was) the child. She drowns.

Bud: Is there a connection with ⎯⎯⎯ (wife's ex-husband) in the 20th Century, in this particular situation at the turn of the century?

LaVedi: He seems to be connected. ⎯⎯⎯ (father) seem(s) to have blamed him (for the drowning), but he wasn't at fault. (Father was) at fault, but . . . could not accept that. Yet, in a sense (he wasn't) either, but therein lies the lesson. ⎯⎯⎯ did not understand, because the child came to teach . . . lesson. She came to teach ⎯⎯⎯ to accept and forgive. In this (he) blamed instead of understanding, because of the pain, the loss . . . felt . . . wrongly took the life of the other entity.

Bud: Does this daughter-father relationship in the past account for the natural bringing together in the present situation between ⎯⎯⎯ (wife) and ⎯⎯⎯ (present husband)?

LaVedi: Yes.

Bud: Is there a reason for her selection of ⎯⎯⎯ (ex-husband) at this time?

LaVedi: They have been together before, he, I keep seeing him as the gardener (person killed). She was actually quite

close to him and quite fond of him; _____ (father) jealous
of this relationship at that time. Though (he) did not say so
. . . , really very possessive of this very loving child, who really
was friends with everyone.

But her circumstances were such that there were not people to
play with, children, there were not many in close association;
she had this special relationship with the gardener. It was
through this association that she died. He was not really to
blame, but _____ thought he was . . . , felt he was. This has
also brought them together; she remembers those happy times
. . . .

Bud: What lesson is to be learned in this 20th Century for
_____ (ex-husband) and _____ (wife)?

LaVedi: Compassion. He has not utilized the opportunity to
do this . . . he is working out another debt . . . the tie between
the three . . . is mostly from . . . unjust feelings. His righteous
indignation at being both unjustly accused and suffering and
dying with that thought, that emotion, that link . . . he had
great love for the child . . . .

The crux of their karmic interaction preceeded even
this episode, for the former father, (present husband), and
the former gardener, (ex-husband), had been feuding and
taking turns killing each other for centuries. The daughter,
who had loved both entities in that former life, through
her death presented an opportunity for them to absolve
their hatred, but the attempt failed. In this lifetime, she
has again brought them together, and this time they are
being more successful. At least the entity requesting the
reading has gained awareness of the situation and is trying

to resolve it through love, patience and forgiveness.

A MESSAGE OF HOPE

Tremendous courage and inspiration may come in small packages. The January 26, 1978, edition of the Los Angeles Times reported the remarkable case of seven-year-old Edouard de Moura Castro, who, dying from leukemia, left an articulate taped message for others facing death, while giving faith and hope to his family. The "Times" reported:

> Two weeks ago, Edouard asked his mother to remove the oxygen mask that was keeping him alive.

> He said, 'Mother, turn off the oxygen, I don't need it anymore,' Barbara de Moura Castro said Tuesday. 'I turned it off,' then he held my hand and a big smile came to his face and he said, 'It is time.'

> 'Then he left.'

> The son of Brazilian diplomat Dr. Claudio de Moura Castro, Edouard lived with his mother and step sister in Santa Barbara and spent his few years amazing those who knew him by the things he said and did.

> When he was 3½, Edouard became associated with a local group that follows the precepts of the ancient Eastern religion Vedanta. By the time Edouard died, the Vendanta swami believed his tiny friend was the reincarnation of a holy man.

> 'He was not a normal little boy .... He was so full of understanding of his suffering, full of understanding of God ....

'I don't know how he got involved with them,' said Mrs. de Moura Castro, who added that her son's faith in reincarnation inspired her to believe also. 'He introduced me to it.'

It was Edouard's fascination with the Vedanta philosophy that gave him the belief that death 'was like a passageway, a walk into another galaxy' as he said on his tape.

His messages were recorded by Kim Downey, a volunteer worker for a group called Hospice, which works with the dying and their families.

When Mrs. Downey asked the boy why he wanted to die, he said:

'Because I am so sick. When you are dead and a spirit in heaven you don't have all the aches and pains. And sometimes if you want to, you can visit this life but you can't come back into your own life.'

'If you don't hang onto your body,' Edouard said on the tape, 'and let yourself ease away it is not so painful.'

There is solace for the boy's mother, 'It was a privilege and an honor to go through this with my son. I hope it helps parents talk things over with their children and doctors. If he's done this in his short life, then it will have been worth it.'

"If he's done this in his short life, then it will have been worth it." Here is our key to children's cancelled roles. It is not the *length* of any particular performance that is important. What counts is fulfillment of the soul's objective. Even an aborted or stillborn infant may accomplish this . . . without a murmur.

INTERMISSION

13

Intermission

Well, how'd that last act go?

>>> *Not bad, but I still need a*
> *break. Come'n . . . , let me*
>>>> *go rest awhile.*

What did you think of
> not being born?

>>> *It's okay, but you really miss*
>>>> *out on dying.*

> That's true.

>>> *I had this super death once in Tibet . . . .*

You told me.

>>> *I reeal-ly understood consciously,*
>> *and I merged with the White Light . . . .*

You told me.

>>> *My teacher kept giving me*
>>>> *instructions . . . .*
>>> *Did I ever tell you about*
>>>> *that one?*

Hmmm . . . .

NOW WHAT DO I DO?

What happens to an entity immediately after death varies considerably. Phases experienced may depend upon the individual's evolutionary background, the degree of awareness during the transition, the desires accumulated during the just-ended life, and very importantly what he *expects* to happen after death. As Jesus said, "In my Father's house there are many mansions." (John 14:2).

After making the transition, you will *probably* continue much as you have lived during your preceding incarnation, reuniting with loved ones and old friends. At the time of your passing, or shortly afterward, you will experience a review of the life just ended. If the death is unexpected, traumatic or you are unprepared, you may enter a sleep state in "limbo" for awhile to rest.

Following this, all of the recent life's unconscious memories will be assimilated. This assimilation process has been named purgatory (meaning to purge) because, once free of the physical body, you gain the emotional sensitivity and awareness to re-experience not only all of your past feelings, but also those you have generated in others. This is worth giving some thought to ahead of time. It is an important reason to make the effort to clear karma and obtain forgiveness prior to death. You will probably experience some rest and healing, but you may skip this altogether if it is not needed or if you have mastered the death transition well enough to move on readily, either to another level or back into incarnation.

DOUBLE VISION

The physical body has a "double" known as the *etheric body,* the lowest vibratory aspect directly above the visible form. This double actually belongs to our dimension and consists of etheric matter that may be referred to as *ectoplasm.* It forms the pattern around which our physical body grows and maintains itself. Amputees, for example, often continue to feel their missing limbs, because the etheric counterparts remain. This etheric body is what is treated through acupuncture, involving complex sensory and energy flows that interpenetrate and nourish the physical form. At death the etheric double normally dies slowly by dissipation, within a few days. It may linger around the physical remains for a time, but it cannot continue living without a physical body to sustain it and supply life force.

Most people can see the etheric double if they try. All you need to do is *gaze* steadily and quietly past someone else, or past your reflection in a mirror. Look toward a point about 12 feet past the body being observed. Soon you should become aware of energy waves or moving tendrils surrounding the body or of emanating gray to bluish light extending out an inch or more.

Another simple experiment is to lie down, completely relax with your eyes closed, and then have someone make a slow "pass" with a hand a few inches above your body from head to toe. You will probably be able to feel the pass and be able to tell the person where his hand is, without looking, even though your physical body is not being touched.

A variation of this that is easy and fun to do is to unexpectedly tap a friend "on his aura" from behind. Watch the reaction. Be sure not to touch skin or clothing and do it on the spur of the moment, so you do not make the person aware of you telepathically.

Cremation of the deceased should not be done until the etheric has been allowed to dissipate, a minimum of three days, or the deceased will be caused pain. Cremation is, however, the ancient accepted way to cleanse and sever connection with the physical world. Earthbound entities with the knowledge and desire that is powerful enough to maintain the etheric double after death, have given rise to the vampire legends. These undesirables must attach themselves to the living or newly dead and draw sustenance from one or more people to keep the etheric form alive. Such entities are usually attempting to evade their karma for past actions, and their drain upon the living can cause death or chronic illness, if the vampire is not sent packing. Many of the vampire stories centered around the Transylvania region of Europe due to active practices by Children of Darkness in this area. We should maintain awareness of the ability of the intelligence to operate without a physical body. As Joan Grant says in *Many Lifetimes*, "The personality," regardless of whether the physical body is dead, alive, awake, asleep, conscious or unconscious, "always retains both form and function."

YOUR ATTENTION PLEASE!

Funerals are not nonsense. Originally they were intended for the benefit of the *dead*, not the living. Most traditions have held that the funeral provides passage into the next world. There have been reasons for this belief, since sometimes it becomes necessary to convince the deceased that he *is* dead. The person may not realize or accept this. Flowers also serve an unsuspected purpose. They are not merely decorative, as they offer etheric "food" or sustenance to help temporarily maintain the etheric body so an entity can attend his own funeral.

Whether entities wait to celebrate this event will vary greatly, depending upon their attachments, success of transition and the depth of grief among people left behind. Most will move on right after death, though confusion may occur, especially if the death was violent or unexpected. Then the entity simply may not realize what has happened. In wartime, for example, a soldier carried forward by his emotional momentum to fight, may continue fighting until he discovers he is having no effect upon the enemy.

It is time we reevaluated our death process and procedures. We take great pains to see that a newborn babe is brought into the world safely, but we are inclined to treat the dying and elderly as expendable, since they have lived their lives. This is a most deplorable attitude, since death is a rebirth into our true estate. We can prepare to die, and each death should be carefully attended, though the methods are nearly a lost art. If this were done, we would have considerably fewer problems with those reincarnating, as they would come back with greater awareness and conscience.

Careful attention was given to dying in Atlantis, Egypt and in the East, especially Tibet. The Tibetans have a breviary known as *The Tibetan Book of the Dead*, a how-to-die manual, to be read aloud for the benefit of both the dying and the surviving. Carl Jung emphasized the importance of a proper attitude about death in the preface of Evans-Wentz' English translation of this book in 1927, stating that death is a science that surpasses all other sciences. He wrote that exploration of the inner life is much more important than the exploration of outer space and that learning to die means learning how to live and how to avoid leaving life "spiritually emptyhanded."

THE PROCESS CALLED DEATH

Death should be faced with a calm, clear state of mind that seeks to achieve a mental balance transcending life's experiences. Jung called the process of transferring the consciousness from this earthly plane to the after-death plane an art, and stated that medical science tends to increase the fears of dying patients while frequently clouding the consciousness with "stupifying drugs and injections." Instead of the *"process called death"* being an illuminating occasion of *"solemn joyousness,"* it is usually an unwilling and fearful episode for everyone involved. Both birth and death transitions should be natural processes, undisturbed by undesirable physical conditions and surroundings or interference from mental influences.

It seems that in our modern age, we may be overlooking the greatest experience available to us. There are excellent books about the afterdeath experience we can benefit from, and the Hospice organization offers trained help that should be taken advantage of and encouraged. In most books on death, the dying consistently report seeing a brilliant blinding *light,* or a glorious *Being of Light.* Referring again to the ancient knowledge in *The Tibetan Book of the Dead*, the dying person is guided into this *light* through stages of invocation, prayer and meditation. For example, instruction is given to experience the "Radiance of the Clear Light of Pure Reality." The light is explained as unobstructed "intellect itself." The union of self merging with Self is called a "state of perfect enlightenment," or union with "Reality, the All-Good."

It is the Tibetan teaching that if, at this moment, one can fully comprehend and accept this union—this mergence of consciousness—then there will be no need for further incarnations. Few are able to accomplish this, however, unless well prepared in advance, due to the intensity of the experience. The blinding *light* or *Being of Light,* perceived at death, is the *One-Self* offering union, if you are ready for it. For most this experience is more than the grosser self can endure; the Presence of perfect love, compassion, intelligence and understanding is overwhelming. The magnificent moment slips by in awe, then the after-death journey continues on into other levels of consciousness.

There have been many reports about this immediate "crossing" and of encounters with friends, relatives, Christ

Reference: *On Death and Dying and Death, The Final Stage of Growth,* Elisabeth Kubler-Ross, Macmillan Publishing Co., 1969 and Prentice-Hall, 1975; *Living Your Dying,* Stanley Keleman Random House, 1978; *Life After Life* and *Reflections on Life After Life,* Raymond A. Moody, Jr., M.D., Bantam Books, 1976 and 1978: *The Tibetan Book of the Dead,* W.Y. Evens-Wentz, Oxford University Press, 1960 (1927); *American Book of the Dead,* E.J. Gold, I.D.H.H.B., Inc. and Doneve Designs, Inc., 1978.

or another Great Being, and even occasionally, a beloved pet. These reports have become fairly easy to obtain, either from the dying who describe what is happening, or from the many people who have returned from clinical death experiences, now that it is socially acceptable to discuss them. But what happens after that? What is living on the "other side" like?

Emmanuel Swendenborg was a natural psychic who wrote extensively about his travels in realms beyond ours. Reporting on the ordinary afterlife most people are likely to experience, he said he found it to be an earth-like world, with population centers similar to those we are familiar with. People there were working for the general good of all, with everyone learning or teaching and helping new arrivals.

As to the "angelic condition" or "wisdom of the dead," Swendenborg wrote that "souls are no better than ourselves; no less mean and no less bodily. . . . " They have occupations similar to ours. He goes on to write, "Death is not change of substantials." The same problems are repeated and must be solved.

What then about all of the fanciful stories of heaven, that place of great peace, love, kindness and bliss? Let's be realistic for a moment. *Who are you?* What kind of life do you lead, now? What are your thoughts, feelings, objectives, hopes and wishes? Are you materialistically inclined, spiritually motivated, humanistic or hedonistic and living for sensation? Whoever and whatever you are, you have a subtle emotional interpenetrating *light* body that usually continues living after you drop your physical form. This emotional body will remain with you, but will be expanded to awareness of all you have ever been. Death is simply a transition. "To the wider consciousness the womb is a grave and the grave is a womb." At rebirth the "evolving soul, bids farwell to his friends . . . and taking courage in both hands . . . enters upon *life*." (*The Cosmic Doctrine*, Dion Fortune).

HEAVEN AND HELL

The desires you have built up during your last incarnation can become critical when you become fully conscious within your astral body after physical death. While on Earth in your physical form, you probably spent your nights in this dimension while sleeping and dreaming. You have a life there that you have built parallel to your waking physical life, so this astral life will reflect your earthly thoughts and desires. This world consists of a higher vibrational substance that is highly reponsive to thought, enabling us to create a familiar world there from our conscious and unconscious thoughts over our many lifetimes.

After death, if you have been physically sick, you can heal your astral counterpart immediately, just by willing it to be whole and well, assuming you are mentally and emotionally ready to be well. If not, you may carry the seeds of illness or disability with you life after life, either as psychosomatic ailments or manifesting physical complaints. The *real* cause ceases to be physical, as the *disorder* becomes just a symptom of *dis-ease* elsewhere in the complex mental-emotional make-up rooted in previous life experiences.

The astral world first created by the angelic beings, has been greatly elaborated upon by mankind through the ages. Largely it is of our own creation. You can find anything there that has ever existed upon Earth. If you believe implicitly in a heaven of golden streets and harps, you will probably have the opportunity to visit such a place, but it is unlikely you will care to remain there. Most likely you will choose to join loved ones as they live out their hopes and dreams.

Addicts may be among the most unfortunate entities, for if they maintain their emotional addictive dependency, they will find themselves without a physical form to satisfy their habits. This can literally be "hell," with torment continuing until the emotions burn themselves out and desire diminishes, or the entity reincarnates. It's much better to rid oneself of serious addictive habits on the physical plane. If they carry-over into the next incarnation, not having been overcome between lifetimes, they will probably manifest as inexplicably powerful compulsions. Such subconscious urges can be much more difficult to conquer than the original habit.

I came across a humorous story of an unhappy alcoholic, who became an earthbound ghost haunting the village where he had lived, held by his desire for alcohol. It seems the natives found an unusual way to stop his haunting, as his grave is heaped with liquor bottles from periodic pourings of alcohol over it. The cure sounds expensive and somewhat dubious, but apparently it worked.

Smoking seems to be a habit that can be continued out-of-body, perhaps when related more to pleasure than physical addiction. My ex-husband was assisted in his astrology work by the "departed" astrologer Jondro. I always knew when Jondro was present, as the aromatic smoke of his pipe filled the room with its scent.

Entities who have serious gross desires to work through, spend much of their afterlife in what is termed the "lower astral." This most unpleasant place was what Dante described in his *Inferno* as the "Hell" he had to pass through to reach "Heaven." We should be grateful that most of us will not have to spend time there, despite religious efforts to convince us we may. This *pit* has been created by mankind from his lower emotions, those of the lowest and most animalistic types. Less than human emotional *creations* wind up in the lower astral. Those who wallow in the mire, may find themselves stuck in it. There is a *hell*, but it is man-made, not an eternal punishment by God. Like attracts like, and what man desires he gets.

For the most part our problems are worked out with the loving assistance of helping entities in relatively normal afterlife surroundings. The helpers behave much like they do in physical form; there are teachers, doctors, counselors and so forth. Hell is only experienced by those who condemn themselves to it by denying others and the helping hands that are always reaching out to them.

People often wonder what happens to children in the afterlife. Most reports indicate that children simply keep on growing normally, frequently into adulthood, before reincarnating. One of the most impressive journeys I have made into these realms at night was a visit to a hospital for handicapped children. These were both *dead* children and children who were visiting in the dream state, while their physical bodies slept. I was surprised to find the assassinated John F. Kennedy there, busy helping these children adjust their lives—learning to speak, walk and lead normal healthy lives. It seems his own disability and sympathy for others may have prompted him to work with these children. We should realize that handicaps and disabilities are not necessarily negative conditions, but may offer tremendous learning experiences for both the person and others in association.

ATTENDING NIGHT SCHOOL

Dimensional "evening classes" are held for both those in physical incarnation and those between lives. Many of us attend or teach these classes in our sleep, remembering only snatches upon awakening, but all we learn is retained unconsciously. It will gradually come to the consciousness as needed or is appropriate. The subject matter is just as broad as in earthly schools, but much more extensive, not being limited to physical knowledge. Teachers may also come from many spheres and realms besides Earth.

The availability of these night classes is another reason why seekers are told, "When you are ready a teacher will come." If one earnestly desires to learn anything, that knowledge is available, but a physical teacher may not appear mysteriously before you. Instead you are expected to do your waking homework by studying available material and seriously working on your life. The more effort you put into this, the more help you will be ready to receive beyond the visible by preparing your unconscious mind.

Rachel MacPherson found an illustration of the potential of some of these inner-dimensional classes when she attempted a past-life *reading* to find out what her connection has been with me in other lifetimes. In the present one she has become my student, friend and assistant. But, instead of discovering any lifetimes, she was surprised to find:

> No scene at all, all subjective impressions. L.L. a teacher, I a pupil, student, chela, but not on the physical plane at all, but rather in a place of light, beautiful golden light, all light and love (formless. . . . Our relationship on that plane—perfect rapport, perfect love and understanding.

This is a description of instruction on a mental dimension, but the majority of classes are conducted on the astral, where familiar forms are available to relate to.

People usually settle down on some level of the astral world, until they are ready to return to a physical body. They enjoy the rest, assimilate new knowledge to use "next time," and they work on the emotional residue carried over from the past. The time period between lives varies greatly. There seem to be some entities who incarnate only occasionally, while others appear to be on a marathon, taking only a few short years between lifetimes.

A number of old Atlanteans, on the other hand, appear to have refused to return to the "lesser" civilizations that have existed preceeding the present one. They seem to be incarnating *en masse* in the United States. Sometimes entities have this choice, but it can limit their progress. For some this becomes possible by moving up beyond the astral world to the mental. By dropping the astral-emotional envelope, they are not drawn back into incarnation by karmic desires. Instead they control their incarnations by thought. When they are ready to incarnate, they must build a new emotional body by attracting matter again, then they will be ready for another physical form. Most entities, though, even if advanced enough to do this, prefer to stay and help in the astral world, where many are needed.

Today there is a shortage of assistance, due to the overly large Earth population. This creates special problems, especially with so many people dying who are unprepared for the death experience. These unprepared entities pose distinct difficulties, often due to their unbelieving and uncooperative attitudes, but they must have help through the transition. This creates "waiting lines" (in limbo) on the "other side," because there are not enough trained entities to help the newly dead.

There is a great and urgent need for more people to study the process of dying, becoming known as "thanatology" (*thantas* comes from the Greek, meaning death). Death education would both make more people knowledgeable at death and enable them to assist others. Those who learn about the death transition would not only be able to help following their own deaths, but before hand, at night while asleep.

After death, or during sleep, we are not limited to just the astral world of Earth. There are also other realms we visit; some people return to their homes upon other planets. Dreamers may return with strange memories, and due to extraterrestrial interest now, many more people are beginning to remember such dreams. Education goes on in these other worlds, too. Exceptional scientists may be from other planets and, upon incarnating here, they may bring their old knowledge with them unconsciously. Inspiration seems to imaginatively well-up from deep within their minds, as if spontaneous.

Dr. Gustaf Stromberg, a Swedish-American astronomer and physicist (1882-1962), expressed his beliefs about the soul and mind in his book, *The Soul of the Universe*, writing, "There is no doubt about the existence of the human soul if we define it properly." He said the soul was the human ego, "a perceiving, feeling, willing, thinking and remembering entity." He felt the soul possessed a group of mostly unconscious memories and gave unity to human mentality. He believed these memories to be "engraved" in the electrical field of the human brain, and that this field disappeared at death from the physical world of "matter, radiation and force fields," going unchanged into a *"nonphysical world."*

HANGOVER

Occasionally entities return to incarnation too fast, especially if they met a premature or violent death and were unprepared to die. These people, who die while still full of life, or who die off schedule, tend to come back as soon as possible, to attempt to resume life where they left off. The only problem in this is that they may not give their emotional wounds from the death experience time to heal. This is common among accident and war victims. After rushing back into incarnation, they may have to work out their emotional shock in dreams, nightmares or, sometimes, through emotional-mental disturbances.

A friend and student of mine in 1971 had such a carry-over from World War II. When I met her she was about 23 and throughout most of her life had suffered from a violent repetitious nightmare of running terrified down a corridor. Finally, after all those years of dreaming, she was ready and able to face the origin of the nightmare. We found that she had been among the Jews to be annihilated in Nazi Germany. She remembered being herded out with her family to be taken to the gas chambers when, for some unknown reason, the guards took the rest of the family, but left her behind. She found herself alone, and as the realization hit her, she began to run down a hallway. Needless to say, she did not get very far and her death at the hands of Nazi soldiers was far from pleasant. With the recall, however, her nightmares at long last ended.

GHOSTS . . .?   (boo!)

Stories and fears of ghostly hauntings appear wherever man has lived and died. In his ignorance, modern man has often rejected these phenomenonal apparitions of the emotional-astral world. They may just be left-over thought forms resulting from intense thoughts or feelings of a dead person in connection with an earthly experience. Or, a ghost may be an actual entity or intelligent *portion* of the emotional body left behind due to emotional attachment. At other times a ghostly remnant may act much like a magnetic videotape, that just keeps reliving thoughts and feelings that surrounded the death scene, caught in a "tape loop"

"Goldrush Ghosts"

In Fairbanks, Alaska we lived in a house with two ghosts, a singing dance hall girl, and a former gold miner who liked to sit and rock through the night in a rocking chair.

of emotion. The degree of awareness and intelligence can vary from highly aware to a total lack of consciousness.

Marcia Moore, in her book *Hypersentience,* gives an example of how a ghost, caught up in the re-enactment of his murder, came to involve a 12-year-old girl named Betty. Following a divorce by her mother, the two of them had moved into a new house. Then Betty's personality seemed to change. She became listless and spent large amounts of time in bed. Having used regression techniques before, Betty asked her mother to work with her to try to find out what was wrong.

During the regression she told her mother that a young bushy-haired young man kept pushing at her. Her mother then asked her if the man was in the spirit world and Betty replied that he was, but that he was "in the dark" and he seemed to be afraid. They then began to realize that Betty had apparently contacted the ghostly spirit of a young man who had experienced a sudden death. As a result he was confused and apparently unaware of where he was.

Betty's mother asked her if she could find anyone to help him and Betty responded that she had found someone. She was then instructed by her mother to try to "take him into the light" and pass him on to the assistance of his "spiritual guide," which she did.

Following this, Betty became her normal self again. What Betty had not known was that the prior year a young man had been murdered at the backdoor of the house. Frightened by a gang of party-crashing motorcycle riders, he had gotten a pistol from the house. A struggle over the gun followed and he was killed by a shot in the head.

Apparently the young ghost was mistaking Betty for the person who had killed him, and he was still trying to push his murderer away, affecting Betty's astral body. This was an earthbound type of ghost, locked into his terror on the lower astral. In this combination it is difficult for those on higher vibratory levels to help, as they cannot reach the entity. It is somewhat like a person locked into a state of hysteria. Betty, however, coming from the slower physical level and acting as a bridge could make contact and pass the entity on into the *light*.

This is a good example of an effective procedure to help an earth-bound entity on his way. An alternate method that works well is to simply talk to the ghost about former loved ones, allowing memory and old desires to surface and move the entity on by the power of attraction and redirected emotional energy.

We had an historically recorded ghost similar to this in the old farmhouse we lived in near Cambridge, England. The house dated back to the 1100s, but the ghost was less than a century old. It was encountered by a visiting sensitive from Australia, when a child appeared to her in the night, pulling at her bedclothes and calling for his mother. It seems that a boy had died from a lingering illness in the next room, and the room where the visitor was sleeping had been his mother's. We had no visitations, so most likely the lady succeeded in sending the child on.

Ghosts are far from imaginary, their manifestation resulting from powerful emotions. A frequent cause is an entity that desires to pass some vital or important information to the living. Another common cause is excessive emotional attachment to something, perhaps hidden money or someone, such as an unrequited love or a desire for vengeance. Sometimes ghosts have appeared to give individuals warnings, such as of impending death. An example of this was the death of the Duke of Buckingham, foretold by an apparition of the Duke's father, who manifested to a servant clad in a suit of armor. This latter type of apparition is not really a ghost, but just someone from the afterlife making an appearance to prepare the dying person for his transition. People frequently make a similar brief appearance to loved ones at the time of death. Again these are not really ghosts, but are simply individuals saying farewell for the time being.

Actual ghosts are not normally anything to fear. They can even be sociable. We had a pair of ghosts who lived with us in an old turn-of-the-century house in Fairbanks, Alaska. We became aware of the first one, a woman, when my daughter heard her singing along with a record of Buffy St. Marie's, with "tra-la-las" coming from the vicinity of the stereo. Later two members of a study group also heard her singing behind them, from the same part of the room. A reading by the highly clairvoyant Patricia-Rochelle Diegel in 1972, revealed that our "singing ghost" had been a local dance hall girl during the "gold rush days" of Alaska. We also discovered we had a second ghost in the same house. I came to realize this after an old rocking chair in the living room kept squeaking over my head at night (my bedroom being directly underneath). We could find no external cause for the stubborn rocking of the chair, so finally one night I got fed up and told the ghostly entity that if he didn't quit and let me sleep, I would banish him. The rocking stopped instantly.

Patricia-Rochelle identified this ghost, too, while visiting with us. Her energies and presence greatly increased the phenomena, so we had noises in the house and heavy footsteps of the man clomping through the attic. Patricia said he had been a gold miner who had frozen to death. Since they both seemed to enjoy living with us and appeared to have a high degree of awareness, she felt they were learning from us. At any rate they stayed on and became very protective of the house.

One weekend we went out of town and a girl friend agreed to stay at the house. Fortunately she knew about the ghosts, only we had not thought to tell them about her. They created quite a racket and generally did their best to scare the "intruder" out of the house, and almost succeeded, until she realized what was happening. Then she explained to them that she was there to take care of the house until we returned. After that everything was fine.

The last time we inquired, the new tenant in the house had also become aware of his ghostly roommates. Perhaps, this is why the house rented so cheaply, but to us the ghosts became close friends. Now the house is being torn down to make room for urban expansion. This should be interesting someday, if a modern commercial structure is built on the site, with "tra-la-las" drifting through it along with piped-in music.

Normally, though, it is desirable to send ghosts on, as

they shouldn't remain attached to the earthly plane. This is usually accomplished by making contact with them and getting them to direct their thoughts and feelings to one or more people they have loved at some time. If they just briefly establish this linkage by redirecting their thoughts and emotions, it is usually enough to pull them away from this physical world and into their own dimension. In the case of the Alaskan ghosts there may have been still more to the story, other sightings in the area indicating an old *astral portal* used by ghostly entities.

DO NOT MOURN

We need to learn about death and how to die correctly. Do not mourn the dead, for by so doing you bring them sorrow. Instead send them loving supportive thoughts and prayers. They are just as sensitive to sadness as those living in physical bodies, while positive thoughts can be very helpful.

I had this pleasantly impressed upon me, after doing some work to clear karma with my parents. They both died within three months of each other in 1978 and 1979, one of a stroke and the other of cancer. My relationship with my mother had been especially difficult, and I felt it was necessary to release it through forgiveness between us. I encountered heavy energy in the process, but when that was dissipated I assumed I had been successful.

It was a few days later, when doing some further work that I knew I had succeeded. My father appeared to me clairvoyantly. I had been carrying the image of them as old and ill, the way I had seen them in their latter years, and they wished to correct this. My father, once again was the dapper, dashing Irishman of his youth, dressed in shirt and tie. I wondered what he was doing in the after-life and was much surprised to find he was raising race horses. I had forgotten he had been an expert horseman, as my paternal grandfather had bred racehorses in Kentucky. Apparently my father had had a secret dream.

So, I then wondered about my mother, and she deigned to appear, lounging in the background, once again her glamorous youthful self, dressed in a luxurious gown, such as she had loved so much. I was extremely happy to find, more importantly, that she was fulfilling her dream that had been crushed during her lifetime. Started on the piano at the age of three by my grandfather, it had been her life. Through her own dedication she put in fifteen years of grueling work to prepare for the concert stage, becoming a protege of one of the known teachers of the period. Then, when World War I burst upon the scene and the world was in upheaval, the family refused her financial backing. My grandfather was dead and his wealth gone, so her career died a withering death. It left her with a life-long bitterness. I was most pleased to find her as her former elegant self and once again rippling the keyboard and ob-viously enjoying her renewed life.

This experience stressed the importance of not carry-ing around old images of deceased family and friends. Instead think about what they were like in their "salad days," and of what their fondest dreams were, and be glad they have a chance to complete them. Death is an opportunity that we should learn to properly understand.

As Alice Bailey wrote in *A Treatise on White Magic*, "it is one of our most practiced activities . . . conscious one moment on the physical plane . . . a moment later we have withdrawn onto another plane," becoming, "actively conscious there." She goes on to say once we realize we are souls and have the ability to focus consciousness on any dimension, we "shall no longer know death."

Death is simply a transition of consciousness. Even in a physical body it is possible for an evolved being to remain conscious night and day, being as aware out-of-body while in the dream state, as he is aware during the daytime waking state. For such a one, death is nothing but the dropping of a form, the shedding of an envelope, for his consciousness remains the same. This is our potential. We can achieve this by reprogramming our thinking, by removing man-made concepts and accepting ourselves as creative entities without limitations of time or space.

STAGE FRIGHT

14

Stage Fright

I've been going through our casting records
and you've been scheduled for a multi-life contract
until you clear up that suicide.

What suicide?

Remember, when you were a woman
in Paris, and you electrocuted yourself with your
curling iron?

It was an eggbeater.

An eggbeater?!

*Yeah, you see my step-sister ran this
pastry shop . . . ,*

*and she accused me
of watering down the dough
for her croissants.*

*Well, that was the last straw,
let me tell you!*

Watering down the dough . . . ?

*I had suffered humiliation before,
but nothing like that!*

(Psst . . . what's a croissant?)

343

SELF-CONDEMNATION BY SUICIDE

Taking one's own life is a very serious business. The person who commits suicide is usually in the emotional basement, the dungeon of life. We have stressed how you create your own afterlife by your thoughts and feelings. Suicide is an attempt to escape life's lessons, and this denial of self and others produces self-condemnation. The life is terminated "off-schedule," so the entity is not likely to be greeted by the *light of the soul* when the transition is made. Instead he will probably find himself plunged into the horror and darkness of the lower-astral world by his own powerfully negative emotions. Suicides tend to be re-born rapidly, and it is small wonder. Who would want to stay in this self-created *hell*? Suicide is never escape, and destroying the body so much effort has been put into creating is a hard way to learn this.

People who have attempted to kill themselves and failed have reported a nightmare world they encountered while clinically dead. The film *Beyond and Back* drama-tized the experience of a woman who, only a few days before her wedding, in a turmoil of emotion, ran her car off a road to her death. She was clinically dead for 30 minutes before returning to her body. During those 30 minutes she reported experiencing a grotesque world of astral horrors, and was shown her future as it might have been. Apparently in her case the potential of new happiness and a desire to escape the lower astral was enough to take her back to her body, which suffered no after-effects, despite having been "dead" for half-an-hour. The soul seems perfectly capable of placing the body in a state of "incubation" that prevents brain damage.

As fast as it can be arranged, the entity is returned to incarnation and circumstances similar to those existing at the time of suicide—to face the same lessons again. This poses an additional problem, as there is no healing time between death and rebirth and the four bodies (physical, mental, emotional and spiritual) will be out of alignment with each other, essentially at war, until the person is able to coordinate them by accepting life, regardless of what it brings. As Joan Grant puts it in *Many Lifetimes,* instead of "instinct, intuition and intellect working smoothly together towards a common goal, they indulge in internecine strife." This can cause trouble, regardless of which one is dominating, since, " . . . they will not be at peace until they choose to integrate."

I am more familiar with this problem than I would like to be, having staged my own suicide in my last life. It seems to have brought to a head a long series of karmic interactions over numerous lifetimes. It was one of the first lives I remembered, stimulated possibly by living in Spain. In that life I was a Spanish soldier stationed in Mexico, and I placed a fellow officer and close friend in the undesirable position of being forced to shoot me for a traitorous act, involving a French naval fleet stationed in the harbor at the time. I recognized my military friend, as he has been my friend again for many years in Alaska. Upon my return I asked him if he remembered this life, and he described it detail by detail as I had seen it.

I had had a perfectly good body with a reasonable future. My *conscious* malaise was a matter of pride and resentment, as I had been born the illegitimate son of a female Spanish prisoner in the late 1800s. By stupidly throwing away the opportunity to work through the karma connected with my mother at that time, I made my present life much more difficult than it need have been. My prisoner mother had, in an earlier life, been the illegitimate son of a brother I had disowned. Pride again was the culprit. I had been embarrassed by my blacksheep brother and had taken my resentment out on his son, as his guardian, following my brother's death.

In this Spanish life I was not raised by my mother, but by the Captain of the Guards at the prison. To add to the intrigue, the Captain actually was my father, but could not claim me due to his compromising position. Instead he raised me as an adopted son, but I never knew this during that lifetime, illustrating why we should accept life's challenges as they are given. There may be reasons behind situations that are totally unsuspected. The webs we weave create confusing knots, and the best way to untangle them is to be as humble, accepting and honest as possible. It is *much* easier to see these things through the first time around, seeking whatever help is needed and making the best of crises, understood or not. For me the failure to do this brought chronic disabling health problems and crises, driving home all of the messages so I would never forget them again.

Russian novelist, Leo Tolstoy, intuited the fate of the suicide very well in 1896, when he wrote in his diary:

How interesting it would be to write the experiences of a

man who killed himself in a previous life; how he now stumbles against the very demands which had offered themselves before, until he arrives at the realization that he must fulfill those demands. Remembering the lesson, this man will be wiser than others.

About the only time taking one's own life can be justified is if it is done for unselfish reasons. An example is those who have killed themselves to avoid betraying others under torture. In some situations allowing one's self to die can be honorable. Suicide does not follow some universal dictum. Motivation is the vital factor. Bud and I found an example of honorable suicide in a reading for a man who had been an Atlantean priest during one of the destructive periods. He was old and stayed behind to protect the city's temple from desecration, while others fled. Little negativity was involved in his decision, rather it demonstrated his faith and trust in his own immortality. A portion of the *reading* describes his death:

Bud: Was the entity still alive in the last days of Atlantis in that incarnation?

LaVedi: He did not leave the city.

Bud: Did the city disappear while he was still in the body?

LaVedi: He died by his own hand, but I'm trying to determine . . . seems to be toward the end, there seems to be quite a panic, there were others involved, but there seems to have been almost a revolt of some of the people in the priesthood and again in the government. I think they killed the ruler, either killed him or imprisoned him, they dethroned him, quite a large number left, but this entity because of his feelings of guilt, conflict between the government, the death of the ruler, his age, and some other factors, stayed too. Someone had to stay to protect the temple, someone had to stay, he stayed. Someone who *knew* had to stay.

Bud: At the soul level at the time of his death in this incarnation, was that an acceptable method of dying?

LaVedi: Yes, in this sense it was an honorable death.

Terminal illnesses and old age may present another exception, when the life is completed and is perhaps being prolonged artifically. While deliberate suicide, or a cutting off too soon is normally unacceptable, undue prolongation of life can be equally harmful. While the body lives, the soul maintains attachment to it, neither able to benefit from the body or free himself from it. A natural, dignified and peaceful death should be our right and privilege, unclouded by excessive drugs that may interfere with a clear transition or create addictions that must be dealt with later.

LEARNING TO APPRECIATE LIFE

What if a suicide doesn't learn his lesson the first time, and tries to escape a second time? This is very possible, because the pressures of life for the post-suicide may be extremely difficult to bear and they may seem extremely unjustified. A second failure will activate the same process again, but the limitations will probably be increased to prevent a third failure and the time span may be increased. For example, the person might, in the future, incarnate with severe physical or mental handicaps resulting from the disturbed bodies. A handicap can act as a preventive measure, making suicide very difficult or impossible. We may then find this recovery process encompassing several lives, allowing the entity to gain strength from life to life.

Marcia Moore gives an example of this type of severe case, involving a woman in her late 30s who was totally crippled. Her husband had to carry her everywhere and attend to all of her personal needs. Using the *hypersentience* recall technique developed by Marcia Moore, the woman found herself as a young girl running away from a soldier. She ran up some stairs to a rooftop and then in anger, more than fear, she spitefully threw herself from the roof with a "don't care" attitude. The fall to the street below killed her.

There is a strong possibility her present husband might be the soldier, who now has the "body" he wanted. As to the woman her purpose in committing the suicide seemed to be based on an indifferent attitude combined with a desire to make the man feel remorse for his actions. In that life she had thrown away a good body, so in her present life she was apparently experiencing paralysis to gain appreciation for the gift of life.

This raises another common emotion, the desire of the suicide to seek revenge by attempting to make someone feel guilty and sorry. Fortunately this often fails, but if it doesn't the suicide has succeeded in tying the karmic knot even tighter. It is much better to tough it out alive and attempt to understand one's own feelings, rather than trying to force feelings within another.

We found less drastic results in a reading mentioned earlier, about a woman who killed herself during the Flapper Days of the 20s, following desertion by her husband because of an unwanted pregnancy.

The present life circumstances of this post-suicide case were quite unusual. She came to us because she wanted to become pregnant by artificial insemination, but she had a weight problem, and her doctor insisted she had to reduce her weight to a set maximum. But every time she would near the designated weight, she would stop losing. She could not reach the necessary weight. She asked us to help, and that was how we happened to discover that she had committed suicide. To achieve her goal, she would have to work through her fears of desertion and suicide caused by the former pregnancy.

To reiterate, though Bud and I prior to the *reading* had no expectations of a suicide problem, the lady did. She was not present when we actually did the past life *reading*, so afterward Bud played a tape back for her. She interrupted him at one point to ask, "I drove off a cliff, didn't I?" Bud confirmed that she had, and then she heard the confirmation on the tape. She went on to describe to Bud how this scene of the car going over the cliff had appeared repeatedly in her dreams and how she hated the 20s. Through her perseverance, this lady can now earnestly work to reverse the negative program she created within herself from that lifetime. With the help and cooperation of her husband she should be able to overcome the effects of the suicide and have the baby she wants so badly now.

THERE IS NO ESCAPE

> I cannot take my life for the Will to accomplish the object
> of Art would draw me back into life again until I realized that
> Object, and so I would only be re-entering this circle of tears
> and misery.
>
> (Richard Wagner, letter to Hans Bulow, Sept. 27, 1858).

We can't run away from our self-created karma. Sometimes we try in other ways that are nearly as harmful as actual suicide—through drugs, alcohol, or by attempting to ignore it all, perhaps living in fantasies. But, since our thoughts are real, and we continually create our life through our thoughts, mental escapism can be a form of indirect suicide. We don't necessarily have to pull a trigger to avoid life's challenges. Negative escapism, however, only compounds circumstances by adding other hurdles to overcome, creating problems that may carry forward through many unhappy lifetimes. An addict, or "dreamer," may be getting "hooked" in more ways than he realizes.

Even though difficult, no situation is ever impossible. We never face more than we can surmount. Keep knocking on the apparently locked door, and it will open. It is vital to hang-on and keep trying. Past failures can make the present seem unsolvable, but be aware that you may only be facing tests to strengthen you and make you prove to yourself that *you can do it.* Nothing succeeds like success, so look for little ways you can succeed. Begin by building a positive momentum.

I remember another life when I tried to escape an intolerably boring life in the Middle East; it contributed to my later suicide karma. I found myself among simple fig farmers as a housewife and mother. In this society relatives lived together, so I shared a home with my farmer husband, his parents and other children. For me it was an exceedingly dull existence and I rejected it, children and all, refusing even to accept the responsibilities of my motherhood.

Instead I spent my time day-dreaming, living on the astral dimension where life was stimulating and interesting. I didn't kill my body, but I wasn't quite "present" either. My indifference created a heavy karmic debt, not only by neglect of my responsibilities, but through misuse of my psychic faculties. Pride was the problem again. I felt I was too good for the life I found myself in. I hadn't learned *Oneness* and lost the opportunity offered at that time to demonstrate self-responsibility, so I had to face future lives that would teach me these lessons. Finally, in the present I have had to re-earn, by hard work and dedication, the clairvoyant abilities I had abused, for the door remained closed to me, until I insisted I would use it for the benefit of others, not myself.

I also had to fully accept the responsibility of parenthood without shirking it. It wasn't easy, and the temptation to give up was great, since I reared my daughter primarily alone and often under adverse circumstances. I rebelled at times, like a high-strung, stubborn filly chaffing at the bit, but I *knew* what I had to do, like it or not.

Eventually the suicide reaches this point, where he realizes there is no escape; the only way is to "face the music" of our own creation and accept the circumstances as justified, even if mystifying. Once we understand how we create our own cycles, we know that whatever happens *is* justified, and egoic denial will only make matters worse. Humility, selflessness and willing acceptance are the answers to releasing the grip of karma. A problem is only a problem if you think of it as one.

J.B. Priestly wrote a play, entitled *I Have Been Here Before,* to dramatize the futility of suicide and the inevitability of man's self-created cycles. Ormund, one of the characters, threatens to shoot himself to get "a good sleep." Another character, Dr. Gortler, tells Ormund it would only be a sleep full of dreams like the present. "Peace is not somewhere just waiting for you . . . you have to create it." He explains to Ormund that the "dreary circle of existence" is really a spiral. Each incarnation is different. The differences between lives may be great or small, but we are always growing. No matter how difficult things may seem, you will be better and stronger for facing them.

IN THE DARK OF THE NIGHT

15

In the Dark

of the Night

Okay, drop that eggbeater—
and put on this cowboy hat and red-checkered bandana.

Say, this is neat!

How do you like those leather chaps
and jingling spurs?

Very, very classy.

This time you play a bank robber in the 1800s
in the Western United States, until you

finally die in a shoot-out.

A shoot-out!?

Yes. Many die because of you
in this incarnation,
but they all need the experience.

Now, wait just a minute . . . .

What's a shoot-out?

You'll see. Are you ready?

Well, I don't . . . , I'm not sure about . . . .

Go on, you'll be great!
Remember you're really a villain this time,
    and a lot of people are counting on you for
        striking contrast.
                            But, a shoot-out?
Here we go now . . . Action!
        Let's try it again . . . . . . Action!
Where is that hypnotist? Will someone find Bud?
He has the next two scenes!
                (Where could . . . ZzzzZzzz. Never mind.)
        TRUMPETS! *RatataTAtaTAAA!*
                Nice work.

GOOD GUYS AND BAD GUYS

Remember when you were a kid and played cowboys
and Indians, and the Indians were always the bad guys?
Someone had to agree to be the Indian. Why? It was
because you needed forces in opposition, or there would
have been no drama, no opportunity for adventure, no
dance. How could you learn to be a courageous hero, if
there were not opportunities to struggle against the villain?
The more fierce the struggle, the greater the chance for
growth.

This child's game is in many respects like the *eternal
dance* of life. In each performance you agree to forget who
you "really" are, and you play your part with so much
enthusiasm and imagination that only under extreme
duress do you remember that it is only a game. The excitement of a chase and a shoot-out may continue until
death signals the end of the performance. Then you get up,

brush yourself off, and perhaps switch roles.

This is a bit of an oversimplification naturally, but the question that could be raised is whether there is such a thing as good and bad. The answer may be determined by the seat and the view that you temporarily select in the cosmic auditorium.

THANKS A LOT, LAVEDI!

We mentioned earlier that LaVedi and I had shared lives in Egypt, where to resist foreign invasion more firmly, she had me murdered . . . tsk, tsk. Equally as important as the information we learned from our individual exploration into the past was that we each uncovered this same life experience independently. I was about to reveal to LaVedi what I had found the night before, when she started explaining that she just discovered that we had shared power as Pharaoh during what she thought was the XV Dynasty. After we put our two stories together and made a quick trip to the library, it seemed that our rather non-glorious reign must have occurred during the Hyksos invasion.

My past-life journey to Egypt began when I was searching for a karmic connection with a very close friend, and I discovered that we were raised there together in a very privileged environment. We ran together, threw spears together at targets, and even practiced together with the bow and arrow (I don't know if this fits historically or not). As we grew, I somewhat reluctantly assumed power and evidently shared it with LaVedi, my sister. My friend was, in his official capacity, my arms-bearer and right-hand man. I strongly feel at the intuitive level, although I have yet to investigate it clairvoyantly, that another mutual friend of ours was my loyal and trustworthy military commander. I also feel the strong desire to thank him for his efforts during this period in Egypt, even though, as of this writing, I still don't consciously know what his specific involvement was.

As I continued my own life *reading,* using our hypnotic technique, I saw the two of us racing across the plains in our horse-drawn chariot. Then we flipped over. Although I was hurt, but not dead, when I failed to get up my friend thought his foolishness had killed me, and he took his life with his sword. I then moved forward through time to view his funeral pyre. My reign, from that time forward until my own death, was rather removed, except to voice my concern for the elderly living in the land and to focus my attention on "feeding my people." (This may account for all of my graduate studies in gerontology.) Unfortunately, I chose to ignore the mounting threat from imminent invasion on our borders.

I next saw myself seated alone in a darkened reception room in contemplation. I then rose and walked through a doorway on my left, entering a small anteroom, where I prepared to bathe in a sunken blue-tiled bathtub. I was then attacked by several armed soldiers. And, while it was a very exciting battle, I lost. (*C'est la vie* . . . .)

This was, at first, one of the tougher past-life memories to accept, because of the high status I attached to the worldly position of a Pharaoh. Consequently, I felt at the time somewhat like the stereotyped "nut" who thinks he is Napoleon. However, try as I might, the scenes remained in my clairvoyant gaze, until I finally consented to review them willingly. It was not until later that I reasoned that there are obviously thousands of leadership positions in the world, and that the role of Pharaoh was just another one of many that each of us gets a chance to play. And besides that, from a karmic standpoint, power and wealth are not necessarily a privilege, but a tremendous responsibility with far-reaching karmic consequences.

Well, what happened to LaVedi in this Egyptian experience after she "bumped off" her future hypnotist-colleague-author-humorist? As it turned out, our country was still overrun and she was left to the mercy of the invaders. If she had the same powerful emotional character and fierce independence then as she does now, then this captivity must have been worse than death for her. But karmically, since her reasons for my premature demise may have been semi-honorable, it is possible that her karmic debt may not have been too severe. Her honest intent to save our country, rather than the negative desire to gain power, would have been the determining factor. Her own soul must be the judge of her true intentions.

MURDER OVER A MISUNDERSTANDING

One soft-spoken lady came to us for a life *reading* to understand how best to deal with her young step-son. This boy had shot and killed another youth and was soon to be released from a correctional institution to once again live with her and the boy's father. She also wanted to understand why she had been surrounded by men and had had difficulties with them most all of her life. The first part of the *reading* answered her question concerning her difficulties with men:

> LaVedi: I see her in the Civil War, in the South, among many men, soldiers, the wounded.
>
> Bud: Is she a nurse?
>
> LaVedi: Yes.
>
> Bud: How does she feel about being a nurse?
>
> LaVedi: I think she hates it. She is revolted by it. The scenes, smells, cries, the horror of it all. She wants to throw up, she can't stand it. (At this point LaVedi was starting to get sick so I suggested she move to a higher level to witness the experience rather than be so close to it.)
>
> Bud: Is there a hatred for men?
>
> LaVedi: That seems to be it. Seems to get even . . . it is the killing. Again, the killing. Views them as animals because they are doing this—what they are doing to their families, the horror of it all, and she hates them. So she kills them, not out of mercy, but with hatred, so they die with this.
>
> Bud: Is this why she is in the karmic position of the present?
>
> LaVedi: Yes.

We knew there was probably a further karmic story explaining why she was placed in this Civil War experience to directly confront her hatred for men. So, as we dug deeper into the problem, we found that she had been abandoned at a very tender age by a man who, unfortunately, had no control over the circumstances. It was not his fault, and this led to the misunderstanding. She did not know this, and blamed him for never returning. Consequently, this hatred for him grew into hatred for all men, and provided the karmic momentum to carry her into the Civil War experience to overcome it. But instead of learning to feel compassion for men, she compounded her hatred and her karmic responsibilities.

Today she is encountering many of her "victims," and is being given the opportunity once again to learn the lessons of compassion and forgiveness. But her main challenge is still unfolding—the boy who is her stepson. When I asked for the karmic explanation for his involvement with her, LaVedi stated, " . . . *for this is he who left her* and she will hate him. She did not realize he did not leave her on purpose."

So now she is in the position to satisfy her old strong desire—to desert the man who she felt deserted her at such a tender age in the past. But if she does desert him, she will tie the karmic knot even tighter and carry it forward into other lives in the future. She must sooner or later face this challenge and overcome it with compassion and forgiveness, both for others involved in the misunderstanding and especially for herself. This does not mean she should become a martyr for the boy or the other men in her life. But through acceptance, she will be able to look deeper within herself and honestly say, "I have tried my best, I forgive you, I forgive myself, I free us all to go in peace."

MURDER FROM A HIGHER VIEW

Before we discuss the highest crime against man—
murder—we should look further at the implications of
passing judgment. After all, who is to say what lessons
another soul is here to learn? Who is to judge the actions
of another soul, without understanding his karmic momentum from the past? It should be pointed out that it is
fundamental to all major religions that we "judge not that
we be judged." But, if we find the urge too strong for our
particular level of consciousness, we should remember
that how we judge others will be how we, in the end, shall
judge ourselves. So once again, the lesson is to evolve to
higher levels of consciousness, to totally demonstrate compassion and forgiveness, in order to overcome the pitfall of
casting judgment.

Obviously, to truly forgive others can be a very difficult task, especially when you mistakenly see the other
person from the ego-personality level and not from the
higher level of pure spirit. You may need to remind yourself that even the most vile personality you can imagine,
such as a Hitler for example, is still in his true essence an
expression of God. But this other person may not remember,
or not understand, his true identity. He may be relating
to his ego-centered and body-centered self. It may even
take many incarnations before he is ready to discover,
or re-discover, this knowledge. If you relate to his ego-
consciousness, you *both* get stuck at this level. If, on the
other hand, you focus on God within, or his Higher-Self,
you will SEE more clearly, and may even assist him out of
his emotional confusion. Even the so-called soulless *"things"*

still have the *light* envelopes of the soul. They only lack the direct contact of *spirit* with *Cosmic-Logoic Consciousness.*

It is much easier for us to relate to our fellow man if we focus on the Higher-Self, our real eternal Identity as pure God-given energy, when we meditate on forgiveness. Avoid focusing on the limited and illusionary ego-personality of the individual. By so doing you can avoid judgments, learn to more fully realize that each soul is at its own stage of unfolding and working on its own particular lessons that most of us have either passed or will pass through. Now, let us look at the drama of murder . . . .

If we view murder in the limited perspective that we each have only one brief 70-year lifespan, then a murderer is a criminal of the highest order, having stolen *time* from his victim. From a higher perspective though, taking into account reincarnation and karma, the drama becomes more complex, and yet more understandable and fair. For example, when the karmic connection is known between the victim and the murderer, we can understand the victim's karma in this single life experience. We can also probably understand the karmic reasons why the victim's family experienced grief, mourning, serious introspection, or even financial hardship. The crime may make sense, whereas before it was an isolated case of extreme unfairness. And besides, *no one really died anyway.*

As you learn to experience scenes from your own past lives, you may well find *you* were in the position of killing someone, or of being killed yourself. Keep in mind that we may misuse and abuse our human equipment, but our spiritual *Self* is beyond all harm. All of our experiences are just part of our soul's education, and generally the tougher the experience, the greater the opportunity for spiritual growth. Also, consider that the "cause" of a karmic tie may stretch back into a complexity of offenses over endless lifetimes. So do not think, for example, that just because you found yourself being murdered by your present father, in a previous life, that now it is your turn for revenge. If you will look more closely, you will probably discover that the two of you have been flunking the lesson in forgiveness with each other for centuries. So do not single out one past-life experience to build an iron-clad case, either for or against anyone. Forgiveness is always the logical, rational and DIVINE lesson.

WE JUDGE OURSELVES

As we evolve through many lifetimes, we seem to grow more harsh in our judgment against ourselves. It could be said that the more advanced soul is more sensitive to its transgressions. Because of this increased sensitivity it must work harder to release its more powerful emotional impressions than a less sensitive soul. This was noticed in a *reading* LaVedi and I did for a young boy when we were trying to discover the karmic explanation for his hemophilia ("bleeder's disease").

> LaVedi: It seems that this has been a problem stemming back from more than one life. I first get: "If you shed blood, you will let blood, or lose blood." And there seems to have been a time he was involved in a considerable amount of bloodshed and . . . see if I can get a word . . . anyway a rather barbaric

situation, where there were a number of people killed in invading towns and villages, sacking the communities. He was only one of many doing this, but the soul was already well developed and consciousness strong before entering into this life, which was apparently one to learn to appreciate . . . to work out certain karma. Anyway, the result of that experience apparently was a rather strong guilt load after that.

Bud: On the soul memory?

LaVedi: Yes, he didn't really realize what had happened, and had difficulty forgiving self for having been involved in such a primitive expression. You could say because this is an already developed entity, and he shouldn't have participated in the activity as he did. But he did, and then felt guilty as a result.

Evidently this soul sentenced itself to "let blood" over several lifetimes, because of all the blood that it had let in others. Perhaps a less sensitive soul would have been less impressionable and thus less harsh on itself. The point is, that he KNEW he was wrong in the earlier period, and this strong emotional guilt is still being expressed today through hemophilia. Interestingly, his blood-related expression of guilt appeared before his present life. We found him in France. Let's resume the *reading* and find out what happened:

LaVedi: . . . . The rather unusual result of this is I find him becoming, in a Christian life, one of those who . . . can't remember the term . . .

Bud: Martyr?

LaVedi: No, shed blood . . . .

Bud: Stigmatic?

LaVedi: That's it. I think it was in France. It wasn't too well
known, but yet it was . . . oh, what was that name? Well, it
was out, kind of in the countryside. He was removed from the
general populace, but people did come to see him and be
blessed by him. He was a monk. Because of his intense feelings
he became a stigmatic. This is carried through to the present
time, when there's still the tendency to leak blood, shed blood
from self to compensate for having previously shed the blood
of others. So now he's come full circle, and he wants . . . he
should now understand this and, perhaps, he's a little young to
fully absorb all this, but he will now learn to control his body,
to forgive himself. Forgiveness is vital. He's done everything he
could have done. It's not essential or important, in fact it's
detrimental, to carry guilt forward from previous lives. It only
hurts the soul. He now needs to forgive the former existence,
send it love, realize it was . . . , it's done. It's past. And now
he'll regain control of his body, and the proper expression of
the blood, the life force flowing through the body. The hemophilia will not be necessary.

Like this young boy who is still shedding his own
blood because of shedding the blood of others, we must
remember that we are constantly "meeting ourselves." We
are also being given continuous opportunities to overcome
our self-created karma by learning the divine qualities of
compassion and forgiveness.

If we can learn to view our experiences from the
higher level of *soul consciousness*, we can then understand
that war, vengeance, selfishness and hatred are the expressions that provide that contrasting backdrop for experiencing peace, forgiveness, compassion and love. Without the

darkness the light cannot be noticed. Thus, *yin-yang*, black-white, male-female, positive-negative, innocence-guilt, are ALL GOD experiencing Himself in the dualistic choreography of the *eternal dance*. Who is at fault? Who is the criminal? Who really dies? Nobody! It has all been produced and staged in the physical theater for the growth of our souls.

The following Taoistic type of Chinese story was retold by Alan Watts on his cassette tape, *The Diamond Way*, by Big Sur Recordings about a farmer whose horse ran away. His neighbors all said to him that it was, "Too bad." The farmer replied, "Maybe." When the horse returned the next day with seven wild horses, they all thought he was lucky. He said, "Maybe." When his son tried to ride one of the wild horses and broke his leg, the neighbors again all said, "That's too bad." The farmer still replied, "Maybe." Next, conscription officers came gathering men for the army, but they rejected the farmer's son because of his broken leg. Now the neighbors all thought this was a great turn of events. The farmer said, "Maybe."

The farmer understood the law of karma and wisdom in maintaining his own inner balance, his Oneness with the *Tao*. In this way he was able to see beyond the worldly claims of good and bad. He knew that divine justice was being met in every instance, and that each soul reaps its own crop from the seeds it has sown in the past.

ONWARD AND UPWARD

Why is crime on the increase in today's society? What would possess a man to hijack an airplane, beat his own child, or throw a bomb into a busy Belfast tavern? How would a murderer face his supposedly innocent victim on the "other side"? And in terms of reincarnation, what is the result of crime? Before we discuss these questions from an individual karmic standpoint, let us first consider the influence on Earth of the *New Age consciousness* being introduced by the Age of Aquarius.

Edgar Cayce mentions that, "Life is continuous and only changes its phases, owing to the state of consciousness or change in vibratory rate of existence." (*Many Mansions,* Gina Cerminara). We on the earth at this time are in the midst of great changes in our vibratory rate. These changes are being triggered by the earth passing from the negative Piscean Age with its 2,000 year emphasis on *building* self, to the positive Aquarian Age with its emphasis on *sharing* Self. We are in transition today, moving from *physical involution* to *spiritual evolution.* Being on this borderline results in a strong unconscious drive toward destroying the *old* to make way for the *new.*

This planetary drive is manifesting itself in the reevaluation of old standards of behavior and in the crumbling of old guard institutions. Excessive influence of this drive appears when there is destruction simply for destruction's sake, with no creative thought for the future. This transition corresponds to the greater cyclic expansion of the cosmic Ring Chaos.

An increase in population has also resulted from this common drive to expand, or in this case, to populate. Unfortunately today, this population drive is drawing many entities into incarnation before they are prepared. They may either have not had enough preparation time between lives, or they may be coming into human incarnation for the first time from another form of evolution. They may, therefore, be emotionally unstable to begin with, and at best ill-prepared to face the tremendous challenges we are experiencing. Thus today we find temptation leading more people to emotional reactions, which in turn leads to commitment of more crimes. All of this is above and beyond the obvious problems created simply by the vast numbers of people being pressed together to jockey for life space.

Compounding this transitional period on our planet are the effects that technology has on the air we breathe and our daily diet. It is difficult at best to remain emotionally balanced and centered in our tension-ridden Western culture. The emotionally disturbed or potentially unstable individual will find that the general pollutants, chemicals, poor diet and especially the indulgence in sugar, overwhelm the glandular system and exaggerate the tendency toward strong emotional reactions. Hence, there is also a direct linkage between pollution and dietary habits to emotional behavior and the increase in crimes against one's self and society.

Two experiences made me personally aware of this important connection between diet and emotional behavior. The first experience was the apparent emotional calming effects of a dual program of rigorous physical exercise, and dietary regulation on hyperactive emotionally handicapped junior high school students. This program was conducted by an old friend now masquerading as a serious administrator for the city of Anchorage, Alaska. In a study he had conducted earlier he had reported that rigorous activity and a modified diet resulted in his students being considerably calmer and better behaved in the classroom. Many of them, for the first time, were mentally stabilized enough to take an interest in learning. Several of these emotionally handicapped students even asked Bill to teach them to read.

The other experience was personal. I discovered quite clearly, after meditating and fasting for a few days, that my own emotional calmness and expanded states of consciousness increased considerably. I could do my own past life *readings* much easier with greater clarity. It was as though I had lived all my life in a covered birdcage, and someone for the first time raised the cover. I then knew for myself how our chemically treated foods agitate the mind and make finding the *Self* even more difficult than it already is.

KARMA INSURES BALANCE AND JUSTICE

For every thought, action or desire there must be an equal response. The universe is exquisitely balanced and fair. Many people mistakenly think of karma as simply negative debts owed to the "Great Accountant in the Sky," but as Meher Baba points out in his *Discourses*, karmic law does not operate as some blind rigorous outside force. We are not helpless victims of karma, but instead, karma involves a "rationality in the scheme of life." It exemplifies "true responsibility," meaning that each and everyone will reap the harvest that is sown life after life. Not only is the universe balanced and fair, it is rational and logical and it teaches complete responsibility for our own condition.

Karma has also been oversimplified to imply that everything is predestined or due to "fate." But, as Madame Blavatsky so aptly put it, the law of karma, whether it is conscious or unconscious, does not produce predestination. "Karma creates nothing . . . " man "plans and creates causes." Karmic law is the manifestation of *harmony adjusting.* It rebalances the scales that man sets into swinging motion.

So, fate is actually one's own self-created karma from past lives that is stored in the mental-emotional bodies and carried forward with a specific momentum seeking release and balance.

Your karmic momentum can be modified and released deliberately and effectively through wise action. If these modifications were not possible, there would be no point in the conscious struggle, the desire to grow, or the joy of participating in the *dance.* Wise and intelligent action may take the form of searching for the eternal truths in the religious and esoteric literature, or internally in meditation, or even by inviting a Master such as Jesus, Meher Baba, or Yogananda to relieve you of these karmic burdens (sins). Whichever path you select will ultimately lead toward God-realization and freedom from the karmic wheel of rebirth. Your Path leads you toward the total realization of your own divinity and unity of ALL THAT IS.

THE SHOW MUST GO ON

16
The Show Must Go On

That was well done, well done.

Why, thank you.

Everyone really benefited from your
superb presentation that time.

All in a life's work.

Now, are you ready to turn inward?
Let's try poor health . . . . Here, take a look
at this almanac of diseases and deformities and
select a few that you think would be most
appropriate and challenging.

Gee, there are so many . . . ,
and they all look so helpful. I just
can't make up my mind.

Here's a hint. Try to select ones
that can push you just up to your emotional
barriers, but not so far as to make things
appear impossible.

373

                                          Say . . . , I think I've found
                                                            one!
                    Good, good.
                                          How about athlete's foot?
              Athlete's . . . foot . . . ? Hmmmm . . . ,
        that's a rather slow method, but . . . ,
                                          Wait a minute, I think I have a
                                                       better one!
                                          Dandruff! That sounds pretty rugged.
                                          Flakes, rejection and all of that!
                                                  What do you think?
              Hmmm . . . , well, better not forget
                          your shampoo.

KARMA AND HEALTH

All of the past-life research LaVedi and I have done, using clairvoyant skills, continually reinforces the direct connection that Edgar Cayce stated very simply, "No one can hate his neighbor and not have stomach and liver trouble." He went on to say jealousy and anger will lead to digestive or heart problems. (*Edgar Cayce's Story of Karma*, Mary Ann Woodward).

Assuming our thoughts and emotions can cause physical illness, we need to look more closely at how this is possible. And more importantly, we need to learn how to reverse our negative thinking and achieve better health. To learn how, let's consider the process involved and take a look at several life *readings* done by LaVedi and myself that directly relate to health problems.

Not only supported in our life *readings*, but by a

wide variety of the esoteric literature, physical health may summarily be described as the end result of all of your past-life impressions filtered through the screen of your chosen spiritual ideals. In other words, poor physical health is a result of poor spiritual attunement; this poor attunement manifests AFTERWARD in your physical body.

This is the reason why our life *readings* focus on the spiritual adjustments to mental and emotional expression. These are the deeper first causes, not the symptoms that later manifest in the physical body itself. The rationale here is that even if the physical body is corrected, without spiritual corrections, the physical problem would probably return. Now, since neither LaVedi or I have medical training, we do not pretend to give medical advice. We instead focus our attention on the effects of spiritual, mental, and emotional karma carried from past lives into the present. We do feel, however, that compiling a karmic recall profile of patients may become an accepted practice of Western medicine in the near future. Let us look at some typical examples of how mental-emotional karma from the past affects the physical body in the present.

THE BITTERNESS OF AN ARM INJURY

A family requested a *reading* for their teenage son who had been in an accident and was in danger of losing the use of one arm. LaVedi received and relayed instructions given to her by *higher sources*, on the *inner planes,* that described the physical and etheric injury. We then turned our attention to the karmic explanation for the injury and found:

Bud: Concerning the entity _____ , is there a karmic explanation for the injury from previous lives?

LaVedi: There was another time, when he lost the use of his arm, even lost part of the arm. His attitude was not correct. There was anger, a sense of privation, cruelty at that time to others, particularly those weaker than himself and suffering. He did not face the situation, but instead reacted with bitterness, created sorrow, in those around him.

Beware you do not slip back into the memory of the loss of the arm from that time period. It would be easy to do, because you did not regain the use at that time. It is not necessary this time. You are only going back to re-experience those sensations, and have the opportunity to view the situation from the proper perspective, accept loss. This is not loss, but opportunity to grow, and not with any bitterness. This apparent loss has occurred as a result of the growth gained. (It) far exceeds any apparent losses, which are only temporary.

Bud: Were the other entities involved in the earlier time period in that sorrow and damage, part of the immediate family of the entity?

LaVedi: Yes. At that time they were also part of the cause of his attitudes, where he felt a burden, and the times were such that it was not an easy period to be one where it would impose such a burden, and he felt this, felt the bitterness of it. And they, too, felt the bitterness of his burden, and therefore, compounded the situation among themselves.

Notice that the injury today is an opportunity for growth to overcome his previous bitterness. Thus the injury is not, and should not be viewed as, punishment, but rather as a divine opportunity for spiritual growth.

A SAINT'S BLESSING

In the last chapter we mentioned a young boy with hemophilia, who is still "letting blood" for having "shed blood" in the past. This time we will share a different aspect of that *reading* with you when the boy, as the stigmatic, healed his present mother. At that time she had a crippling disability and the healing stimulated a karmic bond of love between them that has carried forward into the present. It seems that all our strong desires create karmic ties, whether they be strong feelings of bitterness, or as revealed in this case, love:

> Bud: Okay, we're now looking for the karmic connection between the entity _____ and the mother, _____ in his present incarnation . . . .
>
> LaVedi: She was one of those blessed by him as a monk.
>
> Bud: Stigmatic?
>
> LaVedi: Yes. She came to him crippled and he healed her. Interesting that she has the opportunity, or has had the opportunity to in turn assist him in healing himself. I find a great deal of love flowing back and forth between these two . . . . "

Notice how her response to the blessing of love and healing by the monk (now her son) has placed her in the position today to help him in turn. From her gratitude she generated the desire to be helpful. This very phenomenon— DESIRE—whether we judge it good or bad, binds us to repetitive human experiences. When we fulfill our desires, wear them out or bring them into balance, then we can escape the wheel of rebirth. Then we realize there is no good or bad, just God and His eternal manifestation of Himself.

One young couple, mentioned earlier, came to us to find out the karmic implications of having had an abortion. During the *reading* we found that the soul associated with the aborted fetus had accomplished its two-fold mission to draw these two people together, and to initiate healing changes in the woman. Here are the details connected with a birth defect in the woman's hip:

Bud: Let's move back to _____ in terms of the physical changes that have been induced by the aborted fetus. Is there a connection in that situation with her hip?

LaVedi: I think so . . . . connected with the hormone balance.

Bud: Does there seem to be a karmic explanation for the malformed hip?

LaVedi: To teach her to stand on her own two feet. There was a tendency to be too dependent on others and this caused loss or suffering to others . . . learn inner strength, learning of lessons, to appreciate.

Bud: Would it be relevant to understand consciously her previous situation?

LaVedi: This is the problem that this aspect of the whole is working out, a tendency to be overly dependent. This came . . . , seems to have been concentrated in one of her lives, (an) overcoming. Sometimes we can work things out without being aware that we are also working on inner levels, and that seems to be the case here. But it is almost like a measure in her growth, but at the same time it is a releasing. It is a soul problem.

So, it is again indicated that physical problems are an end result of faulty alignments at the spiritual and mental-emotional levels. The logical method of treatment here should be to first treat the physical symptoms, and then give at least equal attention, if not more, to the less tangible causes behind the apparent problem.

GUILT FOR AN OLD SHIPWRECK

One personable young man, with an extensive educational background, came to us for a life *reading* to find out why he lacked confidence in himself and felt reluctant to accept positions of responsibility connected with his work. His feelings were seriously interfering with his career potential.

The clairvoyant LaVedi found him adrift at sea in a lifeboat full of people, who all, as the story unfolded, died slowly of thirst and exposure. As it turned out, this man had been the officer on the ship responsible for navigation and he blamed himself for the disaster, even though the charts and instruments of the times were crude and inaccurate. Watching the others slowly die evidently branded feelings of guilt and inadequacy deeply into his emotional body. And, consequently, he has carried these subconscious emotions of guilt forward into this life to be played out and released.

While this guilt was an understandable emotional reaction, we decided to investigate the incident further to understand why these apparently innocent passengers had needed to experience such a horrible death. What we found may have helped him release some of his excessive guilt feelings.

> Bud: Let's pursue one thing here, a little bit out of character, but let's see what we come up with here. How many approximately were in the life boat?
>
> LaVedi: A dozen, dozen and a half, something like that, women and children.
>
> Bud: Perhaps it would be important to understand . . . group karma in relation to why this particular group was to undergo this experience. Does there seem to be a common tie?
>
> LaVedi: Kind of unusual . . . . It wasn't specifically connected with water so much as slow death . . . experience . . . .
>
> Bud: Do you see it more or less as an opportunity . . . ?
>
> LaVedi: Let's see if I can get it more specific. I see something here that is unusual. I'm viewing a scene . . . mountains . . . Middle East . . . tribesmen, northern. I keep seeing this one scene, riding on a horse, spear, some sort of arena sport. I can't see what they are really doing, it's like one person on horseback, another on foot . . . The idea is that the one on foot winds up dead. It is a remote sort of thing, but at any rate, this is what it was, like Roman gladiators . . . .
>
> Bud: Do most of the people on the boat seem to have been responsible for this type of action?

LaVedi: That is what I'm getting. In other words, this particular group, tribe, participated in this. This is part of their karma
. . . .

This is a good illustration of how complex karma can become. If you patiently search out cause-1, then cause-2, then cause-3, etc., then these causes seem to stretch into infinity. Thus, it is illogical to carry forward feelings of guilt and ridiculous to blame others for "causing" your difficulties. The goal is to release all guilt, release all blame, and be at peace.

Besides, if we consider the lifeboat episode again, who REALLY died? No one, right? We often tend to have an exaggerated view of our own power and the importance of our acts. Further, if the *reading* is to be believed, the people in the lifeboat brought about their own slow death experience to balance their past karma and, perhaps, learn compassion, mercy, and respect for the God essence within each human temple. We all have our lessons to work on; we should concentrate on learning them, and on growth. As Cayce mentioned, instead of going to heaven, "you grow to heaven!" (*Many Mansions*, Gina Cerminara).

EIGHTEEN YEARS IN MOURNING

As LaVedi mentioned earlier, we worked with a very gentle, but deeply depressed lady and her concerned husband. They both asked us to do a life *reading* to uncover the karmic reasons for her long years of incapacitating depression that required prolonged psychiatric care and, as a last resort, even shock treatments. We knew before the *reading* began that she felt responsible for the accidental death of her infant daughter 18 years before. While her immediate depression after the death would be understandable, her extreme feelings of guilt over so many years about this accidental death indicated to us that she was working through a very strong karmic challenge.

The life *reading,* which was both long and at times complicated, placed her in the role of the man who disposed of dead, or even half-dead bodies by tossing them off of a high cliff, to rocks and human debris below. As we saw before, the infant daughter came into her brief incarnation to reawaken this lady's unconscious memory of having previously killed the daughter's husband. But we didn't describe an important part of the healing process suggested for her use in this lifetime.

That ghastly lifetime occurred during the time of the Master Jesus, and later in Palestine the man embraced the teachings of Jesus, due in part to the influence of a very close comrade. This same comrade is now her present husband in this life, once again placing himself in a position to help his soul-mate. She now needs to overcome this very challenging karmic tie by learning the divine lesson of the forgiveness of others and the forgiveness of self. As we each walk our own Path, we find that the forgiveness of self is definitely the tougher of the two.

To assist her in learning the lessons of forgiveness, the clairvoyant LaVedi suggested that because of her early exposure to the Christian teachings, she should " . . . visualize a cross in front of herself, glowing with *light,* shielding her from the darkness, shedding light all around her, protection, comfort, impenetrable, giving love, forgiveness, mercy," while placing more reliance upon her religious faith.

This family will need to remember that the momentum of a long-standing habit, in this case depression, is not an easy one to change even if some type of cure could be instantly provided. With her family's help she will need to learn and maintain a new healthy self-image. Unfortunately, it may be much easier to retain the depressed self-image and keep the status quo, rather than to battle the discomforts of change. But, over a period of time, she WILL change. If not in this lifetime, the next one, or the one after that . . . . Eventually, the guilt will wear itself out or be overcome, and the soul will be free to move on to other lessons.

We must remember that we have all the time of eternity, so, eventually, not only this nice lady, but all of us will learn to form the *habit of health*. When you have a physical difficulty, you should endeavor to face the challenge as cheerfully as possible, and then use your mental chalkboard to check off another victory for a lesson learned, a karmic debt paid, or even another step closer to Home.

THE VALLEY OF THE KINGS

One of the more fascinating *readings* we have encountered involved the initial search to uncover the karmic causes for a man's alcoholic illness. Much to our surprise, it led us instantly to the Valley of the Kings in Egypt. Here we uncovered this man's disastrous misuse of knowledge concerning the vital forces of the dead as a Priest and

Keeper of the Dead. His abuse involved the theft of etheric energy from the vital organs of the dead. Such theft is a definite misuse of higher knowledge, since the loss of etheric energy could cause many entities to become earth-bound after death by interfering with their normal dissolution. Once freed of the earth plane, they would make their death transition in a weak condition. A side-light to this story was that it also struck an old memory with LaVedi and gave her quite an unexpected reaction. Here is what happened:

> LaVedi: I find the entity first in Egypt. He is related at the present to one of those buried in the Valley of the Kings . . . underground. At the time . . . this was when the vital organs were removed and stored in jars . . . and there's some connection with this and . . . and the knowledge of the body's . . . *ka?* . . . , *ba,* I think?

> Bud: Could be life force?

> LaVedi: *Ka,* I think it's *ba* also, and the oversoul. There was knowledge developed then in these fields and areas of life. The keeper of same . . . .

> Bud: The knowledge?

> LaVedi: Acted as a keeper of . . . the dead? I see, okay, he was involved in ceremonies connected with . . . ooh . . .

> Bud: You can remove yourself from this scene if you choose.

> LaVedi: No. I'm getting reactions. Let's just see what we're getting here . . . .

Bud: Are you okay?

LaVedi: Yes, let's see what this is all about . . . . One who knew how to use the vital forces of the dead. This is . . . dealing with the Valley of the Kings and . . . another site.

Bud: The kings were buried at another site also?

LaVedi: This was the reason why they separated vital organs from the body. They used energy centers—focused energies, like equivalent of chakra centers, to direct power, to accomplish out-of-the-body work. The priesthood did this . . . member of the priesthood dealing with the dead . . . guardian of the dead. I was involved with this, that's why I'm getting a reaction.

Bud: Was this during your incarnation as Anon Hetok?

LaVedi: No. . . . This was an abuse of the bodies of the dead. This was not . . . not favorable . . . not . . . it was an abuse of the etheric energies during the interval after death, when the vital forces of certain areas were directed to accomplish certain ends. The reaction—my reaction, is down through the left side, or excuse me, right side—lower back, I guess it would be the liver . . . and down in the lower intestine area . . . that would be connected with the out-of-body focus through Jupiter forces . . . this was a negative karma attracted, very negative . . . damaging to the vital forces of the body and negative karma through the harm involved with many people . . . interfering with their normal dissolution and path onward after death, holding them to the earth plane and sending them on essentially in weakened condition after death. . . . Even the incenses, preparations they used in the jars for the organs, were connected with this.

Bud: Would this have been more accepted had the entities waited a longer period after death?

LaVedi: No. It was an abuse.

The *reading* explained that the organs they used to enhance their out-of-body work corresponded to various *chakra* centers. It also seemed that these Egyptians selected specific individuals with certain strongly developed traits and "encouraged" their premature death. Then the priests used the etheric energy of their chosen victims for their own purposes. We were also told that their etheric thievery was one of the reasons why kings had themselves sealed and guarded at their death.

It seems we had also "accidently" stumbled upon a serious abuse connected with LaVedi's karmic health problems. In a past-life reading done for her by the clairvoyant Noel Street in 1970,* he had told her about her misuse of out-of-body ability as a priest in a Temple of Capricorn in Egypt. Injury to her astral body was serious enough to carry forward thousands of years, through many lifetimes and into the present. Now its healing is being stressed through forgiveness and karmic balancing.

Returning to our initial purpose, to uncover the karmic reasons for the man's alcoholism, we found:

Bud: What is the connection here — the importance to _____ in his present-life experience?

_____

* *The Man Who Can Look Backward*, Noel Street, Samuel Weiser, Inc., 1969.

LaVedi: He's carrying guilt of this in other experiences. There's the selfish motivation that comes through some of this attainment, knowledge, contacts, abilities, grounding . . . These were abuses of a high level of knowledge, which we call negative forces. With those forces come emotions, reactions, reception of negative impulse. This causes depression, obscures vision, blinds the Light awareness, acts as a veil.

Bud: Is this one of the causes of the drinking problem?

LaVedi: That's right.

SEEK FIRST THE KINGDOM

The life *readings* presented in this chapter indicate the direct connection that exists between past-life karma and present-life mental, emotional and physical health. This is repeatedly indicated in the data of such past-life researchers as Edgar Cayce, Joan Grant, Patricia-Rochelle Diegel and Marcia Moore, as well as in the wealth of Eastern and Western esoteric literature. But, even assuming these karmic connections are true, how it is possible for you to apply this knowledge to face your own health problems?

One of the first things to do is honestly recognize your present condition, honoring it as a situation you have created yourself for growth. You might even view the situation as a detective story, one where you must piece the clues together to discover the karmic lesson. Once you discover your positive lesson or lessons, such as patience, acceptance, forgiveness, moderation or compassion, focus your attention on the necessary spiritual ideals in meditation and internalize them. Work toward achieving balance and harmony within and without.

At the same time consider seriously the possibility that you are NOT your body, but that *YOU ARE PURE LIGHT,* pure energy, pure spirit. Acknowledge that your physical body is *dense light* that can be directed by the strength of your DESIRE *and guided by your* WILL toward at-one-ment (atonement) with your *Source* and *Higher-Self.* Work with this possibility in your moments of meditation, self-hypnosis or deep reflection, and you will learn to discern the levels of truth for yourself. If you are quiet enough—still enough—you will KNOW all you need to know.

It seems that the *dance* we are participating in is so exquisitely choreographed that none of our human experiences inhibit our opportunity to work on our spiritual lessons. For example, intelligence has nothing to do with learning and expressing kindness, compassion or forgiveness. And even the most sickly person, broken of body can still learn kindness, love and positive thought from those caring for him, or it may be that he will be the example and teacher to these people.

Whether our role happens to be male or female, rich or poor, healthy or sick, *we are of our own creation.* We can summarize this in Christian terms as, " . . . seek ye first the kingdom of God, and his righteousness, and all these things shall be added unto you." (Matthew 6:33). Where does one seek this kingdom? The Master Jesus told us plainly in Luke 17:21, " . . . behold, the kingdom of God is within you."

So do not bemoan your physical plight, when, in

reality, your Higher-Self may be using a health condition to gain your attention. STOP feeling sorry for yourself. LOOK for your spiritual lesson, or for the lessons others may be learning from you. LISTEN to your Higher-Self, the small still voice. And then get off your spiritual fanny and get to work! The show must always go on; *injury or illness is no excuse.* So, dance through your tears if you must, but dance!

THE MASKED BALL

17

The Masked Ball

This is going to be great!
A masquerade ball!
Where is my pumpkin?

Your pumpkin?

Certainly, I need transportation, don't I?

But a pumpkin?

And my glass slippers.

Let's see . . . , where did I leave my glass
slippers . . . .

Ah, here's one of them!

Now, where do you suppose the other
one is?

Oh, well . . . ,

if you must have a pumpkin!

(LaVedi, you're on again.)

391

THE PROMENADE

At times we all feel as if we are living behind a mask, projecting images that are not the "real me." We need to work continually at finding our true *Self,* amidst a continual flow of expectations from our egoic self, others and a mirage of unconscious past-life personalities. We often pretend to be what we aren't, attempting to meet life as it is thrust upon us. Sometimes these pretenses become so real, we think the role we are playing is our true *Identity.* Lives that have achieved degrees of fame or notoriety are likely to spill over strongly into following incarnations, because of emotional carryover and karmic interactions with others. Unfortunately the more influential the role, the more likely serious karma, possibly public karma, will be entailed. *Fame* without attachment is considered one of the more difficult initiations that must be passed successfully.

Masks can be very helpful, however, by giving us a certain amount of anonymity. We might compare this to writers who use a pseudonym, which frees them from identifying with their work. This allows a freer flow of creativity, with less ego attachment. Dancing behind a mask helps us to "let go," and give ourselves to the moment. We can become anyone we have ever dreamed of being, just be careful to dream of positive attributes and unselfish motives, or your dream might turn into a nightmare.

> Time brings not death, it brings but changes;
>   I know he rides, but rides afar,
> Today some other planet ranges
>   and camps to-night upon a star

Where all his other comrades are.
> (*A Comrade Rides Ahead:* The memory of
> Emerson Hough by Douglas Malloch, 1877-1938).

FOREIGN AMBASSADORS

Earlier we stressed how periodic cycles bring spiritual leaders and change in the collective consciousness of humanity. Most human activities are affected by such cycles of group incarnations, giving sudden bursts to society, science, literature, the arts, philosophy, reforms, etc. When the time is ripe astrologically and the earthly stage is set, groups will incarnate together to stimulate and support each other and accomplish a particular objective.

Most often these groups are spear-headed by non-earthlings who have been drawn into the evolutionary cycle of Earth. Unconsciously bringing knowledge from other worlds, they periodically attempt to manifest it on Earth, while attempting to reconcile themselves to earthly incarnation and seeking the solution to the human experience. The result of their search and inner struggles has produced great works of art, music, writing and drama. Unconsciously they know the answer to their quest is to conquer the flesh and matter, while also raising the awareness of the entire planet. Their creative response is more intuitive than conscious, since they feel "driven" to self-expression, even though they don't know why.

Sometimes the results have been confusing, since they often retain a deep unconscious fear of the involutionary pull of earthly expression. This has resulted in excessive dedication to causes and resistance to the human roles of love and family. Instead they immersed themselves in creativity, intellectualism, philosophy and ideals as a protective mask. For those who balanced physical and emotional expression, evolution was easier, but many would be plunged into the hot water of human emotions by their very fear of it. The result has been some of the greatest recorded spiritual battles of individuals with the lower-self.

THE GREAT PHILOSOPHERS

As Emerson wrote, "Out of Plato come all things that are still written and debated among men of thought," and behind Plato was his teacher, Socrates. Socrates (467-399 B.C.) has probably affected the course of our Western evolution more than any other philosopher. By his logic, clairvoyance and search for truth, he profoundly influenced Plato and an increasing number of flourishing young philosophers. He taught reincarnation, the inevitability of cycles and the importance of ethics in personal and national conduct. Adored by his students, he was also respected by his enemies. As is customary, history paints a glorified portrait of the famous, afraid to reveal the human being behind the mask. So, who was Socrates, really?

In 1977 I encountered the new updated version of the old philosopher, born in Alaska. He was the surviving twin of the one killed at Pearl Harbor and became the "thread" that took me to Ojai, California and a very special soul-group gathering. I did not immediately recognize the "old man," instead my first karmic recall was of an earlier life in Salonica (now Thessoloniki) in northeastern Greece.

There he also appeared as a philosopher, but the life was more provincial and incredibly idyllic. I was in female form, but was educated equal to the young men my father then taught. There was great equanimity among us and in our relationships. The balance was exquisitely tuned The life was one of those brief islands we are given to show us what is possible and give us motivation, before we are thrown back into the torrent of life to sink or swim.

My next memory of him was, when as Crito, a member of Socrates' academy, I managed his property and kept him financially independent, so he could pursue his teachings. It was Crito who upon Socrates final day, escorted him to his last bath, and Crito who, when Socrates breathed his last breath, closed the eyes of this man his friends all loved more than life itself.

Socrates has had a long lasting effect upon human thought, but, while he taught truth, he overlooked two things. The first was the importance of compassion for individuals, and the second was that we *karmically attract what we fear.*

This great man had a wife, Xanthippe, known for her violent temper. She loved Socrates in her way, and saw his students as competitors for his money, affection and attention. Ignoring a serious karmic debt already existing between himself and Xanthippe from the past, Socrates ignored her. He took to the streets and followed his own pursuits. At the same time, he was a passionate man, but he sought to deny this human side of himself, fearing the power of the flesh and its attractions. He failed to recognize or acknowledge the genuine misery of his wife. Both he and the rest of us judged her, and by so doing, we passed judgment upon ourselves.

We sentenced our future lives to include the torments of Xanthippe, as well as our fears of the sensual and material world. Though carrying the wisdom of Greece subconsciously with us, we would still have to overcome our fears of physical entanglement, by diving deeply into the physical and material expressions of earthly life. We would be forced to conquer the power of the emotions by experiencing and facing them, instead of being permitted to deny and avoid them. By shunning Xanthippe we fell under the powerful feminine *involutionary* tides of Mother Earth, the unconscious fostering of desire for manifested expression.

Socrates reappeared in this lifetime with all the power that might be expected of such an individual. He has a similar sense of humor, the same penetrating wisdom and logic and even the same appearance, but the *dance* is different. Concentration now is upon those two lessons he rejected before, compassion for individuals and his former fear of passion, emotion and sensuality.

To set his direction, Socrates had a recurrent dream before he died that implored him to make music. In this lifetime he finally did, starting with exposure from an early age and later graduating with a university degree in music. Then "fate" took a hand and karma began catching up. His musical background took him into the entertainment world of California and here he found a playground to release the old repressions. His talents brought him wealth, as might be expected, in the film world. Then Xanthippe with all of her old personality traits, appeared to continue her attempts at domesticating the wandering

Socrates to the comforts of home and hearth. He loves the comforts, and while after a fashion he has honored her claim on him, he has not given her an easy time for her pains. Most of all he is trying to find himself again and, in the throws of his struggle, has not made it easy for those around him, friend or foe. Clairvoyant as before, his intuition tells him he must conquer alone. He is one of us who entered the earthly experience during the Venusian cycle. His astrological influences today are predominately Taurian (Venusian), and are nearly identical to those of the former Socrates.

THE RELUCTANT SAINT

Some 700 years later my studies of the Greek philosophers was renewed in Rome. Carrying forward idealism from Greece and feeling overwhelmed by human suffering, religious inclination prompted me to join one of the new orders of monks emerging at the time. Maintaining my strong respect for the written word and the study of the classics, my library was lugged around with me, even as it is today.

Then a burst of clairvoyance and a vision seemed to direct me away from intellectualism and toward deeper spiritual pursuits, very similar to my motivations in this present-life experience. At that time, however, this tended to be channeled into stern asceticism, exchanging one form of mental expression for another. The soul trend continued though, with the collection of manuscripts, language studies and lengthy writings. And, following the early Church Father, Origen, continuation of Greek thought on reincar-

"The Reluctant Saint"
Illustration by artist William (Bill) Berry, 1975.

nation was held.

Later, as a priest and under threat of disfavor from Rome, I gave support to Pope Theophilus in his crusade against the teachings of Origen around 400 A.D. The memory "dropped-in" one day that this priest's name had been Jerome. He became lauded by the Church of Rome for his commentaries correcting "heresies," including the teachings on reincarnation.

That life's insult to *Self* was followed during the Inquisition by the privilege of dying chained to the prison wall in Spain, surrounded by the stench of filth and branded as a heretic by the Church. This time support had been staunchly maintained unto death of the Christian beliefs that included reincarnation. The Catholic Encyclopedia has this to say regarding metempsychosis, or the passing at death of a soul into another body:

> St. Jerome tells us that metempsychosis was a secret doctrine of certain sectaries in his day, but it was too evidently opposed to the Catholic doctrine of Redemption ever to obtain a settled footing. It was held, however, in a Platonic form by the Gnostics, and was so taught by Origen in his great work [*De Principiis*].

Now, over 500 years since that death in Spain, it is time to attempt to set the record straight and again lend support to the original Christian teachings. The time has come for a modern reappraisal of the original Christian beliefs.

ROMANCE IN THE BRITISH ISLES
Another cyclic group emerged in the 18th Century in

England and Scotland as a group of romantic writers. The circle included Lord Byron, Percy Bysshe Shelley, Mary Shelley and Sir Walter Scott. As a literary influence the group nurtured appreciation of individual human worth in a basically stiff-necked, class-conscious society, while Scott introduced the historical novel.

Byron and Shelley threw morality to the winds and espoused free love. They were "getting with the program," and were plunging into life, instead of rejecting human emotion as they had in Greece. As with such sharp swings, they went too far and incurred karma from the pain they caused, but they were reaching deep into their humanity. Shelley, for example, left his wife, Harriet, for Mary and provoked Harriet to suicide. Today Shelley and the former Harriet are remarried and are quietly working out their relationship in obsurity. Mary Shelley is now Barbara Lynn Devlin, and is writing again. At that time she created the character of *Frankenstein,* writing the book by that name. Now she is specializing in writing about astrology and re-incarnation.*

Lord Byron is now Robert Noel Byron, having reincarnated into the same family lineage as before. He looks much the same and possesses the same attitudes and magnetism as before, except that this time instead of one lame leg, he now has two. He is also writing again, but as with the group trend, now it is about reincarnation and related subjects. He has become expert in out-of-body techniques.

---

* *I am Mary Shelley,* Barbara Lynn Devlin, Condor, 1977.

Marcia Moore was a member of the group then, as Lord Byron's mistress. This experience, its memory and her friendship during this lifetime with Byron, prompted her to write *Byron: The Myth and the Man*. In that lifetime she had a low opinion of herself, a circumstance that may have been the impetus that brought her death in this life, when she expected too much too fast. Even so, she became one of America's foremost writers on astrology and reincarnation, and a pioneer in past-life recall.

"SCOTTY"

I began meeting members of this old group soon after moving to Ojai, California, where they were gathered at the time. At first I was unaware of the ties. I didn't know about them, until the day I met Byron and in his classic blunt style, his first question to me was, "Who are you?" I took an emotional step backward and instantly knew the answer, "Scott." At the time I consciously knew nothing about these people, past or present, so didn't even know if Scott and Byron had been contemporaries. Then I was informed that they had not only been contemporaries, but also friends.

Actually the idea of having been Scott wasn't new to me, but I had never pursued it. It was a life I hadn't wanted to face, though it had haunted me mildly since childhood, when I had tried immersing myself in a portrait of Scott, pursuing some unconscious pathway that persisted in eluding me. Then the first time I went to Edinburgh, I went for a walk to see the town and wandered directly to Scott's old Edinburgh home. The memory was fairly close to the surface by then, but I still refused to focus on it. I didn't like the museum. It felt barren, like a home after the movers have left. I much preferred the statue in the business district with my large dog beside me.

Following Byron's question and realizing the implications of the "regathering," I asked Barbara to assist me in doing a *reading* to see if we could find either confirmation or correction of the impressions. Going back in time, I entered Scott's childhood, where I found myself wrapped in a hot wet blanket and could barely breathe. We were using Marcia's *hypersentience* technique, so I was *there*, not acting as an objective observer, as we normally do in our *readings*. It seems I had been sick and my family was trying to make me sweat. It was extremely uncomfortable, so we moved on to another scene. This time we were in a country kitchen and my grandfather was massaging my legs and giving me a hot bath.

As it turned out, upon doing research following this experience, I found that Scott, the same as I in this life, had had polio as a young child. We both had sickly childhoods and, continuing the karmic syndrome into adulthood, we both developed back problems from the polio and both had serious bowel problems. (Actually these were just old manifestation of the former astral abuses and injuries in Egypt).

In the *reading* we next moved through several events, up to the emergence of Byron as a literary success. My views about my friend, expressed under the *hypersentience* technique, were *very* strong about this "young upstart," and I revealed my hidden feelings of inadequacy as a poet, emphatically declaring that I would have to resort to the "inferior form of the novel," to avoid "exposing myself to ridicule." All of this was stated in an extremely thick Scottish brogue, which I couldn't possibly imitate consciously, and was accompanied by what we later learned were characteristic facial expressions. A comparison of handwriting also revealed common characteristics I have used since learning to write in this life, such as the writer's "g" and uncrossed ending "t." Try as they would, my school teachers could not change my irregular habits.

Obviously the streak of stubborn pride had emerged, and the reason for writing the novels anonymously at first became clear. Scott did not want to claim them, but after they succeeded, he felt they were acceptable. He lived very much behind a mask of propriety, unable to resolve his personal inner dilemmas. Charming and entertaining externally, trying much too hard to please everyone, he carried over suppressed feelings he could not "digest."

Part of this related to the life immediately prior, when he had been Pierre Langvoir, an artist, historical writer, political activist and clairvoyant with the ability to extend his consciousness at will. A Parisian born in 1686, by mid-life he thought he was a failure and gave up, not realizing his future still lay before him. One of the difficulties of being under the Capricorn influence is that success rarely surfaces until after mid-life. Scott, though having a Leo Sun, had Saturn conjunct it in his tenth house of careers, and both Pluto and Jupiter were in Capricorn in his third house related to writing. In my present life Leo has moved to my Moon (unconscious), while Jupiter remains in Capricorn, now conjunct the Sun at the Mid-heaven (related to self-knowledge), while Pluto switched signs, so it remains at the bottom of the chart (forced transformation and karmic drain). Neptune remains in Virgo, signifying the bowel problem. Essentially the two charts just flipped, as Scott had Libra rising, now, I have Aries, with Mars placed where the Moon and Ascendant were previously, related to karma.

In the life immediately following Scott, Julianne repeated the strong Capricorn influence, this time with the Moon, Saturn (again) and Mars in this sign, the latter two falling in the fifth house related to theater, with Jupiter also in this house, but in the next sign of Aquarius (freedom of expression).

While Scott's mask appears to have fooled most people, the worldly Lord Byron saw right through him. At a second memory recall, Barbara guided *both* Byron and myself back together into our old personalities. Then Byron began reminiscing, sentimentally summing up our past conversations and his impressions:

> It was like the old philosophers getting together and sharing a piece of chewing gum. . . .

> Insecurity, that's what you had . . . , I've got piercing eyes, and you've got a piercing heart, which would you rather have? I can look at somebody and scare them half to death, and you can look at them and make them feel love. . . . You like to suffer, you know if you don't suffer, you won't be able to give enough.

> You've got to sit down and think about what's really important in life . . . , pen, nipples and . . . (laughter). You were too

damn gentle with everybody, you weren't risque, there wasn't enough zest of life in you. I couldn't imagine any real excitement in your whole life. I bet at five years old you would have been a grandfather figure." (Indignantly Scott replied, "I was an *onery* lad.")

It was all an act. You've got to take a good healthy chunk out of life and taste it and I don't think in your adulthood, you ever took a good healthy chunk out of life. Life loves to be bitten. You had this thing in you, like gentleman down through centuries; it seemed to be born right in you.

I told him [Scott] I would like to read something he wrote when he was really angry, really steaming mad, when there wouldn't be any lead links [typical Saturn symbol] holding him, no restraints.

Tell them about the wine glass, Scotty . . . . (Byron continued) I didn't know this until right now . . . , he took my wine glass and put it behind books, and he wouldn't let it be cleaned, he hid the damn wine glass. I can see this now, but I didn't know it then. That's cute, he probably had a collection of glasses . . . .

You walked near that guy and you really felt secure, everything even if it was topsy-turvy, was still very much organized. Go up to your death, Scotty, and tell me the first thing you see (Scott remembered being met by Byron). . . . One of the biggest dreams this guy had in his whole life was to have a desk the size of the average person's whole room, and that was materialized just out of wishful thinking.

A humorous aspect of this is that I still have my preoccupation over desks, usually using two or three instead of one, and, indeed, taking up an entire room whenever possible. Less humorous was the suppression of temperament to avoid the pain of rejection. This was something that has had to finally be conquered in this lifetime, the power and harshness of the full personality being simply more than many can tolerate. Even Scott with his attempt at pleasing, was still known for being "unconsoling." To go against the crowd means to stand very alone, but it is the only way to stand true in your own Identity, with no man-made masks placed upon you by society or the *expectations* of others and their images of what you *should* be.

As Bud said earlier, it is difficult to claim the experience of any famous lives, because too much importance has been attached to them. It seems presumptuous and is likely to get one classed among the "nuts" of humanity. However, *fame* simply implies that there has been some form of accomplishment or notoriety that received public attention. It does not represent the true qualities of the person.

It should also be born in mind that such experiences are not necessarily those of single personalities, since they may be shared with others in various ways. Reincarnation is much more complex than just simple one to one transfers of personality from body to body. Remember the soul can split, impress aspects of itself on others and seemingly share memories with many people, so apparent *personal* recall of a particular life can have a variety of possible interpretations. It's all part of the game, or the *dance*.

While Julianne's life, following Scott, was not especially successful, she did take the plunge and attempt to learn the meaning of life and love from experience. The sadness and lack of fulfillment carried forward into the life of the

Spanish soldier, and when he gave up the try it carried forward into this life. Eventually it all had to be faced, and like a snowball gathering bulk and momentum, it eventually came crashing down in a "kill or cure" syndrome. The result was touch and go, but I had "gotten the message," this time no giving up, no suicide, no escapism. I had tried them all to no avail. The only way is to "face the music," and what will be will be. No more pleasing the Church, society, public, etc., it is the *Self* that must be faced and merged with. Or, as Jesus said, "Seek ye the kingdom first. . . . "

I rarely speak of these lives, as they are generally painful to me. Scott, overextended financially, spent his latter years working to pay off the bankruptcy debt of his publisher-partner. The stress finally killed him and the debt was cleared from his estate. It was both a physically and emotionally demanding life. Julianne though she didn't quite commit suicide, did tempt fate, by walking on the crumbling edge of a cliff by the English sea, where she fell to her death at the age of 40. I would as soon close the door on this costume closet and leave it locked, after one or two more bits of business.

NORTHERN LIGHTS

Earlier I mentioned that my Spanish mother had been my abused nephew; his uncle was Scott. As might be expected, this drama still had to be played out, since I cut it off short. He turned up again in Alaska, the state being a kind of magnetic karmic melting pot. The relationship has been as difficult as ever, his subconscious motivations producing chaotic situations. The relationship remains to be fully resolved, but hopefully we can both successfully release the grip of the past.

Bud and I did a *reading* for this individual to find out who he had been and found another non-earthling attempting to work his way through the maze of human intanglement. He had had the opportunity to use power politically to benefit a populace as King Gustavus III of Sweden, but instead led his people into ruinous war and himself into disgrace. Having never heard of Gustavus, I looked him up and was amazed at the physique and facial resemblance to the present day personality. We found:

> One who has walked the Halls of Knowledge, a being not of earth origin. There is a problem that often occurs with non-earthlings in the development of earth consciousness. Their minds function normally upon another dimension. In learning earth consciousness, there are often gaps, stresses, places without emphasis in development. This entity is not an exception to this situation.

> There are two avenues of friction. One, attunement to the natural level of consciousness beyond this earth plane. Two, realization of consciousness, the seat of consciousness on this plane, and healthy relating to it. It is like having static, (or) two stations functioning, and this is rather common, that earth-consciousness tends to short-out in essence and walks both avenues of communication. (We might relate this to a "feed-back" syndrome.)

> This entity has an imbalance in his nature brought about by an unhealthy . . . desire for power, causing grief to his people, whom he should have ruled with love and justice. An oppor-

tunity lost and a debt acquired, the seed which bore such bitter fruit must be dug from the make-up of this entity. For it is alien to his purpose. It must be faced, accepted, and self forgiven . . . . Self-pity is not the way, forgive self and ask forgiveness of those damaged, disillusioned. This personality has come with the emotional makeup to bring certain qualities faithfully to the awareness so they may be faced, forgiven and put to good use in redirected positive energies.

Today he is still searching for himself, of an intellectual-scientific-adventuresome bent, he continues to resist the greater *Self*. In that earlier life, he tried to manifest social reforms, but succumbed to political chicanery and war. He's still working on those lessons related to others. His chances of Self-realization are strong, with an evolved soul-mate to help him. I'm sure there is even more to our particular dramatic interaction than has surfaced. We probably killed each other off through the centuries, but it is time to call a screeching halt and say, "No more."

As Bud mentioned earlier, this person was not the only one of our karmic group to succumb to political pressures and failure. We had that humbling experience at the time of the Hyksos invasion of Egypt. At the time we were apparently brother and sister, and while I was for fighting the invaders and saving the greatness that had been Egypt, Bud describes himself as indifferent and uncaring, due to mourning over the death of his dearest friend.

This was a dissipated period and our defenses were badly organized. I had not only to contend with my brother's lassitude, but with division and resistance among my officers and advisers. In my determination, I finally resorted to eliminating my brother's opposition by having him knifed to death in his bath, but it was all for nought. Standing alone, I was forced to take my choice of being killed or abdicating.

Until recently, I was not able to find any confirmation for or against our recall. This period was so tumultuous that records are sparce. It appears, though, that Bud was Amenemhet IV, the heir of Amenemhet III, "but his brief reign of a little over nine years has left few monuments, . . . he was succeeded by the Princess Sebek-nefru-Re . . . . After struggling on for nearly four years she too, the last of her line, disappeared. The family had ruled Egypt two hundred and thirteen years, one month and some days."*

Probably our rule had not actually been joint, but rather I had tried and failed to influence him, explaining more strongly the need to "remove" him. Both reigns were so brief and intertwined, that we took them to be one. I lived that life out in humiliating exile among my oppressors, bearing the burden of my failures. "Rapid dissolution followed, as the provincial lords rose against each other and strove for the throne. Pretender after pretender struggled for supremacy," and "foreign adventurers took advantage of the opportunity . . . King still followed King with unprecedented rapidity . . . . Where preserved at all, the length of the reign is usually but a year or two . . . . " So it was, that Bud and I saw the end of a period of Egyptian greatness. About 1657 B.C. the Hyksos invaders

---

* *A history of the Ancient Egyptians,* James Henry Breasted, Ph.D., John Murray, London, 1929.

came to claim the remains. They remained until finally driven out by Ahmose I about 1580 B.C., when he assumed leadership of the Theban house and delivered Egypt. Then a new empire that eventually produced an attempt at monotheism was built. "The triumph of a Theban family had brought with it the supremacy of Amon. Transformed by the solar theology into Amon-Re . . . he now rose to a unique and supreme position of unprecedented splendor as the state god."

During this period, perhaps my karma caught up with me for killing Bud a couple of centuries earlier. I was doing religious and architectural restoration, and while inspecting a tomb under construction, I had my throat cut from behind by a political enemy. (Bud?) Those were bloody times, and we relied on murder to settle differences. The cycles of life, people, nations and civilizations rise and fall with the tides. The human will and violence are no match for the inevitable. The only real solution is to learn to flow along and ride the crests and falls.

COSTUME EXCHANGE

Anyone who has ever been to a masquerade celebration, such as *Mardi Gras*, knows some very strange costumes appear on the streets. Many of these belong to homosexuals and transvestites. We are often asked about their place in the *dance*, so we will share some basic information that may increase understanding of these special groups, bearing in mind that many cases are unique and cannot be generalized.

We need to go back to the androgynous soul that split

itself into the sexes. Each of us is basically male or female, unless we bypassed this stage or have merged with our twin-half. A common situation that creates difficulty in accepting a sexual role is simply adjusting to the opposite gender, especially if repeated incarnations have been in one sex, or the "natural" sexual role. We find that men, in particular, may have a difficult time even facing that they have lived female roles. Yet the cosmic experience of manifestation requires the development of *balance* between both of these fundamental polarities and they must be integrated to create the third, the unified Self and soul. We cannot merge with our *other half,* if it is undesirable to us to do so.

Many homosexual individuals belong to a particular reincarnating group, having come into physical incarnation under the permanent stamp of its influences. Among the effeminate there seems to be a particular mixture of Lunar, Venusian and Mercurial influence, manifesting in the characteristic speech, gestures, intellectual ability and artistic aptitude of many homosexual men. They have repeatedly appeared in groups, such as in Greece and in Europe. Now a large gathering is in San Francisco, California, where the social and cultural climate is favorable for them.

Condemnation or ridicule is not going to change their elemental composition or their pattern of expression. They are a product of evolution, carrying the karma of a time when sexual energies were diverted. Even the church concept of celebacy is one of these old diversions, stemming from the attempt to keep the *children of God* pure by preventing marriage with the *children of men.* These entities must work through their own lessons. Ironically the present demands for equal rights, will produce karma that will pull them out of their group energy and draw them into emotional interaction with more conventional humanity.

This result will also be true for that vocally militant group of lesbians involved in extremes of women's liberation. This group seems to be stamped with Solar and Martian influences, and have probably appeared in powerfully matriarchal societies. Then there are other homosexuals who are not necessarily members of the original incarnating groups, but became members by association and bonds of affection formed along the way.

When you meet someone you have loved dearly through many lives, you may respond to more than just the sexual mask, as the subconscious memory resonates. This can be rough if roles are confused, but gradually these relationships do sort themselves out and the individuals incarnate into appropriate bodies.

Bud and I ran into a case where this type of homosexual carry-over was evident. In the present life the man's former dominant male partner incarnated as a woman and, following the memory pattern, they married. This at least offered appropriate bodies, but there was a problem, as they had reversed their old roles. Now, instead of the present husband having a chance to develop a male image, he was dominated by his masculine wife.

His subconscious response to this was to return to relationships where he could get the right role support—meaning homosexual, even though he didn't really want to do so. The feeling was compulsive. The two of them will need to develop the characteristics that go with their present sexual roles and it may not be easy. The process must involve the wife working on femininity, while at the same time helping her husband to develop a more secure male image of himself. Then he may be able to begin reversing his subconscious programming.

AFTER THE BALL . . . .

One more group that differs from the norm and who have a problem accepting present sexual roles are the transvestites. Generalizing about these unusual individuals is very difficult, as each case is likely to be unique. Some of them seem to be caught in subconscious "tape-loops," much like the ghosts. They seem to get caught in personality shells or memories of a particular time or place and feel compelled to keep reliving them, until either worn-out or overcome.

In one such case the man was overshadowed by the shell of a powerful female personality from an incarnation in Mesopotamia. His own emotional problems had allowed her to grow stronger and stronger, nearly driving the present personality out of the body. If he doesn't conquer her and send her packing, he will not be able to develop his present masculine incarnation, creating a very serious personality imbalance.

Bud and I did a *reading* for another case where the entity had been one of a set of twins, but then they decided not to incarnate. After the female body had been aborted the over-shadowing female entity decided she wanted to incarnate anyhow, so she took the male body. This really "upset the apple cart," so to speak. She cost her partner his body, taking it herself, and then found herself in a male body she couldn't relate to. Consciously she felt she was female, which she should have been, only she was wearing a male body. Despite heavy family opposition, the young man's feelings were so powerful that he had a sex change operation. It was a complete success, and he (she) now is happy as the woman he was supposed to have been in the first place. *She* is seeking spiritual growth and making normal adjustments to life.

You never know what is really behind another's mask. Nor do you know what cosmic jig-saw puzzles are being worked out. It is best to let well enough alone and simply accept people for whoever, or whatever, they are. There is only one certainty: behind the mask, or in the costume, is one of *us*, striving for the same goals and undergoing the same problems. He or she is trying to understand and work it all out in his or her own personal way. It's great if you can lend a hand, but *don't interfere*, (unless you feel the dubious need for extra karma).

DANCE OF THE SUGAR PLUM FAIRIES

18

Dance of the Sugar Plum Fairies

Cut! Take that mask off and put on
this purple suit and join that small group over there . . . .
Wait a minute . . . , what's with this
round purple costume?
You're doing the intro
to the next scene as a sugar plum.

A sugar plum?

Right! A sugar plum.
What type of sugar plum? A dashing
young sugar plum, or one more on the
wrinkled prune side?
Never mind that. Listen, this time, after
the intro
you go back behind the "veil" to
experience power and money.
Power and money?
Yes.
A lot of power and money?
417

All you could possibly imagine.

I don't think I'm centered
enough for that yet. How about
some big-time poverty, or disease or
something?

Nope. You don't want Scheduling to louse
up the whole cosmos, do you?

Well . . . , no, but . . . .

Just relax and try to
remember who you REALLY are.

Yeah, but that's tough down there
with only five active senses.

So, develop your intuition.
You can do it. Just try to re-tune to
this vibration again, then I'll help you out.

Really?

Sure.

Say, that's really big of you.

Uh . . . . right.

THE CHALLENGE OF WEALTH

Some of the happiest and most intelligent people I
have known have been poor by our material standards,
only they do not view their lives that way. "Wealth" is a
relative man-made value, but time and again I have watched
civilized standards being forced upon other cultures, thereby destroying their own merits. One of the more remarkable poor people (by our standards) I have had the
privilege to know was Pedro Sanchez, an illiterate man
who literally hewed out a self-supporting ranch in the

Chiapa Jungle on the Mexican-Guatamala border.

Recognizing the threat of change to his way of life, he managed to establish a balance between the old and the new. Located over 100 miles from the nearest town, the people travel the powerful Usumacinta River in handmade dugout canoes, wash their clothes in the river, cook over open fires, sleep in hammocks and live in bamboo huts that come alive with roaches at sunset. However, his wife has two or three servants to care for the children, prepare food and do chores. At the time I was there in 1968, the ranch supported 13 people and had visitors from around the world who came to hunt or explore ancient ruins. They arrived by small plane, landing in a strip beside the compound. Pedro has been included in a book on the 10 most remarkable men in Mexico, using a yardstick, I'm sure, very different from those of more modern countries. Pedro chose this way of life rejecting offers to join relatives in settled areas. It's a good life and they are content by choice.

In Alaska we frequently see similar situations, where people come from all walks of life to escape the pressures of civilization and move into remote areas that may be accessible only by air. I've known several who have come from wealthy and prominent families, trading kith, kin and money for a frontier lifestyle. In the old days they married native women and became "squaw men," adopting the Native ways of life. This is less common now that the cultures are merging, but that hasn't stopped the rugged ones from "leaving it all behind."

It's a valuable experience and seeking it brought me

to Alaska and to my home in the McKinley Park area. My husband and I had had it with trying to make a go of business in Oregon and decided to do an experiment in living off of the land. We had strong backgrounds in hunting, fishing and survival techniques, so we opted for adventure. Our first summer in Alaska was spent primarily living on blueberries and grayling, and the first winter's diet was built around moose and caribou. The caribou migrated past our door by the hundreds, each stepping in the tracks of the preceding ones, and the wolves howled their mournful serenade among the snow-covered spruce trees sparkling under the glow of the moon during the long winter nights. Our nearest neighbor was 30 miles away by snowshoe, with the exception of the bears, foxes, wolverines and ptarmigans. Overhead the Northern Lights crackled and snapped, waving their curtains of filmy light. There is no way to place monetary value upon such a life or the effect it has upon the soul. For me it put me in touch with my inner *Self* and pointed to new directions, while for my ex-husband it became home and he remained.

I have also known some really unhappy wealthy people. I later married briefly into such a family. My ex-father-in-law was a tall, youthful, handsome man with extremely good taste, a lovely home and dear wife, but he spent most of his time trying to find contentment on the golf-links of Hawaii or in cocktails. The family was rife with game-playing, hard feelings and suspicions—all over money.

In contrast one of my best childhood friends came from another millionare family (before today's inflationary

THE *Lifestar* HOME STUDY COURSE

SPIRITUAL HYPNOSIS & PAST LIVES

BUD HOLLOWELL, Ph.D., has now prepared twelve written lessons, accompanied by six special cassette tapes for your progressive study of **SPIRITUAL HYPNOSIS at home.**

Please send me more information on this opportunity to study with Bud:

Name _____

Address _____

City, State, Zip _____

COLLEGIANS International Church
P.O. Box 929
Fairbanks, AK 99707-0929

bite), but none of us knew this until years later. They lived just like everyone else, the only difference being a certain attitude of nonchalance and a stable full of Arabian horses that were trailered back and forth between Oregon and Arizona annually. They were lovely people and very dear to all of us. They knew how to enjoy their wealth and not let it run, or even interfere, with their lives.

The great danger, especially of sudden wealth, is falling into all sorts of egoic traps, social expectations, pretentions, extravagance and bad management. The lifestyle itself can become a terrible burden, if allowed to. Artificial standards abound, and the undiscriminating may find money to be like quicksand. Suddenly everyone is a "friend," and paranoia tip-toes into the picture, while pitfalls abound.

On the other hand, for those who have grown accustomed to wealth, its loss can be equally devastating. My maternal grandfather lost his money in a stock market crash at the turn of the century and died of a heart-attack shortly after from the trauma, leaving his family in poverty. He was only 38-years-old. Later, family fortunes recouped, I was born "with a silver spoon in my mouth" and a "future," but all of that vanished like so much vapor in 1941. The material world can treat us very much like a breath-taking roller coaster ride. If personal values and standards have not been firmly established internally, the experience of wealth, or its loss, can be very testing.

While fate seemed to take cruel twists and turns in my mother's life, I shall always be grateful to her for firmly instilling in me attitudes about money and how to properly relate to it. At the same time she also passed on an appreciation for the arts, the value of education and independent creative thought. Though she never fully recovered herself from her life's losses, my father seemed to thrive on his self-reliance and the pioneer quality of rebuilding a life in Oregon. He was more of an adventurer, having even trapped in the Oregon wilderness earlier. An artist as well, and a business man, he taught me an appreciation of nature and a more rugged type of independence, bordering on social rebellion. Their philosophies created a strange blend, separate, yet merging in values of independent free-thought.

The finding of an inner direction and set of values is of enormous help in relating to money. You can toss external values out of the window and be immune to outside influences. To relate to wealth constructively, goals must be set that relate to the *soul's purpose*. Then worldly standards become meaningless and lose their power to affect you.

MONEY EQUALS ENERGY

All to often I find great confusion among spiritually oriented people regarding money. They may be afraid of it, or treat it as if it is a dirty word or something to be ashamed of. "Money" in whatever form it happens to be— paper, metal or property, represents someone's energy. An entire chain of people have gone to great efforts to produce it and the energy it represents. Financial energy should be given its proper respect and handled accordingly. It represents energy made manifest for us to utilize constructively toward the greatest good (assuming this is our orientation).

Attitudes about money should be carefully examined under a magnifying glass. The idea that it is "not spiritual," is nothing but bunk, meaning the individual is not centered enough to use it well. It is precisely as spiritual as its application, representing God's energy just as much as the rays of the sun or the wind in the trees. It is only negative if the ego identifies with it materialistically for self-gratification, driving the individual deeper into illusions and away from *Self.* It is not an easy energy to handle, especially in quanity, but neither is Fire or Water. Money represents the element of Earth, and we need to know how to use it correctly, if we expect to *"master"* matter. We most certainly cannot do this by fearing it, while throwing it away is irresponsibility toward divine manifestation. It is an important subject in this New Age, as groups face the need for money management and best use of funds to achieve purposes.

We have come into a capitalistic material society to learn to correctly relate to financial energy, not attempt to "play ostrich" and bury our heads in vows of poverty taken in the past for different lessons. We slow up our evolutionary progress by getting hung-up on outdated objectives.

In my opinion Americans have been unfortunate to be so poorly educated about financial management and monetary balance, having come to rely on a system built upon shifting sands, instead of themselves. The result today is creating serious social problems, when the elderly and others who have been given the expectation of state support find that this is an illusion and the affluent society can now barely sustain them in poverty.

The result has been great disparity in financial distribution and, therefore imbalance. Excessive wealth and extremes of poverty, both in our own country and worldwide, warn that the karmic balance is seriously out of kilter, with some taking advantage of material wealth at the expense of others. Each person would be adequately provided for, if a relatively fair exchange existed for services rendered or energy expended. But this exchange rate fluctuates, set by the cost of acquiring, manufacturing, producing and distributing goods (energy forms). As some people take advantage of this sequence either by arbitrarily raising prices, or by making payment demands, the energy chain becomes distorted and loses its fair exchange. Then the governments step in with political goals and attempt to "regulate" this imbalance. The result is chaos and the spiraling runaway world inflation we see today, as people everywhere increase expectations. If nothing else, we may be forced to return to a gold standard to put a stop to the ineffectual regulations and worldwide seesaw. If people in general understood the fundamental utilization of financial energy, they could make this an earthly paradise. The present monetary system is flirting with global diseaster.

The possession of wealth is a heavier karmic responsibility than is generally recognized. It absolutely is not a reward, anymore than poverty is punishment, these being worldly standards, not spiritual measures. If financial energy is abused, no heavenly insurance policy exists to pay the losses, making wealth one of the most dangerous earthly experiences. We can hardly think of this as "reward." You don't send your child out to play in the street to protect him. You do, however, allow him to experience a degree of danger, so he can develop a healthy respect for it.

Now, if you flip the coin, this means that wealth can also be one of the most karmically beneficial experiences, when related to under the light of *Self.* In our society, it is impossible to function without money. It took money to publish this book, it takes money to appear before people, to travel or to distribute knowledge and information. There is no "free lunch." What we must be prepared to do is *give up our personal attachment* to "our" money. We do not "own" it, anymore than we own anything else. We are *caretakers,* and if we will just remember this, it will change our entire attitude. Whatever you receive has been given into your charge, whether earned, inherited or won, and it should be treated accordingly. If Jesus appeared before you right now and placed a bag of gold coins in your hand, how would you treat it? Would you bury it, spend it frivilously, throw it away disrespectfully, or would you ask why it was given to you? Under the guidance of the *Self* you would do your best to utilize it constructively. You might not succeed, but you would put forth your best effort if you thought of God as the owner, and yourself only as a manager. The key to handling money is to disassociate egoic identification with it and place the values of the *Self* upon it, realizing that at this level it represents pure energy.

ON THE BEAM

Jesus taught, "Seek ye first the kingdom, and all else will be provided." In the face of starvation, this can be hard to believe. Sometimes it simply requires willingness to drop all pride and, in our humility, ask others for help. A friend of mine told me about watching a young man steal a bottle of milk and a loaf of bread everyday, when supplies were delivered to a store. She finally asked him why he did it, and he replied he had no other way to eat. The incident was referred to a spiritual teacher for comment and the lucid response was, "He hasn't given anyone the *opportunity* to help him."

How often do we think of the needs of others as opportunity for us, or of our own needs as signifying an opportunity for someone else? Once past some of these barriers, you will find that your needs really are met, possibly being fulfilled before you even anticipate them. This is a strong indication that you are "on the beam" and flowing with life under the guidance of the *Self*. When you resist the flow and create egoic desires and blocks, you move "off center," and slip back into earning your living by the "sweat of your brow." This does not mean you will not have to work if in tune, but rather that such work is a pleasure through its service and sense of accomplishment.

GLOBAL CONSCIOUSNESS

Desire is the great illusion. Each time you think "I

want," it is programmed into your unconscious mind for future reference. You are continually creating your future reality, but if you release your personal will and say, "Not I want, but Thy will," then you turn over your personal desires to the greater purposes of your soul. Progress can then be very rapid, without the ego blocks of lower desires in the way to stumble over and find ways around. Each of us needs to develop such an attitude, if we are going to create a global consciousness and bring the New Age, and the "Kingdom," into manifestation on Earth.

We can do this, but we need to direct financial strength toward stopping pollution, developing non-detrimental sources of energy and the rapid production of non-fossil fueled transportation. We need a powerful drive toward all positive forms of education that will increase public awareness and redirected demand. I find it impossible to imagine that anyone can not know what to do with financial energy, when the needs are so vital and urgent. We need to shift our emphasis away from self-gain to survival and evolution for all. A concentrated cooperative effort would work.

This same cooperative attitude needs to extend through all layers of society. We know that simply giving to the poor, for example, is no solution. People must be given the opportunity to learn, earn and accept self-responsibility, otherwise it is like pouring money through a sieve. Hardship creates a desire for self-betterment, if people are only allowed to keep their self-respect and develop pride of accomplishment. The welfare system in the United States has been notoriously detrimental in these respects, creating disincentive after disincentive to prevent recipients from regaining financial independence. No middle ground is permitted, no margin stimulates or encourages recovery.

Meanwhile successful cooperation is being demonstrated among numerous New Age communities worldwide, such as *The Findhorn Foundation* in Scotland, *The Farm* in Tennessee, *Oroville* in India, and *Ananta* in California. All types of communities are developing, with a variety of beliefs and purposes. Each is different, but all are striving toward a vision, a *wholeness* that is greater than the sum of its parts. They show that people can work together harmoniously for the betterment of all, while at the same time accelerating individual development. We grow by placing our goals outside of personal objectives, and by seeing ourselves reflected in those around us. We do not need to stand alone in isolation. Separatism produces poverty of body, mind and spirit, while many hands make all loads lighter.

All groups should be cooperating and showing mutual respect for each other in these critical times of change. Unfortunately even so-called spiritual organizations have had a tendency, very much like the traditional churches, to be highly competitive and slanderous of each other. The time has come to put a stop to this and also to call a halt to a tendency of some of the older groups to stand upon crystallized self-righteousness, in the face of altruistic waves of New Age idealism and unification. By attempting to rigidly preserve the old, they often thwart the new. Both sides need to learn to give more and arrive at compromise for their mutual benefit.

I can't help but think of one such spiritual center

that Marcia Moore had a special interest in. It's construction was financed by her family to support New Age concepts and teachings, but Marcia herself was a good example of the conflict that exists between the older and the newer approaches. From the older view, this center, or receptive channel, was to be kept pure in the strictest sense of the word, promoting writings from early in the century. From the newer point of view, which made Marcia a blacksheep in her own family, everything and anything should be welcome. Then someone like me comes along and says, "Obviously there should be a discriminating middle ground, that permits growth, but does not obliberate the original intent and purpose." Bless Marcia, she had a wistful dream that one day I would return and teach at this center, for despite her clash with it, she had a great love for it.

Cooperation should be the keynote sounded for the *New Age*, not self-righteousness, judgmental criticisms over viewpoints or moralistic bickering. Tolerance and respect for widely differing ideas and ideals is essential. A stiff-neck may find itself breaking instead of bending, as the pressures of this transition period continue to increase. The challenge is before us to manifest a positive alternative society by constructively balancing all of the energies that are at our disposal and of which we are ourselves created— *Fire, Air, Water* and *Earth*, plus the fifth which we are becoming.

THE MORNING REVIEW

19

The Morning Review

I think you are ready now to begin
    remembering some of your past lives.
                But, I already know all of them!
No, no. I don't mean here. I mean
    when you are behind the veil of
        physical illusion.
                The veil . . . ? Oh! THAT veil.
          Right. It's pretty tough to
          remember when you are in a human body,
            unless you can get centered.
True. That's why Scheduling has made
    special arrangements for age 33. By that time
you will have worked with manifestation
    long enough to become suspicious of its limitations.
  Then you will have a very moving
    near-death experience that will convince you that
          YOU are NOT your body!
      Sound about right?

431

Yes, I only have one question . . . .

And that is?

Do you suppose I could remember how I played
the mandolin back in the 17th Century . . . ,
so I could play a guitar this time?

Yes, I suppose so . . . , but . . . ,

We had a little group in Venice then. We called
ourselves the "Venetian Blinds,"
because . . . ,

Please, spare me the details.

Where's Bud? Find that hypnotist! He's on . . . .

CRITICAL APPRAISAL

Several common criticisms against the theory of pre-existence of the soul and its repetitive incarnation into the human form appear. The first one most often given is the observation that people, as a rule, do not remember their past lives. Therefore, it is assumed there are either no lives to remember, or they are forgotten and thus of no value. Another frequent criticism suggests that because of the population explosion there should be a shortage of souls, if reincarnation is true. A third criticism against reincarnation theory involves emotional and religious prejudice. It tries to condemn Eastern teachings and Western esoteric sciences as ignorant, superstitious and above all, anti-Christian.

In responding to these criticisms, we need to first understand that our ability to *forget* our past lives is very important. Sholem Asch, a Jewish scholar and novelist at the turn of this century, was quoted by Head and Cranston in their book, *Reincarnation,* as saying: "Not the power to remember, but its very opposite, the power to forget, is a necessary condition of our existence." Actually many *do* remember scenes from former lives during childhood, but we are seldom encouraged to pursue our "fantasies" (or recurrent dreams). Those who do remember are usually taught culturally to forget. But this may be a blessing, since few people are capable of dealing with information that is socially unacceptable and possibly disturbing psychologically.

The decision to seek *truth*, regardless of cultural inhibitions, family prejudice or individual religious persuasion, always leads progressively INWARD. This inward journey, irregardless of your background, involves raising your level of consciousness with feelings of love, compassion and forgiveness. This can be accomplished by a number of methods, such as *meditating* on a crucifix, a statue of Buddha or a flower; *contemplating* the life-giving sun, the *Tao* or the meaning of life; or *studying* the *Bhagavad-Gita,* the *New Testament,* or the *Kabbala.* Remember that all of these are just methods to raise your consciousness to divine levels of Godliness where oneness with God can be experienced. These methods and their practice and are not the goal; the goal is *Union.*

Without higher feelings of compassion and forgiveness, the knowledge gained from a past-life experience can be wasted or misused. Without spiritual preparation, for example, a man might prematurely discover that in a past life his father had killed him. He might then react at a lower ego-centered level with feelings of anger and resentment.

If he gains spiritual maturity, these areas of knowledge, as they open up, can become part of his natural unfoldment. With this maturity, he will learn to listen quietly and intuitively and KNOW that he is not his body. Instead he will know he is a *being of light,* beyond time and space, a being that merely works through a human form from time to time. He comes to KNOW he has no friends or enemies —only teachers and challenging situations. Plainly put, few people remember their past lives, because few are ready to do so. When you are ready, you will seek out the knowledge you need, including a technique to explore your own past lives. Then you will have the opportunity to find out for yourself, from EXPERIENCE, whether or not your present life will end in the grave.

Another reason why most people have not recalled their past lives, is that they never considered it was possible. Consequently, they have never tried to remember their past lives, or investigated the techniques available to enable them to do so. For example, when was the last time you tried to remember scenes from a past life? Yet, LaVedi can, I can, and hundreds of our workshop friends have learned to do so. This leads me to believe that whoever you are, when you are ready, you too will be able to remember. But as long as you consider this phenomenon to be impossible, it will be for you—not others—but for you.

If you don't feel ready now, perhaps some day, in either this life or a future one, you will be prepared to experience scenes from your former lives. Then you will probably begin to notice that they all say the same thing concerning the immortality of the soul, its need for purification in the physical realm, and its eventual reunification with the *Source*. You might start to relate to the idea of reincarnation, though perhaps still questioning it. Then will come the time to test your thoughts in the laboratory of personal experience.

A beginning interest in reincarnation may only serve to neutralize any previous negative religious or cultural bias against it. But once you are neutral and open, your belief one way or the other is unimportant, except in how you later interpret your findings. You may be surprised to find that the churches are basically right and that you really *are* an immortal soul. You may also find that you really *are* pure spirit, pure consciousness and pure energy that only works through the form of a body, and is not the body itself. If all this is true, then you really may walk away from the grave after all. But how do you know for sure? At this point, let us turn our attention to intuitive validity and personal experience.

One of the methods to prepare yourself for experiencing some of your past lives is to simply become increasingly sensitive to your intuition. For example, you may meet a man for the first time and instantly like or dislike him. Why should you experience such an illogical yet noticeable reaction? You may have had some strong emotional experiences with this man in the distant past, with these subconscious memories still vibrating at the emotional level. In this instance, you may be a "remembering" some past lives intuitively, though below the level of conscious awareness.

These subconscious memories may trigger *déjà vu* experiences, when for an instant you "know" you have been in the situation before, or you "know" exactly what is going to happen next. While *déjà vu* experiences may be explained in various ways, a few of them appear to be an instant past life replay. A good example of *déjà vu* phenomenon was reported by the famous English writer Charles Dickens in his *Pictures From Italy:*

> In the blood-red light, there was a mournful sheet of water, just stirred by the evening wind: upon its margin a few trees. In the foreground was a group of silent peasant girls leaning over the parapet of a little bridge, looking, now up at the sky, now down into the water; in the distance a deep dell: the shadow of approaching night on everything. If I had been murdered there in some former life, I could not have seemed to remember the place more thoroughly, or with more emphatic chilling of the blood: and the real remembrance of it acquired in that minute, is so strengthened by the imaginary recollection, that I hardly think I could forget it.

In discussing the criticism of increase in population, and the theoretical shortage of souls, the mistaken assumption is that there is a certain limited number of souls, that they are all in incarnation continually, and that they are all human and limited to our little planet. Perhaps we should broaden our perspective to consider the possibility that both the number of souls and the amount of time between their physical appearances may be unlimited— infinite by our concepts of time. Should this be the case, then criticism of the number of souls is not a valid argument. Also, if a variable time factor exists between physical incarnations, then it is possible for quite a sizeable "soul bank" to be waiting for proper circumstances to incarnate.

In the West it is frequently assumed that the soul is somehow created at the body's physical birth. But, perhaps, the soul always "was" and always will "be," whether it uses one body or many. It would seem logical that what the soul can do once it can do many times. In addition, the assumption that the soul's experience is limited to the human form could also be wrong. The question arises. "Are there any limits to the soul's possibilities?" According to our *readings* it certainly does not appear so. It seems that *all limits are only self-imposed.*

Not only is there an infinite number of souls waiting to continue their work in the human expression, there are also other souls evolving up through the lower kingdoms, waiting for their first human incarnation. Entities from other galactic systems are also waiting their turn.

As for the religious question concerning reincarnation and its threat to orthodox Christianity, we shall see later on in this chapter how reincarnation was a basic tenet of the early Christian Church for the first few centuries. Now, having discussed these main criticisms about the theory of reincarnation, let's examine some current research in support of it.

REMINISCING

Since the Bridey Murphy episode, thousands of cases of apparent far memory have been reported, scores of which offer even stronger evidence. Many have been scientifically researched by Dr. Ian Stevenson, Chairman of the Department of Neurology and Psychiatry at the University of Virginia. Among 28 cases presented by Dr. Stevenson in a booklet summarizing his research was the case of a young Japanese boy, named Katsugoro. When this boy was about 8-years-old, he began claiming that his name had been Tozo in an earlier life a few years previously. He said his father had been a farmer named Kyubei, his mother had been named Shidzu, and he had lived in a village known as Hodokubo. He went on to say his father had died and his mother had remarried to a man named Hanshiro. He said he had died himself from smallpox a year after his father's death.

The boy went on to describe his burial and the appearance of his old home and of his parents. When he was eventually taken to visit the village, the people he had named were either found or had been known. Unaccompanied by anyone from the village, the boy went to the home of his previous parents, recognizing both them and the house. He correctly noted that there was now a shop and a tree there that had not existed before. A number of affidavits were sworn to from responsible witnesses supporting the facts of the case. *(The Evidence for Survival from Claimed Memories of Former Incarnations)*.

The fact that Katsugoro provided 16 correct items is statistically very strong evidence supporting the theory of reincarnation. Equally significant were Katsugoro's remarks about a shop and a tree that had NOT been there before. This increases the probability of his report being an actual past-life memory.

The next case of far memory, again by a child, was brought to our attention by Shirley Merle, the mother of a young girl who reported very clear recall of scenes of her former life. This occurred in the United States and was also investigated by Dr. Stevenson. In 1976, he wrote to Shirley, "I am glad to have been of some small help to you, because I believe in the importance of your work in enlightening people in our country on the subject of rein-carnation. A lot of people have very strange ideas on that subject!" Shirley had written down her daughter's words as closely as possible in 1969. The story was finally pub-lished in the June 1976 edition of FATE magazine, entitled "Natalie Remembers."

It seems that young Natalie was petrified by sirens and anything having to do with fire. When she was four-years old, after dozens of inquiries, she finally told Shirley, in descriptive detail, how *her last mother* had accidently set their house on fire with a candle. And even though everyone got out safely, when her father came home he hit her mother for her carelessness. The young girl went on to say:

> I don't remember what happened right after that. The next thing I do remember was the orphanage. There were a lot of kids there. I was one of the older ones. I helped the younger ones eat and dress and I played with them. I tucked them in; we slept on straw mats. I changed their diapers.
>
> We didn't like the man who was the manager. There were a lot of us in the big room. It was dirty. There were bars at the window and the door. We were locked inside at night. There was one baby I especially liked, as if she were my little sister. I wouldn't let anyone else take care of her. Her name was Christine. One night a fire broke out. It was all over, even in

our room. We couldn't get out—the door was locked, I held
Christine close to me.

The next thing I remember, I was kind of floating. Below me
there was a funeral procession winding along the road. People
were walking along, not very many of them, some of them
carrying coffins on their shoulders. I floated close to one of
the coffins. I knew it was mine, that I was in there, but how
could I be in there and above it both? The manager was walking with the others, looking sad, but he was only acting. I
floated away, glad to be able to get away from the orphanage
and the manager. I don't remember where I went after
that.

As you might well imagine, Shirley was quite taken
back, if not totally stunned. Yet the story explained quite
logically her daughter's terrible fear of fire and sirens. It
also explained how this small child could know and use
conversationally the unfamiliar words: "orphanage," "funeral
procession" and "coffin." Having had no previous exposure
to reincarnation, this experience prompted Shirley to
launch her own search for an explanation. She began to
consider and explore the possibility that reincarnation
might be more than just a strange and unfounded theory.

LaVedi and I had the pleasure of having Rachel Mac-
Pherson (formerly Shirley Merle) in our Pastlife Memory
Workshop given at World University in Ojai, California.
Since then she has worked diligently with our cassette
tapes, taking the time to record the results of each of her
past-life experiences. As of this writing, she has uncovered
18 former lives. The following report is in Rachel's own
words after she worked with our tape entitled, "Journey

into the Past with a Loved One." The purpose of her inquiry was to understand her unexplained feelings of shame for her present mother.

> In seeking a past life connection with my mother, the next thing I am aware of is names: George Fox. Elizabeth. Margaret. I am a young child in gray, rough textured clothes. It is dark and crowds are shouting, stampeding; people are trampling each other! There are torches, I am frightened and hide in a ditch. The scene changes to a prison, dark, damp, confining. I can smell the dankness, the straw. My mother . . . , I am ashamed of her. Why?

> My father . . . , a prosperous businessman, I remember him standing in the doorway as I walked down the path holding my mother's hand, waving goodbye, tears rolling down my cheeks. My mother left him to follow George Fox, something about a religious movement. Quaker? It seems radical.

> I am with my mother in prison, I think she has a large basket over her arm, but don't know if we are inmates or visiting. I look up through barred windows and see a gallows being constructed.

Rachel had never heard of George Fox at the time she did this *reading*, and knew little of the Quaker religion. The next day, when she went to the library to do some follow-up research, she found that George Fox had been an English religious leader who founded the Society of Friends (Quakers) in about 1647. He was imprisoned many times and publicly punished. In 1699 Fox married *Margaret* Fell, the former wife of Judge Thomas Fell.

We cannot be sure if her present mother was also her

former mother, Margaret, who married George Fox, or if her father in that life was the Thomas Fell, who had been a member of Parliament in the 1600's. But Rachel feels the information gained from this past-life experience gave her conscious understanding for her previously unexplained feelings of shame about her mother. Now she *knows* the source of her illogical feelings and can consciously work to dissolve them with understanding and forgiveness.

FAMOUS CRITICS SPEAK

Of the many Greek and Roman scholars who wrote favorably about reincarnation, I feel Pythagoras, Plato, and Cicero made the most lasting impact on Western thought. What did they have to say about reincarnation? Pythagoras (582-507 B.C.) spoke of himself as having been Aethalides in a previous life. And during that life as Aethalides, he said he received from Mercury, the god of wisdom, not only the memory of his soul's transmigrations, but those of other souls as well. After his death as Aethalides, he recalled being reborn as Euphorbus, dying in that life from wounds received in the siege of Troy.

Plato (427-347 B.C.), however, is generally considered the central figure in the formulation of an actual theoretical framework for reincarnation. It was fundamental to his philosophy. He states in *Phaedrus,*

> Every soul is immortal—for whatever is in perpetual motion is immortal . . . . All that is soul presides over all that is without a soul and patrols all heaven, now appearing in one form and now in another . . . . Every man's soul by the law of his birth has been a spectator of eternal truth, or it would never

have passed into this mortal frame, yet it is no easy matter for all to be reminded of their past by their present existence.

Interestingly, in the following quotation from *On Old Age,* by Cicero (106-43 B.C.), this great Roman thinker speaks of the two preceding famous Greek philosophers, Pythagoras and Socrates. Cicero was convinced of the immortality of the soul and its ability to recall its past experiences, inspiring him to write:

> I used to be told that Pythagoras . . . never doubted that we had souls drafted from the universal intelligence. I used besides to have pointed out to me the discourse delivered by Socrates on the last day of his life upon the immortality of the soul—Socrates . . . the wisest of men. I need say no more. I have convinced myself, and I hold—in view of the rapid movement of the soul, its vivid memory of the past and its prophetic knowledge of the future, its many accomplishments, its vast range of knowledge, its numerous discoveries—that a nature embracing such varied gifts cannot itself be mortal.

Hundreds of famous critics have supported reincarnation in more recent times. These include such people as Bertrand Russell, Sir Arthur Conan Doyle, H.G. Wells. Albert Schweitzer, Francois Voltaire, Victor Hugo, Leo Tolstoy, Ralph Waldo Emerson, Walt Whitman, Mark Twain, and Henry David Thoreau. Thoreau actually recalled some of his past lives. For example, he wrote a letter to his friend Emerson dated July 8, 1843, which read,

> And Hawthorne too, I remember as one with whom I sauntered in old heroic times along the banks of the Scamander amid the ruins of chariots and heroes.

And then again, in a personal letter to his friend Harrison Blake, Thoreau wrote, on April 3, 1850, concerning another previous incarnation memory, this time during the times of the Master Jesus,

> I lived in Judea eighteen hundred years ago, but I never knew that there was such a one as Christ among my contemporaries.

Supporting critics may also be found in the fields of psychology and science. Some of these include such men as Charles Darwin, Sir Oliver Lodge, Carl Jung, J.B. Rhine, Ian Stevenson, Max Plank, Erich Fromm, Benjamin Franklin and Thomas Edison. Edison for example, was asked on his 80th birthday. "Do you believe man has a soul?" His reply was:

> No one understands that man is not a unit of life. He is as dead as granite. The unit of life is composed of swarms of billions of highly charged entities which live in the cells. I believe that when a man dies, this swarm deserts the body and goes out into space, but keeps on and enters another cycle of life and is immortal. (*Reincarnation, a Universal Truth,* R. F. Goudy).

But just because people we consider to be knowledgeable relate to a theory, does not make it true. A theory or hypothesis to be considered experimentally true in the Western sense of the word needs to be captured in the rigid world of measurement, or at least controlled enough to be a repeatable phenomenon. Therefore, if reincarnation is in fact true, people should be alive today who can repeatedly experience their past-life memories, who may remember details that can be provable, and even, perhaps, who can remember the past lives of other souls as well. As it turns out, a growing number of people are remembering some of their past lives, and, on occasion, the lives of others. Only *one* verifiable case of past-life memory should demonstrate the innate potential to remember. The one human being who repeatedly demonstrated this ability thousands of times over in the West, was Edgar Cayce.

EDGAR CAYCE PERFORMS WHILE ASLEEP

Edgar Cayce—the "sleeping prophet"—found that, with the aid of hypnosis, he could move into a trance state and clairvoyantly make medical diagnoses for people he had never met, even involving great distances around the world. He gave thousands of carefully recorded psychic medical *readings* from 1901 to 1923. In the years following 1923, up to the time of bodily death in 1945, Cayce gave life *readings* that explained not only the medical conditions of individuals, but the karmic causes for the difficulties based upon past lives. And usually at the end of his life *readings,* there would be a spiritual prescription for correcting the difficulty. As an example, the following *reading* was given to a young man afflicted with multiple sclerosis, who had received a medical *reading* from Cayce a year earlier. He followed the prescriptions from his first *reading* for four months and noticed marked improvement, but then his health began to take a turn for the worse. The clairvoyant Cayce pulled no punches with him concerning his failure to follow the spiritual prescription, saying the entity would have to change his attitude about "things, conditions," and his "fellow man." He implied the man was self-centered, self-satisfied and refusing spiritual things, and told him to eliminate "hate, malice, injustice [and] jealousy." Cayce then told the man he must develop "patience, long suffering, brotherly love, kindness [and] gentleness" to receive healing.

He emphasized the need for a change of heart, mind, purpose and intent, that the soul is not a body, and that problems arise due to misidentification with the body. The body is a temporary vehicle for the expression of the eternal Identity and the soul. As Gina Cerminara states herself in *Many Mansions,* the "soul is like an actor who takes different roles and wears different costumes on different nights . . . . "

Anyone who has read the Cayce literature will also notice the strong Christian theme throughout his work. There obviously remains a lasting impression from his past life as Luke the physician, who wrote one of the four Gospels in the *New Testament.* But it is also quite evident in his work that Cayce held a universal Christianity, rather than a closed, orthodox one. This is evident in the following *reading*, also from *Many Mansions,* when he says an entity "had companionship with God," and that this companionship was lost by choice. He said the entity had entered again and again, "as the Master did." Cayce went on to say that each soul's heritage is to "know

---

*   *Many Mansions,* Gina Cerminara, New American Library Signet Book, 1967.

itself to be itself," while "one with the Creative Forces."

UNOFFICIALLY BANNED

How is it possible that the enormous amount of reincarnation data provided by Edgar Cayce fits into his Christian beliefs so smoothly and logically? The answer is reincarnation was fundamental in early Christianity. Even the early Church Fathers saw no contradiction between Greek philosophy, which included reincarnation, and Christianity. These teachings were merged under the leadership of Origen (185-254 A.D.), but have you ever heard of Origen? Neither had I, until I started investigating reincarnation in the Christian Church. The Encyclopaedia Britannica states that Origen was " . . . the most prominent of all Church Fathers with the possible exception of Augustine." Even Saint Jerome, before he renounced his belief in reincarnation, considered Origen " . . . the greatest teacher of the Church after the apostles." While Saint Gregory of Nyssa called Origen "the prince of Christian learning in the third century."

Who was this man who received such glowing praise from the early Christian saints and leaders and yet today is virtually unknown? First of all, very few of his own writings escaped a purge by the Church in 556 A.D., three centuries after his death. His support of reincarnation is evident in the following quotes; the first paragraph is from *De Principiis* and the second paragraph is from *Contra Celsum:*

The soul has neither beginning nor end. . . . Every soul . . .

comes into this world strengthened by the victories or weakened by the defeats of its previous life.

The soul, which is immaterial and invisible in its nature, exists in no material place without having a body suited to the nature of that place; accordingly, it at one time puts off one body, which was necessary before, but which is no longer adequate in its changed state, and it exchanges it for a second.

Two central characters responsible for the purge of Origen's teachings from the Christian Church were Emperor Justinian and his prostitute-turned-wife, the powerful Empress Theodora. Theodora, according to the Encyclopaedia Britannica, speedily acquired unbounded influence over her husband. This was important, for not only did this couple control the Roman Empire, but they also dictated Church policy. This fact is confirmed by Columbia Encyclopedia, which states (under "Orthodox Eastern Church"), "From the time of Justinian the emperior controlled the patriarch absolutely." Control of the Church was used to gain political power.

Justinian and Theodora first condemned the teachings of Origen through a local synod, convened in Constantinople in the year 543 A.D. Ten years later the anathemas (curses) were officially submitted for final ratification to the Second Council of Constantinople. Pope Vigilius opposed this attack on Origen by boycotting the Council. With the exception of six Western Bishops from Africa, the remaining 159 Bishops who attended the Council were all from Eastern countries. These Eastern Bishops were against the teachings of Origen. The Pope, who was in

Constantinople during the meeting, refused to attend even though he had previously been jailed by Justinian. And once again, Pope Vigilius' refusal to cooperate with Justinian in the condemnation of Origen nearly cost him his life.

To this day, even though the anathemas appear to have been "railroaded" through the early Church, there is still an open debate in the orthodoxy as to whether or not Origen and the doctrine of pre-existence of the soul were in fact anathematized. In their well researched book *Reincarnation, an East-West Anthology,* Head and Cranston reported the change in the attitude of Catholic scholars regarding the anathemas against Origen and the exclusion of the Christian creed teaching pre-existence of the soul (which implies reincarnation). Scholars are beginning to deny that the Roman Church had any part in this and, therefore, the belief in condemnation of Origen has been an error.

Even more importantly, did Jesus say anything that might indicate that our souls are immortal, that they have existed before and will return again? Ten quotes in the Bible refer to John the Baptist as being the reincarnation of Elijah. Matthew 11:13-15 summarizes them clearly:

> All the prophets and the Law of Moses, until the time of John, spoke about the Kingdom, and if you are willing to believe their message, John is Elijah whose coming was predicted. Listen, then, if you have ears!

Another quote from the Master Jesus indicating that his impending death as Jesus would not be his first death, is taken from Matthew 17:9. Jesus is speaking to Peter,

James and his brother John, as they are walking down a mountain after the Transfiguration experience with Moses and Elijah:

> And as they came down the mountain, Jesus charged them saying, "Tell the vision to no man, until the Son of Man be risen *again* from the dead."

What does Jesus mean risen "again"? He may have been aware of having been dead at least once before, and of having risen before.

Other references in the *Bible* concern reincarnation, but perhaps Mark 4:11 offers more light on the limitations of the written and spoken word during this period, and, by reference, the limitations of the Bible itself. Once again, Jesus, speaking to his disciples, says:

> Unto you it is given to know the mystery of the kingdom of God; but unto them that are without, all these things are done in parables.

Well, we still only have the parables. What happened to the real inner teachings? Where is the straight-forward knowledge that reveals the mystery of the kingdom of God? This is where the strong desire and perseverance to know the *truth* must take over. Lacking knowledge, we have substituted faith to cover the embarrassing lack of logic and reason supporting orthodox Christianity. We have been led to believe that we must "die to find out," rather than being able to gain the knowledge to experience God now. Granted, the laws get more difficult to explain as we work in higher levels of consciousness, but we may follow laws, rules and patterns to find our way "home." Faith is a very important quality, but much too frequently the fallacy of its use as a substitute for knowledge has been seen by an increasingly educated populace. Humanity today is ready for the inner teachings, not just the parables.

Your search for these inner teachings is likely to take you to both the historic and esoteric literature of mystery schools. For centuries these teachings have been preserved and the inner knowledge discretely passed on. Some of the movements which have kept these teachings alive in the West through the centuries have been Gnosticism, Freemasonry, Kabbalism and Rosicrucianism.

It seems the time has arrived to reunite the basic tenets of reincarnation with Christianity, as Edgar Cayce did. It is time to rediscover Christianity's universal compatibility with logic, reason and the spiritual evolution of humanity. A part of this process, or personal unfoldment, involves learning to consciously remember your past lives.

LISTENING TO INTUITION

As mentioned earlier, many of us recall past lives during childhood. Perhaps as a child you may have felt that your name did not really belong to you or your body may have felt foreign. You may even have felt an intuitive certainty that you would never really die. Your intuitive feelings may have been closer to the truth than you realized. Although many people experience these feelings as children, they soon forget them and begin relating more and more to their physical senses. Eventually the physical sensing apparatus wins out and identification with the body becomes complete. Cultural concepts are introduced, constructing views of reality that are limited to acceptable and communicable facts. Anything that does not fit into the right category of observation is shunned. Unfortunately, this includes your intuition.

So, the very important tool of intuitive knowledge has been generally discouraged and allowed to silently atrophy. But, like a jewel dropped in the mud, it is not damaged; it merely waits patiently to be rediscovered. The universe seems to have a way of ignoring unhealthy preconceived ideas, no matter how well intentioned they may be. The problem of preconception was described by Mark Twain when he said, "It's not that people are ignorant, but that they believe so much that ain't so." Well, it seems many of us have been caught "red-handed," believing something about intuition that just "ain't so." It is an extremely valuable faculty. The recent studies with left brain and right brain research is proving the importance of listening to your intuitive nature.

Today many people are breaking through the limitations of sensory knowledge based upon the five physical senses. By so doing, they are developing a closer relationship with their Higher-Self. Besides desire and will, intuition is one of the basic tools to make this breakthrough. For example, we suggest you read this book and *intellectually* analyze it, and next, *intuitively*, be aware of how it "feels" to you. Does it feel off-center, or does it harmonize with something deep in your being?

You might say that we in the West must learn to overcome our formal education. That does not mean we should forget it, or ignore it, but to recognize its limitations. If we fail to do this, it becomes a handicap. We need to keep the left brain tools of reason, logic and scientific method, but we should add to them the right brain tools such as intuition, clairvoyance, out-of-body experience and hypnotic technique. To broaden our perspective we should also add the esoteric literature that is behind most of the world religions. This literature includes books like the *Bhagavad-Gita, The Tibetan Book of the Dead*, numerous publications by the Theosophical Society, and the writings of Alice A. Bailey. Put it all together, and combine it with a study of the *Kabbala* (underlying most Western mysticism), add a touch of soul, bake under pressure for many lifetimes, and PRESTO. . . . Purified Enlightenment!

TEST YOUR MEMORY

In the final analysis you are the ultimate critic. As such you should realize that you use many levels of "knowing," ranging from the weaker levels of opinion, belief and subconscious programming, to the stronger levels of personal experience. The most convincing level of knowledge is, naturally, personal experience. This is why we are keenly aware that unless you EXPERIENCE some of your own past lives, reincarnation will remain only a nice theory at best. Until you gain personal access to your past lives, you will remain without a source of knowledge that could greatly enhance your spiritual growth.

You do not have to use hypnosis and far memory to test intuitive feelings about your past lives. For example, is there a period of time depicted in movies, or in television that you really feel strong about? Or, are you attracted to certain types of period costumes? Give your imagination free-rein and see if you can fantasize yourself in a different time period, clothing or circumstances. While these may only be fantasies at this level, they can help you begin sensitizing yourself to the more subtle vibrations and your intuition.

The most effective way to investigate past-life memories is to learn a method to reach higher levels of consciousness where past memories are stored. While LaVedi and I feel very confident about the technique we have developed and placed on cassette tapes, ours is by no means the only method. Patricia-Rochelle Diegel, for example, teaches Trinity Workshops in California, with people working in groups of three to raise their energy level and gain clairvoyant feedback from each other while they investigate past lives. Dick Sutphen, also now in California, who wrote *You Were Born Again to be Together* has cassettes available, too. Marcia Moore developed the *hypersentience* (high-sensory) techniques, and numerous other past-life researchers are now conducting workshops or doing private consultations. There are many ways to get *home*: the serious student must and *will* find the Path that suits him best.

Whichever methods you may select, we strongly encourage you to keep your focus God-centered: do not fall into the trap of seeking psychic powers to puff the ego In the earlier stages, keeping centered on the Spiritual Path, while moving toward a goal you cannot see, can be very difficult. It requires steadfast determination But even though you can't "see" the goal, you can intuitively "feel" it, and know that it is there.

FANTASY OR MEMORY?

One difficulty in working with past-life memory has been to set up a criteria for distinguishing authentic memories from fantasy or imaginative role playing. Naturally, we have not yet found an absolute objective measurement for such a subjective phenomenon. Since some approach to this problem has seemed necessary, we developed a six criterion evaluation procedure. Four of these criterion are ACTION, EMOTION, SURPRISE and PERSONAL CERTAINTY.

Number four has been dubbed the *IJK Response*, "I Just Know." It is an inexplicable inner knowing, without logical or objective support. It frequently marks legitimate clairvoyant and intuitive experiences, often presenting information the individual is resistant to, or that seems not to make sense. Given time or investigation, the information usually proves to be correct.

Using our evaluation procedure, if a person reported standing beside a pyramid with no action or emotion, we would evaluate that experience as a probable fantasy or mental projection. If, on the other hand, a person reported stepping out of the "blue tunnel" and into a terrifying life or death struggle in a Turkish uprising, then we would evaluate this experience as a probable past-life memory, since it had action, emotion and surprise. Surprise, by the way, seems to be a very useful measurement, since it tends to rule out the probability of fabricating a story line.

Discussion after a probable past-life experience invariably brings out the "IJK" response. Such a discussion might sound something like, "How did you know that the man you were fighting was your present father?" "I just know." "Did he wear a sign?" "No." "Then how did you know it was he?" "I don't know, I JUST KNOW!" This response obviously doesn't mean much to anyone else, but to the experiencer it is often all he can say about his encounter, and it seems all that he needs to say.

It may be noticed here that the individual apparently brings back a great deal more information than he at first realizes. Not only does he tap into the sensory flow of knowledge experienced as memory, but he also seems to tap into his own previous personality's intuitive flow as well. This possible intuitive connection may be one reason why some people often see symbols with, or in place of, actual memory scenes. This reinforces the value of learning to work with intuitive knowledge and symbols.

The fifth criterion is EVALUATION of the reported past-life experience, seeking to determine if it fits into the known facts in the present life. Do the people and situations reported in the experience fit logically into the present? Did the experience help answer the question being researched? Valid past-life experiences tend to offer clearly relevant information in this regard.

And, finally, the proof positive that so often is sought is DOCUMENTATION of historical or other factual evidence in support of the memory. This becomes even more convincing to the analytical mind when the information supplied is of little known or obscure facts previously unknown or unavailable to the past-life experiencer.

Another typical example of a heavily documented memory was reported in a June 1978 edition of the *National Enquirer.* A New Hampshire teenager, George Field, using hypnotic regression, recalled numerous highly obscure details about a life in the small town of Jefferson, North Carolina in the 1800s.

He supplied names and facts that were carefully confirmed, data that was not accessible to the general public from available reference sources. He correctly supplied information about 15 people he had been acquainted with during that life, in reply to questions asked by a local historian. Dr. Banerjee, director of research for the Indian Institute of Parapsychology in Varanasi, India, said, "This is one of the most thoroughly documented cases of reincarnation in the United States!"

In actual practice, this kind of detailed recall is not common. We tend to be much less interested in facts and figures than in our emotional memories, so we are more inclined, at least at first, to report the dramas that have made strong impressions on us when they occurred. Even so, with careful questioning during a memory experience, it is often possible to obtain supporting evidence.

Even more remarkable than such "facts" which may impress the conscious mind, is the endlessly amazing way these particular bits of information fit the complex circumstances and personalities involved. Ultimately, though, real conviction comes from IJK, that intuitive inner certainty of what has been, is, and will be. Each explorer of consciousness has to *go within* and determine for himself alone the authenticity and value of his experiences.

In the final analysis, there is really only ONE person who needs to be convinced and whose opinion is important. Whether or not the public, friends, the family or a therapist believe in the validity of an experience is of no particular consequence. You must determine the validity, the applicable value and the personal significance of your own experience. Ultimately you, and you alone, must decide what to do with this information once you have had the experience.

THE LAST WALTZ

20

The Last Waltz

I just heard that if you get caught
violating Newton's Law of Gravity you
get a suspended sentence . . . .
"Suspended sentence," get it?

Who told you that?

A "Cosmic Cop"?

Who ever heard of
a Cosmic Cop?

Well, do you believe in gravity?

Not really, but . . .

Since we all create our own reality,
I then choose to believe in
Cosmic Cops.

Say, I think you are beginning to catch on.
You may be approaching your last dance
with us.

You mean I'm going to be fired?

461

No, no, no.

> *Back to Central Casting*
> *and all those long lines*
> *and forms to fill out?*

Lines? Forms?
What are you talking about?

> *Oh, just a little*
> *cosmic humor*
> *there.*

Hmmmm, yes, you are ready at last . . .

EVOLUTION VERSUS INVOLUTION

As God made manifest, we have taken the plunge into matter, and have become caught in dense forms that have been very difficult to master. Just when we think we have control, the game changes. Perhaps, as Swami Satchidananda says, we are all God playing hide-and-go-seek with Himself. We think we have found our way, and before we know it, we feel lost again.

There really isn't much left that man can do to himself on this planet, short of blowing everything to bits. We have murder, rape, arson, hate, malice, war, nuclear bombs and a whole complex of secret intrigues and sophisticated ways to eliminate the "enemy." Don't you wonder what an evolved entity would think watching all of this? We may not be living in caves, but sometimes human behavior seems no less primitive.

Thank God, the tide is turning. It may be hard to see between sirens, newscasts and just trying to keep up with living, but it is happening. Behind the scenes, at first hundreds, and now thousands of people have been working for many years to prepare for this tidal change. In the 1800s they began laying a foundation, and from this a frame-work went up in the early 1900s. Construction was slow as the workers were few, but they kept at it, knowing they were only making preparation. Then came the '60s and finally the '70s. Everything they had prepared for began to boom, the workers became many and construction has mushroomed over the globe. Now many "buildings" are up and their doors are open. A new society is developing that welcomes the New Age seekers.

Gradually the stir these people caused has made the populace aware of them. Some have joined them, others are simply mystified by them. For the most part the two "worlds" go along quietly beside each other now, except for occasional negative situations, when the movement gets lumped with a negative group using the New Age momentum for financial gain or personal power. The old Sons of Darkness still know how to lure in flocks for shearing and slaughter.

New Age manifestation has developed so steadily from a "ground-swell" that people in general have simply accepted it, perhaps thinking of it as just another fad. With it has come development of intuitive skills. The old idea of a psychic practicing out of a backroom somewhere has become *passé,* though there are still antiquated laws around against "fortune-telling." Now if you need such assistance, you probably ask a friend or consult a professional specialist.

In the same sense the old idea of seeking a spiritual

guru (perhaps self-styled) is also outdated. Now people are capable of attuning to their own inner teacher, and of learning from each other. This *Self*-dependency and realization has been a little slower developing, but it is rapidly gaining momentum now, as more and more teachers, groups and communities increase awareness of individual and group potential.

This isn't to say there is anything "wrong" in following an established *guru* or any of the older schools or teachings. People are in a multitude of developmental stages. Some, of a devotional nature, need to have a physical teacher to love and learn from, others need to go through disciplinary training in various schools or denominations, or take other parts. Not infrequently an individual will need a "brush-up course" in some phase, so will participate in some conventional or older religious, philosophical or academic school of thought. When it is time for change, the soul will provide the impulse. If the impulse isn't heeded, the *Self* may come through with a good swift kick where it will be most effective.

All of this is part of the *evolutionary* process. The people and groups we are speaking of have moved out of *involution,* and are striving for *Oneness.* They recognize the unity behind superficial differences and understand the basic principles of man's spiritual nature. They are becoming the architects of a new way of life, refashioning themselves and designing new social structures.

ADDITION AND MULTIPLICATION

Even though the course of human evolution has been

complex, only three basic methods have been used as learning processes. These are sometimes referred to as *addition, multiplication,* and *squaring.* The vast majority of people live each life as a step-by-step *addition* process, learning by action and reaction. They enter life and build upon experience after experience, until they have accumulated the necessary unconscious *habit patterns* of action and reaction. While this is a very slow process, they will ultimately learn their lessons over the course of time. For example, they will eventually learn ethics after experiencing both the benefits and pain of ethical and unethical behavior. Like Pavlovian theory, reaction patterns are ingrained in the mind and actions will be taken that avoid pain. Remember we are dealing with a physical body and level of mind that is not in conscious contact with the *Self* and has to learn "right" and "wrong" for itself to express its own free will. *Addition* is the slower, safer and easier method of evolution. Those following it are considered to be about two-thirds of the way along in their process.

A faster method than *addition* has been through initiation processes, comparing to *multiplication.* The same lessons must be learned as in the step-by-step method, but they are condensed and intensified. The old temple initiations were extremely rigorous, and not surprisingly some aspirants fell by the wayside. Like some children's games, if you missed a step, you had to go back and start all over again, meaning you could lose all you had gained.

Once you have entered the initiation process, you cannot change your mind; there is no turning back. You become permanently connected to a Master and his ashram. This contact may be arrested for intervals of time, until your desire to move ahead again builds enough to restimulate the instruction, but it will always be resumed. The entity will probably feel the unconscious urge to enter into studies and to seek the meaning of life or self. Once "on track" the "train of thought" is pulled steadily along, guided toward the *Self*. Many strange quirks of fate are used to get us on track. As often as not we may have had no such conscious intent, but may find ourselves moving along it before we know what happened.

Remember that the earlier initiations were intended to take man deeper into *involution*. In the past this sometimes resulted in what appeared to be "falls" by entities who seemed to be "highly" evolved. The problem was that these entities had held themselves aloof, not fully immersing themselves in the human experience. It was a good try, but not sufficient. By suppressing their human nature in an attempt to be "Godly," they denied the very lessons they were here to learn. Sometimes they were so good at resisting, they had to have the "rug pulled out" from under them. They had to learn the lesson of not denying life, but accepting it, while still retaining awareness of *Self*. You cannot move to higher levels by evading homework and tests.

As we have mentioned earlier, one who denies his passionate or human nature, for example becoming a celibate, or perhaps a strict vegetarian, may learn valuable self-discipline or other lessons. But, if he makes this self-denial out of fear, then he will attract exactly what he has feared, such as a passionate or greedy life in the future. This seems to be a paradox that has created saints, since many of them have described intensely passionate natures that they have had to overcome through experience. They were only able to reach their spiritual nature after passing through the human trials.

We cannot pretend we are what we are not, for we are composed of the clay of the earth and our energy is the same as the powerful energies of the planet. Our role is to know ourselves and these forces intimately, to experience and understand these powers so we can master them and use them creatively and positively. Male-female relationships are stressed, since they are the basic expression of polarity that produces God made manifest. Our relationships today with the opposite sex involves a current initation process of *synthesis*. We are merging, acknowledging equality in polarity, consciousness and expression, becoming aware of who and what we really are.

USHERING IN THE NEW AGE

We are now moving, as a planetary whole, out of the involutionary cycle and back into true evolution. We are passing the bottom, known as the *nadir,* of our evolutionary arc, and we are beginning the journey, as a cosmic group, back toward our Source. This is what is meant by the New Age, of which the Aquarian Age is only one important astrological factor. During the Piscean Age, now passing, many of us paid-off large accumulations of karmic debt in preparation for this time. We underwent persecution, death in revolutions and major wars, along with a variety of equally unpleasant experiences. Suffering, by counter-balancing karma (and imprinting us with lessons that *will be remembered*), can serve greater purposes than are apparent. We should never, from our human viewpoint, *assume* that any situation or circumstance is *BAD,* just because we do not understand why it must be experienced.

Regardless of our origin or the evolutionary process we are following, we have largely been held to Earth by the strong involutionary tides. Occasionally, at other favorable times, a few individuals have managed to complete their evolutionary cycle and free themselves from the wheel of rebirth. We refer to most of these entities as "Masters," working from higher dimensions. Each cycle has produced Masters with their own special attributes, interests and means of expression. They are highly developed specialists, usually working from levels of mental substance and through human consciousness in accordance with its receptivity. Because our level of telepathic, intuitive and psychic receptivity is very high now, they are able to communicate with us powerfully through our collective consciousness.

Strengthening this, *light centers* have developed into a worldwide network that purposely link-up telepathically in meditation to serve as "superconscious" receiving, anchoring and sending stations. Many such groups exist. We have even "seen" their "lights" twinkling across Russia. Some are known this way, intuitively, but many are now consciously aware of each other and are in direct contact. An important focus for this link-up has been the Unity-in-Diversity Council (formerly International Cooperation

Council).* The Council publishes an annual directory of member and supporting organizations, and sponsors an annual conference where group representatives from around the world gather to meet, conduct workshops and exchange information.

SQUARING THROUGH GROUP ENERGY

The third process of evolutionary advancement is known as *squaring,* or the "quantum leap." This is an initiation procedure that is not done individually, but in groups that are merging and balancing their consciousness within the One Will. The present urge to join or form New Age communities is a manifestation of this process.†
This makes these alternative societies more important than they may realize. The more who gather together, the faster the results will be and the more the global awareness will accelerate. Groups can receive much more potent energy than individuals and become channels for knowledge and healing energies. At the same time, by offering themselves in group service, they intensify their own evolution in direct proportion to their work, efforts and awareness.

This means an actual speeding up of individual vibratory rates, until they become as in tune with the next dimension as this one. You may be certain you have met

---

* Unity-in-Diversity Council, World Trade Center, 350 S. Figueroa St., Suite 370, Los Angeles, CA, USA 90071.
† To locate spiritual communities reference: *Spiritual Community Guide,* Spiritual Community Publications, Box 1067, Berkeley, CA 94701 or contact the *Findhorn Foundation Communications Centre,* Drumduan, Forres, Scotland IV360RD, where a computerized referral list is kept of individuals, groups and communities in contact with Findhorn.

an individual who is *squaring* when he or she begins "fading" in-and-out before your very eyes. No, there is nothing wrong with your sight, and this is not your imagination. They are just very loosely attached to this dimension. If we accept dimensional interpenetration, it is not really so remarkable. Sometimes it can be embarrassing though. Patricia-Rochelle Diegel has been doing this sort of thing for years, and she told me about an experience she had one evening, while dining out with her husband, Jon. An acquaintance stopped by their table and nonchalantly sat in her chair, *with her in it.* He was totally unaware of her presence.

Another person, an artist in California, has been scaring her slower vibrational friends by fading in-and-out while talking to them. Moving between dimensions can have its hazards. It takes a little getting used to, while gaining the realization that others may not be aware of your presence. This is another reason for living with people who are moving along at the same rate, since whatever dimension you are on, it seems most natural to be with those of a similar vibration.

Another example of this transmutation process is Anna Lee Skarin, author of *Ye Are Gods* and other highly magnetized books. She has been vanishing and reappearing for many years, and no longer maintains a home on this dimension. Magnetized books, such as hers, have a *cosmic link* that stimulates the receptive unconscious. They can have a profound affect upon readers.

THE COSMIC CHRIST

The dimensional change itself is not what we must seek, as it is a *result* of seeking the *Self* and successful merging of heart and mind with Divine Will. Jesus provided us with the example of this process and the resulting transmutation, demonstrating the power of squared group energies channeled through his disciples. The *Cosmic Christ* represents the christening or annointment by Cosmic Consciousness that is available to all Self-realized individuals, not any one special "Son of God." We are all the "children" of God.

In a *reading* Bud and I did on the *Cosmic Christ* we inquired about the "Second Coming of Christ" and found:

> Bud: Is this particular point in the 20th Century moving toward what is referred to in Revelations as the Coming of the Christ?

> LaVedi: Yes. Not Christ as understood by most today, (but) Christ in spirit.

> Bud: How should one prepare for this period? By seeking the higher planes?

> LaVedi: Time of change is approaching rapidly. There is more in this than can be covered now, much will come naturally, nothing needs to be forced, but preparation should flow as doors open. Accept that which comes.

The second coming of Christ does not refer to the man Jesus, but to the manifestation of the Spirit of the

Cosmic Christ in the hearts and minds of all humanity. The "cloud" Jesus said he would appear as, refers to the dimensional level of mind or consciousness.

If you feel the desire to end your earthly reincarnation cycle, you need to begin looking deeply into yourself and carefully examine your motivations, goals and desires. If you find you really want to undertake the process of merging with *Self*, then the time has come to move toward gaining familiarity with all aspects of yourself and development of a balanced healthy personality. It will be necessary to earnestly seek willing acceptance of life without complaint, realizing that all experiences are, or have been, for your growth and development. It is essential to learn to know yourself, and discover within yourself all the reflected experiences of humanity. To deny any aspect of yourself or others will be to condemn yourself and fail in the assimilation process.

The process is not easy and it doesn't happen overnight. It takes time to assimilate, accept and transmute the emotional residues of physical experience. When you really get with the program, you call in upon yourself the balance of your karma, so choosing to undergo this does not mean life becoming a "bowl of cherries." This choice is not a panacea or cure all, so it can be a serious decision. All of your old unconscious creations and memories will have to be faced and cleared, or possibly surpassed by earned "grace." Life can get rough, if a large accumulation from the past must be cleaned up, calling for dedication, perseverance, determination and willingness. It can require practice to become flexible and strong, ardent and patient, all at the same time.

Since at some point you will need to assimilate your past-life experiences, developing past-life skills can assist the process. A part of *return* requires the recovery of past lives, as you become ready to view them objectively. They will not normally become available to you until you are ready to know them without feeling guilt, egoic attachment, remorse or pride, realizing they have just been a part of your human experience.

We have arrived at the time when this assimilation will help us and will speed up our understanding and release of the past. This is true regardless of your particular evolutionary stage or method of development. Even the memory of a single life can be helpful by convincing the consciousness that death is not something to fear, but only a new beginning. The choice between the learning methods of *addition, multiplication* or *squaring* is yours to make at anytime in the upward direction.

Because the "latter days" have arrived and the involutionary cycle is ending, the "day of judgment" is also upon us. This does not mean condemnation, but it does mean choice. We can remain in the incarnation cycle, though it might not be on this planet, or we can seek to return to *Self*. Each individual will have to face *Self* and be judged whether the earthly experience has been mastered or not. Those who are able to face the brilliant light of the compassionate *Self* with humility and without shame may be able to merge with *Self* in purpose, will, thought and heart—the earthly *mission* accomplished.

ANOTHER OPENING, ANOTHER SHOW

21

Another Opening, Another Show

Well, how did your last performance go?

Very, very beautiful.

The choices are completely yours now.
What would you like to do next?
You can choose from celestial harmonics,
guidance, production, or even
pioneering.
And, of course, there are always a lot of new
systems that need more Light.

Yes, I understand now.
But I think I'd really prefer to
help others in this solar system for a couple
of cycles, just as you have done as a Director.

If that is really what you wish,
you may have my position.

But what will you do?
Where will you go next?

I guess my soul still resonates
to the pioneering vibrations.

475

I've become aware of a small frequency-level beyond
the edge of the *unimaginable* that is just ripe for a
total creation.

> *Sounds pretty challenging,*
> *but that's part of the joy of the*
> *"dance."*

Oh, before I move on, I should tell you
  that there is a New One coming over to try out for
    his part as a fallen angel in the next production.

> *Fine.*

You'll recognize him by his broken wing.

> *His broken wing?*

Right. Here he comes now.

> *He carries around a broken wing . . . ?*

OFFERS AND OPTIONS

Earth has been quite a challenge. Assuming we decide
to "go for it" and try to pass all of the tests and meet
the requirements for advancement, we might like to know
what kind of promotion we can expect. We have seen that
return does not mean annihilation or strumming on a
harp somewhere. But will we have a choice of scripts or be
under another unbreakable contract?

First we can consider the other "theatrical com-
panies," if you will allow the comparison. You might say
you have already specialized in the roles you like best and
you naturally gravitate to playing these. These roles have
been largely predetermined by the universal influences
affecting you when you first came into incarnation upon
Earth. These influences included the rays dominating at

the time, and the combination of star and planetary energies that affected your light envelopes. You cannot change these; they are permanent in your make-up and consciousness.

Next you are influenced by your origin, either earthborn or extraterrestrial and by the group you entered incarnation with. These factors cause you to have your own personal longings for expression, both during and beyond incarnation. Where your desire is, there shall you be, also.

With these influences in mind, we can look at the different options available to us, as perceivable within the limits of our earthly consciousness. I say limited, because we can only partially comprehend the greatness and richness of our potential; it exceeds our imagination. Still, we can try. We will begin with the death transition.

The period after death may simply be a further learning experience for you. Or you may take on a teaching, healing or helping role directed either toward entities in the astral realms, or toward entities still in incarnation upon earth. After death you stop upon a dimensional level where you have prepared yourself to work in accordance with your origin, former incarnations, between life training and soul trend.

We will look at the different levels as they may reveal your future options. If you are going to return to physical incarnation, you will probably stay on the astral level, unless your *Self* is functioning on multi-dimensional levels. If you have been following the step-by-step *addition* method of evolution, you will most likely continue your life in a manner similar to what you have programmed for yourself.

This means if you have made strong identification with *Self,* and have become a disciple of a particular *path,* you will probably continue as either a student or a helper, under the guidance of an ashramic assistant. This assistant will be under a Master who oversees the astral school from the mental dimension. If you should happen to be completing your cycle, one of your choices could be to remain on the astral level as a "guide," assisting individuals still in incarnation. Or you could become an ashramic assistant yourself, moving between the astral and mental levels, as Masters rarely enter either the astral or physical worlds.

Entities who work as guides may or may not be preparing for return to incarnation. The many Indian guides, for example, that have worked with numerous mediums, were actually a group which completed its evolution through native shamanism. The nature of this experience led to the work on the astral level of communication through mediumship. These are considered "greater guides," and should not be confused with "lesser guides," who are also contacted mediumistically. The latter are usually just helpers who are between lifes and may not be working with a school or ashram, which is why their information may be 90 percent platitudes and possibly 10 percent of modest value, or worse, just plain misleading nonsense.

The lesser guides may simply be expounding feelings based upon their own astral experiences, or from remembrance of what they learned while in incarnation. There is no guarantee of validity, which is why such contacts are of dubious value, unless the recipient is highly capable of discrimination. Just because an individual is out-of-body and has made contact with an earthly consciousness does not mean a great amount of awareness is possessed.

Most people do have some lesser guides, but they rarely make contact consciously. They act more as messengers and helpers than as channels of illumination. The greater guides working either as a type of Master. or under a Master, are very different. "By their fruits shall ye know them," and under their help you should find steady, positive growth, but not necessarily easy progress. They should direct you toward developing self-knowledge. Individuals under such guidance are not usually aware of it, until they develop the practice of meditation or skill in remembering their dreams.

On the other hand, if at anytime an entity makes contact and attempts to give you orders, begins building your ego or gives you negative suggestions, you should immediately cut the contact. Place yourself in a cocoon of *white light* as brilliant as you can imagine it, and with the power of your mind visualize the entity's thoughts reflecting off of an impenetrable transparent "glass-like" oval surrounding you. Visualize them returning to the originator. This can be done with any negative thoughts, causing appropriate discomforture to the original sender. An alternative is to visualize the thought-forms as shattered into pure energy, then send this energy back into the *void,* or "empty" space. You are always in the driver's seat, if you don't lose your "cool," because by thought you can control thoughts or emotional-astral creations (thought-forms) directed at you. Remember like attracts like; the reverse of this is you can repel undesirable influences by concentrat

ing on the opposite, as described above. To strengthen this
you can add the clear visualization of a glowing cross in
front of you, or held in your right hand before you. Do
not take this lightly, it is a powerful defense.

For those with mediumistic or natural psychic abilities, such defensive tactics may be particularly needed, if
for no other reason than simply to protect themselves
from the continual bombardment of thoughts and energies
impinging upon them night and day. A tendency also
exists to attract both energy polarities when spiritual work
begins, simply because they are two parts of one whole.
You need to be aware and able to reject or control one,
while receiving and benefiting from the other. This may or
may not come naturally to you. There are no hard and
fast rules, as each person's background and approach varies.
If one has had black magic contacts in the past, these may
attempt to reestablish themselves again as energy builds up
and they must be broken or rejected. Or, as with one highly
evolved entity I know, the entire subject needs to be
left unstimulated. This individual is plagued by nightmares
and astral battles, so needs to rest and concentrate upon
family, service and conscious activities to promote his own
healing and balance. There are many roads, and no one
right way.

When all is said and done, defense rests primarily
upon your attitude. If it is faulty, you are wide open to
falling victim to corresponding negativity in response. To
support development of attitude, becoming a member of
a positive active group can be important. Positive group
energy is both protective and corrective. As you develop,

you may hit snags, or wander out in "left field." A group will tend to reject negative developments and pull you back into balance. This is especially important when dealing with intangible areas, such as are found in esoteric studies. You need constant checks and balances for both confirmation and correction. You cannot do this alone, and to think you can is egoic illusion.

In many ways work in connection with the astral is difficult because of its emotional nature, its illusionary aspects and its relationship to the Collective Unconscious. Even so, it is a natural transition when leaving this incarnation to continue work on the next dimension with friends. We might compare this to joining a greater family, which it actually is. The position of guide can be compared to that of elder brother or sister, while sometimes such guides are loosely termed "guardian angels."

These inner-plane guides should not be confused with still a third type of guide, who are also thought of as guardian angels. In reality these are earthly family members who are concerned about a loved one still in incarnation, such as a parent for a former child. These entities remain in subconscious contact from the astral and play a helping role for a time, sometimes becoming similar to an earth-bound spirit temporarily, but out of selfless love for another.

Still another group of greater guides seem to be frequently encountered today, known simply as "The Brothers." They appear to instruct or teach and can wield a strong influence if needed. They wear long, grayish, belted monks robes. I met them clairvoyantly in a beautiful inner-plane monastery (I assume), where they were quietly strolling through the stone hallways, chanting and creating the most beautiful music and absolutely peaceful atmosphere I have ever encountered. Since, I have talked to so many other people who have met "The Brothers," that I expect the stories. My impression is that this is a Hermetic Brotherhood calling its own, or at least establishing contact and offering assistance and protection.

If you are among those entities who have chosen to speed their evolution by various initiation and learning processes, the choices are wider because you have pushed your development. Through techniques of consciousness expansion, meditation, seeking, devotion, and effort, you have greater potential of re-establishing *Cosmic-Logoic* contact. Learning to "switch levels," or move *intuitively* through the dimensions with ease can greatly accelerate your awareness and evolution (bearing in mind this is not the same as astral psychism).

MASTERSHIP

What about *Mastership*: is it possible for you to move from an earthly incarnation to this level? The answer is, "yes," but *only* if you have mastered the other dimensions through past-life training and present-life assimilation. This is often rigorous, but if this is your destiny, you will attain it. This may be the most natural expression of your energies. Leaving your emotional-astral body behind, you will become a being-of-mind, functioning within a mental body upon a dimension beyond the astral. Masters can appear upon our earth, but they do not do so in bodies such as we know. To do this they use bodies created by mind. They seldom use their energies for such appearances, however, unless it will serve an important specific purpose of evolution. The Masters are mostly evolved humans who have mastered the earthly elements within themselves and focused their attention upon serving the *One Will*.

A number of ashrams under the Masters are established on the dimensional inner planes. Masters concern themselves primarily with groups, religions, technology, education, nations, races, etc. They only rarely work directly with individuals, and even these must have a group expression and group mind to receive and forward a Master's thought. The thoughts of the Masters reach many telepathically, so repeatedly we see group responses around the globe simultaneously. Individuals should realize this, and move beyond thinking they *personally* have received some special dispensation by contacting a Master.

For example, St.-Germain is a very active Master today in relation to the New Age. Many feel drawn to him, believing he is in contact with them. Remember the Masters work with the entire planetary consciousness and do not limit their influence to any exclusive special interest groups. You will receive from this consciousness according to your capacity to absorb, intuit and understand, but it is most unlikely that you are receiving a personal communication, even though it may seem so. Your subconscious mind may allow it to be perceived as personal, but *watch that ego*. Consider that any communication you seem to receive from a Master has been broadcast worldwide, or at least to all of those connected by some common linkage and concern of the Masters at the time.

There is one sure way you can know whether a group is functioning under the Masters and serving, as a whole, the evolutionary growth of the planet. All groups and individuals responsive to thought from the Masters are *inclusive*, not *exclusive*. This means they see *all* as expressive aspects of the *Whole*, not their particular egoic group as "the only way." When you hear this exclusive claim, RUN, don't walk to the nearest exit. It is not the way. We are all *One*, like innumerable individual flowers. Together we are a garden, in various stages of bud, bloom and seed. When we finish our cycle in this garden, we will simply move on to do it all again in other gardens, for the flowering is endless.

Some, then, will move on and become Masters, but this cannot be sought. Only the Kingdom and selfless wisdom, Divine Will, strength, compassion, understanding, love and oneness should be sought, NOT the reward. To attain the goal of Oneness, the ego must be released and self-identification dissolved. At this level there is no thought of personal reward. The only motivation is the driving desire to serve the *One*. Nothing is sought for self, because attention is no longer self-centered. The personal self becomes only a physical servant, completely at the service of the soul reflecting the Divine Will to its personality expression. In turn, the personality will do its best to receive and interpret the Divine Will and follow it, regardless of the life style, for there are many areas where service is vital, not necessarily religious.

DIMENSIONAL CASTING

Entities who attain this level of mastership may have several options open to them. They may, as we have described, work upon another dimension, while maintaining contact with Earth. They may also take the treacherous path of reincarnation back into physical form, in order to be of greater evolutionary help on the physical level. There is always the danger in doing this of being caught-up in the rebirth cycle again. This return, out of love, is called the *Kuan Yin Syndrome*. Kuan Yin was a Chinese woman, who upon reaching the "top of the mountain," turned and heard the cries of suffering humanity. Out of love, she returned to human form to help ease the suffering. Many have done this, and you may choose to do so, too.

Expanded possibilities include working upon other worlds, but I believe we will find most of those who choose to go to other planets are actually only choosing to return home. As we have shown, numerous extraterrestrials are in incarnation upon earth. Many of them already *know* this is their last life here and they are being recalled. Their yearning is not toward earth, but toward other evolved worlds they remember. They came here for different reasons, but now it is time for most of them to return home.

> Maestro!
> Spare me your hapless harps;
> Spare me your troubled trombones,
> I'm tired, and I want to go home.
> > Robert Noel Byron.

Others, hearing "Gabriel's call" may choose to return

to dwell with the Logos, joining others "around the throne," and becoming the equivalent of archangels and angels. Still others may choose to journey into the Cosmos beyond our universe and *become universes* themselves. This is the potential of the fully *conscious* Identity. We cannot be destroyed by a "big bang" because we are continually evolving and expanding new universes beyond existing or dying ones. We just move on.

During an unusual near-death experience, Dr. Ray Brown, the discoverer of the underwater city in the Bermuda Triangle, experienced the level of consciousness we mean. He described it at a lecture in Ojai, California, explaining that when this happened he had no knowledge of spiritual or esoteric cosmology. He had been hit by a sport fishing boat while diving, and the impact of the collision drove him down into the water 40 to 50 feet. Then he drifted as if dead for about three hours.

Though physically immobile, he was consciously aware, and thought, "This is it," sure that he was going to die. So, he decided to see what happens during the death transition. He says that as he began to think this way, a great peace came over him and his body "shut down," just like a switch being turned off. Then he kept waiting and waiting, until he got bored with this "death process," and he started to look around. The first thing he saw was a tiny irridescent jewel fish, and he decided to take a closer look and found his consciousness merging with that of the jewel fish. He became aware of its thoughts and problems and then of other sea creatures, even the plankton. Seeing in 360 degrees around himself, he said, "I could not only communicate, but I could see and feel at the same time with an intensity that went all the way through me and felt good. I could hear, see, feel, touch in a clarity there are no words to describe. . . . "

Then his consciousness began extending beyond the water and over the land, until it included the entire planet. "It was sort of like wearing itself out . . . a potential . . . then it broke loose, like being in an explosion, I was totally free." He said he felt himself going in all directions, still retaining the clarity of the senses. This consciousness "spread through the universe and went on through other galaxies, other cosmoses without end. There is no end to what I saw. It went on and on."

He continued, "In this state there was no time . . . and I found myself working with a group of other beings . . . we developed and passed certain requirements . . . and we were developing our own planets and our own universes." Then one day one of these individuals approached him and told him he would have to leave. Concerned that he might have done something wrong, he was told, "No, you have an uncompleted cycle and you have to go back and complete it." He says he had forgotten all about life on Earth, "It was no part of my existence . . . awareness here is so dim and so dull, compared to the clarity of this other state, that it's easy to forget."

He felt himself being pulled back and gaining awareness of the earth life as he drew closer, until he was back in his body, and it had been found. "They pushed me up on top of a boat and . . . carried me away. . . . " As he listened he heard the paramedics say, "He's dead." They debated over whether to use the respirator or not and finally said, "What the heck," and turned it on. When they did this, the "switch in me that had turned off, turned on, and everything started working . . . . "

The options and roles ahead of us are many and varied, but your choice will be strongly influenced by your origin, your dominant ray and planetary influences, along with your training and human experiences. Each of us has a natural expression that results from these combined factors. All you need to do is flow with your inner being and you will find your way back when it is time. Desire for return can help to awaken the inner life. When this occurs, then the rest of your life will gradually be brought into harmony, as long as you maintain objective perspective and seek the love that transcends by uniting. *Never* use force; simply seek and flow with life.

Where your thoughts are, there you will be—eventually. Take care to focus your thoughts upon the *Self* and its purposes, not yours, seeking the Divine Will, not yours. Earnestly and one-pointedly, "Seek ye the Kingdom." Desire for return and to end your earthy incarnations may be your initial motivation, but ultimately even this will pass, giving way to a greater desire to serve the One Will as you move closer and closer to merging with the *Self*. Gradually the worldly concerns will seem less and less important, even irrelevant, but you must go in, and in, and in, seeking the Divine Spark within that connects you with your compassionate external Source.

"The road back
though long and hard and oft cold,
Is never the less a pleasant journey to your heart,

A dream,
A whisper,
A promise.

When there is a tree,
There is a garden;
When there is a smile,
There is a pardon."

Robert Noel Byron

THE MELODY LINGERS ON . . .

22

The Melody Lingers On

Hello there. . . .

Angel Harvey Crow, Third Class,
reporting for duty, sir!

Ah . . . , Harvey . . . Crow . . . ?

Yes, sir!

Where did you . . . ?

I heard the troops talking, sir,
and this Earth name came up.

Kind of catchy, don't you think, sir?

Yes . . . , catchy . . . , right.
Listen, ah . . . , excuse me, but do you wish
to be called Harvey, or Mr. Crow,
or what?

Harv is fine, sir.

It helps me practice.

Right, practice . . . . Listen, Harv,
this part as a fallen angel
should be real easy . . . , what's *that?*

Oh, this, sir? My broken wing.
It keeps me thinking about my part
and is kind of symbolic, like my name.

Symbolic? I think I'm beginning
to see the . . . ,

Right, sir. You know . . . , fallen angel,
crow, broken wing . . . .
Do you see what I'm saying, sir?

Yes, Harv, I see very clearly.
And I'm sure you will make a wonderful
fallen angel in our next production.

I could fix this wing, if you
really think I should, sir.

No, no, that will be just fine.

But . . . .

Relax, Harv,
Come over here a minute.

Over here?

A little farther this way.

How's this?

Fine.
Have you ever thought of adding
a bent halo?

A bent halo?

You know,
a little more
symbolism?

Great idea, sir!

I thought you'd like it.
Come on, Harv. Let me take you around

and introduce you to the cast.
I think you'll really
enjoy our next show!

HAPPY, HEALTHY AND HOLY

Masses of people today are unable to communicate their Higher-Self, and consequently, they inwardly believe themselves to be victims of their environment, persecuted by their peers or robbed of their dreams by a cruel world. Many of these people demonstrate feelings of hatred and disrespect for themselves by mistreating those around them. Yet how many of these people would continue to do so, if they could understand *why* they have these feelings and *why* they behave in such a non-constructive manner? And more importantly, how many of these people know that *they can change* their feelings, that *they can change* their behavior and that they *can* grow into beautiful communion with their Higher-Self?

While neither LaVedi or myself are officially qualified to perform any medical treatment, we have found in our work that it is possible to uncover basic causes for present-life physical and psychological difficulties by researching past-life memories. Whether these past-life causes are discovered through personal experience or the less personally impressive, but usually more accurate, information given by a skilled past-life *reader* (such as LaVedi), the individual is given the opportunity to move from a position of vagueness and doubt towards a position of clarity and knowledge.

We are not offering past-life memory as a magical formula or "psychological penicillin," but we do feel strongly that in the near future it will be included in Western medicine as an additional method to develop a more total health profile of patients. Already a number of New Age doctors are utilizing regression techniques in their practices. We have found that once a person understands *WHY* he is facing a crisis, then he can work from a knowledgeable position of power and leverage to overcome it. We have found that this past-life knowledge usually leads to understanding, a corresponding decrease in tension, and a subsequent shift from negative emotional reactions to constructive affirmative behavior. These statements are based upon our own subjective observations, and not on any established measureable psychological criteria.

It should also be made clear that past-life experiences are by no means a *cure* for anything. In fact, they do not *solve* problems. They do frequently provide knowledge the individual can utilize to understand and deal more effectively with his problems. This leads us to the basic weakness of any psychological method or treatment—there must be *desire* and *effort* initiated and sustained by the individual himself. No one else can do another person's internal work. Each must shoulder his own responsibilities, face his own karmic challenges and then get to work. If the individual does not have enough desire, or does not choose to work to overcome his difficulties, then neither past-life memories, or any other therapeutic treatment is likely to be of much positive value to him.

Normally we have found that once the knowledge concerning a past-life problem is available, the importance of sincere forgiveness is recognized. If there is one word that could be used to summarize the essence of our work with past-life memory, that word would be *FORGIVENESS*. In his book *Psycho-Cybernetics,* Dr. Maxwell Maltz described forgiveness as an emotional scapel. This is the scalpel that you can use to remove such emotional scars as anger, greed, jealousy and hatred. Past-life memory helps the individual to identify the "dis-ease," and then the scalpel of forgiveness becomes the tool applied to remove and clear it.

Hypnosis, prayer or meditation (personally I combine them), can be used to work on forgiving others and forgiving yourself. These methods can be used to relax away emotional hurts and to consciously ask for forgiveness from those who you in turn may have hurt. The most challenging task, as we have mentioned before, is to work on forgiving yourself. This, I believe, is one of the most important keys in any type of long term healing—self-forgiveness.

The next important benefit of past-life memory, in a therapeutic sense, is to help the individual *EXPERIENCE* the fact that he never dies. While it is obvious that the physical body dies, death as it is generally understood can be recognized for what it is—a change of address. Once the individual experiences a past life, he *knows* that his *uniqueness* (the soul), will survive physical death like it has many times in the past. He proves his own immortality to himself based on personal experience, not on religious theory or wishful thinking. This very knowledge leads the consciously aware person to reevaluate his personal waste of energy concerning worry, tension, frustration or the need to hurry-work-buy-save-spend-rush. It becomes obvious that there is honestly no hurry, since we have an eternity; and as it turns out, everyone is always right on schedule anyway. Loss of tension and the gain in calmness become obvious by-products for people who work with past-life memory.

It also becomes apparent that to carry burdens of ill-feeling toward another is not only immoral, but it is a genuine reflection of spiritual ignorance. Why should any-one, consciously and willfully, develop and maintain a karmic tie to another person or situation life after life? Wouldn't it be wiser, and a great deal more pleasant, to work on the lesson of forgiveness in this life to clear those karmic ties, at the same time tapping into the wondrous joys and divine depths of the Higher-Self?

THE PAST LIFE MEMORY PROGRAM

The *Past Life Memory Program* we have developed is really a complete workshop on cassette tapes. You can learn at your convenience. When practicing the technique, you are *always in control,* always *conscious* and able to return to the present at any time.

You are guided to specific memories by asking to see a past life with someone who is important to you in your present life, or by seeking specific answers to present-life problems or needs. This avoids getting random memories, which may seem to have little practical application. This also helps to avoid traumatic memories, such as a death, that might otherwise be remembered first, simply because of the emotion connected with the memory.

Since the memories are approached from the all knowing superconscious mind, you will recall lifetimes that are the most *relevant* to your present life. These will be memories that will help you to understand yourself, your spiritual growth, your relations with your loved ones, your karma and your potential.

An important part of spiritual growth is the assimilation of all that you have ever been. You can consciously begin this process, actively growing toward wholeness.

The *Past Life Memory Program* is available on a series of five cassette tapes, as described below:

Tape 1. *How Past Lives Affect the Present* contains 60 minutes of actual sample *readings* done by LaVedi and me, explaining some of the unusual and intricate workings of karma and the effects of past lives upon the present incarnation.

Tape 2. *How to Use the Power of Hypnosis* gives a thorough explanation of hypnosis and contains two highly effective hypnotic inductions, "The Quiet Room" and "The Magic Room." These introductory techniques are important to the success of the inductions used for past-life memory recall.

Tape 3. *Journey into the Past with a Loved One* is recommended as the first tape to use in beginning past-life memory work, as our past connections with people are usually the easiest to recall.

Tape 4. *Finding Solutions to Present Life Problems* teaches you how to focus questions and get specific answers to resolve fears, guilts, phobias, psychosomatic pain and other reactions that may be carryovers from previous lifetimes.

Tape 5. *Discover Hidden Talents, Abilities and Knowledge* contains a program to help you tap knowledge and skills you acquired in earlier incarnations. Learning to bring these forward can greatly expand and develop the present life.

On the reverse of tapes 3, 4 and 5 is a spiritually oriented, and universally positive thought program. This is also an important preliminary to the actual use of the memory inductions and has therefore been included on each of these tapes. Especially recommended is at least one usage of the "Body of Light" induction. This greatly assists in transcending identification and limitations connected with the personality and physical body.

HOW TO CLEAR KARMA

We have emphasized the importance of forgiveness to clear away karmic ties, with hypnosis, prayer and meditation all being effective methods to accomplish this. Now I would like to share with you some techniques we recommend. A long time associate of LaVedi's, Paul Dozier, summarized several of these from her letters to him for distribution. Rather than disturb his excellent synthesis of LaVedi's comments, let me present them in his own words:

1. Learn self-hypnosis technique for its basic induction and Body-of-Light induction. (We have cassette tapes which give you this.) Now,

   Center yourself in the Light. Build the Light visually around yourself, until you can actually feel it as warmth and a comfortable surrounding fluidic pressure. You may feel it as a rosy glow.

This relates to the light of love within, the soul contact, universal oneness, the Eternal Flame; it is acknowledged and made manifest in your consciousness. Visualize it expanding every cell of your body, like little ballons inflated with the Light. In this Invocation, you ask the Light to remove all darkness.

2. Visualize all the thought-forms from past ages as being outside of this Light. See them shatter and return to universal energy. These are elementals, emotional body attachments to other people and things; those who seek advancement can make giant strides of attainment by this method. It isn't easy, however.

3. Notice some of the reactions you get from your emotional body: blocks, feeling of resistance, excuses for not proceeding; the process can be both emotionally and physically painful. It cannot be rushed or forced, but requires steady will or resolution: "I will proceed and be cleansed." This is the polishing of the perfect diamond; the jewel on the lotus; the philosopher's stone of eternal life.

4. Take each problem into the Light, discuss it with the Light, and stay centered there until it dissolves into Light. Do not feed the problem any longer with emotional or even mental reactions. Now that the old problem becomes illuminated, you comprehend it; that is, you learn what you were meant to learn from it. Now you are freed from it. All ties exist to TEACH, and they all dissolve when the lesson is accepted and understood.

5. This method is to be your strength; it will result in your becoming a Being-of-Light. As you test it in coming situations, each "win" will make you burn brighter, until nothing exists but the Eternal Light. By this process are spiritual initiations

granted these days; we've come here this time to *be our own initiators.*

You will become transparent—open like a sieve, so things flow through your light and pass out transformed. While you do this, you go through transformation, also. The more difficult the situation and the harder you must struggle to hold your center in the Light, the greater and more rapid will be your own transformation. All aspects of your Being come into alignment: physical, emotional, mental and spiritual.

6. *Accomplish this and you will need no other education.*

In a *reading* we did for an Alaskan friend, he asked LaVedi for information on how to meditate and apply meditation in his life. Here are the instructions she gave:

LaVedi: We are going to go back through the steps of concentration—if you have a question, concentrate on the question. Go back through all the knowledge you have . . . .

You have been concentrating on a particular area, exhausting all the (known facts). That is essentially contemplation.

Then enter into a meditation. Use a mantra, or whatever is best for you. You achieve a super-conscious level, an alpha state.

Don't go into it necessarily expecting the answer (to your question). It may come during the meditation—depends on [your concentration]. You may be completely unaware consciously during the meditation . . . perhaps after the meditation you will know the answer to your question. (But) it may not come at that point; it may come during the next day. It may not even come for weeks. You won't necessarily get an instant answer.

You *will* find that it comes, either in degrees, or from somebody or suddenly you find it in a book. There it is, or whatever avenue is appropriate. Often you just *somehow know*. That is because it has come in from the superconscious through the subconscious—there it is all of a sudden!

. . . you see there is a step in there that isn't conscious, but you *do* direct the mind. This is your handling of it. Take advantage of . . . mind completely . . . this is all genius is about and where inventions come from, where all comes from . . . Anyone who is doing creative work—they do as much as they possibly can, they go to school if need be, they study when they can. You train your consciousness, your body, or whatever it is, to the degree of extent you can . . . the next step is naturally meditation, and then comes inspiration (and finally, illumination.)

Bud: That answers that, we could use a little inspiration and illumination ourselves. Inspire my banker. . . .

A peaceful calming meditation was given by LaVedi in a *reading* for a highly strung individual that would be applicable for most of us in our busy work-a-day world:

LaVedi: Meditate upon a sunlit field, relaxing in the green grass-scent of flowers—buzzing of bees—clouds floating overhead. Release yourself into the perfect peace—in tune with this planet, and the physical self, which is of this earth. In this you will begin to develop balance, this is needed for the release of pain. A simple, highly effective meditation, particularly when stress is felt.

This is the "work" we have talked about that begins after you have gathered the knowledge from your past-life memory experience, analyzed it, and decided upon a deliberate plan of action. It represents the hurdles that many people fail to clear in order to genuinely gain the most from their past-life memory experiences. This is true because, even though discovering the original karmic cause of the present problem may be very beneficial, this discovery is seldom enough to completely overcome it without persistence and sincere forgiveness. We feel that the heartfelt desire to clear karma, and the corresponding work described in meditation, self-hypnosis or prayer is essential to achieve physical, emotional, mental and spiritual healing.

GOD AS THERAPY

As scenes of former lives are repetitively experienced, the existence of God also becomes an unavoidable issue. It becomes apparent that you are not your body, but a *being-of-light,* consisting of soul, spirit and an immortal Self. If you are such a being, then you might conclude that we are all in the process of realizing our own divinity, God experiencing the human form as Self-manifestation. Maybe it is like Seth says of us in *Seth Speaks,* "You are all learning to be co-creators. You are learning to be Gods as you understand the term."

If we are all pure *light,* or "pieces of God," then at some level of awareness we are obviously *ALL ONE.* And, if we are all one, it is unhealthy, as well as illogical to continue to focus on someone's lower ego-self, breeding misunderstandings and ill-feelings. If you can just remember that we are all one, we are *ALL GOD*, focusing on the *Allness* and the Higher-Self in everyone, your reasons to cling to negative feelings will disappear. Eventually all negative feelings towards everyone and everything will dissolve back into the nothingness from which they came.

If we go beyond this view, to an even higher view, it appears that only God is real and all else is illusion. Meher Baba writes about this in *The Everything and the Nothing*, "Ignorance believes: The cosmos is a reality; birth, death, old age, wealth, honour, are real. Knowledge knows: The cosmos is a dream. God alone is Real." This same message rings clear in the *Bhagavad-Gita* written thousands of years earlier, "By all the Vedas am I known; indeed I am the compiler of Vedanta, and I am the knower of the Vedas."

Logic, reason, intuition and the esoteric literature from most world religions indicate that if you think you have "the only way," then your God is too limited. God does not belong to an individual, to a group, to a nation or even to a planet. Rather God *IS* the individual, He *IS* the group, He *IS* the nation and He *IS* the planet!

So, part of the therapeutic value of past-life memory is to experience the reality of survival of bodily death, at the same time gaining personal proof that God exists on an infinitely broader and grander scale than may have been comprehended. Now, I may be a little biased, but I would say that's pretty valuable therapy . . . for those who are ready to earn it.

IS YOUR GOD TOO SMALL?
Neither LaVedi and I, nor anyone else, has all of the

answers, but we have attempted to offer you the obvious and intuitive results of our work to the best of our ability. We have personally discovered we must each endeavor to grow in our conceptual approaches to God and our environment, rather than stagnate behind someone else's experience that eventually gets suffocated and buried in religious dogma. We must attempt to grow beyond the persistent limitations of our language, our culture, our family and even our narrow religious experience.

For example, there are no categories in nature, only in our heads. Yet our language, and therefore our culture, tends to push us towards either-or conclusions. Our sharp-slicing words may appear reasonable on paper, but have little resemblance to the vastness and infinite complexities of the world of experience.

This mistake and narrowness of thinking is especially evident when we try to restrict and confine God's love, compassion and forgiveness to one special group. For example, many believe that *either* you accept Jesus as your personal Master, *or* you will go to hell. This limits the experience of the Christ Consciousness to only one man (Jesus), and denies the universality of God's power within each of us that has been demonstrated by many Masters before, and since, the Master Jesus. This is not to deny the Mastership of Jesus, but it simply confirms what He said Himself, recorded in John 14:12, " . . . He that believeth on me, the works that I do shall he do also; and greater works than these shall he do . . . " It defies not only rational thought, but the doctrine of God's infinite compassion and forgiveness, for organized Christianity to claim ultimate authority by virtually condemning the majority of humanity to hell. Intuitively, most people realize the awkwardness of this position in the orthodoxy and either ignore it, or ignore the Church.

The narrowness of this type of either-or thinking shrinks and compartmentalizes God into an even smaller box, when denominational differences are considered. This "small God" would judge that: *either* you are a Southern Baptist and saved, *or* a Mormon and lost; *either* you are a Mormon and saved, *or* a Jew and lost; *either* you are a Jew and saved, *or*. . . . It goes on and on and on. Can God really be so small as to be limited and "owned" by one group? As Samuel Bois warns throughout his book *The Art of Awareness*, "Beware of hardening of the categories."

God is available to every man, if he looks in the right place. And that place, we are continuously told throughout recorded history, is *inside.* Jesus did not say to look in a book, or in a Church, or a synagogue, or in a special structure of any kind. He said, reported in Luke 17:21, " . . . the kingdom of God is within you." This was known centuries before and was clearly evident when Krishna spoke to Arjuna in the Bhagavad-Gita.

> One whose happiness is within, who is active within, who rejoices within and is illuminated within, is actually the perfect mystic. He is liberated in the Supreme, and ultimately he attains the Supreme.

God is infinitely more forgiving, infinitely more compassionate, and infinitely more understanding than mankind really wants Him to be. From the perspective of many people, God is *"ours"* but not *"theirs."* God is not just a Caucasian American living in Los Angeles, California. God is ALL inclusive, not exclusive just for the privileged few. He is not owned. He is not limited. He is not confined to any national boundary or arbitrary organized religion, no matter how well-intentioned the people involved, or the beauty of their belief system.

THE GOLDEN BUDDHA

At this point I would like to share with you, with Audrey Waterman's permission, her experience in one of our Past Life Memory Workshops in San Francisco. I wish to share it with you not only because of its beauty and its message, but because it is an excellent example of intuitively *going with the flow* of knowledge from the Higher-Self.

Audrey had been meditating for many years, so it was apparently easy for her to achieve a deep state of hypnosis with our basic induction technique. She was also experienced enough with higher levels of consciousness to follow the messages she received from her Higher-Self, recognizing the symbolic correspondences of her experience with the recall suggestions given for a past life with a "loved one." We find this a fitting, symbolic summation of life's *eternal dance*.

> After relaxing my body and passing through the blue light of the tunnel, I entered the huge eye where I found the silver spark of pure light and I was eager to experience a past life with my father, whom I loved deeply. He died when I was a child.

Three lives seemed to vie for recognition at the same time. One was in Atlantis where my father and I were working in a temple of healing. One was in Egypt where my father taught me in the healing mysteries. And the last was on the North American continent in the north east, long before the coming of the white man, where again we worked with healing as shamans. In all three lives I was in the male body.

I tried desperately to decide which life I would pursue because I was really eager to experience this. But the Golden Buddha kept pushing these past lives away, and finally I allowed myself to go with the Buddha and depart from the suggested routine of the workshop.

The Golden Buddha is enormous and fills the entire universe. He sits upon the thousand petaled lotus in meditation. In his right hand he holds a rainbow and in the left hand rests a beautiful electric-blue butterfly. I am the butterfly.

In rapture I rest in the palm of the Buddha. I bathe in the glorious golden white light which surrounds us and I feel such heavenly joy and perfection and love it is beyond description.

"I will rest here in peace forever," I say as I look up at the calm, sweet face of the Buddha.

But suddenly I fall from the Buddha's hand and go down into an infinity of spaces into complete and utter darkness and chaos.

I am blown about by the winds, the tides and the tempests of the blackness, and my delicate gossamer wings are shredded and torn. And I am beaten to bits and destroyed.

There is nothing left but tiny particles of butterfly dust, and I am lost in the desolation of the dark.

Eons pass and time seems to be forever.

After a very long passage of time some of the particles begin to glow with a soft light and are drawn to each other, and as time goes on and on, gradually more and more of the particles reassemble.

It is not possible to count the time that passes. It may be that millions of years came and went as I was buffeted about in the darkness and the storms. But as the time passes, more and more of the particles are drawn together and eventually they form a sphere or ball. It is not a solid ball, but rather a loose one, made up of the tiny separate glowing sparks.

Time goes on and the softly glowing ball commences to rise in the blackness. Gradually, up it goes and I find myself, as the ball, rising into light.

More time passes and the light becomes brighter and brighter and at last I find myself at the foot of the altar in The Temple of Light before the Twelve Teachers. They know me and I seem to have known them from before, but I cannot remember where or when. Their forms are so bright that I cannot look directly at them, but I sense great love and compassion. They welcome me, but the central figure tells me that it is not yet time and that I cannot stay.

Three guardian angels come and lead the glowing ball back down into the lower places. They leave the ball at the foot of the rainbow, and I roll along the rainbow path, up and over the bow. And there is the Golden Buddha!

He sits there, in meditation, just as he did in the beginning. But the rainbow arches from one hand to the other, embracing the universe. And in his upturned palm is the butterfly, more beautiful than ever.

And there I rest, safe in the hand of the Buddha.

FINAL CURTAIN

In closing, we would like to share one final *reading* with you that brings us back to living our daily lives as an experience with God:

Bud: We wish to make contact with _____. We are seeking a past-life experience to explain his present-life situation.

LaVedi: We begin with a life in Attica. There is a purpose . . . . There is a need. . . . A life as a woman, mother. It seems to be involved in some village. She is rather stout; there would seem to be about three children, an older one and two little ones.

The home is stucco-like, stone, very simple. There is a joy in the simplicity of the environment, in the family. A joy in the simple things of life—in living, an attunement with the earth, a closeness in love, the people, the family.

This is someone who could sing as she worked, found no hardship in the rigours of life. She knew and understood. And love was really prevalent. A beautiful life in its utter simplicity. A life that is like a cornerstone to be understood.

Life's lessons are not always complex, esoteric or mysterious. Sometimes the whole truth can be found in the simplest activities.

It is possible now to build a house upon this beautiful, solid foundation. Through (again) attunement with this life, the hearts of people, seeing reality, the apparent is always so obvious and the light glowing within, attunement to the earth, the sky, the feel of the earth.

Once again grow from experience. This is beautiful simplicity, joy, uncomplicated by ideas, concepts, ego—touching the inner heart of the planet—of God.

Bud: Is this particular life in Attica to be the model for _____'s benefit in the rest of his life experience?

LaVedi: In many ways, yes. Obviously it cannot be repeated. It can only be expanded upon, developed. The inner consciousness is growing on earth now. A consciousness which this entity has tuned into very naturally. Now it is a consciousness many are becoming aware of, and one that he can move into very naturally.

Seek the new consciousness. Don't worry about complications, but seek UNION . . . Rise above everyday . . . enjoy once again . . . .

"EN REQUIETORIUM SANCTUM"

Enter the Hidden shrine in the 'holy place.'

BIBLIOGRAPHY

ALEXANDER, THEA, *2150 A.D.*, New York: Warner Books, Inc., 1976.

ARNOLD, SIR EDWIN, *The Light of Asia*, London: Routledge, (1879), 1971.

ARROYO, STEPHEN, *Astrology, Psychology and the Four Elements*, Davis, Calif: CRCS Publications, 1975.

ASSAGIOLI, ROBERTO, M.D.,*Psychosynthesis*, New York: Penguin Books, 1976.

AUROBINDO, SRI, *The Problem of Rebirth*, Ponticherry: Aurobindo Ashram, 1952.

AXMINSTER LIGHT CENTER, *M.R. Scripts*, 66, Willhayes Park, North Street, Axminster, Devonshire, England: Axminster Light Center.

BABA, MEHER, *Discourses* (3 vol.), San Francisco: Sufism Reoriented, Inc., 1973.

BABA, MEHER, *The Everything and the Nothing*, Berkeley, Calif: The Beguine Library, 1971.

BAILEY, ALICE A., *A Treatise on White Magic*, New York: Lucis Publishing Co., (1931) 1972.

BAILEY, ALICE A., *Discipleship in the New Age*, New York: Lucis Publishing Co., (1955) 1972.

BAILEY, ALICE A.,*Esoteric Psychology* (two volumes), New York: Lucis Publishing Co., (1936) 1971.

BAILEY, ALICE A., *The Consciousness of the Atom*, New York: Lucis Publishing Co., (1922) 1968.

BAILEY, ALICE A., *The Soul and It's Mechanism*, New York: Lucis Publishing Co., (1930) 1965.

BAILEY, ALICE A., *The Unfinished Autobiography*, New York: Lucis Publishing Co., (1951) 1970.

BAKER, DR. DOUGLAS, *Esoteric Psychology—The Seven Rays*, Essendon, Herts, England: Little Elephant, 1975.

BAKER, M.E. PENNY, *Meditation: A Step Beyond With Edgar Cayce*, New York: Pinnacle Books, 1975.

BESANT, ANNIE and LEADBEATER, C.W., *Thought Forms*, Wheaton, Illinois: The Theosophical Publishing House, (1925) 1975.

BLAKE, J.F., ed., *Astronomical Myths Based on Flammarion's History of the Heavens*, London: Macmillan, 1877.

BLAVATSKY, HELENA PETROVNA (H.P.B.), *Isis Unveiled*. Pasadena, Calif: Theosophical University Press, (1877) 1960.

BLAVATSKY, HELENA PETROVNA (H.P.B.), *The Secret Doctrine* (two volumes), Pasadena, Calif: Theosophical University Press, (1888) 1963, The Adyar edition (six volumes), Adyar, India, 1971.

BOIS, J. SAMUEL, *The Art of Awareness*, Dubuque, Iowa: Wm. C. Brown Co., 1966.

BREASTED, JAMES HENRY, Ph.D., *A History of the Ancient Egyptians*, London: John Murray, 1929.

BRO, HARMON HARTZELL, Ph.D., *Edgar Cayce on Dreams*, New York: Paperback Library, 1969.

BRUNTON, PAUL, *Search in Secret Egypt*, London: Rider & Company, 1969.

BUDGE, E.A. WALLIS, *Egyptian Book of the Dead*, New York: Dover Publications, Inc., 1967.

CAMPBELL, JOSEPH, *The Hero with a Thousand Faces*, Princeton, New Jersey: Princeton University Press, (1949) 1973.

CAPRA, FRITJOF, *The Tao of Physics*, Boulder, Colorado: Shambhala Publications, Inc., 1975.

CAPT, E. RAYMOND, *The Great Pyramid Decoded*, Thousand Oaks, Calif: Artisan Sales.

CASE, PAUL FOSTER, *The Tarot, A Key to the Wisdom of the Ages*, Richmond, Virginia: Macoy Publishing Co., 1947.

CASE, PAUL FOSTER, *The Book of Tokens*, 5105 North Figueroa Street, Los Angeles, Calif. 90042: Builders of the Adytum, 1968.

CAVENDISH, RICHARD, ed., *Man, Myth and Magic: An Illustrated Encyclopedia of the Supernatural*, New York: Marshall Cavendish Corp., 1970.

CAYCE, EDGAR EVANS, *Edgar Cayce on Atlantis*, New York: Paperback Library, 1968.

CERMINARA, GINA, *Insights for the Age of Aquarius*, Wheaton, Illinois: The Theosophical Publishing House, 1976.

CERMINARA, GINA, *Many Lives, Many Loves*, New York: William Slone Assoc., 1950.

CERMINARA, GINA, *Many Mansions*, New York: William Slone Assoc., 1950.

CERVE, WISHER S., *Lemuria—The Lost Continent of the Pacific*, Kingsport, Tenn: Kingsport Press, Inc., 1958.

CHALLONER, H.K., *Regents of the Seven Spheres*, Wheaton, Illinois: The Theosophical Publishing House (1966) 1976.

CHALLONER, H.K., *The Wheel of Rebirth, An Autobiography of Many Lifetimes*, Wheaton, Illinois: The Theosophical Publishing House, 1977.

CLARK, GLENN, *The Man Who Tapped the Secrets of the Universe*, Waynesboro, Virginia: The University of Science and Philosophy, 1975.

COUÉ, EMILE, *Self Mastery Through Conscious Auto-suggestion*, London: George Allen & Urwin Ltd., 1922.

COUÉ, EMILE and BROOKS, C.H., *Suggestion and Autosuggestion*, New York: Samuel Weiser, (1922) 1974.

DANTE (Alighieri), *The Inferno*, New York: Mentor Books, 1954.

DE MANHAR, NURHO, trans., *Zohar*, San Diego, Calif: Wizards Bookshelf, 1978.

DENNING, MELITA and PHILLIPS, OSBORNE, *Psychic Self-Defense & Well-Being*, P.O. Box 43383, St. Paul, MN, Llewellyn Publications, 1980.

DEVLIN, BARBARA LYNNE., *I Am Mary Shelly*, New York: Condor Publishing Co., Inc., 1977.

DIEGEL, PATRICIA, Ph.D., *Reincarnation & You*, Los Angeles, Calif: Prism Publications, 1970.

DONNELLY, IGNATIUS, *Atlantis: The Antediluvian World*, London: Sanson Low, Merston & Co., Ltd., (1882) 1910.

EDMUNDS, SIMEON, *Hypnotism and Psychic Phenomena*, North Hollywood, Calif: Wilshire Book Co., 1961.

ELMAN, DAVE, *Hypnotherapy*, Los Angeles, Calif: Westwood Publishing Co., 1964.

EVANS-WENTZ, W.Y., *The Tibetan Book of the Dead*, New York: Oxford University Press, (1927) 1960.

EVANS-WENTZ, W.Y., *Tibetan Yoga and Secret Doctrines*, England: Oxford University Press, 1975.

EVERARD, DR., trans., *The Divine Pymander of Hermes Mercurius Trismegistus*, San Diego, Calif: Wizards Bookshelf, 1978.

FERRO, ROBERT and GRUMLEY, MICHAEL, *Atlantis, Autobiography of a Search*, New York: Bell Publishing, 1970.

FINDHORN COMMUNITY, *The Findhorn Garden*, New York: Harper & Row, 1976.

FORTUNE, DION, *Avalon of the Heart*, New York: Samuel Weiser, (1934) 1971.

FORTUNE, DION, *Psychic Self-Defense*, New York: Samuel Weiser, 1930.

FORTUNE, DION, *The Cosmic Doctrine*, New York: Samuel Weiser, 1966.

FORTUNE, DION, *The Mystical Qabalah*, New York: Samuel Weiser, 1957.

FORTUNE, DION, *The Sea Priestess*, New York: Samuel Weiser, 1972.

FORTUNE, DION, *Through the Gates of Death*, New York: Samuel Weiser, 1972.

GOLD, E.J., *American Book of the Dead*, I.D.H.H.B., Inc. & Doneve Designs, Inc., 1978.

GOODAVAGE, JOSEPH F., *Astrology: The Space Age Science*, New York: The New American Library, 1967.

GOUDEY, R.F., *Reincarnation, A Universal Truth*, (The Aloha Press), Wheaton, Illinois: The Theosophical Press, 1928.

GRANT, JOAN, *Far Memory*, New York: Harper & Row, 1965.

GRANT, JOAN, *Winged Pharaoh*, New York: Harper & Row, 1938.

GRANT, JOAN and KELSEY, DENYS, M.B., M.R.C.P., *Many Lifetimes*, London: Corsi Books, a division of Transworld Publishers, Ltd., (1967) 1976.

GRAY, JOHN HENRY, *China: A History of the Laws, Manners and Custom of the People*, New York: Barnes and Noble, (1878) 1974.

GRAY, WILLIAM G., *The Ladder of Lights*, Toddington, Nr. Cheltenham, Glos., England: Helios Book Service, 1968.

GREED, JOHN A., *Glastonbury Tales*, Bristol, England: St. Trillo Publications, 1975.

GUIRDHAM, ARTHUR, *The Cathars and Reincarnation*, Wheaton, Illinois: The Theosophical Publishing House, 1978.

HALEVI, Z'EV BEN SHIMON, *Adam and the Kabbalistic Tree*, London: Rider and Company, 1974.

HALL, MANLY PALMER, *The Secret Teachings of All Ages*, Los Angeles, Calif: The Philosophical Research Society, Inc., 1972.

HAWKEN, PAUL, *The Magic of Findhorn*, New York: Harper & Row, 1975.

HAYES, CHRISTINE, *Red Tree: Insight into Lost Continents of Mu and Atlantis*, San Antonio, Texas: The Naylor Co., 1972.

HEAD, JOSEPH and CRANSTON, S.L., eds., *Reincarnation*, New York: Causeway Books, 1967.

HEAD, JOSEPH and CRANSTON, S.L., eds., *Reincarnation: An East-West Anthology*, Wheaton, Illinois: The Theosophical Publishing House (Quest Book), 1968.

HEAD, JOSEPH and CRANSTON, S.L., eds., *Reincarnation: The Phoenix Fire Mystery*, New York: Julian Press/Crown Publishers, Inc., 1977.

HEINDEL, MAX, *The Rosicrucian Cosmo-Conception*, Oceanside, Calif: The Rosicrucian Fellowship, 1937.

HILGARD, ERNEST R., *The Experience of Hypnosis*, New York: Harcourt, Brace & World, Inc., 1977.

HODSON, GEOFFREY, *Reincarnation, Fact or Fallacy*, Wheaton, Illinois: The Theosophical Publishing House, 1967.

HODSON, GEOFFREY, *The Kingdom of the Gods*, Wheaton Illinois: The Theosophical Publishing House, (1950) 1970.

HUMPHREYS, CHRISTMAS, *Concentration & Meditation*, New York: Penguin, 1970.

IVERSON, JEFFREY, *More Lives Than One?* London: Pan Books, 1976.

JACOLLIOT, LOUIS, *The Bible in India,* New York: G.W. Dillingham, 1887.

JINARAJADASA, C., *The First Principles of Theosophy,* Adyar, Madras, India: Theosophical Publishing House, (1921) 1948.

JOCELYN, JOHN, *Meditations on the Signs of the Zodiac,* Blauvelt, New York: Steinerbooks, 1970.

JUDGE, WILLIAM Q., *The Ocean of Theosophy* (four vols.), Theosophical Society, 1888.

JUNG, CARL GUSTAV, *Man and His Symbols,* New York: Dell Books, 1968.

JUNG, CARL GUSTAV, *Memories, Dreams, Reflections,* New York: Pantheon, 1961.

JUNG, CARL GUSTAV, *The Archetypes and the Collective Unconscious,* Vol. 9, Part 1, Princeton, New Jersey: Princeton University Press, (1959) 1977.

KELEMAN, STANLEY, *Living Your Dying,* New York: Random House, 1978.

KITTER, GLENN D., *Edgar Cayce on the Dead Sea Scrolls,* Paperback Library, 1970.

KLINE, MILTON V., *A Scientific Report on the Search for Bridey Murphy,* New York: Julian Press, 1956.

KRIPPNER, STANLEY and RUBIN, DANIEL, *The Kirlian Aura, Photographing the Galaxies of Life,* Anchor Books, 1974.

KUBLER-ROSS, ELISABETH, *Death: The Final Stage of Growth,* Englewood Cliffs, New Jersey: Prentice-Hall, Inc. 1975.

KUBLER-ROSS, ELISABETH, *On Death and Dying,* New York: Macmillan Publishing Co.. 1969

LePLONGEON, AUGUSTUS, *Sacred Mysteries Among the Mayas and Quiches,* Minneapolis, MN: Wizards Bookshelf, 1973.

LEVI, ELIPHAS, *The Aquarian Gospel of Jesus the Christ,* Los Angeles, Calif: DeVorss & Co., (1970) 1964.

LEWIS, LIONEL SMITHETT, *St. Joseph of Arimathea at Glastonbury,* Cambridge, England: James Clark & Co., Ltd., (1922) 1976.

LILLY, JOHN C., M.D., *The Center of the Cyclone,* New York: Julian Press, 1972.

MAC GREGOR, GEDDES, *Reincarnation in Christianity,* Wheaton, Illinois: The Theosophical Publishing House, 1978.

MALTZ, MAXWELL, *Psycho-Cybernetics,* Los Angeles: Wilshire, 1960.

MARSHALL, GEORGE, *Buddha, The Quest for Serenity,* Boston, Mass: Beacon Press, 1978.

MICHAEL, ARNOLD, D.D., Ph.D., *Blessed Among Women,* Los Angeles, Calif: Devorss & Co., 1973.

MICHELL, JOHN, *The View Over Atlantis,* New York: Ballantine Books, 1969.

MISHRA, RAMMURTI S., M.D., *Fundamentals of Yoga,* New York: Anchor Books, Anchor Press/Doubleday, 1974.

MONAGHAN, PATRICIA, *The Book of Goddesses and Heroines,* New York: E.P. Dutton, 1981.

MONROE, ROBERT A., *Journeys Out of the Body,* Garden City, New York: Doubleday & Co., 1971.

MOODY, Jr., RAYMOND A., M.D., *Life After Life,* New York: Bantam Books, 1975.

MOODY, Jr., RAYMOND A., M.D., *Reflections on Life After Life,* New York: Bantam Books and Mockingbird, 1977, 1978.

MOORE, MARCIA, *Hypersentience,* New York: Crown Publishers, 1976.

MOORE, MARCIA and DOUGLAS, MARK, *Astrology the Divine Science,* York Harbor, Maine: Arcane Publications, 1971.

MOORE, MARCIA and DOUGLAS, MARK, *Reincarnation: Key to Immortality,* York Harbor, Maine: Arcane Publications, 1968.

MURCHIE, GUY, *Music of the Spheres,* New York: Dover Publications, 1967.

MYERS, FREDERIC W.H., *Human Personality and its Survival of Bodily Death,* London: Longmans, Green and Co., 1920.

OSTRANDER, SHEILA and SCHROEDER, LYNN, *Psychic Discoveries Behind the Iron Curtain,* Englewood Cliffs, New Jersey: Bantam Books, 1973.

PARKER, DEREK and JULIA, *The Compleate Astrologer,* New York: McGraw-Hill, 1971.

PEPPER, ELIZABETH and WILCOX, JOHN, *Magical and Mystical Sites,* New York: Harper & Row, 1977.

PERKINS, JAMES S., *Experiencing Reincarnation,* Wheaton Illinois: The Theosophical Publishing House, 1977.

PHYLOS THE THIBETAN, *A Dweller on Two Planets* (written 1884), Great Britain: Neville Spearman, 1970.

PLATT. Jr., RUTHERFORD H., ed., *The Forgotten Books of Eden,* New York: Crown Publishers, Inc., (reprint of 1927 ed.) 1980.

PLAYFAIR, GUY LYON, *The Indefinite Boundary,* Frogmore, St. Albans, Hertz., England: Panther Books, 1977.

POLWHELE, RICHARD, *History of Cornwall,* London: Dorking, Kohler & Combes (reprint of 1803-08 ed.), 1978.

PRABHAVANANDA, SWAMI and ISHERWOOD, CHRISTOPHER, *Bhagavad-Gita,* Hollywood, Calif: Vedanta Press, 1944.

PRABHAVANANDA, SWAMI and ISHERWOOD, CHRISTOPHER, *How to Know God: The Yoga Aphorisms of Patanjali,* New York: The New American Library, 1969.

PRIESTLEY, J.B., *I Have Been Here Before,* London: William Heineman, 1937.

RANDALL-STEVENS, H.C., *Atlantis to the Latter Days,* Jersey, England: The Order of Knights Templars of Aquarius, 1966.

READ, ANNE, *Edgar Cayce on Jesus and His Church,* New York: Paperback Library, 1970.

REGARDIE, ISRAEL, *Twelve Steps to Spiritual Enlightenment,* Dallas, Texas: Sangreal Foundation, 1969.

REISER, OLIVER L., *This Holyest Erthe,* London: Perennial Books, 1974.

REYES, BENITO, *Scientific Evidence for the Existence of the Soul,* Wheaton Illinois: Theosophical Press, 1970.

ROBB, STEWARD, *Prophecies on World Events by Nostradamus,* New York: Liveright Publishing Corp., 1961.

ROBERTS, JANE, *Seth Speaks: The Eternal Validity of the Soul,* Englewood Cliffs, New Jersey: Prentice-Hall, Inc., 1972.

ROBERTS, JANE, *The Education of Oversoul No. 7*, New York: Washington Square Press, 1976.

ROBINSON, LYTLE, *Edgar Cayce's Story of the Origin and Destiny of Man*, New York: Coward, McCann & Geoghegan, Inc., 1972.

ROGO, D. SCOTT, *Man Does Survive Death: The Welcoming Silence*, Secaucus, New Jersey: Citadel Press, 1973.

RUDHYAR, DANE, *Occult Preparation for a New Age*, Wheaton Illinois: The Theosophical Publishing House, 1975.

RUDHYAR, DANE, *The Astrology of Personality*, New York: Doubleday & Co., (1936) 1970.

RUDHYAR, DANE, *The Sun is Also a Star*, New York: E.P. Dutton, 1975.

SATCHIDANANDA, SWAMI, *Beyond Words*, New York: Holt, Rinehart & Winston, 1977.

SCHULMAN, MARTIN, *Karmic Astrology*, New York: Samuel Weiser, 1977.

SCHURE, EDOUARD, *Great Initiates: Secret History of Religion*, Blauvelt, New York: Garber Communications Inc., 1961.

SCOTT-ELLIOT, W., *The Story of Atlantis and the Lost Lemuria*, Wheaton, Illinois: The Theosophical Publishing House, (1896) 1972.

SECHRIST, ELSIE, *Dreams—Your Magic Mirror, With Interpretation of Edgar Cayce*, New York: Dell Publishing Co., 1968.

SHEEHY, GAIL, *Passages*, New York: Bantam Books, 1977.

SHELLY, MARY, *Frankenstein*, New York: Lancer Books, Inc., 1968.

SKARIN, ANNA LEE, *Ye Are Gods*, Los Angeles, Calif: DeVorss, 1973.

SMITH, GEORGE, *The Chaldean Account of Genesis:* (trans. from cuneiform inscriptions in 1870's), Minneapolis, Minn. Wizards Book Shelf, 1977.

SPANGLER, DAVID, *Revelation: The Birth of the New Age*, rev ed., San Francisco, Calif: Rainbow Bridge, 1976.

STEIGER, BRAD, *Atlantis Rising*, London: Sphere Books Ltd., 1977.

STERN, JESS, *The Search for a Soul: Taylor Caldwell's Psychic Lives*, Greenwich, Connecticut: Fawcett Publications, Inc., 1972.

STERN, JESS, *The Sleeping Prophet*, London: Fredrick Ltd., 1967.

STEVENSON, IAN, M.D., *The Evidence for Survival from Claimed Memories of Former Incarnations*, 4 Oakdene, Burgh Heath, Todworth, Surry, England: M.C. Peto Publisher, 1961.

STEVENSON, IAN, M.D., *Twenty Cases Suggestive of Reincarnation*, New York: American Society for Psychical Research, 1966.

STREET, NOEL, *The Man Who Can Look Backward*, New York: Samuel Weiser, Inc., 1969.

STROMBERG, GUSTAF, *The Soul of the Universe*, North Hollywood, Calif: Education Research Institute, 1965.

SUTPHEN, DICK, *How to be a Better Past Life Regression Receiver*, Scottsdale, Ariz: Valley of the Sun, 1977.

SUTPHEN, DICK, *You Were Born Again to be Together*, New York: Pocket Books, 1976.

SYNNESTVEDT, SIG, *The Essential Swedenborg*, New York: *Twayne Publishers, 1970.*

SZEKELY, EDMOND BORDEAUX, *The Essene Gospel of Peace*, San Diego, Calif: Academy Books Publishers, 1973.

THOREAU, HENRY DAVID, *The Writings of Henry David Thoreau*, Cambridge, Mass: Houghton Mifflin, 1894.

TWO DISCIPLES, *The Rainbow Bridge: First Phase Link with the Soul*, Black Mountain, North Carolina: New Age Press, 1975.

WANGDU, SONAM, *The Discovery of the XIVth Dalai Lama*, Bangkok, Thailand: Klett Thai Publications, 1975.

WATTS, ALAN, *The Diamond Way*, Calif: Big Sur Recordings (distributor).

WEST, JOHN ANTHONY and TOONDER, JAN GERHARD, *The Case for Astrology*, New York: Coward-McCann, 1970.

WILHELM, RICHARD, trans., *The I Ching, or Book of Changes*, New Jersey: Princeton University Press, Bollingen Series XIX, 1970.

WOOD, ERNEST, *Concentration, An Approach to Meditation*, Wheaton Illinois: The Theosophical Publishing House, (1949) 1973.

WOODWARD, MARY ANN, *Edgar Cayce's Story of Karma*, New York: Berkeley Publishing Corp., 1971.

YOGANANDA, PARAMAHANSA, *Autobiography of a Yogi*, Los Angeles: Self-Realization Fellowship, 1959.

YRAM, *Practical Astral Projection*, New York: Samuel Weiser, 1972.

MISCELLANEOUS

A Comrade Rides Ahead: The Memory of Emerson Hough, Douglas Malloch.

Aeneid, The, Virgil,

An Idealist View of Life, Sarvelpelli Radhakrishnan.

Broodings on Meditation Mount, G.C., Meditation Mount, P.O. Box 566, Ojai, Calif. 93023.

Byron: The Myth and the Man, Marcia Moore.

Columbia Encyclopedia, 3rd edition, 1963.

Concila, Sir Henry Spelman, London: (1600's).

Contra Celsum and De Principiis, works of Origen.

Corpus Hermeticum, VIII, Hermes.

Critias, Praedo, Phaedrus, Timaeus and *Symposium*, works of Plato.

De Incertitude et Vanitate Scientiarum et Artium, (The Uncertainty and Vanity of the Sciences and Arts), Heinrich Cornelius Agrippa (Von Nettesheim), orig, 1569.

Dhammapada Commentary, F.L. Woodward, trans.

Encyclopaedia Britannica, 1973.

History of the Inquisiiton of the Middle Ages, Henry Lea, (1888) 1955.

Hypersentience Bulletin, Marcia Moore, editor, Ananta Foundation, Ojai, Calif: December 21, 1977.

"Letters to a Disciple," Mohandas Gandhi, *Young India*, April 2, 1931.

London Sunday Times, The, Sir Bernard Lovell, March 15, 1963.

Los Angeles Times, January 26, 1978.

Magie der Zahlen, Hellenbach.

Magister Ludi, Herman Hesse.

Meditations, Marcus Aurelius Antoninus, George Long, M.A., trans.

"Natalie Remembers," Shirley Merle, *FATE* (magazine), June 1976.

New Catholic Encyclopedia, Publishers Guild Inc., in assoc. with McGraw Hill, Wash. D.C., 1967.

"New Essenes, The," Sir George Travelyan, *One Earth,* vol. 2, issue 3, Findhorn Foundation, The Park, Forres, Moray, Scotland.

New Scientist, April 25, 1968.

New York Herald Tribune, December 15, 1956.

New York Times, Science and Review, August 10, 1958.

On Old Age, Cicero.

Pictures From Italy, Charles Dickens.

Protoevangelium, The (Gospel of James).

"Sacrificial Tide, The", LaVedi Lafferty, *Beyond Reality,* 1980.

Special Studies, "A Lecture on Power Points by Roc," "The Iona Report" and *"The Plan of Light,"* Findhorn Foundation, Findhorn: unpublished.

Spiritual Community Guide, Parmatma Singh Khalsa, ed., Box 1080, San Rafael, Calif. 94902: Spiritual Community Publications, annual.

Sunday Express, May 26, 1935.

Teachings of the Essenes, from Enoch to the Dead Sea Scrolls, Edmond Bordeaux Szekely.

The Gospel of the Essenes, Edmond Bordeaux Szekely.

The Upanishads.

World Book Encyclopedia, 1978 ed.,

INDEX

STAY IN TOUCH

On the following pages you will find listed, with their current prices, some of the books and tapes now available on related subjects. Your book dealer stocks most of these, and will stock new titles in the Llewellyn series as they become available. We urge your patronage.

However, to obtain our full catalog, to keep informed of new titles as they are released and to benefit from informative articles and helpful news, you are invited to write for our bi-monthly news magazine/catalog. A sample copy is free, and it will continue coming to you at no cost as long as you are an active mail customer. Or you may keep it coming for a full year with a donation of just $5.00 in U.S.A. ($7.00 for Canada & Mexico, $10.00 overseas, first class mail). Many bookstores also have *The Llewellyn New Times* available to their customers. Ask for it.

Stay in touch! In *The Llewellyn New Times'* pages you will find news and reviews of new books, tapes and services, announcements of meetings and seminars, articles helpful to our readers, news of authors, advertising of products and services, special money-making opportunities, and much more.

The Llewellyn New Times
P.O. Box 64383-Dept. 436, St. Paul, MN 55164-0383, U.S.A.

★   ★   ★

TO ORDER BOOKS AND TAPES

If your book dealer does not have the books and tapes described on the following pages readily available, you may order them direct from the publisher by sending full price in U.S. funds, plus $1.00 for handling and 50¢ each for postage within the United States; outside USA surface mail add $1.00 per item. Outside USA air mail add $7.00 per item.

FOR GROUP STUDY AND PURCHASE

Because there is a great deal of interest in group discussion and study of the subject matter of this book, we feel that we should encourage the adoption and use of this particular book by such groups by offering a special "quantity" price to group leaders or "agents".

Our Special Quality Price for a minimum order of five copies of THE ETERNAL DANCE is $29.85 Cash-With-Order. This price includes postage and handling within the United States. Minnesota residents must add sales tax. For additional quantities, please order in multiples of five. For Canadian and foreign orders, add postage and handling charges as above. Credit Card (VISA, MasterCard, American Express, Diners' Club) Orders are accepted. Charge Card Orders only may be phoned free within the U.S.A. by dialing 1-800-THE MOON. Customer Service calls dial 1-612-291-1970 and ask for "Kae". Mail Orders to:

LLEWELLYN PUBLICATIONS
P.O. Box 64383-Dept. 436 / St. Paul, MN 55164-0383, U.S.A.

COLLEGIANS INTERNATIONAL CHURCH

Collegians is a Church Universal of the New Age, dedicated to increasing spiritual unity and awareness through knowledge, love, understanding and well-being. Collegians is part of the New Age movement whereby the ancient Mysteries will be understood through a combination of exoteric knowledge and esoteric wisdom. Within the Mysteries are hidden the secrets of science, while the key to intuitively understanding them lies in self-less service and spiritual love. As intellect and the positive will-to-good are fused, New Age revelations will be attained and new religious understanding realized.

Many individuals today are initiates or disciples (though they may not be aware of it) of the Mysteries, meaning they have reached levels of physical, emotional and mental illumination. Initiation is a process that renders the mind capable of registering higher impressions and produces a rejection of that which is devoid of truth. Spiritual illumination and initiations will be realities of the New Age religion.

At Collegians we approach higher sources of inspiration through meditation, group activities and celebration of the Full Moon periods. We recognize those entities who have progressed along the Path, known as Masters, who are seeking to bridge between Universal Consciousness and evolving human consciousness. The New Age, in its full meaning, will be attained as humanity individually and collectively moves past self-centered awareness to Self-realization of human and Universal Oneness. We are in the process of this shift in awareness now, as consciousness changes from a negative emotional polarization to a positive mental one. The time is arriving for presentation of Divine truth to catch up with the human spirit.

Humanity is evolving from control by illusions of form and ignorance into knowledge, where information produced by the senses and experimentation is correlated and defined. From knowledge we are able to gain wisdom as we develop the ability to intuit and harmonize it with universal purposes. Understanding then enables us to adapt the things of form to the spirit.

The formation of New Age religion is necessary to fill the void left by the inability of old religious forms to meet the modern spiritual needs. The churches have demanded devotion to an external Transcendent God, while irrationally turning away from God Immanent in space and all life and forms. Religion in the New Age will no longer deny the Law of Rebirth, while illogically teaching immortality. The common practice of attempting to make the Christ exclusive to certain religious bodies will cease as well, as the true meaning of Christ Consciousness is revealed, centered as Presence in the human heart.

At Collegians we acknowledge the World Teacher who appeared as Jesus the Christ, also known variously as the Lord Maitreya and the Bodhisattva, as well as other appearances of the Christ through such personalities as Melchizedek, Krishna and Mithra. The Sacraments of Remembrance are celebrated in service and are recognized as a door to initiation. Modern initiation refers to those who have moved from the animal kingdom into human individualization and are now passing into fourth dimensional spiritual awareness, the last stage of a fivefold progression.

The new religion will combine devotional qualities with intelligent comprehension. Service work will be recognized as a necessary activity. Balance must be established between the life of the spirit, increasing mental power and actions to produce individual and global health. Groups have responded worldwide to the urgent need. They have created a *Light Network* that radiates New Age energy impulses promoting increased awareness of each person's role and responsibility in solving present world conditions.

Collegians began as a *Light Center* in 1971, organizing formally in 1972 as a non-profit corporation. The present church was organized in 1977, while the name Collegians was adopted with a reorganization in 1981, based upon a Church originally founded in the Netherlands from the teachings of Jocobus Arminius.

Arminius was a respected theologian of the Dutch Reformed Church who became entangled in a theological controversy regarding the right understanding of Calvinism. The heated issue nearly caused civil war. Shortly after the death of Arminius, in 1619, the "Canon of Dort" was drawn up at a general synod condeming his "errors" advocating, (1) conditional predestination, (2) universal atonement, (3) renewal of faith through the Holy Spirit, (4) resistable, uncompelling Divine grace, and (5) the uncertainty of potentially falling from grace and faith. The defeat of these five articles of the Arminian "Remonstrance" resulted in the excommunication of some three hundred ministers.

The Collegiants (or Collegians) were a branch of the Arminian "Remonstrants" who continued to hold services following the removal of their clergymen. They prayed, read and any one who wished could address the congregation. *Collegia* were formed in various places, patterned after the first example in Rynsburg, with one lasting until 1787 in Rotterdam. The Collegiants claimed freedom of speech for all and mutual tolerance. They admitted all Christians to their meetings and defended the rights of individuals against those seeking to limit those rights.

In 1634 an edict of tolerance allowed the Church to gain separate legal status and a Remonstrant College was opened in Amsterdam. There the theories of Arminius were expanded upon toward Universalism and Rationalism. One after another the doctrines held by orthodox theologians were eliminated, until it was eventually held that each person has the right to regulate personal beliefs.

In England the Arminian followers studied Greek philosophy and natural religion, and by the eighteenth century Arminianism was being advocated by Great Britian's leading writers. It became related to the unitarian movement on the Continent and to Methodism in Great Britain and America, primarily because of its attack on the rigid doctrines of Calvinism and its advocacy for freedom of thought. It leavened the Christian thought of america, associating Collegialism with liberal religion versus conservative.

The term Collegialism is derived from Roman law, which considered the early Christian congregations to be *collegia illicita* (illegal associations). As ecclesiastical theory, Collegialism maintains that the visible Church represents voluntary association, a *collegium* that develops within a State. The concept is that the State is not a Divine institution and that separation of Church and State permits a variety of religious associations of equal status within a State. Such a church only has two classes of members, teachers and hearers, which stand side by side with equal rights.

The strength of Collegialism has been its refusal to be bound by rigid doctrinal systems, but this has also resulted in a weakness from the lack of a definite body of doctrine to call its own. Today this problem is nearing resolution by the New Age approaches that seek to dissolve crystallizing dogmas, while penetrating to the universal principles behind them in both Eastern and Western teachings.

Collegians International Church conducts its services in the manner of the original Collegiants and recognizes personal illumination as necessary to spiritual and philosophical teachings that are finding support from modern science.

Membership in Collegians is open to all interested persons and may be applied for by writing to the Church. Such membership is a service that extends the *Light Network*, offering increased support to New Age activities and establishing lines of communication.

CORRESPONDENCE STUDIES

Correspondence studies available from Collegians to members that expand upon the material in *The Eternal Dance*. Emphasis is placed upon spiritual synthesis and studies that lead to personal illuminations and corresponding initiations. Initiations are a part of the synthesis process, not documentable by degrees of study or knowledge, because they involve wisdom and love manifesting in a devoted life. As they are achieved, they become apparent in the activities and expressions of the personality.

The Age of Aquarius is to become predominately an age of synthesis and sight, opening the way to global healing. Synthesis is one of the "presented attributes" of God. Among these attributes *Wisdom* began to emerge through *soul consciousness* in the name of Buddha as the forerunner of love. *Love* is the attribute that has been working into manifestation for the past two thousand years, the Christ offering himself to illustrate its significance. *Synthesis*, presented by Plato as a concept of Wholeness, is the attribute evoking a response now in awakening humanity.

Synthesis involves a series of twelve illuminations and five corresponding initiations that stimulate and open the heart and head energy centers. The illuminations reached are: (1) awareness that *you* are not your physical body, (2) awareness of your emotional reactions and responses, (3) awareness of the workings and conditionings of the mind, (4) revitalization of the physical body, (5) cleansing of the emotional body, (6) illusions disappear and light is entered, (7) fusion of the personality with the soul, (8) establishment of communication between personality, soul and Universal Consciousness, (9) awareness of the Divine Plan and Purpose in evolution, (10-12) increasing Oneness with the Light of "the Ancient of Days."

Studies with Collegians are designed to assist individuals in assimilating all that they have been into the present, as well as providing instruciton to go forward and create the future, the Path is that of Western esoterics corresponding to the Eastern Path of Raja Yoga. Further information is available by request.

THE PAST LIFE MEMORY PROGRAM

The Past Life Memory Program is a series of cassette tapes that offers you an opportunity to easily experience past lives, often in vivid color and detail. If you daydream, remember your nighttime dreams or visualize imaginatively, you should be able to remember some of your previous lives, just as some of the following participants using the *Past Life Memory Program* have done:

> " . I went back to a scene I observed or saw in China; there were a couple of concubines and others I felt were back in another room doing sewing and like that. Then this huge Chinaman...was standing there waiting for me to direct him... I was wearing a Chinese robe; I saw beautiful embroidery work. It was very easy, just go through a transition period and you are there."
>
> "... I was trying to ascertain why my head hurts [in present life] and I found myself in Egypt, where someone was drilling a hole in my head behind my right ear... I felt that my son... was the priest who was drilling behind my ear."
>
> "... I found myself riding on a camel in Egypt near the pyramids. I could smell the sweat of the camel and see the wooden and leather seat on the camel's back. Then I asked who I was and I entered an adobe house where I lived with servants. I knew, then, that my name was Abdul Ben Alla; I had been a trader in North Africa."

Hypnosis is a proven way to reach hidden levels of mind. It was used by Edgar Cayce to develop his clairvoyant abilities and by author Taylor Caldwell to remember previous lives, and who hasn't heard of Bridey Murphy, the first case of past-life memory using hypnosis?

The Past Life Memory Program offers you the opportunity to attain deep states of mental awareness, eliminate fears, reach complete relaxation and become an objective observer of your own past lives.

You remain clearly aware of your surroundings, protected by the programming and able to return to your normal state of consciousness at anytime. All you will need to do is relax, listen to the tape and follow the instructions.

TAPE 1: HOW PAST LIVES AFFECT THE PRESENT

A fascinating justice operates in reincarnation. On this tape you will hear portions of actual past-life *readings* by LaVedi Lafferty, with explanations of how previous lives affect the present. You will have the unique opportunity to visit lost civilizations through Universal Consciousness and glimpse the hidden past of our planet.

TAPE 2: HOW TO USE THE POWER OF HYPNOSIS

Learn what hypnosis REALLY is and how to establish dynamic programs to improve your life and reach higher levels of mind. This tape is a vital preliminary to successful past-life memory, teaching you first to achieve total relaxation and then to reach a state of peace and contact with your inner being.

TAPE 3: JOURNEY INTO THE PAST WITH A LOVED ONE

Love is one of the strongest attachments we form from life to life. We rarely incarnate with strangers, tending to return with those we have known before. This tape will enable you to pick a person you know now—mate, parent, child, friend or other loved one and journey into the past to experience a life that will be revealing and helpful to you today.

TAPE 4: FINDING SOLUTIONS TO PRESENT LIFE PROBLEMS

Present life situations stem from past experiences and involvements. Often difficulties seem to vanish, once the past causes are consciously known. This is one of the greater values past-life knowledge offers. This tape is designed to help you solve problems and find increased meaning and purpose in your life.

TAPE 5: DISCOVER HIDDEN TALENTS, ABILITIES, AND KNOWLEDGE

As we progress life after life, we acquire many skills and a varied education. Often we can apply this previously learned knowledge to our work, career, hobbies and spiritual growth in the present. This tape will help you discover new directions in your life.

TAPES 3, 4 and 5: HYPNOSIS AND HIGHER LEVELS OF CONSCIOUSNESS

The reverse side of each of these tapes offers an outstanding positive thought program and an opportunity to experience your Body of Light. This will assist you in applying and expanding the past-life knowledge you gain from your journeys into former lives and help you take control of your life and destiny.

COLLEGIANS International Church
P.O. Box 929
Fairbanks, AK 99707-0929

Please send me information as indicated. Enclosed is $1.00 to cover cost of handling and postage.

☐ Collegians Correspondence Studies
☐ Spiritual Hypnosis Correspondence Course
☐ Summer Sessions in Alaska
☐ Personal Appearances by Authors
☐ Karmic recall *Reading* Consultations
☐ Study Group Formation
☐ Collegians International Church Membership

PLEASE PRINT

Name _____

Address _____

City, State, Zip _____
　　　　　　　　　☐ P.S. Please put me on your mailing list.

COLLEGIANS International Church
P.O. Box 929
Fairbanks, AK 99707-0929

Please send me information as indicated. Enclosed is $1.00 to cover cost of handling and postage.

☐ Collegians Correspondence Studies
☐ Spiritual Hypnosis Correspondence Course
☐ Summer Sessions in Alaska
☐ Personal Appearances by Authors
☐ Karmic *Reading* Consultations
☐ Study Group Formation
☐ Collegians International Church Membership

PLEASE PRINT

Name _____

Address _____

City, State, Zip _____
　　　　　　　　　☐ P.S. Please put me on your mailing list.